# GOVERNING THE COMMONS

# THE POLITICAL ECONOMY OF INSTITUTIONS AND DECISIONS

*Editors*
*James E. Alt, Harvard University*
*Douglass C. North, Washington University in St. Louis*

Other books in the series
James E. Alt and Kenneth Shepsle, eds., *Perspectives on Positive Political Economy*
Yoram Barzel, *Economic Analysis of Property Rights*
Robert Bates, *Beyond the Miracle of the Market: The Political Economy of Agrarian Development in Kenya*
Gary W. Cox, *The Efficient Secret: The Cabinet and the Development of Political Parties in Victorian England*
Leif Lewin, *Ideology and Strategy: A Century of Swedish Politics* (English Edition)
Gary Libecap, *Contracting for Property Rights*
Matthew D. McCubbins and Terry Sullivan, eds., *Congress: Structure and Policy*
Douglass C. North, *Institutions, Institutional Change, and Economic Performance*
Charles Stewart III, *Budget Reform Politics: The Design of the Appropriations Process in the House of Representatives, 1865–1921*

# GOVERNING THE COMMONS

## The evolution of institutions for collective action

ELINOR OSTROM

*Indiana University*

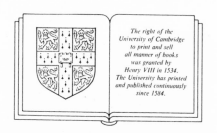

The right of the
University of Cambridge
to print and sell
all manner of books
was granted by
Henry VIII in 1534.
The University has printed
and published continuously
since 1584.

CAMBRIDGE UNIVERSITY PRESS

Cambridge

New York   Port Chester   Melbourne   Sydney

Published by the Press Syndicate of the Univeristy of Cambridge
The Pitt Building, Trumpington Street, Cambridge CB2 1RP
40 West 20th Street, New York, NY 10011, USA
10 Stamford Road, Oakleigh, Melbourne 3166, Australia

First published 1990

Printed in the United States of America

*Library of Congress Cataloging-in-Publication Data*
Ostrom, Elinor.
Governing the commons : the evolution of institutions for
collective action / Elinor Ostrom.
p.   cm. – (Political economy of institutions and decisions)
Includes bibliographical references.
ISBN 0-521-37101-5     ISBN 0-521-40599-8 (pbk.)
1. Commons.   2. Commons – Case studies.   3. Social choice.
4. Social choice – Case studies.   I. Title.
HD1286.O87     1991
333.2 – dc20                                          90-1831
                                                          CIP

*British Library Cataloguing in Publication Data*
Ostrom, Elinor
Governing the commons : the evolution of institutions for
collective action. – (Political economy of institutions and decisions)
1. Natural resources : Water. Management
I. Title
333.9117

ISBN 0-521-37101-5 hardback
ISBN 0-521-40599-8 paperback

To Vincent
For his love and contestation

# Contents

# Contents

# Contents

# Series editor' preface

The Cambridge series on the Political Economy of Institutions and Decisions is built around attempts to answer two central questions: How do institutions evolve in response to individual incentives, strategies, and choices, and how do institutions affect the performace of political and economic systems? The scope of the series is comparative and historical rather than international or specifically American, and the focus is positive rather than normative.

In this pioneering book Elinor Ostrom tackles one of the most enduring and contentious questions of positive political economy, whether and how the exploration of common-pool resources can be organized in a way that avoids both excessive consumption and administrative cost. These cases, where a resource is held in common by many individuals – that is, well-defined individual property rights over the resource are absent – are often held by economists to be exploitable only where the problem of over-consumption is solved by privatization or enforcement imposed by outside force. Ostrom, by contrast, argues forcefully that other solutions exist, and that stable institutions of self-government can be created if certain problems of supply, credibility, and monitoring are solved. She provides a close study of a uniquely broad range of cases, including high mountain meadows in Japan and Switzerland, water projects in the Philippines and California, and fisheries in Canada and Turkey. Some of these cases involve stable institutions; in other cases the institutions were fragile and failed. Basing her conclusions on comparisons of sources of success and failure in self-government, Ostrom describes some fundamental characteristics of successful common-pool management schemes, and concludes with a challenge to other social scientists to build on her original theoretical work.

# Preface

It is difficult to say when I began work on this study. If one asks when I first began to study problems of collective action faced by individuals using common-pool resources, then identifying the beginning is easier. In the early 1960s, I took a graduate seminar with Vincent Ostrom, who was to become my closest colleague and husband. The seminar focused on the development of institutions related to water resources in southern California. I began my dissertation focusing on the entrepreneurship involved in developing a series of public enterprises to halt the process of saltwater intrusion into a groundwater basin underlying a portion of the Los Angeles metropolitan area. A fellow graduate student, Louis Weschler, conducted a parallel study in an adjacent groundwater basin that adopted different institutional arrangements to cope with similar problems. As Weschler and I completed our studies, it appeared that both institutional arrangements had been successful in enabling the water producers to avoid the catastrophic economic loss that would have occurred if both basins had been inundated by the Pacific Ocean (E. Ostrom 1965; Weschler 1968).

In the late 1960s, Vincent and I participated in the Great Lakes Research Program initiated by the Batelle Memorial Institute (V. Ostrom and E. Ostrom 1977b), but most of my work as a young faculty member focused on problems of urban service delivery and public economies in metropolitan areas. In 1981 I was asked by Paul Sabatier, a colleague for a year at the Center for Interdisciplinary Research at the University of Bielefeld, to make a seminar presentation on "organizational learning." I used as my example of organizational learning the set of rules that groundwater producers had developed in the southern California groundwater basins. Paul then wanted to know why I was so confident that the systems I had studied

xiii

15 years earlier were still operating and performing well. At the time, I had no effective answer other than that the institutions had been so well crafted to fit local circumstances that I presumed they had survived and were faring well.

When I returned from Bielefeld, I suggested to one of my doctoral students, William Blomquist, that he answer Sabatier's question as his dissertation. Blomquist (1987b) found that the institutions that the water producers themselves had designed were still in place and operating effectively. The physical condition of the basins had improved substantially. The very substantial "success" involved in these cases led us to undertake a study, funded by the U.S. Geological Survey (grant number 14-08-0001-G1476), of a larger set of groundwater basins in southern California and a limited set in northern California to ascertain what factors were associated with the successful evolution of new institutions and with the efficiency and equity of those institutions. Eventually, we will have completed a comparative study of institutional, economic, and physical changes in 12 groundwater basins over a 30–50-year period.

Although I have been excited about what one can learn from a concentrated effort to study a dozen groundwater basins and the institutions that have evolved for their governance and management over time, such studies alone are not sufficient for the development of a broader theory of institutional arrangements related to the effective governance and management of common-pool resources (CPRs). One needs similar information from many other settings to begin to gain the empirical base necessary to improve our theoretical understanding of how institutions work and how individuals change their own institutions.

My awareness of the possibility of using detailed case studies written by other authors to obtain a sufficiently rich empirical base for understanding CPRs came about as a result of joining the National Academy of Sciences' "Panel on Common Property Resource Management" in 1985. By the time I was asked to join the panel, its members had commissioned a series of papers to be written by field researchers. The authors were all asked to organize their papers using a framework prepared by Ronald Oakerson (1986). That meant that all of the papers would address not only the physical properties of the resource systems but also what types of rules were used to regulate entry and use of these systems, what types of interactions resulted, and what types of outcomes were obtained. The papers were presented at an international conference in Annapolis and were published by the National Academy Press (National Research Council 1986). Some of those papers and some new chapters have been brought together in a new volume (Bromley in press).

# Preface

Reading those studies, as well as some of the studies cited by those authors, made me aware of two major facts: First, an extraordinarily rich case-study literature already existed, written by field researchers who had invested years of effort in obtaining detailed information about the strategies adopted by the appropriators of CPRs and the rules they used. Second, that literature had been written by authors in diverse fields and frequently had appeared in obscure publications. Almost no syntheses of the findings from that literature had been undertaken.

Several colleagues at Indiana University began to collect citations to relevant cases, and within a short time Fenton Martin, who compiled the resultant bibliography, had identified nearly 1,000 cases. More recently, the number was approaching 5,000 (Martin 1989). The disciplines represented in the bibliography include rural sociology, anthropology, history, economics, political science, forestry, irrigation sociology, and human ecology; included also are area studies, such as African studies, Asian studies, West European studies, and so forth. Scholars had cited primarily studies conducted by others in their own disciplines and perhaps others focusing on the same resource sector or geographic region. Few citations had come from outside each author's disciplinary, sectoral, or regional frame of reference. Consequently, a vast amount of highly specialized knowledge had been accumulated without much synthesis or application of the knowledge to the policy problems involved.

Given the importance of understanding how institutions help users cope with CPR problems, and given the existence of a rich theoretical literature concerning these problems, it seemed to me that it was important to use these case studies as an empirical basis for learning more about the effects of institutions on behaviors and outcomes in diverse field settings. With the help of a grant from the U.S. National Science Foundation (grant number SES 8619498), several colleagues and I have been able to gather many of these cases into an archive. We have systematically screened these cases and selected a much smaller subset for further scrutiny, coding, and analysis. Our selection criteria required that the case be written as a result of extended fieldwork and that information be provided about (1) the structure of the resource system, (2) the attributes and behaviors of the appropriators, (3) the rules that the appropriators were using, and (4) the outcomes resulting from the behaviors of the appropriators. We have now developed a structured coding form that enables us to transform the indepth qualitative data into a structured data base amenable to quantitative analysis.

The development of the coding forms was itself an exercise in theory development. We used the method of institutional analysis that had grown out of our earlier work (E. Ostrom 1986a,b) as the organizing framework for the design of these coding forms. In addition, we paid serious attention to the hypotheses stated by field researchers who had conducted multiple studies or were themselves reviewing findings from multiple studies. We tried to include ways of measuring their concepts and proposed relationships in our coding forms. Because we were working with qualitative data, most of our concepts had to be formulated as variables with ordinal or nominal values. Some years of hard work were required simply to read sufficient numbers of cases, study earlier efforts to synthesize findings from specialized fields, and develop the coding forms.

During this process, several papers were written in an attempt to elucidate a theory that would help us understand the patterns we were beginning to see in reading these diverse materials (Gardner and E. Ostrom 1990; Gardner, E. Ostrom, and Walker 1990; E. Ostrom 1985b, 1987, 1989; Schlager and E. Ostrom 1987; Walker, Gardner, and E. Ostrom 1990). It is my conviction that knowledge accrues by the continual process of moving back and forth from empirical observation to serious efforts at theoretical formulation. This book can thus be viewed as an intermediate "progress report" for an ongoing research effort. Given the complexity of the empirical phenomena being studied and the type of theory that is needed to explain these phenomena, the effort may well continue for another decade.

The stimulus to write this volume came from James Alt and Douglass North after I presented a lecture at Washington University in St. Louis during the fall of 1986. Given that the CPR project was still "in process," I would never have dreamed of writing a book without their continued prodding. When Kenneth Shepsle and James Alt asked me to present a series of lectures at Harvard University, during a semester of sabbatical leave, the die was cast.

Actual work on the manuscript began in January 1988, when again I was fortunate to spend a sabbatical semester at the Center for Interdisciplinary Research at the University of Bielefeld. During that time I participated in a Research Group on Game Theory and the Behavioral Sciences organized by Dr. Reinhard Selten, Department of Economics, University of Bonn. I benefited greatly from the opportunity to participate in that research group. Although only a few game-theoretical examples are used in this book, the way that game theorists think about strategic possibilities in social settings strongly influences the way I analyze the central questions addressed here. Working with Roy Gardner and Franz Weissing on two game-theoretical analyses of CPR situations greatly increased my apprecia-

# Preface

tion for the power and utility of game theory as a general theoretical tool for scholars interested in studying the consequences of diverse institutions.

The writing of this book was undertaken in tandem with participation in the "Decentralization: Finance and Management Project" sponsored by the Office of Rural and Institutional Development of the Bureau for Science and Technology (ST&RD) of the U.S. Agency for International Development. The challenge of making theoretical ideas relevant for application, the support for fieldwork in Nepal, Bangladesh, and Pakistan, and the opportunity to discuss these ideas with Larry Schroeder, Susan Wynne, Jamie Thomson, Louis Siegel, James Wunsch, Ed Connerley, Jerry Miner, Ken Kornher, and Eric Chetwynd, as well as mission personnel and host-government officials, have been of considerable value to me, and I hope that this volume is of value to the project.

I have also benefited greatly from the opportunity to present lectures based on parts of this work while the manuscript was in process. Besides the lectures at Harvard in April 1988, I have made presentations based on one or more chapters at the following places: the Sociology Department at the University of Bielefeld; the first Udall Lecture at the University of Arizona; a conference on "Democracy and Development" organized by the Sequoia Institute; a Liberty Fund summer series held in Victoria, British Columbia, May 15–20, 1989; and several different occasions at the Workshop in Political Theory and Policy Analysis at Indiana University.

Many people have commented on earlier papers or draft copies of this book, and I am deeply appreciative of their frank and helpful critiques. I hope I have responded adequately to their suggestions. Readers of the whole manuscript included Arun Agrawal, James Alt, Oliver Avens, Fikret Berkes, Elizabeth Case, David Feeny, Roy Gardner, Larry Kiser, Hartmut Kliemt, Robert Netting, Douglass C. North, Vincent Ostrom, Christine Picht, Russell Roberts, Edella Schlager, Jane Sell, Michael Taylor, Norman Uphoff, James Walker, Franz Weissing, and Rick Wilson. Readers of the individual chapters, drawing on their own prior research, included Paul Alexander, Fikret Berkes, William Blomquist, Peter Bogason, Thomas F. Glick, Arthur Maass, Robert Netting, and Norman Uphoff. Readers of prior papers that were drawn on in preparing the manuscript included Wulf Albers, Christi Barbour, William Blomquist, James Coleman, James Cooper, David Feeny, Margaret McKean, Fritz Scharpf, Kenneth Shepsle, Rick Wilson, and James Wunsch. I extend a special note of appreciation to those colleagues who have been associated with the CPR project from the beginning – William Blomquist, Roy Gardner, Edella Schlager, S. Y. Tang, and James Walker – and have spent hours refining concepts, developing models, designing instruments and experiments, and discussing how we

*Preface*

can better search out variables from what we are reading and gathering. The help of Elizabeth Case, associate editor for this series, Sophia Prybylski at Cambridge University Press, and Emily Loose, editor at Cambridge University Press, is gratefully acknowledged. Patty Dalecki has, as always, provided professional editorial and production support that has greatly improved the quality of the manuscript. Her cheerful spirit has relieved pressures on many occasions.

# 1

## *Reflections on the commons*

Hardly a week goes by without a major news story about the threatened destruction of a valuable natural resource. In June of 1989, for example, a *New York Times* article focused on the problem of overfishing in the Georges Bank about 150 miles off the New England coast. Catches of cod, flounder, and haddock are now only a quarter of what they were during the 1960s. Everyone knows that the basic problem is overfishing; however, those concerned cannot agree how to solve the problem. Congressional representatives recommend new national legislation, even though the legislation already on the books has been enforced only erratically. Representatives of the fishers argue that the fishing grounds would not be in such bad shape if the federal government had refrained from its sporadic attempts to regulate the fishery in the past. The issue in this case – and many others – is how best to limit the use of natural resources so as to ensure their long-term economic viability. Advocates of central regulation, of privatization, and of regulation by those involved have pressed their policy prescriptions in a variety of different arenas.

Similar situations occur on diverse scales ranging from small neighborhoods to the entire planet. The issues of how best to govern natural resources used by many individuals in common are no more settled in academia than in the world of politics. Some scholarly articles about the "tragedy of the commons" recommend that "the state" control most natural resources to prevent their destruction; others recommend that privatizing those resources will resolve the problem. What one can observe in the world, however, is that neither the state nor the market is uniformly successful in enabling individuals to sustain long-term, productive use of natural resource systems. Further, communities of individuals have relied on institutions resembling neither the state nor the market to govern some resource systems with reasonable degrees of success over long periods of time.

## Governing the commons

We do not yet have the necessary intellectual tools or models to understand the array of problems that are associated with governing and managing natural resource systems and the reasons why some institutions seem to work in some settings and not others. This book is an effort to (1) critique the foundations of policy analysis as applied to many natural resources, (2) present empirical examples of successful and unsuccessful efforts to govern and manage such resources, and (3) begin the effort to develop better intellectual tools to understand the capabilities and limitations of self-governing institutions for regulating many types of resources. To do this, I first describe the three models most frequently used to provide a foundation for recommending state or market solutions. I then pose theoretical and empirical alternatives to these models to begin to illustrate the diversity of solutions that go beyond states and markets. Using an institutional mode of analysis, I then attempt to explain how communities of individuals fashion different ways of governing the commons.

### THREE INFLUENTIAL MODELS

#### The tragedy of the commons

Since Garrett Hardin's challenging article in *Science* (1968), the expression "the tragedy of the commons" has come to symbolize the degradation of the environment to be expected whenever many individuals use a scarce resource in common. To illustrate the logical structure of his model, Hardin asks the reader to envision a pasture "open to all." He then examines the structure of this situation from the perspective of a rational herder. Each herder receives a direct benefit from his own animals and suffers delayed costs from the deterioration of the commons when his and others' cattle overgraze. Each herder is motivated to add more and more animals because he receives the direct benefit of his own animals and bears only a share of the costs resulting from overgrazing. Hardin concludes:

> Therein is the tragedy. Each man is locked into a system that compels him to increase his herd without limit – in a world that is limited. Ruin is the destination toward which all men rush, each pursuing his own best interest in a society that believes in the freedom of the commons. (Hardin 1968, p. 1,244)

Hardin was not the first to notice the tragedy of the commons. Aristotle long ago observed that "what is common to the greatest number has the least care bestowed upon it. Everyone thinks chiefly of his own, hardly at all of the common interest" (*Politics,* Book II, ch. 3). Hobbes's parable of man in a state of nature is a prototype of the tragedy of the commons: Men

2

## Reflections on the commons

seek their own good and end up fighting one another. In 1833, William Forster Lloyd (1977) sketched a theory of the commons that predicted improvident use for property owned in common. More than a decade before Hardin's article, H. Scott Gordon (1954) clearly expounded similar logic in another classic: "The Economic Theory of a Common-Property Research: The Fishery." Gordon described the same dynamic as Hardin:

> There appears then, to be some truth in the conservative dictum that everybody's property is nobody's property. Wealth that is free for all is valued by no one because he who is foolhardy enough to wait for its proper time of use will only find that it has been taken by another.... The fish in the sea are valueless to the fisherman, because there is no assurance that they will be there for him tomorrow if they are left behind today. (Gordon 1954, p. 124)

John H. Dales (1968, p. 62) noted at the same time the perplexing problems related to resources "owned in common because there is no alternative!" Standard analyses in modern resource economics conclude that where a number of users have access to a common-pool resource, the total of resource units withdrawn from the resource will be greater than the optimal economic level of withdrawal (Clark 1976, 1980; Dasgupta and Heal 1979).

If the only "commons" of importance were a few grazing areas or fisheries, the tragedy of the commons would be of little general interest. That is not the case. Hardin himself used the grazing commons as a metaphor for the general problem of overpopulation. The "tragedy of the commons" has been used to describe such diverse problems as the Sahelian famine of the 1970s (Picardi and Seifert 1977), firewood crises throughout the Third World (Norman 1984; Thomson 1977), the problem of acid rain (R. Wilson 1985), the organization of the Mormon Church (Bullock and Baden 1977), the inability of the U.S. Congress to limit its capacity to overspend (Shepsle and Weingast 1984), urban crime (Neher 1978), public-sector/private-sector relationships in modern economies (Scharpf 1985, 1987, 1988), the problems of international cooperation (Snidal 1985), and communal conflict in Cyprus (Lumsden 1973). Much of the world is dependent on resources that are subject to the possibility of a tragedy of the commons.

### The prisoner's dilemma game

Hardin's model has often been formalized as a prisoner's dilemma (PD) game (Dawes 1973, 1975).[1] Suppose we think of the players in a game as being herders using a common grazing meadow. For this meadow, there is an upper limit to the number of animals that can graze on the meadow for

3

a season and be well fed at the end of the season. We call that number *L*. For a two-person game, the "cooperate" strategy can be thought of as grazing *L*/2 animals for each herder. The "defect" strategy is for each herder to graze as many animals as he thinks he can sell at a profit (given his private costs), assuming that this number is greater than *L*/2. If both herders limit their grazing to *L*/2, they will obtain 10 units of profit, whereas if they both choose the defect strategy they will obtain zero profit. If one of them limits his number of animals to *L*/2, while the other grazes as many as he wants, the "defector" obtains 11 units of profit, and the "sucker" obtains −1. If each chooses independently without the capacity to engage in a binding contract, each chooses his dominant strategy, which is to defect. When they both defect, they obtain zero profit. Call this the Hardin herder game, or Game 1. It has the structure of a prisoner's dilemma game.[2]

The prisoner's dilemma game is conceptualized as a noncooperative game in which all players possess complete information. In noncooperative games, communication among the players is forbidden or impossible or simply irrelevant as long as it is not explicitly modeled as part of the game. If communication is possible, verbal agreements among players are presumed to be nonbinding unless the possibility of binding agreements is explicitly incorporated in the game structure (Harsanyi and Selten 1988, p. 3). "Complete information" implies that all players know the full structure of the game tree and the payoffs attached to outcomes. Players either know or do not know the current moves of other players depending on whether or not they are observable.

In a prisoner's dilemma game, each player has a dominant strategy in the sense that the player is always better off choosing this strategy – to defect

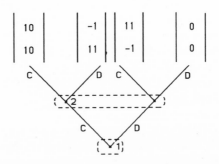

Figure 1.1. Game 1: The Hardin herder game.

# Reflections on the commons

– no matter what the other player chooses. When both players choose their dominant strategy, given these assumptions, they produce an equilibrium that is the third-best result for both. Neither has an incentive to change that is independent of the strategy choice of the other. The equilibrium resulting from each player selecting his or her "best" individual strategy is, however, not a Pareto-optimal outcome. A Pareto-optimal outcome occurs when there is no other outcome strictly preferred by at least one player that is at least as good for the others. In the two-person prisoner's dilemma game, both players prefer the (cooperate, cooperate) outcome to the (defect, defect) outcome. Thus, the equilibrium outcome is Pareto-inferior.

The prisoner's dilemma game fascinates scholars. The paradox that individually rational strategies lead to collectively irrational outcomes seems to challenge a fundamental faith that rational human beings can achieve rational results. In the introduction to a recently published book, *Paradoxes of Rationality and Cooperation*, Richmond Campbell explains the "deep attraction" of the dilemma:

Quite simply, these paradoxes cast in doubt our understanding of rationality and, in the case of the Prisoner's Dilemma suggest that it is impossible for rational creatures to cooperate. Thus, they bear directly on fundamental issues in ethics and political philosophy and threaten the foundations of the social sciences. It is the scope of these consequences that explains why these paradoxes have drawn so much attention and why they command a central place in philosophical discussion.
(Campbell 1985, p. 3)

The deep attraction of the dilemma is further illustrated by the number of articles written about it. At one count, 15 years ago, more than 2,000 papers had been devoted to the prisoner's dilemma game (Grofman and Pool 1975).

## The logic of collective action

A closely related view of the difficulty of getting individuals to pursue their joint welfare, as contrasted to individual welfare, was developed by Mancur Olson (1965) in *The Logic of Collective Action*. Olson specifically set out to challenge the grand optimism expressed in group theory: that individuals with common interests would voluntarily act so as to try to further those interests (Bentley 1949; Truman 1958). On the first page of his book, Olson summarized that accepted view:

The idea that groups tend to act in support of their group interests is supposed to follow logically from this widely accepted premise of rational, self-interested behavior. In other words, if the members of some group have a common interest or object, and if they would all be better off if that objective were achieved, it has been

5

thought to follow logically that the individuals in that group would, if they were rational and self-interested, act to achieve that objective.     (Olson 1965, p.1)

Olson challenged the presumption that the possibility of a benefit for a group would be sufficient to generate collective action to achieve that benefit. In the most frequently quoted passage of his book, Olson argued that

unless the number of individuals is quite small, or unless there is coercion or some other special device to make individuals act in their common interest, *rational, self-interested individuals will not act to achieve their common or group inter-ests.*                              (Olson 1965, p. 2; emphasis in original)

Olson's argument rests largely on the premise that one who cannot be excluded from obtaining the benefits of a collective good once the good is produced has little incentive to contribute voluntarily to the provision of that good. His book is less pessimistic than it is asserted to be by many who cite this famous passage. Olson considers it an open question whether intermediate-size groups will or will not voluntarily provide collective benefits. His definition of an intermediate-size group depends not on the number of actors involved but on how noticeable each person's actions are.

The tragedy of the commons, the prisoner's dilemma, and the logic of collective action are closely related concepts in the models that have de-fined the accepted way of viewing many problems that individuals face when attempting to achieve collective benefits. At the heart of each of these models is the free-rider problem. Whenever one person cannot be excluded from the benefits that others provide, each person is motivated not to contribute to the joint effort, but to free-ride on the efforts of others. If all participants choose to free-ride, the collective benefit will not be produced. The temptation to free-ride, however, may dominate the decision process, and thus all will end up where no one wanted to be. Alternatively, some may provide while others free-ride, leading to less than the optimal level of provision of the collective benefit. These models are thus extremely useful for explaining how perfectly rational individuals can produce, under some circumstances, outcomes that are not "rational" when viewed from the perspective of all those involved.

What makes these models so interesting and so powerful is that they capture important aspects of many different problems that occur in diverse settings in all parts of the world. What makes these models so dangerous – when they are used metaphorically as the foundation for policy – is that the constraints that are assumed to be fixed for the purpose of analysis are taken on faith as being fixed in empirical settings, unless external authorities change them.³ The prisoners in the famous dilemma cannot change the constraints imposed on them by the district attorney; they are in jail. Not all users of natural resources are similarly incapable of changing their constraints. As long as individuals are viewed as prisoners, policy prescriptions will address this metaphor. I would rather address the question of how to enhance the capabilities of those involved to change the constraining rules of the game to lead to outcomes other than remorseless tragedies.

## THE METAPHORICAL USE OF MODELS

These three models and their many variants are diverse representations of a broader and still-evolving theory of collective action. Much more work will be needed to develop the theory of collective action into a reliable and useful foundation for policy analysis. Considerable progress has been made during the past three decades by theorists and empirically oriented social scientists. The sweeping conclusions of the first variants of this theory have given way to a more qualified body of knowledge involving many more variables and explicit base conditions.

As an evolving, rather than completed, theory, it provokes disagreement regarding the importance or insignificance of some variables and how best to specify key relationships.⁴ The results from more recent work, particularly work focusing on the dynamic aspects of relevant empirical settings, have begun to generate more optimistic predictions than did earlier models; see, in particular, the work of Axelrod (1981, 1984) and Kreps and Wilson (1982). This is one of the most exciting areas in the social sciences, for although considerable cumulation has already occurred, some deep questions remain unanswered. Some of these puzzles are key to understanding how individuals jointly using a common-pool resource might be able to achieve an effective form of governing and managing their own commons. These puzzles are examined in Chapter 2.

Much that has been written about common-pool resources, however, has uncritically accepted the earlier models and the presumption of a remorseless tragedy (Nebel 1987). Scholars have gone so far as to recommend that "Hardin's 'Tragedy of the Commons' should be required reading for all students . . . and, if I had my way, for all human beings."⁵ Policy prescriptions have relied to a large extent on one of the three original models, but those attempting to use these models as the basis for policy prescription frequently have achieved little more than a metaphorical use of the models.

When models are used as metaphors, an author usually points to the similarity between one or two variables in a natural setting and one or two

7

variables in a model. If calling attention to similarities is all that is intended by the metaphor, it serves the usual purpose of rapidly conveying information in graphic form. These three models have frequently been used metaphorically, however, for another purpose. The similarity between the many individuals jointly using a resource in a natural setting and the many individuals jointly producing a suboptimal result in the model has been used to convey a sense that further similarities are present. By referring to natural settings as "tragedies of the commons," "collective-action problems," "prisoner's dilemmas," "open-access resources," or even "common-property resources," the observer frequently wishes to invoke an image of helpless individuals caught in an inexorable process of destroying their own resources. An article in the December 10, 1988, issue of *The Economist* goes so far as to assert that fisheries can be managed successfully only if it is recognized that "left to their own devices, fisherman will overexploit stocks," and "to avoid disaster, managers must have effective hegemony over them."

Public officials sometimes do no more than evoke grim images by briefly alluding to the popularized versions of the models, presuming, as self-evident, that the same processes occur in all natural settings. The Canadian minister of fisheries and oceans, for example, captured the color of the models in a 1980 speech:

If you let loose that kind of economic self-interest in fisheries, with everybody fishing as he wants, taking from a resource that belongs to no individual, you end up destroying your neighbour and yourself. In free fisheries, good times create bad times, attracting more and more boats to chase fewer and fewer fish, producing less and less money to divide among more and more people.

(Romeo LeBlanc, speaking at the 50th anniversary meeting
of the United Maritime Fishermen, March 19, 1980;
quoted by Matthews and Phyne 1988)

The implication, of course, was that Canadian fisheries universally met that description – an empirically incorrect inference.[6] But many observers have come to assume that most resources are like those specified in the three models. As such, it has been assumed that the individuals have been caught in a grim trap. The resulting policy recommendations have had an equally grim character.

## CURRENT POLICY PRESCRIPTIONS

### *Leviathan as the "only" way*

Ophuls (1973, p. 228) argued, for example, that "because of the tragedy of the commons, environmental problems cannot be solved through co-operation ... and the rationale for government with major coercive

8

powers is overwhelming." Ophuls concluded that "even if we avoid the tragedy of the commons, it will *only* be by recourse to the tragic necessity of Leviathan" (1973, p. 229; emphasis added).[7] Garrett Hardin argued a decade after his earlier article that we are enveloped in a "cloud of ignorance" about "the true nature of the fundamental political systems and the effect of each on the preservation of the environment" (1978, p. 310). The "cloud of ignorance" did not, however, prevent him from presuming that the only alternatives to the commons dilemma were what he called "a private enterprise system," on the one hand, or "socialism," on the other (1978, p. 314). With the assurance of one convinced that "the alternative of the commons is too horrifying to contemplate" (1968, p. 1,247), Hardin indicated that change would have to be instituted with "whatever force may be required to make the change stick" (1978, p. 314). In other words, "if ruin is to be avoided in a crowded world, people must be responsive to a coercive force outside their individual psyches, a 'Leviathan,' to use Hobbes's term" (Hardin 1978, p. 314).

The presumption that an external Leviathan is necessary to avoid tragedies of the commons leads to recommendations that central governments control most natural resource systems. Heilbroner (1974) opined that "iron governments," perhaps military governments, would be necessary to achieve control over ecological problems. In a less draconian view, Ehrenfeld (1972, p. 322) suggested that if "private interests cannot be expected to protect the public domain then external regulation by public agencies, governments, or international authorities is needed." In an analysis of the problems involved in water resource management in developing countries, Carruthers and Stoner (1981, p. 29) argued that without public control, "overgrazing and soil erosion of communal pastures, or less fish at higher average cost," would result. They concluded that "common property resources *require* public control if economic efficiency is to result from their development" (1981, p. 29; emphasis added).[8] The policy advice to centralize the control and regulation of natural resources, such as grazing lands, forests, and fisheries, has been followed extensively, particularly in Third World countries.

One way to illustrate these proponents' image of centralized control is to modify the Hardin herder game using the assumptions that underlie this policy advice. The proponents of centralized control want an external government agency to decide the specific herding strategy that the central authority considers best for the situation: The central authority will decide who can use the meadow, when they can use it, and how many animals can be grazed. Let us assume that the central authority decides to impose a penalty of 2 profit units on anyone who is considered by that authority to be using a defect strategy. Assuming that the central agency knows the sustainable yield of the meadow (L) and can unfailingly discover and penalize any herder using the defect strategy, the newly restructured game imposed by the central authority is represented in Game 2. Now, the solution to Game 2 is (cooperate, cooperate). Both players receive 10 profit units each, rather than the zero units they would have received in Game 1. If an external authority accurately determines the capacity of a common-pool resource, unambiguously assigns this capacity, monitors actions, and unfailingly sanctions noncompliance, then a centralized agency can transform the Hardin herder game to generate an optimally efficient equilibrium for the herders. Little consideration is given to the cost of creating and maintaining such an agency. This is seen as exogenous to the problem and is not included as a parameter of Game 2.[9]

The optimal equilibrium achieved by following the advice to centralize control, however, is based on assumptions concerning the accuracy of information, monitoring capabilities, sanctioning reliability, and zero costs of administration. Without valid and reliable information, a central agency could make several errors, including setting the carrying capacity or the fine too high or too low, sanctioning herders who cooperate, or not sanctioning defectors. The implications of all forms of incomplete information are interesting. However, as an example, I shall focus entirely on the implications arising from a central agency's incomplete information about the herders' strategies. The implicit assumption of Game 2 is that the central agency monitors all actions of the herders costlessly and imposes sanctions correctly.

In Game 3, we assume that the central agency has complete information about the carrying capacity of the meadow, but incomplete information about the particular actions of the herders. The central agency conse-

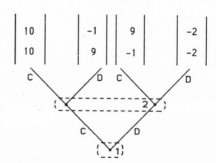

Figure 1.2. Game 2: The central-authority game with complete information.

10

quently makes errors in imposing punishments. Let us assume that the central agency punishes defections (the correct response) with probability $y$ and fails to punish defections with probability $1 - y$ (the erroneous response). Let us also assume that the central agency punishes cooperative actions (the erroneous response) with probability $x$ and does not punish cooperative actions (the correct response) with probability $1 - x$. The payoff parameters are illustrated in Figure 1.3.

A central agency with complete information would make no errors in its punishment level; in that case, $x = 0$ and $y = 1$. Game 2 would then be a special case of Game 3 in which $x = 0$ and $y = 1$. However, if the central agency does not have complete information about the actions of the herders, it imposes both types of sanctions correctly with a probability of 0.7 ($x = 0.3$, $y = 0.7$). An example of the specific payoffs for this game is shown as Game 4 in Figure 1.4. Given this payoff structure, the herders again face a prisoner's dilemma game. They will defect (overgraze) rather than cooperate (graze within the carrying capacity). In Game 4, as in the original Game 1, the equilibrium outcomes for the herders were (0, 0). In a game in which a central agency sanctions correctly with a probability of 0.7, the equilibrium outcomes are ($-1.6$, $-1.6$). The equilibrium of the regulated game has a lower value than that of the unregulated game. Given the carrying capacity and profit possibilities of Game 1, the central agency must have sufficient information so that it can correctly impose sanctions with a probability greater than 0.75 to avoid pushing the herders to the ($D$, $D$) equilibrium.[10]

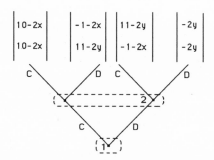

Figure 1.3. Game 3: The central-authority game with incomplete information.

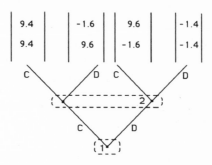

Figure 1.4. Game 4: An example of the central-authority game with incomplete information.

## Privatization as the "only" way

Other policy analysts, influenced by the same models, have used equally strong terms in calling for the imposition of private property rights whenever resources are owned in common (Demsetz 1967; O. Johnson 1972). "Both the economic analysis of common property resources and Hardin's treatment of the tragedy of the commons" led Robert J. Smith (1981, p. 467) to suggest that "the *only* way to avoid the tragedy of the commons in natural resources and wildlife is to end the common-property system by creating a system of private property rights" (emphasis added); see also the work of Sinn (1984). Smith stressed that it is "by treating a resource as a common property that we become locked in its inexorable destruction" (1981, p. 465). Welch advocated the creation of full private rights to a commons when he asserted that "the establishment of full property rights is necessary to avoid the inefficiency of overgrazing" (1983, p. 171). He asserted that privatization of the commons was the optimal solution for all common-pool problems. His major concern was how to impose private ownership when those currently using a commons were unwilling to change to a set of private rights to the commons.

Those recommending the imposition of privatization on the herders would divide the meadow in half and assign half of the meadow to one herder and the other half to the second herder. Now each herder will be playing a *game against nature* in a smaller terrain, rather than a game against another player in a larger terrain. The herders now will need to invest in fences and their maintenance, as well as in monitoring and sanctioning activities to enforce their division of the grazing area (B. Field 1984, 1985b). It is presumed that each herder will now choose $X/2$ animals

12

to graze as a result of his own profit incentive.[11] This assumes that the meadow is perfectly homogeneous over time in its distribution of available fodder. If rainfall occurs erratically, one part of the grazing area may be lush with growth one year, whereas another part of the area may be unable to support $X/2$ animals. The rain may fall somewhere else the next year. In any given year, one of the herders may make no profit, and the other may enjoy a considerable return. If the location of lush growth changes dramatically from year to year, dividing the commons may impoverish both herders and lead to overgrazing in those parts where forage is temporarily inadequate. Of course, it will be possible for the herder who has extra fodder in one year to sell it to the other herder. Alternatively, it will be possible for the herders to set up an insurance scheme to share the risk of an uncertain environment. However, the setup costs for a new market or a new insurance scheme would be substantial and will not be needed so long as the herders share fodder and risk by jointly sharing a larger grazing area.

It is difficult to know exactly what analysts mean when they refer to the necessity of developing private rights to some common-pool resources (CPRs). It is clear that when they refer to land, they mean to divide the land into separate parcels and assign individual rights to hold, use, and transfer these parcels as individual owners desire (subject to the general regulations of a jurisdiction regarding the use and transfer of land). In regard to nonstationary resources, such as water and fisheries, it is unclear what the establishment of private rights means. As Colin Clark has pointed out, the "'tragedy of the commons' has proved particularly difficult to counteract in the case of marine fishery resources where the establishment of individual property rights is virtually out of the question" (1980, p. 117). In regard to a fugitive resource, a diversity of rights may be established giving individuals rights to use particular types of equipment, to use the resource system at a particular time and place, or to withdraw a particular quantity of resource units (if they can be found). But even when particular rights are unitized, quantified, and salable, the resource *system* is still likely to be owned in common rather than individually.[12] Again, referring to fisheries, Clark has argued that "common ownership is the fundamental fact affecting almost every regime of fishery management" (1980, p. 117).

## The "only" way?

Analysts who find an empirical situation with a structure presumed to be a commons dilemma often call for the imposition of a solution by an external actor: The "only way" to solve a commons dilemma is by doing

13

*X*. Underlying such a claim is the belief that *X* is necessary and sufficient to solve the commons dilemma. But the content of *X* could hardly be more variable. One set of advocates presumes that a central authority must assume continuing responsibility to make unitary decisions for a particular resource. The other presumes that a central authority should parcel out ownership rights to the resource and then allow individuals to pursue their own self-interests within a set of well-defined property rights. Both centralization advocates and privatization advocates accept as a central tenet that institutional change must come from outside and be imposed on the individuals affected. Despite sharing a faith in the necessity and efficacy of "the state" to change institutions so as to increase efficiency, the institutional changes they recommend could hardly be further apart.

If one recommendation is correct, the other cannot be. Contradictory positions cannot both be right. I do not argue for either of these positions. Rather, I argue that both are too sweeping in their claims. Instead of there being a single solution to a single problem, I argue that many solutions exist to cope with many different problems. Instead of presuming that optimal institutional solutions can be designed easily and imposed at low cost by external authorities, I argue that "getting the institutions right" is a difficult, time-consuming, conflict-invoking process. It is a process that requires reliable information about time and place variables as well as a broad repertoire of culturally acceptable rules. New institutional arrangements do not work in the field as they do in abstract models unless the models are well specified and empirically valid and the participants in a field setting understand how to make the new rules work.

Instead of presuming that the individuals sharing a commons are inevitably caught in a trap from which they cannot escape, I argue that the capacity of individuals to extricate themselves from various types of dilemma situations *varies* from situation to situation. The cases to be discussed in this book illustrate both successful and unsuccessful efforts to escape tragic outcomes. Instead of basing policy on the presumption that the individuals involved are helpless, I wish to learn more from the experience of individuals in field settings. Why have some efforts to solve commons problems failed, while others have succeeded? What can we learn from experience that will help stimulate the development and use of a better theory of collective action – one that will identify the key variables that can enhance or detract from the capabilities of individuals to solve problems?

Institutions are rarely either private or public – "the market" or "the state." Many successful CPR institutions are rich mixtures of "private-like" and "public-like" institutions defying classification in a sterile dichotomy.

14

## Reflections on the commons

By "successful," I mean institutions that enable individuals to achieve productive outcomes in situations where temptations to free-ride and shirk are ever present. A competitive market – the epitome of private institutions – is itself a public good. Once a competitive market is provided, individuals can enter and exit freely whether or not they contribute to the cost of providing and maintaining the market. No market can exist for long without underlying public institutions to support it. In field settings, public and private institutions frequently are intermeshed and depend on one another, rather than existing in isolated worlds.

### An alternative solution

To open up the discussion of institutional options for solving commons dilemmas, I want now to present a fifth game in which the herders themselves can make a binding contract to commit themselves to a cooperative strategy that they themselves will work out. To represent this arrangement within a noncooperative framework, additional moves must be overtly included in the game structure. A binding contract is interpreted within noncooperative game theory as one that is unfailingly enforced by an

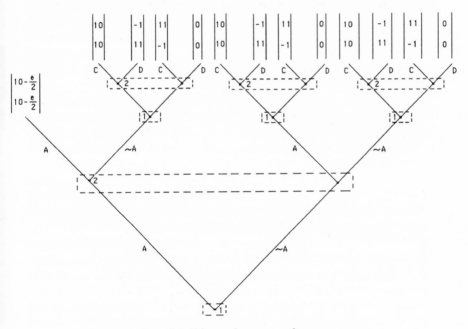

Figure 1.5. Game 5: Self-financed contract-enforcement game.

15

external actor – just as we interpreted the penalty posited earlier as being unfailingly enforced by the central authority.

A simple way to represent this is to add one parameter to the payoffs and a strategy to both herders' strategy sets.[13] The parameter is the cost of enforcing an agreement and will be denoted by $e$. The herders in Game 5 must now negotiate prior to placing animals on the meadow. During negotiations, they discuss various strategies for sharing the carrying capacity of the meadow and the costs of enforcing their agreement. Contracts are not enforceable, however, unless agreed to unanimously by the herders. Any proposal made by one herder that did not involve an equal sharing of the carrying capacity and of enforcement costs would be vetoed by the other herder in their negotiations. Consequently, the only feasible agreement – and the equilibrium of the resulting game – is for both herders to share equally the sustainable yield levels of the meadow and the costs of enforcing their agreement so long as each herder's share of the cost of enforcement is less than 10.[14]

Further, in Game 5, players can *always* guarantee that the worst they will do is the (defect, defect) outcome of Game 1. They are not dependent on the accuracy of the information obtained by a distant government official regarding their strategies. If one player suggests a contract based on incomplete or biased information, the other player can indicate an unwillingness to agree. They determine their own contract and ask the enforcer to enforce only that on which they have agreed. If the enforcer should decide to charge too much for its services [any number equal to or greater than $P_i(C, C) - P_i(D, D)$, $i = 1, 2$], neither player would agree to such a contract.

The "solution" of a commons-dilemma game through instrumentalities similar to Game 5 is not presented as the "only way" to solve a commons dilemma. It is merely one way. But this way has been almost totally ignored in both the policy-analysis literature and the formal-theory literature. Contemplating such an option raises numerous questions. First, might it be possible for the herders to hire a private agent to take on the role of enforcer? This is not as farfetched as it might seem at first. Many long-term business exchanges have the structure of a prisoner's dilemma.[15] Businesses are hesitant to accept promises of future performance rather than enforceable contracts, especially when beginning new business relationships. To reduce enforcement costs, however, a frequent practice is to use a private arbitrator rather than a civil court as the mechanism to achieve enforcement.[16] In N-person settings, all professional athletic leagues face problems similar to those illustrated here. During the play of a professional game, the temptation to cheat and break the rules is ever present. Further,

16

accidents do happen, and rules get broken, even by players who were intending to follow the rules. Athletic leagues typically employ private monitors to enforce their rules.[17]

As soon as we allow the possibility of a private party to take on the role of an external enforcer, the nature of the "solution" offered by Game 5 to the commons dilemma begins to generate a rich set of alternative applications. A self-financed contract-enforcement game allows the participants in the situation to exercise greater control over decisions about who will be allowed to graze and what limits will be placed on the number of animals, as compared with either Game 2 or Game 3. If the parties use a private arbitrator, they do not let the arbitrator impose an agreement on them. The arbitrator simply helps the parties find methods to resolve disputes that arise within the set of working rules to which the parties themselves have agreed. Arbitrators, courts, and other arrangements for enforcement and dispute resolution make it possible for individuals to initiate long-term arrangements that they could not otherwise undertake.[18] Further, as soon as one thinks about a "solution" like Game 5, it is a small step to thinking about the possibility of several arbitrators offering enforcement services at varying charges during the negotiation stage. The payoff-dominant equilibrium is to agree on that arbitrator who will enforce the contract at the lowest $e$.

The key difference between Game 5 and Games 2 and 3 is that the participants themselves design their own contracts in Game 5 in light of the information they have at hand. The herders, who use the same meadow year after year, have detailed and relatively accurate information about carrying capacity. They observe the behavior of other herders and have an incentive to report contractual infractions. Arbitrators may not need to hire monitors to observe the activities of the contracting parties. The self-interest of those who negotiated the contract will lead them to monitor each other and to report observed infractions so that the contract is enforced. A regulatory agency, on the other hand, always needs to hire its own monitors. The regulatory agency then faces the principal–agent problem of how to ensure that its monitors do their own job.

The proponents of the central-authority "solution" presume that such agencies have accurate information and are able to change incentives to produce something like Game 2. It is difficult for a central authority to have sufficient time-and-place information to estimate accurately both the carrying capacity of a CPR and the appropriate fines to induce cooperative behavior. I believe that situations like that in Game 3, in which incomplete information leads to sanctioning errors, occur more frequently than has been presumed in the policy literature. The need for external monitors and enforcers is particularly acute when what is being enforced is a decision by an external agent who may impose excess costs on participants.

A further problem for consideration is that games in which enforcers have been arranged for by mutual agreement may be mistaken by analysts and public officials for games in which there have been *no* agreements about how to cooperate and enforce agreements. In other words, some examples of a "Game 5" may be mistaken for a "Game 1."[19] These situations may be construed to be "informal," carrying a presumption that they are not lawful. This goes to fundamental presumptions about the nature of governments as external authorities governing over societies.

As will be seen in the later discussion of empirical cases, users of CPRs have developed a wide diversity in their own agreements, which are enforced by many mechanisms. Some of the enforcement mechanisms are external governmental agencies. Some enforcement mechanisms involve members of the users' community who have been employed as monitors and enforcers. Some enforcement mechanisms involve the users themselves as their own monitors. When the enforcement mechanism is not an external governmental agency, some analysts presume that there is no enforcement. That is why Game 5 is mistaken for Game 1.

A self-financed contract-enforcement game is no panacea. Such institutional arrangements have many weaknesses in many settings. The herders can overestimate or underestimate the carrying capacity of the meadow. Their own monitoring system may break down. The external enforcer may not be able to enforce ex post, after promising to do so ex ante. A myriad of problems can occur in natural settings, as is also the case with the idealized central-regulation or private-property institutions.

The structure of the institutional arrangements that one finds in natural settings is, of course, far more complicated than the structure of any of the extremely simple games presented here for discussion. What I attempt to do with these simple games is to generate different ways of thinking about the mechanisms that individuals may use to extricate themselves from commons dilemmas – ways different from what one finds in much of the policy literature. To challenge this mind-set, one needs only simple mechanisms that illustrate alternatives to those that normally are presented as the dominant solutions.

### An empirical alternative

Game 5 illustrated a theoretical alternative to centralization or privatization as ways to solve CPR problems. Let us now briefly consider a solution devised by participants in a field setting – Alanya, Turkey – that cannot be characterized as either central regulation or privatization. The inshore fishery at Alanya, as described by Fikret Berkes (1986b), is a relatively small operation. Many of the approximately 100 local fishers operate in two- or three-person boats using various types of nets. Half of the fishers belong to a local producers' cooperative. According to Berkes, the early 1970s were the "dark ages" for Alanya. The economic viability of the fishery was threatened by two factors: First, unrestrained use of the fishery had led to hostility and, at times, violent conflict among the users. Second, competition among fishers for the better fishing spots had increased production costs, as well as the level of uncertainty regarding the harvest potential of any particular boat.

Early in the 1970s, members of the local cooperative began experimenting with an ingenious system for allotting fishing sites to local fishers. After more than a decade of trial-and-error efforts, the rules used by the Alanya inshore fishers are as follows:

- Each September, a list of eligible fishers is prepared, consisting of all licensed fishers in Alanya, regardless of co-op membership.
- Within the area normally used by Alanya fishers, all usable fishing locations are named and listed. These sites are spaced so that the nets set in one site will not block the fish that should be available at the adjacent sites.
- These named fishing locations and their assignments are in effect from September to May.
- In September, the eligible fishers draw lots and are assigned to the named fishing locations.
- From September to January, each day each fisher moves east to the next location. After January, the fishers move west. This gives the fishers equal opportunities at the stocks that migrate from east to west between September and January and reverse their migration through the area from January to May (Berkes 1986b, pp. 73–4).

The system has the effect of spacing the fishers far enough apart on the fishing grounds that the production capabilities at each site are optimized. All fishing boats also have equal chances to fish at the best spots. Resources are not wasted searching for or fighting over a site.[20] No signs of over-capitalization are apparent.

The list of fishing locations is endorsed by each fisher and deposited with the mayor and local gendarme once a year at the time of the lottery. The process of monitoring and enforcing the system is, however, accomplished by the fishers themselves as a by-product of the incentive created by the

19

Governing the commons

rotation system. On a day when a given fisher is assigned one of the more productive spots, that fisher will exercise that option with certainty (leaving aside last-minute breakdowns in equipment). All other fishers can expect that the assigned fisher will be at the spot bright and early. Consequently, an effort to cheat on the system by traveling to a good spot on a day when one is assigned to a poor spot has little chance of remaining undetected. Cheating on the system will be observed by the very fishers who have rights to be in the best spots and will be willing to defend their rights using physical means if necessary. Their rights will be supported by everyone else in the system. The others will want to ensure that their own rights will not be usurped on the days when they are assigned good sites. The few infractions that have occurred have been handled easily by the fishers at the local coffeehouse (Berkes 1986b, p. 74).

Although this is not a private-property system, rights to use fishing sites and duties to respect these rights are well defined. And though it is not a centralized system, national legislation that has given such cooperatives jurisdiction over "local arrangements" has been used by cooperative officials to legitimize their role in helping to devise a workable set of rules. That local officials accept the signed agreement each year also enhances legitimacy. The actual monitoring and enforcing of the rules, however, are left to the fishers.

Central-government officials could not have crafted such a set of rules without assigning a full-time staff to work (actually fish) in the area for an extended period. Fishing sites of varying economic value are commonly associated with inshore fisheries (Christy 1982; Forman 1967), but they are almost impossible to map without extensive on-site experience. Mapping this set of fishing sites, such that one boat's fishing activities would not reduce the migration of fish to other locations, would have been a daunting challenge had it not been for the extensive time-and-place information provided by the fishers and their willingness to experiment for a decade with various maps and systems. Alanya provides an example of a self-governed common-property arrangement in which the rules have been devised and modified by the participants themselves and also are monitored and enforced by them.

The case of the Alanya inshore fishery is only one empirical example of the many institutional arrangements that have been devised, modified, monitored, and sustained by the users of renewable CPRs to constrain individual behavior that would, if unconstrained, reduce joint returns to the community of users. In addition to the case studies discussed in Chapters 3, 4, and 5, productive CPR institutional arrangements have been well documented for many farmer-managed irrigation systems, communal forests, inshore fisheries, and grazing and hunting territories.[21]

Game 5 and empirical cases of successfully governed CPRs provide theoretical and empirical alternatives to the assertion that those involved cannot extricate themselves from the problems faced when multiple individuals use a given resource. The key to my argument is that some individuals have broken out of the trap inherent in the commons dilemma, whereas others continue remorsefully trapped into destroying their own resources.[22] This leads me to ask what differences exist between those who have broken the shackles of a commons dilemma and those who have not. The differences may have to do with factors *internal* to a given group. The participants may simply have no capacity to communicate with one another, no way to develop trust, and no sense that they must share a common future. Alternatively, powerful individuals who stand to gain from the current situation, while others lose, may block efforts by the less powerful to change the rules of the game. Such groups may need some form of external assistance to break out of the perverse logic of their situation.

The differences between those who have and those who have not extricated themselves from commons dilemmas may also have to do with factors *outside* the domain of those affected. Some participants do not have the autonomy to change their own institutional structures and are prevented from making constructive changes by external authorities who are indifferent to the perversities of the commons dilemma, or may even stand to gain from it. Also, there is the possibility that external changes may sweep rapidly over a group, giving them insufficient time to adjust their internal structures to avoid the suboptimal outcomes. Some groups suffer from perverse incentive systems that are themselves the results of policies pursued by central authorities. Many potential answers spring to mind regarding the question why some individuals do not achieve collective benefits for themselves, whereas others do. However, as long as analysts presume that individuals cannot change such situations themselves, they do not ask what internal or external variables can enhance or impede the efforts of communities of individuals to deal creatively and constructively with perverse problems such as the tragedy of the commons.

## Policy prescriptions as metaphors

Policy analysts who would recommend a single prescription for commons problems have paid little attention to how diverse institutional arrangements operate in practice. The centrists presume that unified authorities will operate in the field as they have been designed to do in the textbooks – determining the best policies to be adopted for a resource based on valid scientific theories and adequate information. Implementation of these policies without error is assumed. Monitoring and sanctioning activities are viewed as routine and nonproblematic.

Those advocating the private-property approach presume that the most efficient use patterns for CPRs will actually result from dividing the rights to access and control such resources. Systematic empirical studies have shown that private organization of firms dealing in goods such as electricity, transport, and medical services tends to be more efficient than governmental organization of such firms; for a review of this literature, see De Alessi (1980). Whether private or public forms are more efficient in industries in which certain potential beneficiaries cannot be excluded is, however, a different question. We are concerned with the types of institutions that will be most efficient for governing and managing diverse CPRs for which at least some potential beneficiaries cannot be excluded. Privatizing the ownership of CPRs need not have the same positive results as privatizing the ownership of an airline. Further, privatizing may not mean "dividing up" at all. Privatization can also mean assigning the exclusive right to harvest from a resource system to a single individual or firm.

Many policy prescriptions are themselves no more than metaphors. Both the centralizers and the privatizers frequently advocate oversimplified, idealized institutions – paradoxically, almost "institution-free" institutions. An assertion that central regulation is necessary tells us nothing about the way a central agency should be constituted, what authority it should have, how the limits on its authority should be maintained, how it will obtain information, or how its agents should be selected, motivated to do their work, and have their performances monitored and rewarded or sanctioned. An assertion that the imposition of private property rights is necessary tells us nothing about how that bundle of rights is to be defined, how the various attributes of the goods involved will be measured, who will pay for the costs of excluding nonowners from access, how conflicts over rights will be adjudicated, or how the residual interests of the right-holders in the resource system itself will be organized.

An important lesson that one learns by carefully studying the growing number of systematic studies by scholars associated with "the new institutionalism" is that these "institutional details" are important.[23] Whether or not any equilibria are possible and whether or not an equilibrium would be an improvement for the individuals involved (or for others who are in turn affected by these individuals) will depend on the particular structures

22

of the institutions. In the most general sense, all institutional arrangements can be thought of as games in extensive form. As such, the particular options available, the sequencing of those options, the information provided, and the relative rewards and punishments assigned to different sequences of moves can all change the pattern of outcomes achieved. Further, the particular structure of the physical environment involved also will have a major impact on the structure of the game and its results. Thus, a set of rules used in one physical environment may have vastly different consequences if used in a different physical environment.

## Policies based on metaphors can be harmful

Relying on metaphors as the foundation for policy advice can lead to results substantially different from those presumed to be likely. Nationalizing the ownership of forests in Third World countries, for example, has been advocated on the grounds that local villagers cannot manage forests so as to sustain their productivity and their value in reducing soil erosion. In countries where small villages had owned and regulated their local communal forests for generations, nationalization meant expropriation. In such localities, villagers had earlier exercised considerable restraint over the rate and manner of harvesting forest products. In some of these countries, national agencies issued elaborate regulations concerning the use of forests, but were unable to employ sufficient numbers of foresters to enforce those regulations. The foresters who were employed were paid such low salaries that accepting bribes became a common means of supplementing their income. The consequence was that nationalization created *open-access resources* where limited-access *common-property resources* had previously existed. The disastrous effects of nationalizing formerly communal forests have been well documented for Thailand (Feeny 1988a), Niger (Thomson 1977; Thomson, Feeny, and Oakerson 1986), Nepal (Arnold and Campbell 1986; Messerschmidt 1986), and India (Gadgil and Iyer 1989). Similar problems occurred in regard to inshore fisheries when national agencies presumed that they had exclusive jurisdiction over all coastal waters (Cordell and McKean 1986; W. Cruz 1986; Dasgupta 1982; Panayoutou 1982; Pinkerton 1989a).

## A CHALLENGE

An important challenge facing policy scientists is to develop theories of human organization based on realistic assessment of human capabilities and limitations in dealing with a variety of situations that initially share

23

some or all aspects of a tragedy of the commons. Empirically validated theories of human organization will be essential ingredients of a policy science that can inform decisions about the likely consequences of a multitude of ways of organizing human activities. Theoretical inquiry involves a search for regularities. It involves abstraction from the complexity of a field setting, followed by the positing of theoretical variables that underlie observed complexities. Specific models of a theory involve further abstraction and simplification for the purpose of still finer analysis of the logical relationships among variables in a closed system. As a theorist, and at times a modeler, I see these efforts at the core of a policy science.

One can, however, get trapped in one's own intellectual web. When years have been spent in the development of a theory with considerable power and elegance, analysts obviously will want to apply this tool to as many situations as possible. The power of a theory is exactly proportional to the diversity of situations it can explain. All theories, however, have limits. Models of a theory are limited still further because many parameters must be fixed in a model, rather than allowed to vary. Confusing a model – such as that of a perfectly competitive market – with the theory of which it is one representation can limit applicability still further.

Scientific knowledge is as much an understanding of the diversity of situations for which a theory or its models are relevant as an understanding of its limits. The conviction that all physical structures could be described in terms of a set of perfect forms – circles, squares, and triangles – limited the development of astronomy until Johannes Kepler broke the bonds of classical thought and discovered that the orbit of Mars was elliptical – a finding that Kepler himself initially considered to be no more than a pile of dung (Koestler 1959). Godwin and Shepard (1979) pointed out a decade ago that policy scientists were doing the equivalent of "Forcing Squares, Triangles and Ellipses into a Circular Paradigm" by using the commons-dilemma model without serious attention to whether or not the variables in the empirical world conformed to the theoretical model. Many theoretical and empirical findings have been reported since Godwin and Shepard's article that should have made policy scientists even more skeptical about relying on a limited set of models to analyze the diversity of situations broadly referred to as CPR problems. Unfortunately, many analysts – in academia, special-interest groups, governments, and the press – still presume that common-pool problems are all dilemmas in which the participants themselves cannot avoid producing suboptimal results, and in some cases disastrous results.

What is missing from the policy analyst's tool kit – and from the set of accepted, well-developed theories of human organization – is an ade-

24

quately specified theory of collective action whereby a group of principals can organize themselves voluntarily to retain the residuals of their own efforts. Examples of self-organized enterprises abound. Most law firms are obvious examples: A group of lawyers will pool their assets to purchase a library and pay for joint secretarial and research assistance. They will develop their own internal governance mechanisms and formulas for allocating costs and benefits to the partners. Most cooperatives are also examples. The cases of self-organized and self-governed CPRs that we consider in Chapter 3 are also examples. But until a theoretical explanation – based on human choice – for self-organized and self-governed enterprises is fully developed and accepted, major policy decisions will continue to be undertaken with a presumption that individuals cannot organize themselves and always need to be organized by external authorities.

Further, all organizational arrangements are subject to stress, weakness, and failure. Without an adequate theory of self-organized collective action, one cannot predict or explain when individuals will be unable to solve a common problem through self-organization alone, nor can one begin to ascertain which of many intervention strategies might be effective in helping to solve particular problems. As discussed earlier, there is a considerable difference between the presumption that a regulatory agency should be established and the presumption that a reliable court system is needed to monitor and enforce self-negotiated contracts. If the theories being used in a policy science do not include the possibility of self-organized collective action, then the importance of a court system that can be used by self-organizing groups to monitor and enforce contracts will not be recognized.[24]

I hope this inquiry will contribute to the development of an empirically supported theory of self-organizing and self-governing forms of collective action. What I attempt to do in this volume is to combine the strategy used by many scholars associated with the "new institutionalism" with the strategy used by biologists for conducting empirical work related to the development of a better theoretical understanding of the biological world.

As an institutionalist studying empirical phenomena, I presume that individuals try to solve problems as effectively as they can. That assumption imposes a discipline on me. Instead of presuming that some individuals are incompetent, evil, or irrational, and others are omniscient, I presume that individuals have very similar limited capabilities to reason and figure out the structure of complex environments. It is my responsibility as a scientist to ascertain what problems individuals are trying to solve and what factors help or hinder them in these efforts. When the problems that I observe involve lack of predictability, information, and trust, as well as high levels of complexity and transactional difficulties, then my efforts to explain must take these problems overtly into account rather than assuming them away. In developing an explanation for observed behavior, I draw on a rich literature written by other scholars interested in institutions and their effects on individual incentives and behaviors in field settings.

Biologists also face the problem of studying complex processes that are poorly understood. Their scientific strategy frequently has involved identifying for empirical observation the simplest possible organism in which a process occurs in a clarified, or even exaggerated, form. The organism is not chosen because it is representative of all organisms. Rather, the organism is chosen because particular processes can be studied more effectively using this organism than using another.

My "organism" is a type of human situation. I call this situation a CPR situation and define exactly what I mean by this and other key terms in Chapter 2. In this volume, I do not include all potential CPR situations within the frame of reference. I focus entirely on small-scale CPRs, where the CPR is itself located within one country and the number of individuals affected varies from 50 to 15,000 persons who are heavily dependent on the CPR for economic returns. These CPRs are primarily inshore fisheries, smaller grazing areas, groundwater basins, irrigation systems, and communal forests. Because these are relatively small-scale situations, serious study is more likely to penetrate the surface complexity to identify underlying similarities and processes. Because the individuals involved gain a major part of their economic return from the CPRs, they are strongly motivated to try to solve common problems to enhance their own productivity over time. The effort to self-organize in these situations may be somewhat exaggerated, but that is exactly why I want to study this process in these settings. Further, when self-organization fails, I know that it is not because the collective benefits that could have been obtained were unimportant to the participants.

There are limits on the types of CPRs studied here: (1) renewable rather than nonrenewable resources, (2) situations where substantial scarcity exists, rather than abundance, and (3) situations in which the users can substantially harm one another, but not situations in which participants can produce major external harm for others. Thus, all asymmetrical pollution problems are excluded, as is any situation in which a group can form a cartel and control a sufficient part of the market to affect market price.

In the empirical studies, I present a synopsis of important CPR cases that have aided my understanding of the processes of self-organization and self-governance. These cases are in no sense a "random" sample of cases. Rather, these are cases that provide clear information about the processes involved in (1) governing long-enduring CPRs, (2) transforming existing institutional arrangements, and (3) failing to overcome continued CPR problems. These cases can thus be viewed as a collection of the most salient raw materials with which I have worked in my effort to understand how individuals organize and govern themselves to obtain collective benefits in situations where the temptations to free-ride and to break commitments are substantial.

From an examination and analysis of these cases, I attempt to develop a series of reasoned conjectures about how it is possible that some individuals organize themselves to govern and manage CPRs and others do not. I try to identify the underlying design principles of the institutions used by those who have successfully managed their own CPRs over extended periods of time and why these may affect the incentives for participants to continue investing time and effort in the governance and management of their own CPRs. I compare the institutions used in successful and unsuccessful cases, and I try to identify the internal and external factors that can impede or enhance the capabilities of individuals to use and govern CPRs.

I hope these conjectures contribute to the development of an empirically valid theory of self-organization and self-governance for at least one well-defined universe of problematical situations. That universe contains a substantial proportion of renewable resources heavily utilized by human beings in different parts of the world. It is estimated, for example, that 90% of the world's fishermen and over half of the fish consumed each year are captured in the small-scale, inshore fisheries included within the frame of this study (Panayoutou 1982, p. 49). Further, my choice of the CPR environment for intensive study was based on a presumption that I could learn about the processes of self-organization and self-governance of relevance to a somewhat broader set of environments.

Given the similarity between many CPR problems and the problems of providing small-scale collective goods, the findings from this volume should contribute to an understanding of the factors that can enhance or detract from the capabilities of individuals to organize collective action related to providing local public goods. All efforts to organize collective action, whether by an external ruler, an entrepreneur, or a set of principals who wish to gain collective benefits, must address a common set of problems. These have to do with coping with free-riding, solving commitment problems, arranging for the supply of new institutions, and monitoring individual compliance with sets of rules. A study that focuses on how individuals avoid free-riding, achieve high levels of commitment, arrange for new institutions, and monitor conformity to a set of rules in CPR environments should contribute to an understanding of how in-

27

dividuals address these crucial problems in some other settings as well.

Let me now give a brief sketch of how this book is organized. In Chapter 2, I define what I mean by a CPR situation and individual choice in a CPR situation. Then I examine a series of crucial questions that any theory of collective action must answer. To conclude the chapter, I examine two assumptions that have framed prior work and discuss the alternatives that frame my analysis. The empirical part of this volume is contained in Chapters 3, 4, and 5, where I examine specific cases of long-enduring CPR institutions and resources, the origin and development of CPR institutions, and CPR failures and fragilities. At the end of each empirical chapter, I consider what can be learned from the cases in that chapter that will contribute toward the development of a better theory of self-organization related to CPR environments. In Chapter 6, I pull together the theoretical reflections contained at the ends of Chapters 3, 4, and 5 and address the implications of these conjectures for the design of self-organizing and self-governing institutions.

# 2

## An institutional approach to the study of self-organization and self-governance in CPR situations

In Chapter 1, I described my strategy as that of a "new institutionalist" who has picked small-scale CPR situations to study because the processes of self-organization and self-governance are easier to observe in this type of situation than in many others. The central question in this study is how a group of principals who are in an interdependent situation can organize and govern themselves to obtain continuing joint benefits when all face temptations to free-ride, shirk, or otherwise act opportunistically. Parallel questions have to do with the combinations of variables that will (1) increase the initial likelihood of self-organization, (2) enhance the capabilities of individuals to continue self-organized efforts over time, or (3) exceed the capacity of self-organization to solve CPR problems without external assistance of some form.

This chapter has several objectives. First, I define what I mean by CPRs and how I view individual behaviors in complex and uncertain CPR situations. Then I examine the general problem facing individuals in CPR situations: how to organize to avoid the adverse outcomes of independent action. This general problem is solved by external agents in two well-accepted theories: the theory of the firm and the theory of the state. These explain how new institutions are supplied, how commitments are obtained, and how the actions of agents and subjects are monitored effectively, using in one case the firm, and in the other state, as an organizational device. How a group of principals – a community of citizens – can organize themselves to solve the problems of institutional supply, commitment, and monitoring is still a theoretical puzzle. Given that some individuals solve this puzzle, whereas others do not, a study of successful and unsuccessful efforts to solve CPR problems should address important issues related to the theory of collective action and the development of better policies related to CPRs. Many efforts to analyze collective-action problems have framed the analysis by presuming that all such problems can be represented as prisoner's dilemma (PD) games, that a single level of analysis is sufficient, and that transactions costs are insignificant and can be ignored. In the last section of this chapter, I propose assumptions that are alternatives to those that normally frame the analysis of collective action.

## THE CPR SITUATION

### *CPRs and resource units*

The term "common-pool resource" refers to a natural or man-made resource system that is sufficiently large as to make it costly (but not impossible) to exclude potential beneficiaries from obtaining benefits from its use. To understand the processes of organizing and governing CPRs, it is essential to distinguish between the *resource system* and the flow of *resource units* produced by the system, while still recognizing the dependance of the one on the other.

Resource systems are best thought of as stock variables that are capable, under favorable conditions, of producing a maximum quantity of a flow variable without harming the stock or the resource system itself. Examples of resource systems include fishing grounds, groundwater basins, grazing areas, irrigation canals, bridges, parking garages, mainframe computers, and streams, lakes, oceans, and other bodies of water. Resource units are what individuals appropriate or use from resource systems. Resource units are typified by the tons of fish harvested from a fishing ground, the acre-feet or cubic meters of water withdrawn from a groundwater basin or an irrigation canal, the tons of fodder consumed by animals from a grazing area, the number of bridge crossings used per year by a bridge, the parking spaces filled, the central processing units consumed by those sharing a computer system, and the quantity of biological waste absorbed per year by a stream or other waterway. The distinction between the resource as a *stock* and the harvest of use units as a *flow* is especially useful in connection with *renewable* resources, where it is possible to define a replenishment rate. As long as the average rate of withdrawal does not exceed the average rate of replenishment, a renewable resource is sustained over time.[1]

Access to a CPR can be limited to a single individual or firm or to multiple individuals or teams of individuals who use the resource system at the same time. The CPRs studied in this volume are used by multiple individuals or firms. Following Plott and Meyer (1975), I call the process of withdrawing resource units from a resource system "appropriation." Those who withdraw such units are called "appropriators."[2] One term –

"appropriator" – can thus be used to refer to herders, fishers, irrigators, commuters, and anyone else who appropriates resource units from some type of resource system. In many instances appropriators use or consume the resource units they withdraw (e.g., where fishers harvest primarily for consumption). Appropriators also use resource units as inputs into production processes (e.g., irrigators apply water to their fields to produce rice). In other instances, the appropriators immediately transfer ownership of resource units to others, who are then the users of the resource units (e.g., fishers who sell their catch as soon as possible after arrival at a port).

The analysis of scarce, renewable resources is made from the perspective of the appropriators. This is not the only perspective that can be used in an analysis of complex CPR problems. If the appropriators of a resource unit gain considerable market power, such as by creating a cartel to influence price, their strategies affect themselves as well as others. This analysis relates to situations in which CPR appropriators have no power in a final-goods market, nor do their actions have significant impact on the environment of others living outside the range of their CPR.

The term I use to refer to those who arrange for the provision of a CPR is "providers." I use the term "producer" to refer to anyone who actually constructs, repairs, or takes actions that ensure the long-term sustenance of the resource system itself. Frequently, providers and producers are the same individuals, but they do not have to be (V. Ostrom, Tiebout, and Warren 1961). A national government may provide an irrigation system in the sense of arranging for its financing and design. It may then arrange with local farmers to produce and maintain it. If local farmers are given the authority to arrange for maintenance, then they become both the providers and the producers of maintenance activities related to a CPR.

A resource system can be jointly provided and/or produced by more than one person or firm. The actual process of appropriating resource units from the CPR can be undertaken by multiple appropriators simultaneously or sequentially. The resource units, however, *are not subject to joint use or appropriation.* The fish harvested by one boat are not there for someone else. The water spread on one farmer's fields cannot be spread onto someone else's fields. Thus, the resource units are not jointly used, but the resource system is subject to joint use. Once multiple appropriators rely on a given resource system, improvements to the system are simultaneously available to all appropriators. It is costly (and in some cases infeasible) to exclude one appropriator of a resource system from improvements made to the resource system itself. All appropriators benefit from maintenance performed on an irrigation canal, a bridge, or a computer system whether they contribute or not.

31

Failure to distinguish between the subtractability of the resource units and the jointness of the resource system has in the past contributed to confusion about the relationship of CPRs to public or collective goods.[3] Michael Taylor recognized the difference between CPRs and collective goods when he wrote the following:

There is, in particular, a very important class of collective action problems which arise in connection with the use of resources to which there is open access – resources, that is, which nobody is prevented from using. These resources need not be public goods.                                         (M. Taylor 1987, p. 3)

The relatively high costs of physically excluding joint appropriators from the resource or from improvements made to the resource system are similar to the high costs of excluding potential beneficiaries from public goods. This shared attribute is responsible for the ever present temptation to free-ride that exists in regard to both CPRs and public goods. There is as much temptation to avoid contributing to the provision of a resource system as there is to avoid contributing to the provision of public security or weather forecasts. Theoretical propositions that are derived solely from the difficulty of exclusion are applicable to the *provision* of both CPRs and collective goods.

But one's use of a weather forecast does not subtract from the availability of that forecast to others, just as one's consumption of public security does not reduce the general level of security available in a community.[4] "Crowding effects" and "overuse" problems are chronic in CPR situations, but absent in regard to pure public goods. The subractability of the resource unit leads to the possibility of approaching the limit of the number of resource units produced by a CPR. When the CPR is a man-made structure, such as a bridge, approaching the limit of crossing units will lead to congestion. When the CPR is a biological resource, such as a fishery or a forest, approaching the limit of resource units not only may produce short-run crowding effects but also may destroy the capability of the resource itself to continue producing resource units. Even a physical resource, such as a bridge, can be destroyed by heavier use than was allowed for in its engineering specifications.

Thus, propositions derived from a theory of public goods that are based on the nonsubtractive attributes of those goods are *not* applicable to an analysis of *appropriation* and *use* of subtractable resource units. Appropriation and use of the resource units are more closely related to the theory of private goods than to the theory of public goods. On the other hand, the process of designing, implementing, and enforcing a set of rules to co-ordinate provision activities is equivalent to the provision of a local collective good. CPR appropriators who organize themselves to govern and manage a CPR are faced with some problems that are similar to those of appropriating private goods and other problems that are similar to those of providing public goods. Both aspects are intimately bound together physically and analytically. In a particular CPR, if problems associated with the appropriation of subtractable resource units become severe, local appropriators may refuse to undertake provision activities.[5] No appropriation of resource units can occur without a resource system. Without a fair, orderly, and efficient method of allocating resource units, local appropriators have little motivation to contribute to the continued provision of the resource system.

## Rational appropriators in complex and uncertain situations

The decisions and actions of CPR appropriators to appropriate from and provide a CPR are those of broadly rational individuals who find themselves in complex and uncertain situations. An individual's choice of behavior in any particular situation will depend on how the individual learns about, views, and weighs the benefits and costs of actions and their perceived linkage to outcomes that also involve a mixture of benefits and costs.[6]

Organizing appropriators for collective action regarding a CPR is usually an uncertain and complex undertaking. Uncertainty has many external sources: the quantity and timing of rainfall, the temperature and amount of sunlight, the presence or absence of disease-bearing vectors, and the market prices of various inputs or final products. Other sources of uncertainty are internal to the CPR and the appropriators using the CPR. A major source of uncertainty is lack of knowledge. The exact structure of the resource system itself – its boundary and internal characteristics – must be established. Ascertaining the structure of the resource system may come about as a by-product of extended use and careful observation, as in the case of appropriating from a fishing ground or grazing range. Moreover, this folk knowledge must be preserved and passed along from one generation to the next. For a groundwater basin, on the other hand, the discovery of the internal structure may require a major investment in research by geologists and engineers.

How appropriators' actions affect the resource system, the yield of resource units, and each other's outcomes must also be ascertained.[7] It is not immediately apparent, for example, how one irrigator's forbearance in taking water from a canal will affect the yield obtained by that farmer or by other farmers. In some cases, a farmer located near the head of a system may be able to curtail his water use substantially without a major impact on his own yield, while substantially enhancing the yields of downstream farmers. In other cases, the excess water taken by the farmer located near the headworks may subsequently also flow to farmers located lower in the system. Restraint by the farmer located higher in the system may not increase total yield. Uncertainties stemming from lack of knowledge may be reduced over time as a result of skillful pooling and blending of scientific knowledge and local time-and-place knowledge. Uncertainty reduction is costly and never fully accomplished. The uncertainty stemming from strategic behavior by the appropriators remains even after one acquires considerable knowledge about the resource system itself.

Given these levels of uncertainty about the basic structure of the problems appropriators face, the only reasonable assumption to make about the discovery and calculation processes employed is that appropriators engage in a considerable amount of trial-and-error learning. Many actions are selected without full knowledge of their consequences. Some dams wash out after the first heavy rains. Some rules cannot be enforced because no one is able to monitor conformance to them. By definition, trial-and-error methods involve error, perhaps even disasters. Over time, appropriators gain a more accurate understanding of the physical world and what to expect from the behavior of others.

Appropriators in many settings are strongly motivated to find better solutions to their problems if they can. The economic livelihood of the appropriators depends on their ingenuity in solving individual and joint problems. How complete and accurate the information local appropriators obtain about their situation will vary from one situation to another, depending on the number of appropriators involved, the complexity of the situation, and the stability of factors affecting individual behaviors and resource-system responses. The symmetry of information available to appropriators will also vary from situation to situation, depending on how expensive it is to acquire information and the rules used for disseminating information to appropriators.

Collective-action problems related to the provision of CPRs and appropriation from CPRs extend over time. Individuals attribute less value to benefits that they expect to receive in the distant future, and more value to those expected in the immediate future. In other words, individuals discount future benefits – how severely depends on several factors. Time horizons are affected by whether or not individuals expect that they or their children will be present to reap these benefits, as well as by opportunities they may have for more rapid returns in other settings. The discount rates applied to future yields derived from a particular CPR may differ substantially across various types of appropriators. In a fishery, for example, the discount rates of local fishers who live in nearby villages will differ from the discount rates of those who operate the larger trawlers, who may fish anywhere along a coastline. The time horizons of the local fishers, in relation to the yield of the inshore fishery, extend far into the future. They hope that their children and their children's children can make a living in the same location. More mobile fishers, on the other hand, can go on to other fishing grounds when local fish are no longer available.

Discount rates are affected by the levels of physical and economic security faced by appropriators. Appropriators who are uncertain whether or not there will be sufficient food to survive the year will discount future returns heavily when traded off against increasing the probability of survival during the current year. Similarly, if a CPR can be destroyed by the actions of others, no matter what local appropriators do, even those who have constrained their harvesting from a CPR for many years will begin to heavily discount future returns, as contrasted with present returns.[8] Discount rates are also affected by the general norms shared by the individuals living in a particular society, or even a local community, regarding the relative importance of the future as compared with the present.

Discount rates are not the only aspects of human choice that are affected by shared norms of behavior. Although I stress the importance that the expected consequences will have on one's decisions, individuals vary in regard to the importance they place on acting in ways that they and others view as right and proper. Norms of behavior reflect valuations that individuals place on actions or strategies in and of themselves, not as they are connected to immediate consequences.[9] When an individual has strongly internalized a norm related to keeping promises, for example, the individual suffers shame and guilt when a personal promise is broken. If the norm is shared with others, the individual is also subject to considerable social censure for taking an action considered to be wrong by others.

Norms of behavior therefore affect the way alternatives are perceived and weighed. For many routine decisions, actions that are considered wrong among a set of individuals interacting together over time will not even be included in the set of strategies contemplated by the individual. If the individual's attention is drawn to the possibility of taking such an action by the availability of a very large payoff for doing so, the action may be included in the set of alternatives to be considered, but with a high cost attached. Actions that are strongly proscribed among a set of individuals will occur less frequently (even though they promise to yield high net payoffs to individuals) than will those same actions in a community that does not censure such actions.

The most important impact that the type and extent of shared norms will have on the strategies available to individuals has to do with the level of opportunistic behavior that appropriators can expect from other appropriators. Opportunism is defined as "self-interest with guile" (Williamson 1975). In a setting in which few individuals share norms about the impropriety of breaking promises, refusing to do one's share, shirking, or taking other opportunistic actions, each appropriator must expect all other appropriators to act opportunistically whenever they have the chance. In such a setting it is difficult to develop stable, long-term commitments. Expensive monitoring and sanctioning mechanisms may be needed. Some long-term arrangements that once were productive are no longer feasible, given their costs of enforcement. In a setting in which there are strong norms against opportunistic behavior, each appropriator will be less wary about the dangers of opportunism.

In every group there will be individuals who will ignore norms and act opportunistically when given a chance. There are also situations in which the potential benefits will be so high that even strongly committed individuals will break norms. Consequently, the adoption of norms of behavior will not reduce opportunistic behavior to zero. Opportunistic behavior is a possibility that must be dealt with by all appropriators trying to solve CPR problems.

In some settings, however, rampant opportunistic behavior severely limits what can be done jointly without major investments in monitoring and sanctioning arrangements. Substantial benefits have to be obtained to make costly monitoring and sanctioning activities worthwhile. In other settings, long-term joint commitments can be undertaken with only a modest investment in monitoring and sanctioning arrangements. Shared norms that reduce the cost of monitoring and sanctioning activities can be viewed as social capital to be utilized in solving CPR problems.

Because CPR settings extend over time, and individuals adopt internal norms, it is possible for individuals to utilize contingent strategies, not simply independent strategies, in relating to one another. By "contingent strategies" I mean a whole class of planned actions that are contingent on conditions in the world. The contingent strategy that has been the object of the most scholarly attention is tit for tat in a two-person game in which an individual adopts a cooperative action in the first round and then mimics the action of the opponent in future rounds (Axelrod 1981, 1984). There are many other contingent strategies that can be adopted; they vary in terms of the level of initial cooperation extended and the actions of others required for switching behavioral patterns. That individuals utilize contingent strategies in many complex and uncertain field settings is an important foundation for later analysis.

Thus, I use a very broad conception of rational action, rather than a narrowly defined conception. The internal world of individual choice that I use is illustrated in Figure 2.1. Four internal variables – expected benefits, expected costs, internal norms, and discount rates – affect an individual's choice of strategies. Individuals selecting strategies jointly produce outcomes in an external world that impinge on future expectations concerning the benefits and costs of actions. What types of internal norms an individual possesses are affected by the shared norms held by others in regard to particular types of situations. Similarly, internal discount rates are affected by the range of opportunities that an individual has outside any particular situation.

This general model of individual choice is thus open to many particular specifications. The particular assumptions made about the completeness, shape, and differentiability of preference functions depend on the situation of relevance for a particular model in this theory. In simple, highly constrained situations where individuals have interacted for long periods of time, assumptions about convex, twice-differentiable preference functions

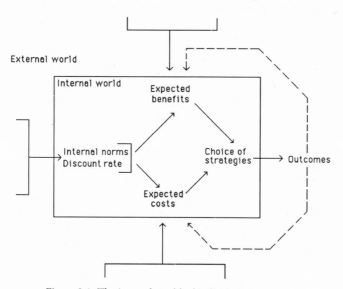

Figure 2.1. The internal world of individual choice.

may be appropriate. In complex situations involving unstructured problems, assuming complete preference functions of any shape is not meaningful. The most one can say is that the individuals in such situations are engaged in a trial-and-error effort to learn more about the results of their actions so that they can evaluate benefits and costs more effectively over time.

This general conception is one way of fulfilling Popper's advice to make the rationality principle "an almost empty principle" (Popper 1967). It places the primary weight of theoretical analysis on specifying rigorously and fully the models of the situations in which individuals find themselves. It accepts Popper's methodological advice to emphasize the way we describe the situations in which individuals find themselves so that we can use observable variables to reject our theories, rather than internal, in-the-mind, subjective variables, which are far more difficult to measure.

Thus, most of the analysis contained in this volume examines the combinations of situational variables that are most likely to affect individuals' choices of strategies and how those situational variables occur.

## INTERDEPENDENCE, INDEPENDENT ACTION, AND COLLECTIVE ACTION

When multiple appropriators are dependent on a given CPR as a source of economic activity, they are jointly affected by almost everything they do. Each individual must take into account the choices of others when assessing personal choices. If one fisher occupies a good fishing site, a second fisher arriving at the same location must invest more resources to travel to another site, or else fight for the first site. If one irrigator allocates time and materials to repairing a broken control gate in an irrigation canal, all other irrigators using that canal are affected by that action, whether or not they want the control gate fixed and whether or not they contribute anything to the repair. The key fact of life for coappropriators is that they are tied together in a lattice of interdependence so long as they continue to share a single CPR. The physical interdependence does not disappear when effective institutional rules are utilized in the governance and management of the CPR. The physical interdependence remains; what changes is the result the appropriators obtain.

When appropriators act independently in relationship to a CPR generating scarce resource units, the total net benefits they obtain usually will be less than could have been achieved if they had coordinated their strategies in some way. At a minimum, the returns they receive from their appropriation efforts will be lower when decisions are made independently than they

38

would have been otherwise. At worst, they can destroy the CPR itself. As long as the appropriators stay "unorganized," they cannot achieve a joint return as high as they could have received if they had organized in some way to undertake collective action. Mancur Olson stated the key problem facing appropriators who rely on a single CPR:

> ... when a number of individuals have a common or collective interest – when they share a single purpose or objective – individual, *unorganized* action [either will] not be able to advance that common interest at all, or will not be able to advance that interest adequately.               (Olson 1965, p. 7; emphasis added)

Prisoners who have been placed in separate cells and cannot communicate with one another are also in an interdependent situation in which they must act independently. Acting independently in this situation is the result of coercion, not its absence. The herders in Hardin's model also act independently. Each decides on the number of animals to put on the meadow without concern for how that will affect the actions chosen by others.

At the most general level, the problem facing CPR appropriators is one of organizing: how to change the situation from one in which appropriators act independently to one in which they adopt coordinated strategies to obtain higher joint benefits or reduce their joint harm. That does not necessarily mean creating an organization. Organizing is a process; an organization is the result of that process. An organization of individuals who constitute an ongoing enterprise is only one form of organization that can result from the process of organizing.

The core of organization involves changes that order activities so that sequential, contingent, and frequency-dependent decisions are introduced where simultaneous, noncontingent, and frequency-independent actions had prevailed.[10] Almost all organization is accomplished by specifying a sequence of activities that must be carried out in a particular order.[11] Because of the repeated situations involved in most organized processes, individuals can use contingent strategies in which cooperation will have a greater chance of evolving and surviving. Individuals frequently are willing to forgo immediate returns in order to gain larger joint benefits when they observe many others following the same strategy. By requiring the participation of a minimal set of individuals, organizations can draw on this frequency-dependent behavior to obtain willing contributions on the part of many others. Changing the positive and negative inducements associated with particular actions and outcomes and the levels and types of information available can also encourage coordination of activities.[12]

Unlike prisoners, most CPR appropriators are not coerced into acting independently. Making the switch, however, from independent to co-

39

ordinated or collective action is a nontrivial problem. The costs involved in transforming a situation from one in which individuals act independently to one in which they coordinate activities can be quite high. And the benefits produced are shared by all appropriators, whether or not they share any of the costs of transforming the situation. Empirically, we know that some appropriators are able to solve this problem, and some are not. Theoretically, we do not have a coherent explanation for why some succeed and others fail.

The theory of the firm and the theory of the state can each provide an explanation for one way in which collective action can be achieved. Each involves the creation of a new institutional arrangement in which the rules in use are fundamentally different from those that structure independent action. Let us briefly and in a stylized fashion consider how each theory can "solve" the problem of independent action in an interdependent situation. By doing this, we can better illustrate the absence of a similar theory that would identify the mechanisms by which a group of individuals could organize themselves.

## The theory of the firm

In the theory of the firm, an entrepreneur recognizes an opportunity to increase the return that can be achieved when individuals are potentially involved in an interdependent relationship.[13] The entrepreneur then negotiates a series of contracts with various participants that specify how they are to act in a coordinated, rather than independent, fashion. Each participant voluntarily chooses whether or not to join the firm, but gives up to the entrepreneur discretion over some range of choices. The participants become the agents of the entrepreneur. After paying each of the agents, the entrepreneur retains residual profits (or absorbs losses).

Consequently, the entrepreneur is highly motivated to organize the activity in a manner as efficient as possible. The entrepreneur attempts to craft contracts with agents that will induce them to act so as to increase the returns to the entrepreneur, and the entrepreneur monitors the agents' performances. The entrepreneur can terminate the contract of an agent who does not perform to the satisfaction of the entrepreneur. Because agents freely decide whether or not to accept the terms of the entrepreneur's contract, the organization is considered private, voluntary, and, at least by some individuals, nonexploitative. If there are large residuals to be obtained, however, it is the entrepreneur, not the agents, who receives them.[14] When a firm is located in an open market, one can presume that external competition will pressure the entrepreneur toward developing efficient internal institutions.

## The theory of the state

The theory of the state can also be presented in a brief and stylized version. Instead of an entrepreneur, we posit a ruler who recognizes that substantial benefits can be obtained by organizing some activities. As Hobbes first formulated the theory, individuals who independently engage in protection activities overinvest in weapons and surveillance and consequently live in constant fear. If a ruler gains a monopoly on the use of force, the ruler can use coercion as the fundamental mechanism to organize a diversity of human activities that will produce collective benefits. The ruler obtains taxes, labor, or other resources from subjects by threatening them with severe sanctions if they do not provide the resources.

The "wise" ruler uses the resources thus obtained to increase the general level of economic well-being of the subjects to a degree sufficient that the ruler can increase tax revenues while being able to reduce the more oppressive uses of coercion. Rulers, like entrepreneurs, keep the residuals. Subjects, like agents, may be substantially better off as a result of subjecting themselves to the coercion exercised by rulers. If the effort is highly successful, the ruler captures a substantial portion of the surplus.[15] There is no mechanism, such as a competitive market, that would exert pressure on the ruler to design efficient institutions. The ruler may face rebellion if the measures selected are too repressive, or military defeat if the realm is not adequately organized to do well in warfare.

In both the theory of the firm and the theory of the state, the burden of organizing collective action is undertaken by one individual, whose returns are directly related to the surplus generated. Both involve an outsider taking primary responsibility for supplying the needed changes in institutional rules to coordinate activities. The entrepreneur or the ruler makes credible commitments to punish anyone who does not follow the rules of the firm or the state. Because they gain the residuals, it is in their interest to punish nonconformance to their rules if they are confronted with nonconformance. Consequently, their threats to punish are credible (Schelling 1960; Williamson 1983). It is also in their interest to monitor the actions of agents and subjects to be sure they conform to prior agreements. Both theories thus address how a new institutional arrangement can come about, how credible commitments can be made, and why monitoring must be supplied.[16]

# Governing the commons

## THREE PUZZLES: SUPPLY, COMMITMENT, AND MONITORING

Although the theory of the firm and the theory of the state can resolve these problems, no equivalently well developed and generally accepted theory provides a coherent account for how a set of principals, faced with a collective-action problem, can solve (1) the problem of supplying a new set of institutions, (2) the problem of making credible commitments, and (3) the problem of mutual monitoring.

### *The problem of supply*

In a recent commentary on contractarianism and the new institutionalism, Robert Bates (1988) raises the issue that modern institutional theories do not adequately address the problem of supply. As he points out, "the new institutionalism is contractarian in spirit. Institutions are demanded because they enhance the welfare of rational actors. The problem is: Why are they supplied?" Bates first examines assurance games, where suppling new rules is considered easier to accomplish than it is in PD games, because there are mutually beneficial outcomes that are potential equilibria in the sense that once reached, no one has an incentive independently to switch strategies. Equilibria in assurance games do not, however, necessarily reward participants equally. Participants prefer a set of rules that will give them the most advantageous outcome. Although all will prefer a new institution that will enable them to coordinate their activities to achieve one of these equilibria, in contrast to continuing their independent actions, a fundamental disagreement is likely to arise among participants regarding which institution to choose. "The proposed solution to coordination – or assurance – games thus itself constitutes a collective dilemma" (Bates 1988, p. 394).[17]

Bates then turns to problems faced by a set of symmetric principals facing a collective dilemma in which all would benefit from a change in rules. Because supplying a new set of rules is the equivalent of providing another public good, the problem faced by a set of principals is that obtaining these new rules is a second-order collective dilemma.

Even if the payoffs were symmetric and all persons were made [equally] better off from the introduction of the institutions, there would still be a failure of supply, since the institution would provide a collective good and rational individuals would seek to secure its benefits for free. The incentives to free-ride would undermine the incentives to organize a solution to the collective dilemma. It is subject to the very incentive problems it is supposed to resolve.

(Bates 1988, pp. 394–5)

42

## An institutional approach to CPR self-governance

Because Bates presumes that the second-order dilemma is no easier to solve than the initial dilemma, he concludes that a new set of rules to solve the collective dilemma will not be provided by a set of principals (M. Taylor 1987).

Bates finds this deeply puzzling as it is obvious to him that some individuals in field settings *do* solve the problem of supply. Bates wishes to remain an institutionalist and a rational-choice theorist. His approach to addressing the inadequacy of current theories to explain how individuals supply their own rules is to turn for inspiration to some of the recent work in the theory of repeated games under uncertainty. Kreps and associates (1982) have demonstrated that in a finitely repeated PD game, some uncertainty about the exact payoff to a player can produce cooperative equilibria, as well as many other equilibria. Given this, it will pay one player to signal to other players an intention to cooperate, in the hope that they will reciprocate for a series of mutually productive plays. Thus, establishing trust and establishing a sense of community are, in Bates's view, mechanisms for solving the problem of supplying new institutions.

Driven by a concern with institutions, we re-enter the world of the behavioralists. But we do so not in protest against the notion of rational choice, but rather in an effort to understand how rationality on the part of individuals leads to coherence at the level of society. (Bates 1988, p. 399)

Bates's approach is similar to the approach taken in this volume.

### The problem of credible commitment

A second puzzle to be solved in explaining how a set of principals can organize themselves to obtain long-term collective benefits is the problem of commitment.[18] To understand the heart of the "commitment" problem, let us consider a highly simplified picture of the choices available to appropriators in CPR situations.[19] In all cases in which individuals have organized themselves to solve CPR problems, rules have been established by the appropriators that have severely constrained the authorized actions available to them. Such rules specify, for example, how many resource units an individual can appropriate, when, where, and how they can be appropriated, and the amounts of labor, materials, or money that must be contributed to various provisioning activities. If everyone, or almost everyone, follows these rules, resource units will be allocated more predictably and efficiently, conflict levels will be reduced, and the resource system itself will be sustained over time.

During an initial time period, an appropriator, calculating his or her estimated future flow of benefits if most appropriators agree to follow a proposed set of rules, may agree to abide by the set of rules in order to get others to agree. During later time periods, the immediate return to the appropriator for breaking one or another of the rules frequently can be high. When an irrigator's crops are severely stressed, the financial benefit of taking water "out of turn" can be substantial. Breaking the rules may save an entire crop from drought. On many occasions after an initial agreement to a set of rules, each appropriator must make further choices. Minimally, the choice at each decision time subsequent to the agreement can be thought of as the choice between complying to a set of rules, $C_t$, or breaking the set of rules in some fashion, $B_t$. On many occasions, $B_t$ will generate a higher immediate return for the appropriator than will $C_t$, unless $B_t$ is detected and a sanction, $S$, is imposed that makes $C_t > B_t - S$.[20]

At the beginning of the process, all appropriators know the general configuration of the commitment problem. If they wish to change their appropriation rules, for example, to rotate the authority to withdraw water from an irrigation system among authorized appropriators, how does one appropriator credibly commit himself or herself to follow a rotation system when everyone knows that the temptation to break that commitment will be extremely strong in future time periods? Each appropriator can pledge: "I will keep my commitment if you keep yours." But when the temptation arises, how do past commitments bind the appropriator to future sacrifices? And given that it may be possible to steal water without being observed, how do the other appropriators know that commitments are actually being kept? No one wants to be a "sucker," keeping a promise that everyone else is breaking.

External coercion is a frequently cited theoretical solution to the problem of commitment (Schelling 1984). The presumption is made that if individuals commit themselves to a contract whereby a stiff sanction ($S > B_{max}$) will be imposed by an external enforcer to ensure compliance during all future time periods, then each can make a credible commitment and obtain benefits that would not otherwise be attainable. External coercion is at times a sleight-of-hand solution, because the theorist does not address what motivates the external enforcer to monitor behavior and impose sanctions. That is not, however, the issue at hand; it will be discussed later. The immediate issue is that a self-organized group must solve the commitment problem without an external enforcer. They have to motivate themselves (or their agents) to monitor activities and be willing to impose sanctions to keep conformance high.

These puzzles cumulate. Even if one appropriator took the time and effort to analyze the problems they faced and to devise a set of rules that

44

could improve their joint returns, the effort at supply would be pointless unless the appropriators could commit themselves to follow the rules. Unless the monitoring problem can be solved, credible commitments cannot be made. So let us now address the problem of mutual monitoring.

## The problem of mutual monitoring

The question of how a set of principals can engage in mutual monitoring of conformance to a set of their own rules is not easily addressed within the confines of collective-action theory. In fact, the usual theoretical prediction is that they will not do so. The usual presumption that individuals will not themselves monitor a set of rules, even if they have devised those rules themselves, was summarized by Jon Elster in a recent discussion of the motivations for workers to monitor each other's participation in a union:

Before a union can force or induce workers to join it must overcome a free-rider problem in the first place. To assume that the incentives are offered in a decentralized way, by mutual monitoring, gives rise to a second-order free-rider problem. Why, for instance, should a rational, selfish worker ostracize or otherwise punish those who don't join the union? What's in it for him? True, it may be better for all members if all punish non-members than if none do, but for each member it may be even better to remain passive. Punishment almost invariably is costly to the punisher, while the benefits from punishment are diffusely distributed over the members. It is, in fact, a public good: To provide it, one would need second-order selective incentives which would, however, run into a third-order free-rider problem.                                        (Elster 1989, pp. 40–1)[21]

Dilemmas nested inside dilemmas appear to be able to defeat a set of principals attempting to solve collective-action problems through the design of new institutions to alter the structure of the incentives they face. Without monitoring, there can be no credible commitment; without credible commitment, there is no reason to propose new rules. The process unravels from both ends, because the problem of supply is presumed unsolvable in the first place. But some individuals have created institutions, committed themselves to follow rules, and monitored their own conformance to their agreements, as well as their conformance to the rules in a CPR situation. Trying to understand how they have done this is the challenge of this study.

## FRAMING INQUIRY

Understanding how individuals solve particular problems in field settings requires a strategy of moving back and forth from the world of theory to the world of action. Without theory, one can never understand the general

45

underlying mechanisms that operate in many guises in different situations. If not harnessed to solving empirical puzzles, theoretical work can spin off under its own momentum, reflecting little of the empirical world.

When theoretical predictions and empirical observations are inconsistent, adjustments in theory are needed.[22] Predictions that individuals will not devise, precommit to, and monitor their own rules to change the structure of interdependent situations so as to obtain joint benefits are inconsistent with evidence that some individuals have overcome these problems, though others have not.

Theories affect the way that a problem is framed, not simply the particular assumptions used in an explanation. The way a problem is framed affects which questions are asked and what one looks for in conducting empirical inquiries. Several of the presumptions that have framed the way that scholars have approached the analysis of collective action have led them to an overly pessimistic view of the capacity of individuals to restructure their own interdependent situations.

Scholars addressing the problem of collective action frequently presume (1) that the underlying structure is always that of a PD game and (2) that one level of analysis is sufficient. When CPR problems are conceptualized as collective-action problems – a useful way to think of them – these same presumptions continue to frame the analyses, leading to the policy prescriptions described in Chapter 1. Consequently, part of the strategy pursued in this inquiry is to start from an alternative set of initial presumptions:

1 Appropriators in CPR situations face a variety of appropriation and provision problems whose structures vary from one setting to another, depending on the values of underlying parameters.

2 Appropriators must switch back and forth across arenas and levels of analysis.

These presumptions lead me to examine questions in a manner somewhat different from that of an analyst using the "normal" presuppositions of collective-action theory, although I still rely heavily on the work of other scholars.

## Appropriation and provision problems

Although some interdependent CPR situations have the structure of a PD game, many do not. Several scholars have shown how some simple situations facing appropriators may be better characterized as "assurance" games and as the game known as "chicken" (Runge 1981, 1984a; M.

46

Taylor 1987; M. Taylor and Ward 1982). The underlying problem facing the appropriators in the Alanya fishing grounds discussed in Chapter 1 cannot be represented as a PD game. A formal analysis shows that it has the structure of an "assignment" game (Gardner and E. Ostrom 1990). In many irrigation systems similar to those discussed in Chapter 3, the fundamental choices facing appropriators are whether or not to steal water and whether or not to monitor the behaviors of others who might be stealing. The resulting game structure is complex and does not reduce down to any simple game. It does not have a single equilibrium. The amounts of stealing and monitoring that occur will depend on the values of parameters such as the number of appropriators, the cost of monitoring, the benefit from stealing, the punishment imposed when stealing is discovered, and the reward that a monitor receives for detecting a rule-breaker (Weissing and E. Ostrom 1990).

Consequently, instead of presuming that all CPR situations involve one underlying structure, I presume that the appropriators relying on any CPR face a variety of problems to be solved. The structure of these problems will depend on the values of underlying parameters, such as the value and predictability of the flow of resource units, the ease of observing and measuring appropriator activities, and so forth. In an effort to develop a unified framework within which to organize the analysis of CPR situations using the tools of game theory and institutional analysis and the findings from empirical studies in laboratory and field settings, Roy Gardner, James Walker, and I have found it most useful to cluster the problems facing CPR appropriators into two broad classes: appropriation problems and provision problems (Gardner et al. 1990).

When appropriators face appropriation problems, they are concerned with the effects that various methods of allocating a fixed, or time-independent, quantity of resource units will have on the net return obtained by the appropriators. Provision problems concern the effects of various ways of assigning responsibility for building, restoring, or maintaining the resource system over time, as well as the well-being of the appropriators. Appropriation problems are concerned with the allocation of the flow; provision problems are concerned with the stock. Appropriation problems are time-independent; provision problems are time-dependent. Both types of problems are involved in every CPR to a greater or lesser extent, and thus the solutions to one problem must be congruent with solutions to the other. The structure of an appropriation problem or a provision problem will depend on the particular configuration of variables related to the physical world, the rules in use, and the attributes of the individuals involved in a specific setting.

47

*Appropriation problems.* In regard to appropriation, the key problem in a CPR environment is how to allocate a fixed, time-independent quantity of resource units so as to avoid rent dissipation and reduce uncertainty and conflict over the assignment of rights. Rents are dissipated whenever the marginal returns from an appropriation process are smaller than the marginal costs of appropriation. Rent dissipation can occur because too many individuals are allowed to appropriate from the resource, because appropriators are allowed to withdraw more than the economically optimal quantity of resource units, or because appropriators overinvest in appropriation equipment (e.g., fishing gear).

In an open-access[23] CPR, in which no limit is placed on who can appropriate, the time-independent appropriation process frequently can be characterized as a PD game.[24] Rent dissipation is likely to be endemic. No appropriator has any incentive to leave any resource units for other appropriators to harvest (Gordon 1954; Scott 1955). In a limited-access CPR, in which a well-defined group of appropriators must jointly rely on a CPR for access to resource units, the incentives facing the appropriators will depend on the rules governing the quantity, timing, location, and technology of appropriation and how these are monitored and enforced. The structure of a limited-access CPR is not a PD game (Dasgupta and Heal 1979, p. 59) and lacks a dominant strategy for each participant. The incentives of appropriators who act independently, however, will lead them to overinvest in any input factor that is not constrained under the current rules (Townsend and Wilson 1987).

A second type of appropriation problem relates to assignment of spatial or temporal access to the resource. This occurs because spatial and temporal distributions of resource units frequently are heterogeneous and uncertain. Many fishing grounds, such as Alanya, are characterized by "fishing sites" that vary in their productivity. In grazing areas, one region may be drowned out in one year, but lush with growth in another year. Farmers who extract water from the head of an irrigation system can obtain more water than farmers who are located at the tail end. The risks associated with geographic or temporal uncertainty can be very high. Physical works, particularly those with storage, involve somewhat reduced risks, but well-enforced rules to allocate time or location of use or the quantity of resource units to specific users can reduce risks still further if the rules are well crafted to fit the physical attributes of the resource system. If risks are sufficiently reduced, appropriators can invest in productive enterprises that would not otherwise be economically viable. Physical violence occurring among the users of fisheries and irrigation systems is symptomatic of inadequate assignments of spatial or temporal slots to appropriators. When appropriators consider the assignment of access rights and duties to be unfair, uneconomic, uncertain, or inappropriately enforced, that can adversely affect their willingness to invest in provision activities. The particular rules used to regulate appropriation will affect monitoring and policing costs and the type of strategic behavior that will occur between appropriators and monitors (the detection/deterrence game).[25]

*Provision problems.* Analyses of provision problems focus on the time-dependent, productive nature of investment in the resource itself. Provision problems may occur on the supply side, on the demand side, or on both sides. The supply-side problem faced in a CPR environment is related to the construction of the resource itself and its maintenance. Construction problems are like any long-term investment in capital infrastructure. Maintenance problems involve determining the type and level of regular maintenance (and reserves for emergency repair) that will sustain the resource system over time. Given that an investment in maintenance will affect the future rate at which a capital infrastructure will deteriorate, decisions about these activities are difficult to make even when a single entrepreneur makes them. When this difficult long-term problem is combined with the free-riding incentives of multiple appropriators, we see that organizing to maintain a system is a challenging task.

Supply-side provision problems are similar to the supply-side problems in providing a continuing, rather than a one-shot, public good. If appropriators act independently, they can expect that less than an optimal effort will be devoted to the construction, and particularly to the maintenance, of the system because of free-riding. What makes the problem more difficult in a CPR situation than in a public-goods situation is that unless appropriation problems are resolved, the provision problems may prove intractable. In a public-goods situation, appropriation problems do not exist, because resource units are not subtractable.

Demand-side provision problems involve regulating withdrawal rates so that they do not adversely affect the resource itself. Many of the dynamic models of "rent dissipation" in the fisheries literature (Clark 1980; Clark, Munro, and Charles 1985) have focused on the time-dependent relationship between current withdrawals and future yields. The same rules that affect the allocation of this year's resource units will have an impact on the availability of resource units next year and the years thereafter.

The underlying uniformities of all CPR situations relate to the non-separability of one's choice of strategy and the choices made by others, as well as the fact that solving provision problems depends on achieving adequate solutions to appropriation problems, not the particular game-theoretical representations for these commonalities.[26] Many factors affect the strategic structure of a particular appropriation or provision problem, including the physical structure of a particular CPR, the technology available to the appropriators, the economic environment, and the sets of rules that affect the incentives that appropriators face. As Oliver (1980, p. 1,359) stressed after reviewing many of the efforts to present "the" model of collective action, "there is no one 'right' way to model collective action: different models imply different assumptions about the situation and lead to substantively different conclusions."

## Multiple levels of analysis

Most current analyses of CPR problems and related collective-action problems focus on a single level of analysis – what can be called the operational level of analysis (Kiser and E. Ostrom 1982). At the operational level of analysis, one assumes that both the rules of the game and the physical, technological constraints are given and will not change during the time frame of analysis: The actions of individuals in an operational situation directly affect the physical world. Resource units are withdrawn from a CPR. Inputs are transformed into outputs. Goods are exchanged. Appropriation and provision problems occur at an operational level. When doing an analysis of an operational situation, it is necessary for the analyst to assume that the technology and the institutional rules are known and unchanging. Both technology and rules are, however, subject to change over time. Analysis of technological changes has proved to be far more difficult than analysis of production and consumption decisions within a fixed technology (Dosi 1988; Nelson and Winter 1982). Analysis of institutional change is also far more difficult than analysis of operational decisions within a fixed set of rules.[27] The rules affecting operational choice are made within a set of collective-choice rules that are themselves made within a set of constitutional-choice rules. The constitutional-choice rules for a micro-setting are affected by collective-choice and constitutional-choice rules for larger jurisdictions. Individuals who have self-organizing capabilities switch back and forth between operational-, collective-, and constitutional-choice arenas, just as managers of production firms switch back and forth between producing products within a set technology, introducing a new technology, and investing resources in technology development. Given that CPR appropriators in some of the cases to be discussed in this volume do switch back and forth between arenas, we must drop the framing assumption that analysis at a single level will be sufficient. It is also essential to clarify what is meant by "institutions" in the first place.

"Institutions" can be defined as the sets of working rules that are used to determine who is eligible to make decisions in some arena, what actions are allowed or constrained, what aggregation rules will be used, what procedures must be followed, what information must or must not be provided, and what payoffs will be assigned to individuals dependent on their actions (E. Ostrom 1986a). All rules contain prescriptions that forbid, permit, or require some action or outcome. Working rules are those actually used, monitored, and enforced when individuals make choices about the actions they will take (Commons 1957). Enforcement may be undertaken by others directly involved, agents they hire, external enforcers, or any combination of these enforcers. One should not talk about a "rule" unless most people whose strategies are affected by it know of its existence and expect others to monitor behavior and to sanction nonconformance. In other words, working rules are common knowledge and are monitored and enforced. Common knowledge implies that every participant knows the rules, and knows that others know the rules, and knows that they also know that the participant knows the rules.[28] Working rules are always monitored and enforced, to some extent at least, by those directly involved. In any repetitive situation, one can assume that individuals come to know, through experience, good approximations of the levels of monitoring and enforcing involved.

Working rules may or may not closely resemble the formal laws that are expressed in legislation, administrative regulations, and court decisions. Formal law obviously is a major source of working rules in many settings, particularly when conformance to them is actively monitored and sanctions for noncompliance are enforced. When one speaks about a system that is governed by a "rule of law," this expresses the idea that formal laws and working rules are closely aligned and that enforcers are held accountable to the rules as well as others. In many CPR settings, the working rules used by appropriators may differ considerably from legislative, administrative, or court regulations (Wade 1988). The difference between working rules and formal laws may involve no more than filling in the lacunae left in a general system of law. More radically, operational rules may assign de facto rights and duties that are contrary to the de jure rights and duties of a formal legal system. My primary focus in this study will be on the de facto rules actually used in CPR field settings, in an effort to understand the incentives and consequences they produce.

All rules are nested in another set of rules that define how the first set of rules can be changed.[29] This nesting of rules within rules at several levels is similar to the nesting of computer languages at several levels. What can be done at a higher level will depend on the capabilities and limits of the software (rules) at that level, on the software (rules) at a deeper level, and on the hardware (the CPR). Whenever one addresses questions about *institutional change*, as contrasted to action within institutional constraints, it is essential to recognize the following:

1 Changes in the rules used to order action at one level occur within a currently "fixed" set of rules at a deeper level.

2 Changes in deeper-level rules usually are more difficult and more costly to accomplish, thus increasing the stability of mutual expectations among individuals interacting according to a set of rules.

It is useful to distinguish three levels of rules that cumulatively affect the actions taken and outcomes obtained in using CPRs (Kiser and E. Ostrom 1982). *Operational rules* directly affect the day-to-day decisions made by appropriators concerning when, where, and how to withdraw resource units, who should monitor the actions of others and how, what information must be exchanged or withheld, and what rewards or sanctions will be assigned to different combinations of actions and outcomes. *Collective-choice rules* indirectly affect operational choices. These are the rules that are used by appropriators, their officials, or external authorities in making policies – the operational rules – about how a CPR should be managed. *Constitutional-choice rules* affect operational activities and results through their effects in determining who is eligible and determining the specific rules to be used in crafting the set of collective-choice rules that in turn affect the set of operational rules. One can think of the linkages among these rules and the related level of analysis at which humans make choices and take actions, as shown in Figure 2.2. The processes of appropriation, provision, monitoring, and enforcement occur at the operational level. The processes of policy-making, management, and adjudication of policy decisions occur at the collective-choice level. Formulation, governance, adjudication, and modification of constitutional decisions occur at the constitutional level.[30]

This nesting of rules within rules is the source of considerable confusion and debate. Institutional theorists, who have attempted to make the choice of rules endogenous to an analysis, have been criticized because it is necessary to assume the presence of some rules that govern the choice of other rules.[31] Making the choice of operational-level rules endogenous does not imply making the choice of collective-choice or constitutional-choice rules endogenous at the same time. For purposes of analysis, the theorist has to assume that some rules already exist and are exogenous for purposes of a particular analysis. The fact that they are held constant and unchanging

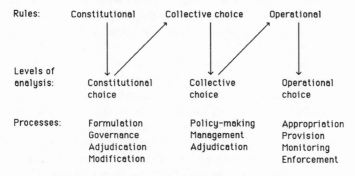

Figure 2.2. Linkages among rules and levels of analysis.

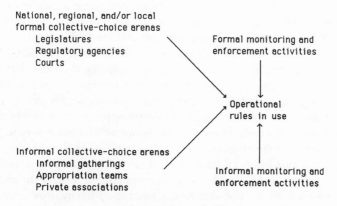

Figure 2.3. Relationships of formal and informal collective-choice arenas and CPR operational rules.

during analysis, however, does not mean that they cannot be changed. Those very same rules may themselves be the objects of choice in a separate analysis or in the context of a different area of choice. At the end of every season, for example, intercollegiate sports leagues consider whether or not to alter the rules of the game for the next season.

On the other hand, rules are changed less frequently than are the strategies that individuals adopt within the rules. Changing the rules at any level of analysis will increase the uncertainty that individuals will face. Rules provide stability of expectations, and efforts to change rules can rapidly reduce that stability. Further, it is usually the case that operational rules are easier to change than collective-choice rules, and collective-choice rules are easier to change than constitutional-choice rules. Analyses of deeper layers of rules are more difficult for scholars and participants to make. Deciding whether an irrigation association should use a legislative body of five or nine members will depend on the physical and historical environment and the analyst's speculation about different outcomes at several levels.[32]

When doing analysis at any one level, the analyst keeps the variables of a deeper level fixed for the purpose of analysis. Otherwise, the structure of the problem would unravel. But self-organizing and self-governing individuals trying to cope with problems in field settings go back and forth across levels as a key strategy for solving problems. Individuals who have no self-organizing and self-governing authority are stuck in a single-tier world. The structure of their problems is given to them. The best they can do is to adopt strategies within the bounds that are given.

At each level of analysis there may be one or more arenas in which the types of decisions made at that level will occur. The concept of an "arena" does not imply a formal setting, but can include such formal settings as legislatures and courts. An arena is simply the situation in which a particular type of action occurs. Policy-making regarding the rules that will be used to regulate operational-level choices is carried out in one or more collective-choice arenas. If the appropriators using a CPR change at least some of the working rules used to organize appropriation and provision, the arena in which collective-choice decisions will be made may be a local coffeehouse, the meetings of a producers' co-op, or the meetings of an organization that has been set up specifically for the purpose of managing and governing this CPR and possibly others related to it. If the appropriators using a CPR cannot change the rules used to organize operational choices, then the only arenas for collective choice are external to the CPR appropriators. In such cases, choices about the rules to be used will be made by government officials in bureaucratic structures, by elected representatives in local or national legislatures, and by judges in judicial arenas.

The relationships among arenas and rules rarely involve a single arena related to a single set of rules. Most frequently, several collective-choice arenas affect the set of operational rules actually used by appropriators for making choices about harvesting and investment strategies in a CPR. Decisions made in national legislatures and courts concerning access to all resources of particular types, when given legitimacy in a local setting and enforced, are likely to affect the operational rules actually used in particular locations. The relationships among formal and informal collective-choice arenas and the resulting operational rules are illustrated in Figure

An institutional approach to CPR self-governance
2.3. Similarly, formal and informal constitutional-choice processes may occur in local, regional, and/or national arenas.

That the working rules used by appropriators may have multiple sources, and may include de facto as well as de jure rules, greatly complicates the problem of understanding behaviors and outcomes in particular locations and the problem of improving outcomes. The absence of national, formal laws regulating the appropriation from and provision of a CPR is not ·quivalent to the absence of effective rules. Over a long period of time, local appropriators may have developed working rules that constrain the entry to and use of a CPR. Such rules may or may not lead appropriators to manage their resource efficiently and fairly, but they will affect the strategies that appropriators perceive to be available to them and the resulting outcomes.

STUDYING INSTITUTIONS IN FIELD SETTINGS

In the cases described in Chapters 3, 4, and 5, I present only a fraction of the detailed information to be found in the in-depth case studies from which I draw. A reader is justified in wanting to know how I approach the task of reading in-depth case materials and abstracting from them for the purpose of studying how individuals supply their own institutions, how they commit themselves to conform to their own rules, and how they monitor each other's conformance to these rules. In general, I am relying on the method of institutional analysis that has been described elsewhere (Kiser and E. Ostrom 1982; Oakerson 1986; E. Ostrom 1986a,b) and applied in many papers, doctoral dissertations, and books (Blomquist 1988a–d; Gardner and E. Ostrom 1990; Kaminski in press; V. Ostrom 1989; V. Ostrom, Feeny, and Picht 1988; Sawyer 1989; Schaaf 1989; Tang 1989; Wynne 1988; Yang 1987).

The basic strategy is to identify those aspects of the physical, cultural, and institutional setting that are likely to affect the determination of who is to be involved in a situation, the actions they can take and the costs of those actions, the outcomes that can be achieved, how actions are linked to outcomes, what information is to be available, how much control individuals can exercise, and what payoffs are to be assigned to particular combinations of actions and outcomes. Once one has all the needed information, one can then abstract from the richness of the empirical situation to devise a playable game that will capture the essence of the problems individuals are facing.

To solve appropriation and provision problems, for example, individuals must learn about the structure of the physical system on which they jointly rely, about their own appropriation and use patterns, about the norms of

55

behavior that are followed in a community, about the incentives they will encourage or discourage as they change rules, and about how all of these factors will cumulatively affect their net benefits and costs over time. Individuals must assess what types of transactions costs will be involved in adopting various strategies within a set of rules or in changing those rules. If the analyst is to understand the structure of the situation, the analyst must learn about the same set of variables.

For the cases that I discuss in Chapter 3, I do not know what the structures of the situations were like before some appropriators in the mists of time began to experiment with various rules to allocate resource units and provisioning responsibilities. What I do know is that the appropriators in the "success" cases described in Chapter 3 were able to allocate resource units and at the same time avoid the conflict, uncertainty, and perceived unfairness of a poorly solved assignment problem, the overinvestment in appropriation efforts involved in an inadequately solved rent-dissipation problem, or the deterioration or destruction of the resources involved when provision problems remain unsolved.

Obviously, I do not know if these appropriators reached optimal solutions to their problems. I strongly doubt it. They solved their problems the way that most individuals solve difficult and complex problems: as well as they were able, given the problems involved, the information they had, the tools they had to work with, the costs of various known options, and the resources at hand. I see my task as one of learning about the structures of the problems they faced and why the rules they adopted seem to work.

This means that I first try to understand something about the structure of the resource itself – its size, clarity of boundary, and internal structure. Then I try to discover the flow patterns involved in the resource units: How much predictability is involved over time, across space, and in quantity? Given the economic circumstances of the appropriators, how reliant are they on the resource, and what are the risks involved in various potential types of allocation schemes? Lastly, I try to ascertain key attributes of the individuals: How many are involved? What are their time horizons likely to be? Are they involved in multiple activities together? Are their interests roughly similar or heterogeneous? Have they established prior norms of behavior that can be drawn on (or pose a disadvantage) in trying to solve these problems? Then I examine the rules that they have devised and try to understand how they work by searching for the design principles that are involved and how these affect the incentives of participants. Given that the appropriators in these cases have engaged in mutual monitoring and generally have kept their commitments to follow their rules to a substantial degree, I try to understand how they have been able to do this.

In Chapter 4, I use this framework again to identify the structure of the situation that existed before a group of appropriators attempted to change their rules to solve several interrelated provision and appropriation problems. Then I examine the process of devising new institutions, in order to address the question of the supply of institutions. The "failure" cases in Chapter 5 are characterized by extreme rent dissipation, unresolved disagreements leading to physical violence, or resource deterioration. The same framework is used to identify the variables that account for that lack of success in solving appropriation and provision problems. I again assume that the individuals involved tried to do as well as they could, given the constraints of the situation. Thus, the problem is to identify what those constraints were, using the same framework for analysis.

In the concluding portions of this study, I discuss how the findings derived from an analysis of these cases can be used to advance theoretical understanding of a theory of self-organized collective action to complement the existing theories of externally organized collective action: the theory of the firm and the theory of the state.

# 3

## Analyzing long-enduring, self-organized, and self-governed CPRs

A direct attack on several of the key questions posed in this book can be launched by an examination of field settings in which (1) appropriators have devised, applied, and monitored their own rules to control the use of their CPRs and (2) the resource systems, as well as the institutions, have survived for long periods of time. The youngest set of institutions to be analyzed in this chapter is already more than 100 years old. The history of the oldest system to be examined exceeds 1,000 years. The institutions discussed in this chapter have survived droughts, floods, wars, pestilence, and major economic and political changes. We shall examine the organization of mountain grazing and forest CPRs in Switzerland and Japan and irrigation systems in Spain and the Philippine Islands.

By indicating that these CPR institutions have survived for long periods of time, I do not mean that their operational rules have remained fixed since they were first introduced. All of the environmental settings included in this chapter are complex and have varied over time. In such settings, it would be almost impossible to "get the operational rules right" on the first try, or even after several tries. These institutions are "robust" or in "institutional equilibrium" in the sense defined by Shepsle. Shepsle (1989b, p. 143) regards "an institution as 'essentially' in equilibrium if changes transpired according to an *ex ante* plan (and hence part of the original institution) for institutional change." In these cases, the appropriators designed basic operational rules, created organizations to undertake the operational management of their CPRs, and modified their rules over time in light of past experience according to their own collective-choice and constitutional-choice rules.

The cases in this chapter are particularly useful for gaining insight regarding how groups of self-organized principals solve two of the major puzzles discussed in Chapter 2: the problem of commitment and the problem of mutual monitoring. (The problem of supply of institutions is addressed in Chapter 4.) The continuing commitments of the appropriators to their institutions have been substantial in these cases. Restrictive rules have been established by the appropriators to constrain appropriation activities and mandate provisioning activities. Thousands of opportunities have arisen in which large benefits could have been reaped by breaking the rules, while the expected sanctions were comparatively low. Stealing water during a dry season in the Spanish *huertas* might on occasion save an entire season's crop from certain destruction. Avoiding spending day after day maintaining the Philippine irrigation systems might enable a farmer to earn needed income in other pursuits. Harvesting illegal timber in the Swiss or Japanese mountain commons would yield a valuable product. Given the temptations involved, the high levels of conformance to the rules in all these cases have been remarkable.

Sizable resources are invested in monitoring activities in these cases, but the "guards" are rarely "external" agents. Widely diverse monitoring arrangements are used. In all of them, the appropriators themselves play a major role in monitoring each other's activities. Even though mutual monitoring has aspects of being a second-order dilemma, the appropriators in these settings somehow solve this problem. Further, the fines assessed in these settings are surprisingly low. Rarely are they more than a small fraction of the monetary value that could be obtained by breaking the rules. In the conclusion to this chapter, I argue that commitment and monitoring are strategically linked and that monitoring produces private benefits for the monitor as well as joint benefits for others.

In explaining the robustness of these institutions and the resource systems themselves over time in environments characterized by high levels of uncertainty, one needs to search for the appropriate specificity of underlying commonalities that may explain this level of sustainability. Given the differences in environments and historical developments, one would hardly expect the particular rules used in these settings to be the same. And they are not. Given the length of time that they have had for trial-and-error learning about operational rules, the harshness of these environments as a stimulus toward improvement, and the low transformation costs in changing their own operational rules, one can, however, expect that these appropriators have "discovered" some underlying principles of good institutional design in a CPR environment. I do not claim that the institutions devised in these settings are in any sense "optimal." In fact, given the high

## Governing the commons

levels of uncertainty involved and the difficulty of measuring benefits and costs, it would be extremely difficult to obtain a meaningful measure of optimality.[1]

On the other hand, I do not hesitate to call these CPR institutions successful. In all instances the individuals involved have had considerable autonomy to craft their own institutions. Given the salience of these CPRs to the appropriators using them, and their capacity to alter rules in light of past performance, these appropriators have had the incentives and the means to improve these institutions over time. The Swiss and Japanese mountain commons have been sustained, if not enhanced, over the centuries while being used intensively. Ecological sustainability in a fragile world of avalanches, unpredictable precipitation, and economic growth is quite an accomplishment for any group of appropriators working over many centuries. Keeping order and maintaining large-scale irrigation works in the difficult terrain of Spain or the Philippine Islands have been similarly remarkable achievements. That record has not been matched by most of the irrigation systems constructed around the world during the past 25 years. Consequently, I have attempted to identify a set of underlying design principles shared by successful CPR institutions and to determine how those design principles affect the incentives of appropriators so that the CPRs themselves and the CPR institutions can be sustained over time. When in Chapter 5 we discuss cases in which appropriators were not able to devise or sustain institutional arrangements to solve CPR problems, we shall consider to what extent the design principles used by appropriators in the "success" cases also characterize the "failure" cases.

The cases discussed in this chapter also help us to examine two other questions. First, the CPR institutions related to the use of precarious and delicately balanced mountain commons to provide fodder and forest products in Switzerland and Japan, in particular, help us to confront the question of the presumed superiority of private-property institutions for most allocational purposes, and specifically those related to the uses of land. Although many resource economists admit that technical difficulties prevent the creation of private property rights to fugitive resources, such as groundwater, oil, and fish, almost all share the presumption that the creation of private property rights to arable or grazing land is an obvious solution to the problem of degradation. Dasgupta and Heal (1979, p. 77), for example, assert that when private property rights are introduced in areas of arable or grazing land, "the resource ceases to be common property and the problem is solved at one stroke."

Many property-rights theorists presume that one of two undesirable outcomes is likely under communal ownership: (1) the commons will be

60

destroyed because no one can be excluded, or (2) the costs of negotiating a set of allocation rules will be excessive, even if exclusion is achieved.[2] On the contrary, what one observes in these cases is the ongoing, side-by-side existence of private property and communal property in settings in which the individuals involved have exercised considerable control over institutional arrangements and property rights. Generations of Swiss and Japanese villagers have learned the relative benefits and costs of private-property and communal-property institutions[3] related to various types of land and uses of land. The villagers in both settings have *chosen* to retain the institution of communal property as the foundation for land use and similar important aspects of village economies. The economic survival of these villagers has been dependent on the skill with which they have used their limited resources. One cannot view communal property in these settings as the primordial remains of earlier institutions evolved in a land of plenty. If the transactions costs involved in managing communal property had been excessive, compared with private-property institutions, the villagers would have had many opportunities to devise different land-tenure arrangements for the mountain commons.

Second, I have frequently been asked, when giving seminar presentations about the Swiss, Japanese, and Spanish institutions, if the same design principles are relevant for solving CPR problems in Third World settings. The last case discussed in this chapter – the *zanjera* institutions of the Philippines – provides a strong affirmative answer to this question. All of the design principles present in the Swiss, Japanese, and Spanish cases are also present in the Philippine case. An analysis of the underlying similarities of enduring CPR institutions, though based on a limited number of cases, may have broader applications.

## COMMUNAL TENURE IN HIGH MOUNTAIN MEADOWS AND FORESTS[3]

### *Törbel, Switzerland*

Our first case concerns Törbel, Switzerland, a village of about 600 people located in the Vispertal trench of the upper Valais canton, as described by Robert McC. Netting in a series of articles (1972, 1976) that were later incorporated into his book *Balancing on an Alp* (1981). Netting (1972, p. 133) identifies the most significant features of the general environment as "(1) the steepness of its slope and the wide range of microclimates demarcated by altitude, (2) the prevailing paucity of precipitation, and (3) the exposure to sunlight." For centuries, Törbel peasants have planted their privately owned plots with bread grains, garden vegetables, fruit trees, and hay for winter fodder. Cheese produced by a small group of herdsmen, who tend village cattle pastured on the communally owned alpine meadows during the summer months, has been an important part of the local economy.

Written legal documents dating back to 1224 provide information regarding the types of land tenure and transfers that have occurred in the village and the rules used by the villagers to regulate the five types of communally owned property: the alpine grazing meadows, the forests, the "waste" lands, the irrigation systems, and the paths and roads connecting privately and communally owned properties. On February 1, 1483, Törbel residents signed articles formally establishing an association to achieve a better level of regulation over the use of the alp, the forests, and the waste lands.

> The law specifically forbade a foreigner (*Fremde*) who bought or otherwise occupied land in Törbel from acquiring any right in the communal alp, common lands, or grazing places, or permission to fell timber. Ownership of a piece of land did *not* automatically confer any communal right (*genossenschaftliches Recht*). The inhabitants currently possessing land and water rights reserved the power to decide whether an outsider should be admitted to community membership.
>
> (Netting 1976, p. 139)

The boundaries of the communally owned lands were firmly established long ago, as indicated in a 1507 inventory document.

Access to well-defined common property was strictly limited to citizens, who were specifically extended communal rights.[4] As far as the summer grazing grounds were concerned, regulations written in 1517 stated that "no citizen could send more cows to the alp than he could feed during the winter" (Netting 1976, p. 139). That regulation, which Netting reports to be still enforced, imposed substantial fines for any attempt by villagers to appropriate a larger share of grazing rights. Adherence to this "wintering" rule was administered by a local official (*Gewalthaber*) who was authorized to levy fines on those who exceeded their quotas and to keep one-half of the fines for himself. The wintering rule is used by many other Swiss villages as a means for allocating appropriation rights (frequently referred to as "cow rights") to the commons. This and other forms of cow rights are relatively easy to monitor and enforce. The cows are all sent to the mountain to be cared for by the herdsmen. They must be counted immediately, as the number of cows each family sends is the basis for determining the amount of cheese the family will receive at the annual distribution.

The village statutes are voted on by all citizens and provide the general legal authority for an alp association to manage the alp. This association includes all local citizens owning cattle. The association has annual meetings to discuss general rules and policies and elect officials. The officials hire the alp staff, impose fines for misuse of the common property, arrange for distribution of manure on the summer pastures, and organize the annual maintenance work, such as building and maintaining roads and paths to and on the alp and rebuilding avalanche-damaged corrals or huts. Labor contributions or fees related to the use of the meadows usually are set in proportion to the number of cattle sent by each owner. Trees that will provide timber for construction and wood for heating are marked by village officials and assigned by lot to groups of households, whose members then are authorized to enter the forests and harvest the marked trees.

Private rights to land are well developed in Törbel and other Swiss villages. Most of the meadows, gardens, grainfields, and vineyards are owned by various individuals, and complex condominium-type agreements are devised for the fractional shares that siblings and other relatives may own in barns, granaries, and multistory housing units. The inheritance system in Törbel ensures that all legitimate offspring share equally in the division of the private holdings of their parents and consequently in access to the commons, but family property is not divided until surviving siblings are relatively mature (Netting 1972). Prior to a period of population growth in the nineteenth century, and hence severe population pressure on the limited land, the level of resource use was held in check by various population-control measures such as late marriages, high rates of celibacy, long birth spacing, and considerable emigration (Netting 1981).

Netting (1976, p. 140) dismisses the notion that communal ownership is simply an anachronistic holdover from the past by showing that for at least five centuries these Swiss villagers have been intimately familiar with the advantages and disadvantages of both private and communal tenure systems and have carefully matched particular types of land tenure to particular types of land use. He associates five attributes to land-use patterns with the differences between communal and individual land tenure. He argues that communal forms of land tenure are better suited to the problems that appropriators face when (1) the value of production per unit of land is low, (2) the frequency or dependability of use or yield is low, (3) the possibility of improvement or intensification is low, (4) a large territory is needed for effective use, and (5) relatively large groups are required for capital-investment activities. See Runge (1984a, 1986) and Gilles and Jamt-gaard (1981) for similar arguments.

Communal tenure "promotes both general access to and optimum production from certain types of resources while enjoining on the entire community the conservation measures necessary to protect these resources from destruction" (Netting 1976, p. 145). Although yields are relatively low, the land in Törbel has maintained its productivity for many centuries. Overgrazing has been prevented by tight controls. The CPR not only has been protected but also has been enhanced by investments in weeding and manuring the summer grazing areas and by the construction and maintenance of roads.

Netting is clear that Törbel should not be considered the prototype for all Swiss alpine villages. A recent review of the extensive German literature on common-property regimes in Swiss alpine meadows reveals considerable diversity of legal forms for governing alpine meadows (Picht 1987). However, Netting's major findings are consistent with experience in many Swiss locations. Throughout the alpine region of Switzerland, farmers use *private* property for agricultural pursuits and a form of *common* property for the summer meadows, forests, and stony waste lands near their private holdings. Four-fifths of the alpine territory is owned by some form of common property: by local villages (*Gemeinden*), by corporations, or by cooperatives. The remaining alpine territory belongs either to the cantons or to private owners or groups of co-owners (Picht 1987, p. 4). Some villages own several alpine meadows and reallocate grazing rights to the use of a specific meadow every decade or so (Stevenson 1990).

In addition to defining who has access to the CPR, all local regulations specify authority rules to limit appropriation levels (Picht 1987). In most villages, some form of proportional-allocation rule is used. The proportion is based on (1) the number of animals that can be fed over the winter,[5] (2) the amount of meadowland owned by a farmer, (3) the actual amount of hay produced by a farmer, (4) the value of the land owned in the valley, or (5) the number of shares owned in a cooperative. A few villages allow all citizens to send equal numbers of animals to the summer alp (Picht 1987, p. 13). Overuse of alpine meadows is rarely reported.[6] Where overuse has occurred, the combined effects of entry rules and authority rules have not sufficiently limited grazing practices, or else several villages have owned and used a single alp without an overarching set of rules (Picht 1987, pp. 17–18; Rhodes and Thompson 1975; Stevenson 1990).[7]

All of the Swiss institutions used to govern commonly owned alpine meadows have one obvious similarity – the appropriators themselves make all major decisions about the use of the CPR.

The users/owners are the main decision making unit. They have to decide on all matters of importance and seem to have a considerable degree of autonomy. They can set up statutes and revise them, they can set limits for the use of the pastures and change them, they can adapt their organizational structure. . . . It can also be said that the user organizations are nested in a set of larger organizations (village, Kantone, Bund) in which they are perceived as legitimate.    (Picht 1987, p. 28)

# Analyzing long-enduring CPRs

Thus, residents of Törbel and other Swiss villages who own communal land spend time governing themselves. Many of the rules they use, however, keep their monitoring and other transactions costs relatively low and reduce the potential for conflict. The procedures used in regard to cutting trees for timber – a valuable resource unit that can be obtained from communal forests – illustrate this quite well. The first step is that the village forester marks the trees ready to be harvested. The second step is that the households eligible to receive timber form work teams and equally divide the work of cutting the trees, hauling the logs, and piling the logs into approximately equal stacks. A lottery is then used to assign particular stacks to the eligible households. No harvesting of trees is authorized at any other time of the year. This procedure nicely combines a careful assessment of the condition of the forest with methods for allocating work and the resulting products that are easy to monitor and are considered fair by all participants. Combining work days or days of reckoning (where the summer's cheese is distributed and assessments are made to cover the costs of the summer's work) with festivities is another method for reducing some of the costs associated with communal management.

In recent times, the value of labor has risen significantly, thus representing an exogenous change for many Swiss villages. Common-property institutions are also changing to reflect differences in relative factor inputs. Villages that rely on unanimity rules for changing their common-property institutions are not adjusting as rapidly as are those villages that rely on less inclusive rules for changing their procedures.

## Hirano, Nagaike, and Yamanoka villages in Japan

In Japan, extensive common lands have existed and have been regulated by local village institutions for centuries. In an important study of traditional common lands in Japan, Margaret A. McKean (1986) estimates that about 12 million hectares of forests and uncultivated mountain meadows were held and managed in common by thousands of rural villages during the Tokugawa period (1600–1867) and that about 3 million hectares are so managed today. Although many villages have sold, leased, or divided their common lands in recent times, McKean (1986, p. 534) indicates that she has "not yet turned up an example of a commons that suffered ecological destruction while it was still a commons" (McKean 1982).[8]

McKean provides both a general overview of the development of property law in Japan and a specific view of the rules, monitoring arrangements, and sanctions used in three Japanese villages – Hirano, Nagaike, and Yamanoka – for regulating the commons. The environmental conditions of the villages studied by McKean are remarkably similar to those of Törbel. The villages are established on steep mountains where many microclimates can be distinguished. Peasants cultivate their own private lands, raising rice, garden vegetables, and horses. The common lands in Japan produce a wide variety of valuable forest products, including timber, thatch for roofing and weaving, animal fodder of various kinds, and decayed plants for fertilizer, firewood, and charcoal. The land held in communal tenure meets the previously cited five conditions that Netting posits as conducive to communal property rather than private property.

Each village in earlier times was governed by an assembly, usually composed of the heads of all the households that had been assigned decision-making authority in the village. The basis for political rights differed from one village to another. Rights were variously based on cultivation rights in land, taxpaying obligations, or ownership rights in land. In some villages, almost all households had political rights and rights to the use of the commons.[9] In others, such rights were more narrowly held (McKean 1986, p. 551; Troost 1985).

Ownership of the uncultivated lands near a village devolved from the imperial court to the villages through several intermediate stages involving land stewards and locally based warriors. National cadastral surveys were conducted late in the sixteenth century at a time of land reform that assigned "most of the rights that we today consider to be 'ownership' of arable land to peasants who lived on and cultivated that land" (McKean 1986, p. 537). Owners of large estates in the earlier systems had employed agents in the various villages and authorized those agents to regulate access to uncultivated lands. As villages asserted their own rights to these lands, they shared a clear image of which lands were private and which were held in common. They took the view that those lands held in common needed management in order to serve the long-term interests of the peasants dependent on them.

In traditional Japanese villages, the household was the smallest unit of account, but the *kumi*, composed of several households, was frequently used as an accounting and distributional unit related to the commons. Each village contained a carefully recorded, defined number of households. A household could not subdivide itself into multiple households without permission from the village. Rights of access to the communally held lands were accorded only to a household unit, not to individuals as such. Consequently, households with many members had no advantage, and considerable disadvantages, in their access to the commons. Population growth was extremely low (0.025% for the period 1721–1846), and ownership patterns within villages were stable (McKean 1986, p. 552).

## Analyzing long-enduring CPRs

In addition to delimiting the ownership status of all lands, village assemblies created detailed authority rules specifying in various ways how much of each valued product a household could harvest from the commons and under what conditions. The rules used in these villages, like those in the Swiss villages, were tailored to the specific environment, to the particular economic roles that various forest products played in the local economy, and to the need to minimize the costs of monitoring labor inputs, resource-unit outputs, and compliance with the rules. A village headman usually was responsible for determining the date when the harvesting of a given product could begin. For abundant plants, the date would be selected simply to ensure that plants had matured and had propagated themselves. No limit was placed on the amount to be gathered. For scarce products, various harvesting rules were used. The rules for allocating winter fodder for draft animals by one village from a closed reserve are illustrative:

... each *kumi* was assigned a zone according to an annual rotation scheme, and each household had to send one, but only one adult. On the appointed day, each representative reported to the appropriate *kumi* zone in the winter fodder commons and waited for the temple bell as the signal to begin cutting. However, this grass was cut with large sickles, and since it would be dangerous to have people distributed unevenly around their *kumi* zone swinging sickles in all directions, the individuals in each *kumi* lined up together at one end of their zone and advanced to the other end, whacking in step with each other like a great agricultural drill team. The grass was left to dry ... and then two representatives from each household entered the fodder commons to tie the grass up into equal bundles. The haul for each *kumi* was grouped together and then divided evenly into one cluster per household. Each household was then assigned its cluster by lottery.

(McKean 1986, pp. 556–7)

Villagers were required to perform collective work to enhance and maintain the yield of the commons, such as annual burning or specific cutting of timber or thatch. Each household had an obligation to contribute a share to such efforts:

There were written rules about the obligation of each household to contribute a share to the collective work to maintain the commons – to conduct the annual burning (which involved cutting nine-foot firebreaks ahead of time, carefully monitoring the blaze, and occasional fire-fighting when the flames jumped the firebreak), to report to harvest on mountain-opening days, or to do a specific cutting of timber or thatch. Accounts were kept about who contributed what to make sure that no household evaded its responsibilities unnoticed. Only illness, family tragedy, or the absence of able-bodied adults whose labor could be spared from routine chores were recognized as excuses for getting out of collective labor. ... But, if there was no acceptable excuse, punishment was in order.

(McKean 1986, p. 559)

# Governing the commons

Each of the villages also devised its own monitoring and sanctioning systems. Given that the mountain usually was closed, except for specified periods, anyone caught in the communally owned territories at other times obviously was not following the rules. Most of the villages hired "detectives" who daily patrolled the commons on horseback in groups of two looking for unauthorized users. In some villages, this position was considered "one of the most prestigious and responsible available to a young man" (McKean 1986, p. 561). In other villages, all eligible males rotated into these positions on a regular basis. One village that did not use formal detectives relied on a form of "citizen's arrest," and anyone was authorized to report violations.

The written codes for each village specified a series of escalating penalties for various violations of the rules to protect the commons, depending on the past behavior of the offender. An occasional infraction would be handled by the detective in a quiet and simple manner. "It was considered perfectly appropriate for the detective to demand cash and saké from violators and to use that as their own entertainment cache" (McKean 1986, p. 561). In addition to the fines paid to the detectives, violators were deprived of their contraband harvest, their equipment, and their horses. The village retained the illegal harvest. The rule-breaker had to pay a fine to the village to retrieve equipment and horses. Fines were graduated from very low levels to extremely high levels to reflect the seriousness of the offense and the willingness of the culprit to make adequate and rapid amends. The most serious sanctions that could be and occasionally were imposed involved complete ostracism or ultimately banishment from the village.

Although the level of rule compliance was very high, violations certainly occurred. McKean reports several types of infractions. Impatience with waiting for mountain-opening day was one reason. In the period just before the official opening of the commons for harvesting a particular plant, the detectives expected – and found – a higher level of infractions and were able to keep themselves well supplied with saké.

A second reason for rule violation sometimes was genuine disagreement about the management decisions of a village headman. McKean illustrates this type of infraction in the following way:

One former detective in Hirano, now a respected village elder, described how he had been patrolling a closed commons one day and came upon not one or two intruders but thirty, including some of the heads of leading households. It was not yet mountain-opening day, but they had entered the commons en masse to cut a particular type of pole used to build trellises to support garden vegetables raised on private plots. If they could not cut the poles soon enough, their entire vegetable crop might be lost, and they believed that the village headman had erred in setting opening day later than these crops required.                     (McKean 1986, p. 565)

In that instance, fines were imposed, but they involved making a donation to the village school, rather than the usual payment of saké. In her conclusion, McKean stresses that the long-term success of these locally designed rule systems indicates "that it is not necessary for regulation of the commons to be imposed coercively from the outside" (McKean 1986, p. 571).

## *HUERTA* IRRIGATION INSTITUTIONS

On May 29, 1435, about 50 years before the residents of Törbel signed their formal articles of association, 84 irrigators served by the Benacher and Faitanar canals in Valencia gathered at the monastery of St. Francis to draw up and approve formal regulations. Those regulations specified who had rights to water from these canals, how the water would be shared in good years as well as bad, how responsibilities for maintenance would be shared, what officials they would elect and how, and what fines would be levied against anyone who broke one of their rules. The canals themselves, like many others in the region, had been constructed in even earlier times. Many rules concerning the distribution of irrigation water were already well established in customary practices. Valencia had been recaptured from the Muslims in 1238 – two centuries before that meeting of the Benacher and Faitanar irrigators. Some of the rules carried into medieval and modern practice were developed *prior* to that reconquest.[10] Thus, for at least 550 years, and probably for close to 1,000 years, farmers have continued to meet with others sharing the same canals for the purpose of specifying and revising the rules that they use, selecting officials, and determining fines and assessments.

Given the limited quantity of rainfall throughout this semiarid region and the extreme variation in rainfall from year to year, its highly developed agriculture would not have been possible without irrigation works bringing water to the farmers' fields. Water was never abundant in this region, not even after major canals were constructed. Given the high stakes, conflict over water has always been just beneath the surface of everyday life, erupting from time to time in fights between the irrigators themselves, between irrigators and their own officials, and between groups of irrigators living in the lower reaches of the water systems and their upstream neighbors. Despite this high potential for conflict – and its actual realization from time to time – the institutions devised many centuries ago for govern-

69

ing the use of water from these rivers have proved adequate for resolving conflicts, allocating water predictably, and ensuring stability in a region not normally associated with high levels of stability. Maass and Anderson (1986) have devoted much effort to studying the institutions used in the

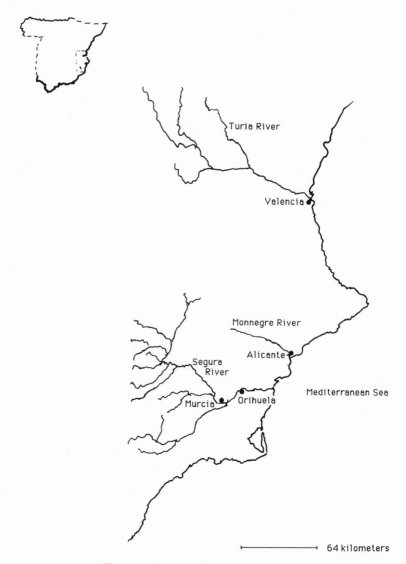

Figure 3.1. Location of Spanish *huertas*.

70

*huertas* (well-demarked irrigation areas surrounding or near towns) of Valencia, Murcia, Orihuela, and Alicante, and Glick (1970) has provided us with an authoritative study of the *huerta* of Valencia during the Middle Ages.

## Valencia

Near the city of Valencia, the waters of the Turia River are divided into eight major canals serving the 16,000-hectare *huerta*. The farms in Valencia have always been small, but they have become extremely fragmented during the past century. Over 80% of the farms are less than 1 hectare, and few exceed 5 hectares (Maass and Anderson 1986, p. 11). Most winters are frost-free, and the summers are hot and sunny. Farmers are able to harvest two or three crops each year and concentrate largely on potatoes, onions, and a wide diversity of vegetable crops. Each farmer is free to select the cropping patterns he prefers.

Given the low rainfall in Valencia itself, the extensive agriculture of this region would not have been possible without effective use of the Turia River. The variation in the flow of the Turia River has historically been quite high. Years of low water flow have been followed by years of extensive flooding. Until the turn of this century, no dams had been constructed on the Turia River serving the Valencian *huerta*. It was not until 1951, when the Generalisimo Dam was completed, with 228 million cubic meters of storage, that substantial upstream storage was provided to regulate the extreme fluctuations in the river's flow. Some groundwater has been developed in the region to supplement the river's supply, but this has never been a major factor in the supply of irrigation water.

In Valencia, the right to water inheres in the land itself. Land that was watered before the time of the reconquest is specified as irrigated land (*regadiu*), and the remaining lands in these *huertas* are dry lands (*seca*).[11]Some land is entitled to water only in times of abundance (*extremales*). The basic allocation principle in Valencia is that each piece of *regadiu* land is entitled to a quantity of canal water proportionate to its size.

In Valencia, the irrigators from seven of the major canals are organized into autonomous irrigation communities whose syndic,[12] or chief executive, participates in two weekly tribunals. The Tribunal de las Aguas is a water court that has for centuries met on Thursday mornings outside the Apostles' Door of the Cathedral of Valencia. The many Islamic features of its traditions have led scholars to argue that the court evolved during the period of Islamic rule.[13] Its proceedings are carried on without lawyers, but with many onlookers. A presiding officer questions those who are involved in a dispute and others who may be able to provide additional information, and the members of the court, excluding the syndic whose canal is involved, make an immediate decision regarding the facts of the case in light of the specific rules of the particular canal. Fines and damages are assessed consistent with the rules of the particular canal. The final decisions of the court are recorded, but not the proceedings. After the court session, the syndics may also convene a second tribunal, which serves as a coordinating committee encompassing all seven of the canals to determine when to institute operating procedures related to seasonal low waters or to discuss other intercanal problems.

The farmers (*hereters*) who own lands eligible to receive water from each of these seven canals meet every second or third year to elect the syndic and several other officials for their canal. Besides his role in the two tribunals, the syndic is the executive officer of the individual irrigation unit. His responsibilities include the basic enforcement of the regulations of his own unit. He has the power to make authoritative physical allocations of water when disputes arise in the day-to-day administration of the waterworks, to levy fines, and to determine the order and timing of water deliveries during times of severe shortages (subject to weekly review by the Tribunal de las Aguas). The syndic must own and farm land served by the canal. The syndic usually has a small staff of ditch-riders and guards whom he appoints to help him carry out these assignments.[14]

In medieval times, the *hereters* also elected two or more inspectors (*veedors*) who were representatives of the community of irrigators and were to consult with the syndic about the daily operation of the canal and assist in rendering physical judgments when conflicts between farmers or between a syndic and a farmer erupted. In modern times, the *hereters* elect an executive committee (*junta de gobierno*) to consult with the syndic until the next biannual meeting. The executive committee is composed of delegates from all of the canal's major service areas. Decisions about when to shut down the canals for annual maintenance and how the maintenance work will be organized are made by the members of this committee of irrigators.

The basic rules for allocating water are dependent on the decisions made by the officials of the irrigation community concerning three environmental conditions: abundance, seasonal low water, and extraordinary drought. In years of declared abundance – a relatively infrequent event – farmers are allowed to take as much water as they need whenever water is present in the canal serving their land.

The most frequent condition under which the canals operate is that of seasonal low water. When the low-water condition is in effect, water is distributed to specific farmers through a complex, rule-driven hydraulic

72

system. Each distributory canal is positioned in a rotation scheme in relation to the other distributory canals.[15] Each farm on a distributory canal receives water in a set rotation order, starting from the head of the canal and culminating in the tail end of the canal:

> On days when water is running in a lateral . . . those farmers who want to irrigate will take it in turn (*por turno*), generally in order from the head to the tail of the channel. Once a farmer opens his headgate, he takes all the water he needs, without any restriction of time; and he defines his own needs, principally in terms of the water requirements of the crops he has chosen to plant. The only limitation is that he may not waste water. If a farmer fails to open his headgate when the water arrives there, he misses his turn and must wait for the water to return to the farm on the next rotation. When a lateral operates in rotation and all users who want water at a given time cannot be served before the rotation passes to another lateral, distribution will begin, when water returns, at the point where it previously terminated. (Maass and Anderson 1986, p. 28)

The basic elements of the *turno* system are that (1) the order in which irrigators receive water is fixed, and (2) each farmer can decide how much water to take as long as water is not wasted. Consequently, no irrigator can tell exactly when his turn will come, because that depends on the volume of water in the canal and the quantity needed by those ahead of him. On the other hand, each irrigator knows that he can take as much water as he needs when his turn eventually comes.

In periods of extraordinary drought, these procedures are modified so that farms whose crops are in the most need of water are given priority over farms whose crops require less water. At the beginning of a drought period, the farmers themselves are expected to apply water only to those crops in most need to shorten their turns in order to allow other farmers in need to obtain the scarce water. As a drought period continues, the syndic and his representatives take more and more responsibility for determining how long each farmer may have water, in light of the condition of the farmer's crops and the needs of others. In recent years, procedures to be used in extraordinary drought have been needed less frequently than in earlier times, because of the increased regulatory capacity of the Generalisimo Dam. Even so, an established procedure is in place for switching rule regimes when environmental conditions change.

The level of monitoring that is used in the *huertas* is very high. In this environment of water scarcity and risk, many temptations occur to take water out of turn, or in some way obtain illegal water. As the time approaches for a farmer to take his turn at the water, he will tend his fields near to the canal so that he can be prepared to open his own gate when the water arrives; if not prepared, he misses his turn entirely and must wait for the next round. While waiting, it is relatively easy to watch what those ahead of him are doing and watch the ditch-riders, whom he is paying. The ditch-riders patrol the canals regularly and are watched over by the syndic, who can lose respect, and his job, if the allocation of water is not handled fairly and according to the farmers' rules. Challenges to the actions of a syndic, a ditch-rider, or another irrigator can be aired weekly before the Tribunal de las Aguas, with many of the other farmers watching the confrontation with interest. The reciprocal monitoring relationships in Valencia are shown in Figure 3.2. Given that everyone is watching everyone else, there is considerable potential for violence among irrigators and between irrigators and their agents. In medieval times, the norms related to honor probably exacerbated the potential for conflict, and *hereters* "were willing to fight in an instant if they felt that their water supply was jeopardized in any way" (Glick 1970, p. 70). The actual violence never approached the potential.

The survival of the books in which fines were recorded for the years 1443 and 1486 for the nearly similarly structured *huerta* of Castellón, some of the detail of which has been reproduced by Glick, provides a picture of the types of infractions discovered, the high level of monitoring undertaken, and the low level of actual fines during an earlier era.[16] In 1443 there were 441 fines assessed; in 1486 there were 499 fines (Glick 1970, p. 54). The similarity in the distributions of offenses and the numbers of fines for these two periods more than 40 years apart testifies to the stability of the system. Guards assessed fines at a rate of more than one per day.[17]About two-thirds of the actions were initiated by the guards, and the remaining third by farmers. Forty-two percent concerned infractions that clearly were motivated by the temptation to obtain water not legally available to the farmer (taking forbidden water, stealing water, installing or undoing canal checks illegally, taking water by force, irrigating without

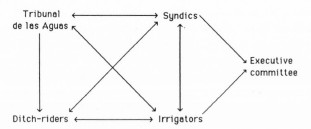

Figure 3.2. Patterns of monitoring and accountability among key actors in the Valencia *huerta*.

right). The remainder of the infractions related to actions that caused harm to others (flooding a road or a fallow field, wasting water) and were also forbidden by the community. Farmers were held publicly accountable for the errors they committed that caused harm to others. Two-thirds of those fined in a year were "one-time offenders" and were not mentioned again in the fine book. Of those who were repeaters, 41% were involved in two actions, 25% in three, 15% in four, 8% in five, and 12% in more than five (Glick 1970, p. 59).

Sufficient data exist to estimate the rate of conformance to the rules for Castellón. There were approximately 1,000 hearths in Castellón in the fifteenth century (T. F. Glick, personal communication). If the rotation system took about two weeks, each of the roughly 1,000 irrigators would have had about 25 opportunities during the year to take water illegally. Thus, approximately 25,000 opportunities for theft occurred, as contrasted to 200 recorded instances of illegal taking of water. That would give a recorded infraction rate of 0.008. One must assume that the guards did not detect all infractions. One could double, triple, or even quadruple the recorded rate, however, and still have a remarkable conformance rate.[18]

Although the conformance rate was high, about one-third of the *hereters* would have had one encounter with a guard at some time during a full year.[19] Consequently, information about the extensive monitoring was regularly conveyed to irrigators. We do not have as detailed a picture of the enforcement patterns in modern times, but both the number of ditch-riders employed and the necessity of holding a weekly court session lead one to suspect that high enforcement levels have been required to dampen the ever present temptation to steal water, as well as the potential for inter-farmer conflict and violence. The stability of this system has been achieved in spite of personal temptations to cheat and engage in violent behavior.

The books of fines also reveal that even though the syndic received two-thirds of the fine (the other third going to the accuser) and the authorized levels for fines were set high, the actual fines assessed "were very low (a few pennies at the most) and also variable, depending on the gravity of the offense, on general economic conditions, and probably on the individual's ability to pay" (Glick 1970, p. 56). Glick comments that this introduced some flexibility into the relatively rigid rotation systems. From time to time, the cost to a farmer of waiting for his next legal turn to receive water, as contrasted to stealing water available in the canal, would be extraordinarily high. Because the fines actually assessed were kept relatively low, the guards did not deeply antagonize the farmers, who generally adhered to the rules. A farmer would suffer some humiliation if detected cheating, but the monetary fine for cooperative farmers would be quite

Governing the commons

low. Assessing harsh punishment to someone who usually follows the rules, but in one instance errs in the face of a desperate situation, can engender considerable antagonism and resentment (Oliver 1980).

Only rarely did farmers engage in ongoing harassment of one another. Glick notes one "particularly fractious individual" who made 5 accusations of theft and was himself similarly accused 13 times during 1486; 10 of the 18 incidents were conflicts between members of two families. But such cases are extremely rare in the archival data, and the absence of chronic conflict between farmers is considered by Glick to be "a tribute to both the efficiency of the distribution system and the vigilance of the guards" (Glick 1970, p. 64).[20]

## Murcia and Orihuela

The Segura River runs from west to east as it approaches the Mediterranean, flowing first through the *huerta* of Murcia and then through the *huerta* of Orihuela. Of the 13,300 farms included within the service area of the *huerta* of Murcia, 83% are less than a single hectare. Of the 4,888 farms in the *huerta* of Orihuela, 64% are less than a single hectare, and 86% are less than 5 hectares. As in Valencia, water rights in Murcia and Orihuela are tied to the land. *Regadiu* and *seca* lands were designated long ago and have remained stable for centuries. The quantity of rainfall in the *huertas* of Murcia and Orihuela is, on the average, considerably less than in Valencia, and it occurs with greater variation. The terrain in Murcia and Orihuela is more varied than the terrain in Valencia, and local procedures involve much more emphasis on the problem of watering highlands and lowlands from the same canal.

Each farmer is assigned a *tanda*, a fixed time period during which he may withdraw water. Thus, each farmer knows exactly when and for how long he may obtain water, but he does not know exactly how much water may be available at that time. The *tanda* procedure has some advantages over the *turno* procedure used in Valencia. Each farmer can plan his activities with a greater degree of certainty as to when he will be able to irrigate. Each farmer is more motivated to economize on the use of water within his own fields because he must make the decision how to allocate a limited time-slice of water to his own fields. On the other hand, the *tanda* procedure is itself quite rigid, particularly as farms are bought and sold, divided or combined.

The officials of the irrigation community, in consultation with city officials, are responsible for declaring when there is insufficient water to continue the regular *tanda* procedure. When extraordinary low-water conditions are in effect, the officials of each community post a new schedule for each rotation of the season – approximately every two weeks – indicating which crops will be given precedence and the schedule and special rules to be followed for the next rotation period.

There are about 30 irrigation communities in Murcia, 10 in Orihuela, and several more that take from canals just below Orihuela. In both *huertas*, the communities employ guards, who most frequently come from the canal sections where they are employed and are nominated by the farmers of that section.

The guards patrol the canal and report any violations of the ordinances they observe; act as witnesses where one farmer charges another with a violation or themselves bring charges against farmers; and assist in the distribution of water, frequently opening and closing the principal canal checks and the turnout gate of the principal laterals. (Maass and Anderson 1986, p. 80)

The irrigation communities within both *huertas* have formed *huerta*-wide organizations. The syndics of the canal communities of Murcia meet yearly in a general assembly and elect members to an executive commission, in addition to approving an annual budget and taxes. The syndics of the canals in Orihuela meet in a general assembly of its *huerta*-wide organization every three years to elect a water magistrate, his lieutenant, and a solicitor. The water magistrate presides at all assemblies within Orihuela. The *huerta*-wide agency performs activities similar to those undertaken in Murcia. The city of Orihuela is hardly involved in irrigation activities within its limits.

Both *huertas* have established water courts in which farmers can bring charges against each other or in which officials can charge a farmer with an offense. Murcia's water court – which has the felicitous name of the Council of Good Men (Consejo de Hombres Buenos) – is composed of five canal syndics and two inspectors. Because Murcia has 30 organized communities, the names of all syndics and inspectors for all systems are placed in two bowls at the beginning of each year, and each month a new court is selected by lottery so that each canal will be represented in an equitable fashion. The Murcian court meets every Thursday morning in the City Hall and is presided over by the mayor of Murcia (or his deputy), who votes only in case of a tie. Not only is the day of meeting similar to that in Valencia, but the general procedures are the same: "oral, public, summary, and cheap" (Maass and Anderson 1986, p. 82).

The water court in Orihuela has only a single judge, and its procedures differ substantially from those in Murcia and Valencia. Those who wish to bring charges against others do so to an officer of the court. The person accused is then summoned to appear before the magistrate within a few days. A sentence is imposed immediately if the person accused confesses to the charge. Otherwise, the magistrate tries to get those involved to come to an agreement that he can accept.

### Alicante

Whereas the Segura and Turia rivers drain large watersheds, including mountain ranges where winter precipitation is stored in the form of snow and released later, the Monnegre River serving Alicante rises near the sea and drains only a small area. The even greater shortage of water in this *huerta*, as contrasted to Valencia and Murcia-Orihuela, which themselves do not have an abundant supply of water, has affected the strategies that the irrigators in Alicante have adopted. The basic water right in Alicante is closer to that of Murcia than to that of Valencia. All water rights are to a fixed time period. Originally, these time allocations were tied to land ownership. Shortly after Alicante was recovered from the Muslims, rights to withdraw water for fixed time periods were separated from ownership of land, and a market in these rights existed apart from the market for land. Alicante farmers took the initiative to construct the Tibi Dam in 1594, which at times has led to greater involvement of national and regional authorities in the management of irrigation in Alicante than in Valencia or Murcia-Orihuela. Local irrigators have sought out still other sources of water, and that has involved them in extensive contractual arrangements with large-scale private water companies.

The 3,700 hectares of *huerta* land are divided among 2,400 farms, 63% of which are less than 1 hectare, and 93% of which are less than 5 hectares (Maass and Anderson 1986, p. 101). Alicante farmers have adopted a mixed strategy of growing cereals and vegetables between rows of fruit and nut trees. Prior to the construction of the Tibi Dam, many owners of land sold their water rights to others or regularly rented their rights. Consequently, a fixed quantity of water rights existed prior to construction of the dam, and those rights were traded independently of land transactions. Tibi Dam made available twice as much usable irrigation water as the unregulated river had provided. The rights to the "new water" created by the Tibi Dam were assigned to owners of *huerta* land whose assessments paid for the dam.[21] The rights to the other half of the water supply – the "old water" – were held by those who had already acquired rights prior to construction of the dam. A new proviso was added to these rights that they could be sold or rented only to those who owned land eligible to receive new water. Consequently, the water rights could not be sold to individuals whose land lay outside the *huerta*. Although the rights to new water were

78

originally attached to the land, those rights were soon "rented" from time to time by farmers who did not need all of their water for a particular rotation.

Prior to a full rotation of water through the irrigation community's canals, a notice is posted by the syndicate providing information about the dates of the next rotation and the times during which "scrip" will be issued. Holders of both new and old water rights obtain scrip equivalent to their recorded water rights in denominations from one hour down to one-third of a minute. All scrip for Tibi water is fully exchangeable. Farmers who hold new-water rights, and thus land within the *huerta*, rarely have sufficient scrip to obtain enough water to irrigate their crops. They can purchase scrip in three ways: at an informal market among holders of rights conducted on Sunday morning before a formal auction is held; at the formal auction; and on market days, when farmers are congregating for trade.

In the formal auction, the irrigation community sells the approximately 90 hours of water that it owns – water rights assigned to it by the irrigators in 1926 to provide a regular income for the syndicate's operations.[22] The syndicate also sells any surplus scrip that was not claimed by right-holders during the previous allotted time period. The minimum quantity of water offered in the formal auction is a full hour, but the purchased scrip is fully divisible and negotiable. Considerable information is made available by the irrigation community to enable farmers to make intelligent choices.

The ditch riders are present . . . and can tell a farmer when the water is likely to reach his property. The organization posts on a bulletin board outside the tavern a current report of water storage in the reservoir; a full account of all water delivered in the previous rotation, including the names of irrigators and the amounts of water delivered to each; and a full accounting of all water sold at auction in the previous rotation, including the names of all successful bidders, the number of hours each purchased, and the prices paid.

(Maass and Anderson 1986, p. 116)

A farmer who wants to irrigate his land during a particular rotation tells his ditch-rider – who opens and closes all of the relevant control structures – how much time he wishes to use. The ditch-rider, in turn, informs the farmer approximately when the water will be available. The farmer is supposed to pay the ditch-rider when water is delivered, but the practice is to allow a farmer up to three days after a rotation has been completed. At that time, the ditch-rider's report of all water delivered and equivalent scrip must be turned in. Thus, farmers purchase scrip not only for future deliveries but also to cover fully what they have used during the current rotation. The price of water is consequently higher toward the end of a

79

rotation than at the beginning of one.[23] The price of water also varies in relation to the amount of water available. In years of abundant rainfall, farmers need less irrigation water, and the price of Tibi water falls. In times of extreme drought, there may not be any water to distribute, and the auction will not occur until water is available. In periods of seasonal low water, the price of water may become very high and can be a source of considerable conflict between holders of old rights versus holders of new rights. Alicante farmers may also purchase water from several other sources.[24]

The organization of the irrigation community in Alicante differs significantly from that for the *huertas* discussed earlier. First, there is only one irrigation community for the entire *huerta*. Second, to vote in the general assembly of the community, a farmer must own 1.8 hectares of land; to vote for the executive commission, 1.2 hectares of land; and to be eligible to serve on the commission, 3.6 hectares of land (Maass and Anderson 1986, p. 117). Whereas a farmer must own a minimum of land to participate, the votes of farmers owning more land are not weighted to reflect differences in the amounts of land owned. The executive commission is composed of 12 representatives (*sindicos*) who serve four years each (half rotating every second year). One member from this body is selected as the director.

The general assembly meets annually to approve the budget and taxes and to decide matters brought before it by the executive commission. Special meetings can be called when problems arise requiring action between the annual meetings. Both the executive commission and the assembly have been extremely active in Alicante in the repeated efforts to find new water and to attempt to develop better contractual arrangements with the private firms using the community's canal to sell water in the *huerta*. The regular expenses of the community are assessed against the holders of all water rights. Three rotations each year are designated as those during which regular taxes will be collected, and a right-holder must pay the assessment at the time of applying for scrip. Extraordinary expenses, which at times have been quite high, are also assessed in the same manner, except that the payment is due at a different set of rotations during the year.

The commission employs an executive secretary, as well as all those who operate the control structures and deliver the water directly to the farmer. The ditch-riders open and close all farm headgates in Alicante. The farmers do this themselves in Valencia and Murcia-Orihuela. The ditch-riders of Alicante, however, exercise less discretion in determining who shall receive water and when. One employee is given the responsibility of accounting for

80

the water that has left the regulating basins until it reaches a ditch-rider, who is again accountable for all of the water that is assigned to him.

National authorities have exerted more control over irrigation matters in Alicante than in the other *huertas*. A large structure, such as Tibi Dam, can be seized and used as a source of revenue and power by a rent-seeking ruler. Although Philip II did not attempt to exercise control over the Tibi Dam when it was built, the dam was transferred to royal ownership for a century in 1739. When control of the dam and responsibility for distributing its water were returned to Alicante in 1840, farmers did not win the right to select syndicate officers for another 25 years. The Spanish Civil War also interrupted the control that farmers exercised over the irrigation syndicate. It was not until 1950 that farmers again selected their own officials.

It should be noted that the degree of freedom to devise and change their own institutions, successfully asserted by the irrigators of eastern Spain, was not typical of the Castilian part of Spain, whose far more centralized institutions were the major influences on the evolution of Spanish national institutions.[25] By the end of the thirteenth century, the *cortes* of the kingdom of Aragon (roughly comprising Valencia, Aragon, and Catalonia) had "already secured the power to legislate and even to limit the king's power to issue legislation under certain conditions" (Veliz 1980, p. 34). The *cortes* in Castile, at the same time in history, was seldom summoned. By the time the centralized monarchy based on the Castilian model came to dominate Spain and Latin America, the autonomy of the *huertas* was well established. The continuing willingness of the irrigators in these regions to stand up for their rights attests that they had greater autonomy than did those in other parts of Spain. One can only wonder if the course of history in Latin America might have differed substantially if the Spanish monarchy established by Ferdinand and Isabella had been modeled on Aragon and not on Castile.[26]

Maass and Anderson have conducted an interesting evaluation of the comparative efficiencies of the Spanish *huertas* and several systems operating in the western part of the United States. Without including the costs of water or the administrative costs associated with governing and managing the canals, they find that the system that has evolved in Alicante enables farmers to be most efficient in using other input factors. The system devised in Valencia is the least efficient of the Spanish systems, with the Murcia-Orihuela systems coming in between. All of the systems generate positive benefits for the farmers they serve, and all have shown an amazing capacity to survive. In 1887, the Murcian historian Diaz Cassou concluded that "the democratic and representative character of the agricultural commune of Murcia had shown a remarkable stability, for a succession of very different

81

national political epochs had offered no serious obstacles to its continued function" (Maass and Anderson 1986, p. 83). A century later, Cassou's reflection remains valid.

ZANJERA IRRIGATION COMMUNITIES
IN THE PHILIPPINES

The earliest recorded reference to the existing irrigation societies in the Ilocanos area of Ilocos Norte in the Philippines derives from Spanish priests writing in 1630 (H. Lewis 1980, p. 153). No serious effort has been made to determine if similar organizations were in existence before the Spanish colonial period, but it would not be unreasonable to assume that the modern *zanjeras* are derived from a mixture of traditions, including that of the Spanish. The most striking similarity between the *huerta* and *zanjera* systems is in the central role given to small-scale communities of irrigators who determine their own rules, choose their own officials, guard their own systems, and maintain their own canals. The internal organization of each *zanjera* has been tailored to its own history, and thus the specific rules in use vary substantially (Keesing 1962). In 1979 there were 686 communal irrigation systems in Ilocos Norte (Siy 1982, p. 25).[27]

*Zanjeras* have been established both by landowning farmers wanting to construct common irrigation works and by individuals organizing themselves so as to acquire land. The technologies used in *zanjera* systems are relatively crude and labor-intensive. The large number of operating systems and the amount of labor put into these by farmers – tenants as well as landowners – have meant that technological knowledge of how to construct dams and other works has been widely shared. With this knowledge, it has been possible for enterprising tenant farmers to band together to construct an irrigation system on previously nonirrigated land in return for the right to the produce from a defined portion of the newly irrigated land.

This type of contract – called a *biang ti daga* or a "sharing of the land" – allows the landowner to retain ownership. Use rights are extended to the *zanjera* dependent on continued maintenance of the irrigation system. At the time of forming an association, each original participant in the *zanjera* is issued one membership share or *atar*. The total number of *atars* is set at that point.[28] The share gives each member one vote and the right to farm a proportionate share of the land acquired by the *zanjera*, and it defines the obligation of the member for labor and material inputs. Each *atar*-holder is obligated to contribute one day's work during each work season declared by the *zanjera*, plus a share of the material required at construction time. The system was thus developed as a mode of acquiring long-term use rights

82

to land and the water to irrigate it without prior accumulation of monetary assets.

Each *zanjera* is laid out differently, but all that were set up by a *biang ti daga* contract share an underlying pattern. The area is divided into three or more large sections. Each farmer is assigned a plot in each section. All members are thus in fundamentally symmetrical positions in relation to one another. Not only do they own rights to farm equal amounts of land, but they all farm some land in the most advantageous location near the head of the system, and some near the tail. In years when rainfall is not sufficient to irrigate all of the fields, a decision about sharing the burden of scarcity can be made rapidly and equitably by simply deciding not to irrigate the bottom section of land.

Several parcels are set aside for communal purposes. A few parcels, located at the tail end of the system, are assigned to officials of the association as payment for their services. This system not only provides a positive reward for services rendered but also enhances the incentives for those in leadership positions to try to get water to the tail end of the system. Other lands are retained to secure income for the *zanjera* itself. See the work of Coward (1979, 1985) for a detailed description of this system.

The members of each *zanjera* elect a *maestro* as their executive officer, a secretary, a treasurer, and a cook.[29] In the larger associations, they also select foremen and team leaders to supervise the construction activities. The *maestro* has the challenging job of motivating individuals to contribute many hours of physically exhausting labor in times of emergency, when control structures have been washed out, and for routine maintenance. Given the backbreaking efforts required during the monsoon season or during extremely hot weather, this motivational task is of substantial proportions. The *maestro* is, of course, not dependent simply on his persuasive powers. Many real inducements and sanctions are built into these systems by the rules that *zanjera* members have constructed for themselves.

To illustrate the task involved in governing these systems, we shall consider one of these systems – actually, a federation of nine *zanjeras* – in more detail, based on the work of Robert Siy (1982). The Bacarra-Vintar federation of *zanjeras* constructs and maintains a 100-meter-long brush dam that spans the Bacarra-Vintar River, located on the northwestern tip of Luzon Island approximately 500 kilometers north of Manila. The unpredictable and destructive Bacarra-Vintar River drains the northeastern parts of the provinces. During the rainy season each year, the river destroys the federation's dam, which is constructed of bamboo poles, banana leaves, sand, and rock. During some years the dam will be destroyed three or four times.

83

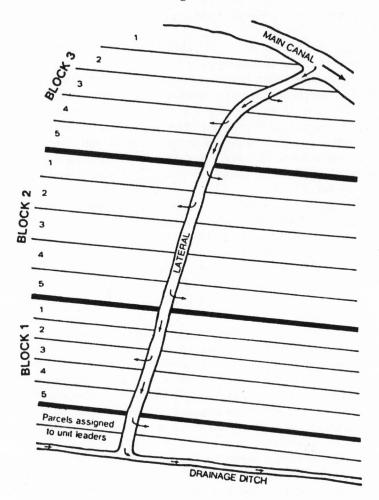

Figure 3.3. Typical layout of *zanjera* fields. (Adapted from Coward 1979.)

The histories of the nine component *zanjeras*, like that of the federation itself, have not been well preserved. What is known is that most of them were established independently and tried to construct and maintain their own diversion works from the river. The river has changed course several times in its history, and at various times some of the *zanjeras* have been cut off from their source of water by such changes. Two of the *zanjeras* were already associated during the nineteenth century and jointly constructed

84

one dam and canal. A formal agreement dated 1906 was written when a third *zanjera* joined their federation. Other existing systems joined slowly through the 1950s. The last two *zanjeras* entered at the time of their formation (Siy 1982, pp. 67-8).

In 1978 the federation formally incorporated as a private corporation in response to the 1976 Philippine Water Code, which defined only individuals or "juridical persons" as eligible to obtain water rights. Given the history of litigation in the area (M. Cruz, Cornista, and Dayan 1987), members of the federation wanted secure water rights in the name of the federation itself, rather than in the name of individual *zanjeras*. The heads of all the component *zanjeras* form the board of directors, with the *maestro* of the Surgui *zanjera* – one of the founding *zanjeras* – named as the president and chairman of the board. In 1980 there were 431 individuals who owned shares, or parts of shares, in at least one *zanjera*. Many members were involved in more than one of the *zanjeras*. The smallest component *zanjera* had 20 members, and the largest had 73 members (Siy 1982, p. 85). Each *zanjera* is responsible for its own financial and internal affairs and owes no financial obligations to the federation.

The board of directors determines when the dam should be rebuilt or repaired. Rebuilding takes about a week – somewhat more when the weather is unfavorable – and involves several hundred persons. Each *zanjera* is responsible for bringing construction materials and providing work teams (and the cooks and food to feed them). After spending a day preparing banana and bamboo mats, work teams in heavy boats confront the swirling waters to begin pounding in the poles that form the foundation for the dam. Then the mats are woven around the poles and reinforced with sand and rock.

Each of the five *zanjeras* with the largest numbers of *atars* provides one work team. The four smaller associations form two work teams. As the dam is laid out, it is divided, by the use of a "flexible" rod, into seven sections that are roughly proportional to the sizes of the work teams and the difficulty of the terrain. This work assignment pattern allows each group to monitor the progress of other groups and engenders some spirited competition among them. The work of maintaining the main canal is also assigned in a similar manner. Work on distributory canals is organized by each *zanjera*, which has divided itself into smaller work teams called *gunglos*, composed of 5 to 10 members.

Siy computed the total obligations (including work as well as attendance at meetings and celebrations) of *zanjera* members to their own associations and to the federation for 1980. The owner of a full *atar* share of the Santo Rosario *zanjera* was obligated to contribute 86 days during 1980 (the largest obligation), whereas an owner of a full share in the Nibinib *zanjera* was obligated to contribute 32 days (the lowest). The average across the federation was 53 days (Siy 1982, p. 92). Given that some *atars* are held jointly by several farmers, the average number of days per working member is somewhat less – around 39 days for the year.

In terms of the contemporary schedule of 5 days per week, this amounts to two months of work supplied without direct monetary payment.[30] About 16,000 man-days were supplied by members to their own *zanjera* or federation during the year.[31] As Siy reflects, "there are definitely few rural organizations in the developing world which have been able to regularly mobilize voluntary [*sic*] labor to such extent" (Siy 1982, p. 95).[32] Given the rigorous and at times dangerous nature of the work, the level of attendance at these obligatory sessions is rather amazing.[33] On average, members were absent somewhat over 2 days out of their required 39, making the attendance rate about 94%. Fines assessed for nonattendance were fully paid in five of the *zanjeras*, and only one of the *zanjeras* had a substantial problem with the payment of fines (Siy 1982, p. 98).[34]

Over time, *zanjeras* face the problem of increased fragmentation of the original shares. A founding member with three sons, for example, may bequeath his plots to be distributed evenly among his sons, each of whom then assumes one-third of the obligations that their father had to fulfill (and having access to only one-third of the land). The individual *zanjeras* have responded to fragmentation in several ways. Some *zanjeras* appoint one person to be responsible for the fulfillment of *atar* responsibilities so that the associations do not have to monitor intra-*atar* work contributions or shirking. Some of the *zanjeras* now require prior approval before a share is sold or tenants are allowed to work *zanjera* land.

Prospective members are "screened," and made to understand the full extent of their obligations to the zanjera before the transaction or tenancy agreement is approved. In a few cases, new members have been required to sign an agreement affirming their recognition of the zanjera's by-laws. These by-laws usually stipulate that erring members may be suspended or expelled from the zanjera, and their lands, confiscated. (Siy 1982, p. 101)

Given the great numbers of the landless population in the area, there is still fierce competition to gain access to land.

Water-allocation rules are not quite as restrictive in these systems as are work-contribution rules. In general, the supply of water to the irrigation system is more than adequate to meet the needs of the farmers, given the current cropping patterns and soil types involved. When water is abundant, water flows throughout the entire system, and anyone can irrigate at will. When water is scarce, rotation systems are established among the *zanjeras*, and within *zanjeras* among the various distributory canals. During extremely dry periods, downstream *zanjeras* are allowed the full flow of the system for several nights in a row. After notification and agreement, the downstream *zanjera* sends its *gunglos* upstream to set up checks and close turnouts. "Other members 'stand guard' to ensure that such temporary control devices remain in place. Other groups attend to the actual delivery of water to individual parcels" (Siy 1982, p. 122). Precedence is given to parcels with the greatest need, and then a regular rotation system is established.

Several of the downstream *zanjeras* harvest only one crop per year, but two crops are possible in the higher *zanjeras*. Siy presents clear evidence that it would be possible to reallocate water among the nine *zanjeras* so as to increase the productivity of the lower *zanjera* lands without a loss in productivity by the head-end *zanjeras* (Siy 1982, pp. 122–45). On the other hand, the distribution of water is roughly proportional to the contributions of labor and materials and to *atar* shares. Thus, the three *zanjeras* that contribute most of the labor and materials (48%) receive 55% of the water, the three *zanjeras* that contribute 30% of the labor and materials receive 25% of the water, and the three *zanjeras* that contribute 22% of the labor and materials receive 20% of the water.[35]

From the perspective of technical efficiency, the system is not as efficient in its water-allocation scheme as it could be. Siy is, however, extremely careful to point out that many costs besides those of output forgone are involved in designing and running such systems:

The costs may be in the form of the time and energy expended in deciding on an acceptable arrangement or in adjusting to an externally-imposed procedure. . . . For example, a shift in the distribution of water may necessitate a shift in the distribution of obligations among zanjeras. A zanjera that ends up receiving more water may then be required to contribute a larger proportion of labor and materials for system maintenance in order to satisfy the demands for sharing obligations in proportion to the increased benefits received. However, there is always the danger that the individual zanjera involved may not possess the immediate capability to meet such requirements, and, as such, these new demands on their resources may actually undermine the stability or solidarity of the whole organization.                                              (Siy 1982, p. 146)

The major criterion used by irrigation engineers to evaluate the performance of an irrigation system is whether or not a system is technically efficient in the sense that water is allocated optimally to enhance crop production. The federation falls short in regard to this criterion, but it performs well in regard to mobilization of personnel for construction and maintenance activities. The members of the federation perceive the alloca-

87

tion of water to conform to legitimate formulas that they have themselves devised, rather than to formulas devised by external experts. As we shall see in Chapter 5, when external experts, working without the participation of the irrigators, have designed systems with the primary aim of achieving technical efficiency, they frequently have failed to achieve either the hoped-for technical efficiency or the level of organized action required to allocate water in a regular fashion or to maintain the physical system itself.

Because many members of the lower *zanjeras* also participate in other *zanjeras*, many own lands that receive adequate or more than adequate quantities of water, thus offsetting those lands that are left dry part of the year. In a survey of *zanjera* members, respondents from the lower *zanjeras* were more likely than members of upstream *zanjeras* to report a lack of water during part of the year. But when asked what major irrigation problems they faced, none "had anything to say about the way water was allocated or about the fairness of water distribution" (Siy 1982, p. 141). The problem cited by 65% of the irrigators surveyed was the hardship associated with the annual damage to their dam.

## SIMILARITIES AMONG ENDURING, SELF-GOVERNING CPR INSTITUTIONS

Despite all of the differences among the CPR settings described in this chapter – and substantial differences exist – all share fundamental similarities. One similarity is that all face uncertain and complex environments. In the mountain commons, the location and timing of rainfall cannot be predicted. In the irrigation systems, erratic rainfall is again a major source of uncertainty. Whereas the construction of physical works tends to reduce the level of uncertainty, it tends to increase the level of complexity in these systems. Irrigators must have practical engineering skills as well as farming skills.

In contrast to the uncertainty caused by these environments, the populations in these locations have remained stable over long periods of time. Individuals have shared a past and expect to share a future. It is important for individuals to maintain their reputations as reliable members of the community. These individuals live side by side and farm the same plots year after year. They expect their children and their grandchildren to inherit their land. In other words, their discount rates are low. If costly investments in provision are made at one point in time, the proprietors – or their families – are likely to reap the benefits.

Extensive norms have evolved in all of these settings that narrowly define "proper" behavior. Many of these norms make it feasible for individuals to live in close interdependence on many fronts without excessive conflict. Further, a reputation for keeping promises, honest dealings, and reliability in one arena is a valuable asset. Prudent, long-term self-interest reinforces the acceptance of the norms of proper behavior. None of these situations involves participants who vary greatly in regard to ownership of assets, skills, knowledge, ethnicity, race, or other variables that could strongly divide a group of individuals (R. Johnson and Libecap 1982).

The most notable similarity of all, of course, is the sheer perseverance manifested in these resource systems and institutions. The resource systems clearly meet the criterion of sustainability. The institutions meet Shepsle's (1989b) criterion of institutional robustness, in that the rules have been devised and modified over time according to a set of collective-choice and constitutional-choice rules. These cases were specifically selected because they have endured while others have failed. Now the task is to begin to explain their sustainability and robustness, given how difficult it must have been to achieve this record in such complex, uncertain, and interdependent environments in which individuals have continuously faced substantial incentives to behave opportunistically.

The specific operational rules in these cases differ markedly from one another. Thus, they cannot be the basis for an explanation across settings. In the Japanese mountain commons, for example, appropriation rights and provision duties are assigned to established family units in a village instead of to individuals. In the Swiss mountains, appropriation rights and provision duties are inherited by individual males who own private property in the village and remain citizens of the village. In eastern Spain, a farmer's right to irrigation water is based on the parcel of land inherited, purchased, or leased, not on a relationship to a village. In the Philippines, a complex contract among long-term usufructuary right-holders determines rights and provision duties. The rules defining when, where, and how an individual's allotted resource units can be harvested or how many labor days are required also vary considerably across cases.

Although the particular rules that are used within these various settings cannot provide the basis for an explanation of the institutional robustness and sustainability across these CPRs, part of the explanation that I offer is based on the fact that the particular rules differ. The differences in the particular rules take into account specific attributes of the related physical systems, cultural views of the world, and economic and political relationships that exist in the setting. Without different rules, appropriators could not take advantage of the positive features of a local CPR or avoid potential pitfalls that might be encountered in one setting but not others.

Instead of turning to the specific rules, I turn to a set of seven design principles that characterize all of these robust CPR institutions, plus an eighth principle used in the larger, more complex cases. These are listed in Table 3.1. By "design principle" I mean an essential element or condition that helps to account for the success of these institutions in sustaining the CPRs and gaining the compliance of generation after generation of appropriators to the rules in use. This list of design principles is still quite speculative. I am not yet willing to argue that these design principles are necessary conditions for achieving institutional robustness in CPR settings. Further theoretical and empirical work is needed before a strong assertion of necessity can be made. I am willing to speculate, however, that after

Table 3.1. *Design principles illustrated by long-enduring*
*CPR institutions*

1. Clearly defined boundaries
   Individuals or households who have rights to withdraw resource units from the CPR must be clearly defined, as must the boundaries of the CPR itself.

2. Congruence between appropriation and provision rules and local conditions
   Appropriation rules restricting time, place, technology, and/or quantity of resource units are related to local conditions and to provision rules requiring labor, material, and/or money.

3. Collective-choice arrangements
   Most individuals affected by the operational rules can participate in modifying the operational rules.

4. Monitoring
   Monitors, who actively audit CPR conditions and appropriator behavior, are accountable to the appropriators or are the appropriators.

5. Graduated sanctions
   Appropriators who violate operational rules are likely to be assessed graduated sanctions (depending on the seriousness and context of the offense) by other appropriators, by officials accountable to these appropriators, or by both.

6. Conflict-resolution mechanisms
   Appropriators and their officials have rapid access to low-cost local arenas to resolve conflicts among appropriators or between appropriators and officials.

7. Minimal recognition of rights to organize
   The rights of appropriators to devise their own institutions are not challenged by external governmental authorities.

*For CPRs that are parts of larger systems:*
8. Nested enterprises
   Appropriation, provision, monitoring, enforcement, conflict resolution, and governance activities are organized in multiple layers of nested enterprises.

further scholarly work is completed, it will be possible to identify a set of necessary design principles and that such a set will contain the core of what has been identified here.[36]

For these design principles to constitute a credible explanation for the persistence of these CPRs and their related institutions, I need to show that they can affect incentives in such a way that appropriators will be willing to commit themselves to conform to operational rules devised in such systems, to monitor each other's conformance, and to replicate the CPR institutions across generational boundaries. I shall discuss each of the design principles in turn.

### Clearly defined boundaries

1 Individuals or households who have rights to withdraw resource units from the CPR must be clearly defined, as must the boundaries of the CPR itself.

Defining the boundaries of the CPR and specifying those authorized to use it can be thought of as a first step in organizing for collective action. So long as the boundaries of the resource and/or the specification of individuals who can use the resource remain uncertain, no one knows what is being managed or for whom. Without defining the boundaries of the CPR and closing it to "outsiders," local appropriators face the risk that any benefits they produce by their efforts will be reaped by others who have not contributed to those efforts. At the least, those who invest in the CPR may not receive as high a return as they expected. At the worst, the actions of others could destroy the resource itself. Thus, for any appropriators to have a minimal interest in coordinating patterns of appropriation and provision, some set of appropriators must be able to exclude others from access and appropriation rights. If there are substantial numbers of potential appropriators and the demand for the resource units is high, the destructive potential should all be allowed to freely withdraw units from the CPR could push the discount rate used by appropriators toward 100%. The higher the discount rate, the closer the situation is to that of a one-shot dilemma in which the dominant strategy of all participants is to overuse the CPR.

Since the work of Ciriacy-Wantrup and Bishop (1975), the presence of boundaries concerning who is allowed to appropriate from the CPR has been used as the single defining characteristic of "common-property" institutions as contrasted to "open-access" institutions. The impression is sometimes given that this is all that is necessary to achieve successful regulation. Making this attribute one of seven, rather than a unique attribute, puts its importance in a more realistic perspective. Simply closing the boundaries is not enough. It is still possible for a limited number of appropriators to increase the quantity of resource units they harvest so that they either dissipate all potential rents or totally destroy the resource (Clark 1980). Consequently, in addition to closing the boundaries, some rules limiting appropriation and/or mandating provision are needed.

### Congruence between appropriation and provision rules and local conditions

2  Appropriation rules restricting time, place, technology, and/or quantity of resource units are related to local conditions and to provision rules requiring labor, materials, and/or money.

Adding well-tailored appropriation and provision rules helps to account for the perseverance of these CPRs. In all these cases, the rules reflect the specific attributes of the particular resource. Among the four Spanish *huertas* that are located in fairly close proximity to one another, the specific rules for the various *huertas* differ rather substantially. It is only in the one system (Alicante) where there has been substantial storage available since the construction of Tibi Dam in 1594 that a water auction is held. At the time of the Sunday morning auction, substantial information about the level of water in the dam is made available to the Alicante irrigators. Consequently, they can know about how much water they will receive if they purchase an hour of water. In the systems without storage, water is strictly tied to the land, and some form of rotation is used. In Valencia, each farmer takes as much water as he can put to beneficial use in a defined order. Thus, each farmer has a high degree of certainty about the quantity of water to be received, and less certainty about the exact timing. In Murcia and Orihuela, where water is even more scarce, a tighter rotation system is used that rations the amount of time that irrigators can keep their gates open. Further, the rules attempt to solve the problem of getting water to a more diversified terrain than in Valencia. Subtly different rules are used in each system for assessing water fees used to pay for water guards and for maintenance activities, but in all instances those who receive the highest proportion of the water also pay the highest proportion of the fees. No single set of rules defined for all irrigation systems in the region could deal with the particular problems in managing each of these broadly similar, but distinctly different, systems.[37]

*Collective-choice arrangements*

3 Most individuals affected by the operational rules can participate in modifying the operational rules.

CPR institutions that use this principle are better able to tailor their rules to local circumstances, because the individuals who directly interact with one another and with the physical world can modify the rules over time so as to better fit them to the specific characteristics of their setting. Appropriators who design CPR institutions that are characterized by these first three principles – clearly defined boundaries, good-fitting rules, and appropriator participation in collective choice – should be able to devise a good set of rules if they keep the costs of changing the rules relatively low.

The presence of good rules, however, does not ensure that appropriators will follow them. Nor is the fact that appropriators themselves designed and initially agreed to the operational rules in our case studies an adequate explanation for centuries of compliance by individuals who were not involved in the initial agreement. It is not even an adequate explanation for the continued commitment of those who were part of the initial agreement. Agreeing to follow rules ex ante is an easy commitment to make. Actually following rules ex post, when strong temptations arise, is the significant accomplishment.

The problem of gaining compliance to the rules – no matter what their origin – often is assumed away by analysts positing all-knowing and all-powerful *external* authorities who enforce agreements. In the cases described here, no external authority has had sufficient presence to play any role in the day-to-day enforcement of the rules in use.[38] Thus, external enforcement cannot be used to explain these high levels of compliance.

Some recent theoretical models of repeated siutations do predict that individuals will adopt contingent strategies to generate optimal equilibria without external enforcement, but with very specific information requirements rarely found in field settings (Axelrod 1981, 1984; Kreps et al. 1982; T. Lewis and Cowens 1983). In these models, participants adopt resolute strategies to cooperate so long as everyone else cooperates. If anyone deviates, the models posit that all others will deviate immediately and forever. Information about everyone's strategies in a previous round is assumed to be freely available. No monitoring activities are included in these models, because information is presumed to be already available.

It is obvious from our case studies, however, that even in repeated settings where reputation is important and where individuals share the norm of keeping agreements, reputation and shared norms are insufficient by themselves to produce stable cooperative behavior over the long run. If they had been sufficient, appropriators could have avoided investing resources in monitoring and sanctioning activities. In all of the long-enduring cases, however, active investments in monitoring and sanctioning activities are quite apparent. That leads us to consider the fourth and fifth design principles:

### Monitoring

4  Monitors, who actively audit CPR conditions and appropriator behavior, are accountable to the appropriators or are the appropriators.

### Graduated sanctions

5  Appropriators who violate operational rules are likely to be assessed graduated sanctions (depending on the seriousness and context of the offense) by other appropriators, by officials accountable to these appropriators, or by both.

Now we are at the crux of the problem – and with surprising results. In these robust institutions, monitoring and sanctioning are undertaken not by external authorities but by the participants themselves. The initial sanctions used in these systems are also surprisingly low. Even though it is frequently presumed that participants will not spend the time and effort to monitor and sanction each other's performances, substantial evidence has been presented that they do both in these settings. The appropriators in these CPRs somehow have overcome the presumed problem of the second-order dilemma.

To explain the investment in monitoring and sanctioning activities that occurs in these robust, self-governing CPR institutions, the term "quasi-voluntary compliance" can be useful, as applied by Margaret Levi (1988a, ch. 3) to describe the behavior of taxpayers in systems in which most taxpayers comply. Paying taxes is voluntary in the sense that individuals choose to comply in many situations in which they are not being directly coerced. On the other hand, it is *"quasi-*voluntary because the noncompliant are subject to coercion – if they are caught" (Levi 1988a, p. 52). Taxpayers, according to Levi, will adopt a strategy of quasi-voluntary compliance when they have

confidence that (1) rulers will keep their bargains and (2) the other constituents will keep theirs. Taxpayers are strategic actors who will cooperate only when they can expect others to cooperate as well. The compliance of each depends on the compliance of the others. No one perfers to be a "sucker." (Levi 1988a, p. 53)

94

Levi stresses the *contingent* nature of a commitment to comply with rules that is possible in a repeated setting. Strategic actors are willing to comply with a set of rules, Levi argues, when (1) they perceive that the collective objective is achieved, and (2) they perceive that others also comply. Levi is not the first to point to contingent behavior as a source of stable, long-term cooperative solutions. Prior work, however, had viewed contingent behavior as an *alternative* to coercion; see, for example, Axelrod (1981, 1984) and T. Lewis and Cowens (1983). Levi, on the other hand, views coercion as an *essential condition* to achieve quasi-voluntary compliance as a form of contingent behavior. In her theory, enforcement increases the confidence of individuals that they are not suckers. As long as they are confident that others are cooperating and the ruler provides joint benefits, they comply willingly to tax laws. In Levi's theory, enforcement is normally provided by an external ruler, although her theory does not preclude other enforcers.

To explain commitment in these cases, we cannot posit external enforcement. CPR appropriators create their own internal enforcement to (1) deter those who are tempted to break rules and thereby (2) assure quasi-voluntary compliers that others also comply.[39] As discussed in Chapter 2, however, the normal presumption has been that participants themselves will not undertake mutual monitoring and enforcement because such actions involve relatively high personal costs and produce public goods available to everyone. As Elster (1989, p. 41) states, "punishment almost invariably is costly to the punisher, while the benefits from punishment are diffusely distributed over the members." Given the evidence that individuals monitor, then the relative costs and benefits must have a different configuration than that posited in prior work. Either the costs of monitoring are lower or the benefits to an individual are higher, or both.

The costs of monitoring are low in many long-enduring CPRs as a result of the rules in use. Irrigation rotation systems, for example, usually place the two actors most concerned with cheating in direct contact with one another. The irrigator who nears the end of a rotation turn would like to extend the time of his turn (and thus the amount of water obtained). The next irrigator in the rotation system waits nearby for him to finish, and would even like to start early. The presence of the first irrigator deters the second from an early start, the presence of the second irrigator deters the first from a late ending. Neither has to invest additional resources in monitoring activities. Monitoring is a by-product of their own strong motivations to use their water rotation turns to the fullest extent. The fishing-site rotation system used in Alanya has the same characteristic that cheaters can be observed at low cost by those who most want to deter cheaters at that particular time and location.

Many of the ways that work teams are organized in the Swiss and Japanese mountain commons also have the result that monitoring is a natural by-product of using the commons. Institutional analysis that simply posits an external, zero-cost enforcer has not addressed the possibility that the rules devised by appropriators may themselves have a major effect on the costs, and therefore the efficiency, of monitoring by internal or external enforcers.

Similarly, it is apparent that personal rewards for doing a good job are given to appropriators who monitor. The individual who finds a rule-infractor gains status and prestige for being a good protector of the commons. The infractor loses status and prestige. Private benefits are allocated to those who monitor. When internal monitoring is accomplished as part of a specialized position accountable to the other appropriators, several mechanisms increase the rewards for doing a good job or exposing slackards to the risk of losing their positions. In the Spanish *huertas*, a portion of the fines is kept by the guards; the Japanese detectives also keep the saké they collect from infractors.[40] All of the formal guard positions are accountable to the appropriators, and thus the monitors can be fired easily if discovered slacking off. Because the appropriators tend to continue monitoring the guards, as well as each other, some redundancy is built into the monitoring and sanctioning system. Failure to deter rule-breaking by one mechanism does not trigger a cascading process of rule infractions, because other mechanisms are in place.

Consequently, the costs and benefits of monitoring a set of rules are not independent of the particular set of rules adopted. Nor are they uniform in all CPR settings. When appropriators design at least some of their own rules (design principle 3), they can learn from experience to craft enforceable rather than unenforceable rules. This means paying attention to the costs of monitoring and enforcing, as well as the benefits that accrue to those who monitor and enforce the rules.

In repeated settings in which appropriators face incomplete information, appropriators who undertake monitoring activities obtain valuable information for themselves that can improve the quality of the strategic decision they make. In most theoretical models, where contingent strategies are shown to lead to optimal and stable dynamic equilibria, actors are assumed to have complete information about past history. They know what others did in the last round of decisions and how those choices affected outcomes. No consideration is given to how this information is generated. In the settings we have examined in this chapter, however, obtaining information about behavior and outcomes is costly.

If the appropriators adopt contingent strategies – each agreeing to follow a set of rules, so long as most of the others follow the rules – each one needs to be sure that others comply and that their compliance produces the expected benefit. Thus, a previously unrecognized "private" benefit of monitoring in settings in which information is costly is that one obtains the information necessary to adopt a contingent strategy. If an appropriator who monitors finds someone who has violated a rule, the benefits of that discovery are shared by all who use the CPR, and the discoverer gains an indication of compliance rates. If the monitor does *not* find a violator, previously it has been presumed that private costs are involved without any benefit to the individual or the group. If information is not freely available about compliance rates, then an individual who monitors obtains valuable information from monitoring. The appropriator-monitor who watches how water is distributed to other appropriators not only provides a public good for all but also obtains information needed to make future strategic decisions.

By monitoring the behavior of others, the appropriator-monitor learns about the level of quasi-voluntary compliance in the CPR. If no one is discovered breaking the rules, the appropriator-monitor learns that others comply and that no one is being taken for a sucker. It is then safe for the appropriator-monitor to continue to follow a strategy of quasi-voluntary compliance. If the appropriator-monitor discovers a rule infraction, it is possible to learn about the particular circumstances surrounding the infraction, to participate in deciding the appropriate level of sanctioning, and then to decide whether or not to continue compliance. If an appropriator-monitor finds an offender who normally follows the rules but in one instance happens to face a severe problem, the experience confirms what everyone already knows: There will always be instances in which those who are basically committed to following the set of rules may succumb to strong temptations to break them.

The appropriator-monitor may want to impose only a modest sanction in this circumstance. A small penalty may be sufficient to remind the infractor of the importance of compliance. The appropriator-monitor might be in a similar situation in the future and would want some understanding at that time. Everyone will hear about the incident, and the violator's reputation for reliability will depend on complying with the rules in the future. If the appropriator-monitor presumes that the violator will follow the rules most of the time in the future, the appropriator-monitor

Governing the commons

can safely continue a strategy of compliance. The incident will also confirm for the appropriator-monitor the importance of monitoring even when most others basically are following the rules.

A real threat to the continuance of quasi-voluntary compliance can occur, however, if an appropriator-monitor discovers individuals who break the rules repeatedly. If this occurs, one can expect the appropriator-monitor to escalate the imposed sanctions in an effort to halt future rule-breaking by such offenders and any others who might start to follow suit. In any case, the appropriator-monitor has up-to-date information about compliance and sanctioning behavior on which to base future decisions about personal compliance.

Let us also look at the situation through the eyes of someone who breaks the rules and is discovered by a local guard (who will eventually tell everyone) or another appropriator (who also is likely to tell everyone). Being apprehended by a local monitor after having succumbed to the temptation to break the rules will have three results: (1) It will stop the infraction from continuing and may return contraband harvest to others. (2) It will convey information to the offender that someone else in a similar situation is likely to be caught, thus increasing confidence in the level of quasi-voluntary compliance. (3) A punishment in the form of a fine, plus loss of reputation for reliability, will be imposed. A large monetary fine may not be needed to return an occasional offender to the fold of those who are quasi-voluntary compliers with the rules. A large monetary fine imposed on a person facing an unusual problem may produce resentment and unwillingness to conform to the rules in the future. Graduated punishments ranging from insignificant fines all the way to banishment, applied in settings in which the sanctioners know a great deal about the personal circumstances of the other appropriators and the potential harm that could be created by excessive sanctions, may be far more effective than a major fine imposed on a first offender.

If quasi-voluntary compliance is contingent on the compliance rate of others, then the question is, What rate must be maintained to ensure that the commitment to comply will continue over time? Previous theoretical work has assumed that 100% is needed; but also see M. Taylor (1987, pp. 89–90), who posits less than 100%. It is assumed that any infraction (or error) will trigger a relentless process: Everyone will resolutely punish the offender (and themselves) by breaking their previous agreement. Although these trigger-strategy models have the attractive theoretical property of stable equilibria, they do not describe the behavior observed in our case studies (or any of the other cases I have read or observed in the field). Acceptable quasi-voluntary compliance rates that will lead appropriators to continue their own quasi-voluntary compliance will differ from one setting to another and will depend on economic or other circumstances within the CPR. Tolerance for rules infractions may be very high during a depression, so long as the higher rate appears temporary and not threatening to the survival of a CPR. This appears to have happened in one of the Japanese villages studied by McKean during the depression of the 1930s:

Almost all the villagers knew that almost all the other villagers were breaking the rules: sneaking around the commons at night, cutting trees that were larger than the allowed size, even using wood-cutting tools that were not permitted. This is precisely the behavior that could get a tragedy of the commons started, but it did not happen in Yamanaka. Instead of regarding the general breakdown of rules as an opportunity to become full-time free riders and cast caution to the winds, the violators themselves tried to exercise self-discipline out of deference to the pre- servation of the commons, and stole from the commons only out of desperation. Inspectors or other witnesses who saw violations maintained silence out of sympa- thy for the violators' desperation and out of confidence that the problem was temporary and could not really hurt the commons. (McKean 1986, pp. 565–6)

In other situations, the harm that a single infraction can inflict on others may be so substantial, and the potential for private gain so great, that 100% compliance is essential. McKean (1986, p. 565) describes a situation in the village of Shiwa when it suffered a severe drought. The temptation to break the dikes, in order to obtain water illegally, was so great for those serving as guards, as well as for the remaining farmers, that all adult males patrol- led the dikes every night in mutual surveillance until the emergency was over.

The fourth and fifth design principles – monitoring and graduated sanc- tions – thus take their place as part of the configuration of design principles that can work together to enable appropriators to constitute and recon- stitute robust CPR institutions. Let me summarize my argument to this point. When CPR appropriators design their own operational rules (design principle 3) to be enforced by individuals who are local appropriators or are accountable to them (design principle 4), using graduated sanctions (design principle 5) that define who has rights to withdraw units from the CPR (design principle 1) and that effectively restrict appropriation activ- ities, given local conditions (design principle 2), the commitment and monitoring problem are solved in an interrelated manner. Individuals who think that a set of rules will be effective in producing higher joint benefits and that monitoring (including their own) will protect them against being suckered are willing to make a contingent self-commitment[41] of the fol- lowing type:

I commit myself to follow the set of rules we have devised in all instances except dire emergencies if the rest of those affected make a similar commitment and act accordingly.

Once appropriators have made contingent self-commitments, they are then motivated to monitor other people's behaviors, at least from time to time, in order to assure themselves that others are following the rules most of the time. Contingent self-commitments and mutual monitoring reinforce one another, especially when appropriators have devised rules that tend to reduce monitoring costs. We are now ready to discuss the sixth design principle.

### Conflict-resolution mechanisms

6 Appropriators and their officials have rapid access to low-cost local arenas to resolve conflicts among appropriators or between appropriators and officials.

In theoretical models of rule-governed behavior, the rules that structure the strategies available to participants are unambiguous and are enforced by external, all-knowing officials. In field settings, applying the rules is never unambiguous, even when the appropriators themselves are the monitors and sanctioners. Even such a simple rule as "each irrigator must send one individual for one day to help clean the irrigation canals before the rainy season begins" can be interpreted quite differently by different individuals. Who is or is not an "individual" according to this rule? Does sending a child below age 10 or an adult above age 70 to do heavy physical work meet this rule? Is working for four hours or six hours a "day" of work? Does cleaning the canal immediately next to one's own farm qualify for this community obligation? For individuals who are seeking ways to slide past or subvert rules, there are always various ways in which they can "interpret" a rule so that they can argue they have complied with the rule, but in effect subverting its intent. Even individuals who intend to follow the spirit of a rule can make errors. What happens if someone forgets about a labor day and does not show? Or what happens of the only able-bodied worker is sick, or unavoidably in another location?

If individuals are going to follow rules over a long period of time, there must be some mechanism for discussing and resolving what constitutes an infraction. If some individuals are allowed to free-ride by sending less able workers to a required labor day, others will consider themselves to be suckers if they send their strongest workers, who could be using that time to produce private goods rather than communal benefits. Should that continue over time, only children and old people would be sent to do work

100

that would require strong adults, and the system would break down. If individuals who make honest mistakes or face personal problems that occasionally prevent them from following a rule do not have access to mechanisms that will allow them to make up for their lack of performance in an acceptable way, rules may come to be viewed as unfair, and conformance rates may decline.

Although the presence of conflict-resolution mechanisms does not guarantee that appropriators will be able to maintain enduring institutions, it is difficult to imagine how any complex system of rules could be maintained over time without such mechanisms. For those cases discussed earlier, such mechanisms sometimes are quite informal, and those who are selected as leaders are also the basic resolvers of conflict. In some cases – such as the Spanish *huertas* – the potential for conflict over a very scarce resource is so high that well-developed court mechanisms have been in place for centuries.

### Minimal recognition of rights to organize

7 The rights of appropriators to devise their own institutions are not challenged by external governmental authorities.

Appropriators frequently devise their own rules without creating formal governmental jurisdictions for this purpose. In many inshore fisheries, for example, local fishers devise extensive rules defining who can use a fishing ground and what kind of equipment can be used. Provided the external governmental officials give at least minimal recognition to the legitimacy of such rules, the fishers themselves may be able to enforce the rules themselves. But if external governmental officials presume that only they have the authority to set the rules, then it will be very difficult for local appropriators to sustain a rule-governed CPR over the long run. In a situation in which one wishes to get around the rules created by the fishers, one may go to the external government and try to get local rules overturned. In Chapter 5 we shall examine several cases in which this design principle is not met.

### Nested enterprises

8 Appropriation, provision, monitoring, enforcement, conflict resolution, and governance activities are organized in multiple layers of nested enterprises.

All of the more complex, enduring CPRs meet this last design principle. In the Spanish *huertas*, for example, irrigators are organized on the basis of three or four nested levels, all of which are then also nested in local, regional, and national governmental jurisdictions. There are two distinct levels in the Philippine federation of irrigation systems. The problems facing irrigators at the level of a tertiary canal are different from the problems facing a larger group sharing a secondary canal. Those, in turn, are different from the problems involved in the management of the main diversion works that affect the entire system. Establishing rules at one level, without rules at the other levels, will produce an incomplete system that may not endure over the long run.

In the last part of this chapter I have identified a set of design principles that characterize the long-enduring CPR institutions described in the first part. I have also attempted to examine why individuals utilizing institutional arrangements characterized by these design principles will be motivated to replicate the institutions over time and sustain the CPR to which they are related. We shall continue to discuss these design principles throughout the remainder of this study. In the next chapter we shall examine how individuals supply themselves with new institutions to solve CPR problems.

# 4

## Analyzing institutional change

In the preceding chapter I examined institutions for governing CPRs in which appropriators have devised governance systems that have survived for long periods of time in environments characterized by considerable uncertainty and change. Although the particular problems involved in governing mountain commons vary from those involved in governing irrigation systems, all of these long-enduring institutional arrangements have shared commonalities. These cases clearly demonstrate the feasibility (but obviously not the likelihood) of robust, self-governing institutions for managing complex CPR situations, but the origins of these systems are lost in time. It is not possible to reconstruct how earlier users of Swiss alpine meadows, Japanese mountain commons, the Spanish *huertas*, or the Philippine *zanjeras* devised rules that have survived such long periods. We do not know who originated or opposed various proposals, or anything about the process of change itself.

A study of the origins of institutions must address the problem of supply raised in Chapter 2. As Bates (1988) points out, the presence of collective benefits as a result of designing new institutions is itself a second-order collective dilemma. A proposed new institution "is subject to the very incentive problems it is supposed to resolve" (Bates 1988, p. 395). Many questions need to be addressed. How many participants were involved? What was their internal group structure? Who initiated action? Who paid the costs of entrepreneurial activities? What kind of information did participants have about their situation? What were the risks and exposures of various participants? What broader institutions did participants use in establishing new rules? These questions are rarely answered in the extensive case-study literature describing behavior within ongoing institutional arrangements. Once a set of rules is in place, the incentives facing

103

appropriators are entirely different from the incentives that faced an earlier set of appropriators when confronted with severe appropriation or provision suboptimalities.

In this chapter, the origins of a set of institutions to manage a series of groundwater basins located beneath the Los Angeles metropolitan area are examined. Louis Weschler and I did extensive fieldwork in these areas during the late 1950s and early 1960s, when many changes were occurring (E. Ostrom 1965; Weschler 1968). We attended meetings, read internal memoranda, and interviewed participants to obtain information about the strategies of groundwater producers to organize voluntary associations, to undertake litigation, to create special districts, and to constitute a complex public-private governance system to regulate their basins. Recently, William Blomquist (1987a, 1988a–e) has expanded the number of groundwater basins studied and updated the available information. For these groundwater basins, we have a good understanding of the processes involved in changing the rules, and sufficient time has elapsed to allow us to evaluate the stability and efficiency of the results obtained in using these rules to govern and manage these basins. In this chapter we examine the processes of changing the rules in three basins (Raymond, West, and Central) that have relied on negotiated settlements of water rights as a key element in the transformation of their situation.[1] See Figure 4.1 for a map of the area.

## THE COMPETITIVE PUMPING RACE

### The setting

In an earlier geologic era, rivers and streams draining the mountains surrounding what has now become the Los Angeles metropolitan area laid down wide and deep bands of sand and gravel that were then partially overlaid by hard layers of clay. The former streambeds are now deep, water-bearing strata that can be thought of as underground reservoirs. These reservoirs are replenished by the rains that fall in the foothills and upper valleys and, to a more limited extent, by precipitation and drainage on the flat coastal plain itself.

In a semiarid region such as Los Angeles, groundwater basins are extremely valuable when used in conjunction with surface supply systems. First, they are sources of inexpensive and high-quality water, as compared with the cost of importing water from long distances. In 1985, the Metropolitan Water District charged $240 per acre-foot (the volume of water that would cover one acre of land with one foot of water) as the wholesale price for imported water from northern California and from the Colorado

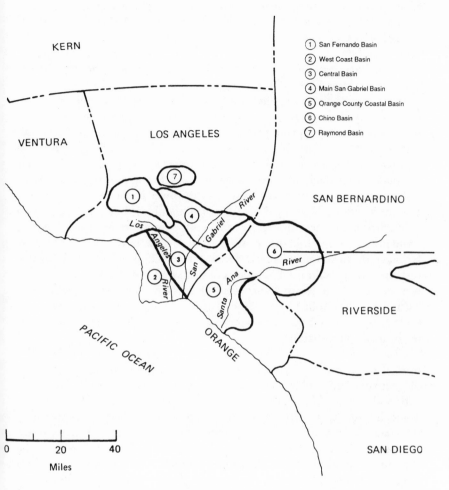

KERN

VENTURA

LOS ANGELES

① San Fernando Basin
② West Coast Basin
③ Central Basin
④ Main San Gabriel Basin
⑤ Orange County Coastal Basin
⑥ Chino Basin
⑦ Raymond Basin

SAN BERNARDINO

RIVERSIDE

SAN DIEGO

PACIFIC OCEAN

ORANGE

0    20    40
Miles

Figure 4.1. Groundwater basins underlying the south coastal plain in California. (Adapted from Lipson 1978.)

River. The cost of pumping groundwater in the Los Angeles area averaged around $134 per acre-foot – a saving of more than $100 per acre-foot. If the 282,458 acre-feet of groundwater that were pumped in 1985 from the three basins discussed in this chapter had been replaced with surface water, it would have cost the industrial users, the urban households, and the irrigators at least $28 million more per year.[2]

The value of the basins as sources of water supply is overshadowed, however, by their even greater value as natural storage vessels that can retain water for use during periods of peak demand.[3] Every surface-water system must have available some type of short-term storage so that it can rapidly meet the accelerated demands of water users that occur at regular intervals during each day and each week, and during the course of a year. The current construction costs for a water tower in the Los Angeles area average around $57,500 per acre-foot (Blomquist 1987a). The minimum amount of short-term storage recommended by the relevant engineering standards is 16% of the total water used in an area. In the area of the West Basin, with an annual demand for water of 327,435 acre-feet, storage reservoirs that could hold 52,400 acre-feet would be required if the basin were not available for this purpose. The replacement costs for this single basin would be about $3.01 billion. The loss of all the groundwater basins underlying the Los Angeles metropolitan area would be an economic disaster of major proportions.

Groundwater basins can be destroyed by overextraction and/or pollution. If more water is withdrawn per year than the average level of replenishment (referred to as the safe yield of a basin), eventually the gravel and sand in the water-bearing strata will compact so that they cannot hold as much water as they formerly did. If a groundwater basin is located near the ocean, and its water level is drawn down below sea level, saltwater intrusion will occur along the coast. Wells along the coastline must be abandoned. If intrusion is not halted, eventually the entire basin will no longer be usable as a source of supply or for its storage capacity. Overextraction threatened all of the groundwater basins in this region until institutional changes were initiated by those affected.

### The logic of the water-rights game

Overextraction was the logical outcome of the way groundwater rights were defined prior to the institutional changes described in this chapter. Water rights in California had been defined on the basis of whether a producer owned the overlying land and used the water on that land (an overlying landowner) or used the water to serve areas other than land

106

owned by the water producer (an appropriator). Under the common law, an overlying landowner held a riparian right to the "full flow" of the water supply underlying his or her land (Nunn 1985). In a region of extreme scarcity of water, the common law does not provide secure rights for an overlying landowner. Water underlying any parcel of land (e.g., parcel A) can be siphoned to a neighbor's land if the neighbor withdraws water more rapidly than does the owner of parcel A. In *Katz v. Walkinshaw* [141 Cal. 116, 74 P. 766 (1903)], the doctrine of "correlative rights" was developed to replace the strict interpretation of riparian rights. That doctrine held that in times of shortage, if the court was called on to adjudicate among competing interests, the court would treat all overlying owners as correlative and coequal owners. In times of scarcity, each would gain a *proportionate* share of the water rather than an *absolute* share of the water. That doctrine was modified somewhat in *San Bernardino v. Riverside* [186 Cal. 7 (1921)], in which overlying landowners were limited to taking only water that they could put to "beneficial" use.

Thus, overlying landowners facing only other overlying landowners knew that if they went to court to settle a dispute over water rights during a time of shortage, they would all share proportionately in any cutback in the total water available to them. In most groundwater basins, however, overlying landowners faced other water users called "appropriators," whose claim to water was on a different basis than that of an overlying landowner. Appropriators pumped groundwater to be used on land not owned by those withdrawing the water. Most private and public water companies were legally classified as appropriators, because the water they pumped was used by their customers, not by the water companies themselves. Nonoverlying landowners were allowed, if not encouraged, by the appropriative-rights doctrines made part of the statutory law in 1872 to withdraw "surplus water" or water that was not being put to beneficial use by the overlying landowners. The key elements in defining the rights of an appropriator had to do with

1  when the appropriator began to withdraw water from the source,
2  how much water was actually put to beneficial use, and
3  whether or not the use was continuous.

Under the doctrine of "first in time, first in right," appropriators acquired rights depending on their history of use. Among appropriators, a court-resolved conflict over a scarce supply would exclude use by the most junior appropriator, and then the next most junior appropriator, and so forth. The most senior appropriators would be fully protected against encroachment on their rights by more junior appropriators. However, the rights of the most senior appropriators were potentially subordinate to those of overlying landowners.

The simultaneous existence of the doctrines of correlative and appropriative rights in the same state introduced considerable uncertainty about the relative rights of one groundwater producer against others. The uncertainty was compounded by the presence of a third common-law doctrine that enabled groundwater producers to gain rights through "adverse use" or prescription. In regard to land, prescriptive rights are relatively straightforward: If one person occupied someone else's land in an open, notorious, and continuous manner for a set period of time (five years in California), and the owner makes no effort to eject the occupier, the original owner loses the right to the land.

In regard to groundwater, possession of water was not enough to establish open and *adverse* use. Any junior appropriator could legally use any water that was surplus water. Surplus water was defined as a part of the "safe yield" of a basin that was not of beneficial use to overlying landowners or senior appropriators. The safe yield of a basin is the average, long-term supply of water to the basin. If that quantity of water was put to beneficial use, no surplus was available to others. An appropriator had to take nonsurplus water openly and continuously for more than five years to perfect prescriptive rights. Once perfected, prescriptive rights were superior to those of overlying owners and appropriators. The same actions of an appropriator – openly taking water continuously from a basin – could lead to the acquisition of rights *superior* to those of overlying landowners or, alternatively, to the *inferior* rights of a junior appropriator relative to an overlying landowner in time of scarcity. The key difference between these outcomes was whether the court ruled that a surplus did or did not exist for the five-year period prior to litigation. Given that all producers suffered from lack of information concerning the safe yield of a basin and the pumping rates of other producers, no one knew at the time of making such decisions what the pumping rates were or whether or not a surplus existed.

The situation in these basins can be characterized as an open-access CPR for which clear limits have not been established regarding who can withdraw how much water. In such situations, two strong pressures encourage pumpers to adopt inefficient strategies. The first is a pumping-cost externality. The second is a strategic externality (Negri 1989). Pumping costs increase as the pumping lift increases, because of falling water levels, and therefore each person's withdrawals increase the pumping costs for others. No one bears the full cost of personal actions. Each pumper is consequently

# Analyzing institutional change

led toward overexploitation. The strategic externality involved in an open-access groundwater basin is aptly described by Negri (1989, p. 9).

> With property rights undefined and access nonexclusive, the "rule of capture" governs the "ownership" of the reserve stock. The rule of capture grants [pumpers] exclusive rights to that portion of the groundwater that they pump. What an operator does not withdraw today will be withdrawn, at least in part, by rival[s]. The fear that [pumpers] cannot capture tomorrow what they do not pump today undermines their incentive to forgo current pumping for future pumping.

The two incentives reinforce one another to aggravate the intensity of the pumping race. Without a change of institutions, pumpers in such a situation acting independently will severely overexploit the resource. Over-exploitation can lead to destruction of the resource itself.

Current institutions affect not only the intensity of a pumping race but also the relative incentives of different participants to initiate institutional change. Given the legal structure of rights in California, overlying landowners were more motivated than appropriators to launch court action so as to keep appropriators from obtaining prescriptive rights. The decision about when to start litigation, however, involved high risks of being too soon or too late. The overlying owner faced two possibilities:

(1)  If he went to court before all "surplus" water had been appropriated, and the court ruled that the water being diverted by the defendant was indeed surplus water, the overlying owner would suffer the costs of the litigation and receive no remedy;

(2)  If he waited too long to go to court, the overlying owner might find that the defendant had perfected a prescriptive right if the court ruled that the water being diverted was non-surplus water. There was, in other words, no way for the overlying owner, on whom the burden of initiating litigation rested, to succeed in protecting his right until it had been invaded, and yet within a short time after the right had been invaded, the overlying owner would have lost the right he sought to protect due to prescription.

(Blomquist 1988a, p. 19)

The uncertainty of the competing water doctrines was compounded by the uncertainty shared by all water producers about the actual supply of water to a basin and the quantity of water withdrawn by all of the parties. It was essential to know the quantities supplied and demanded from a basin to determine the presence or absence of a surplus. Both types of information were costly to obtain. Both could be obtained at the time of litigation

109

by asking the court to appoint a watermaster to make a geologic survey of the basin and determine its water supply and to obtain information about the past water uses of all producers. When determined in this manner, the cost would be shared by all producers involved in the litigation. But that did not solve the problem of uncertainty prior to the initiation of litigation. In past cases, signs of potential problems – such as falling water tables – had not been accepted by the court as sufficient evidence of a water shortage to declare a lack of surplus and uphold the rights of overlying owners as against junior appropriators [*San Bernardino v. Riverside*, 186 Cal. 7 (1921)].

Given these compound uncertainties, it is easy to explain the behavior of groundwater pumpers in the Los Angeles metropolitan area during the first 50 years of this century. To obtain any kind of water right, one needed to show continuous withdrawal of water and application to beneficial use. In that environment of legal uncertainty, attorneys advised producers to pump as much as they needed and to defend later (Krieger 1955). A pumping race occurred in each of the groundwater basins underlying the Los Angeles area.

Given those incentives, many water producers and local government officials during the 1940s and 1950s worried that all of the basins would be severely overdrawn and that those basins located adjacent to the ocean – West Basin and Central Basin – would be lost to the sea. By the 1960s, however, the pumping race had been halted in all of the coastal basins. Water rights were eventually established in all the basins, except in Orange County, which continues to rely on a pump tax for regulation.[4]

Special water districts have been established throughout the area to obtain surface water, to levy pump taxes on water production, and to replenish the basins through a variety of artificial means. A series of injection wells has been constructed along the coast to create a barrier of fresh water against the sea, enabling the coastal districts to regulate the uses of their basins in a manner similar to the use of a surface reservoir. In other words, diverse private and public actors have extricated themselves from the perversity of the pumping race and transformed the entire structure of the incentives they face. Public arenas were involved in many stages of these developments. The initial steps were taken in the shadow of a court order. Elections and public hearings were held at key stages. The solutions to the pumping race, however were not imposed on the participants by external authorities. Rather, the participants used public arenas *to impose constraints on themselves*. Because litigation to gain defined water rights was involved in all of the basins, except in Orange County, we first discuss this strategy to transform the pumping race.

110

# Analyzing institutional change

## THE LITIGATION GAME
### The Raymond Basin negotiations[5]

The Raymond Basin is a small basin, with a surface area of 40 square miles, located inland and thus protected from saltwater intrusion. The area was already highly developed by the turn of the century. Later studies have revealed that the safe yield of the basin was steadily exceeded from 1913 onward. The cities of Pasadena, Sierra Madre, Arcadia, Altadena, La Cañada–Flintridge, South Pasadena, San Marino, and Monrovia are located on the surface of the basin. The city of Alhambra lies on its borders and appropriates water from the basin for use within its boundaries. The city of Pasadena was by far the largest producer of water from the basin – its production equaled the production of the other 30 producers combined. Pasadena thus approached, but did not reach, the position of a dominant actor in a privileged group (Olson 1965). According to Olson's model, if the Raymond Basin producers had been a privileged group, the city of Pasadena would have borne all of the costs associated with stopping the pumping race. The prediction one derives from Olson's model is consistent with some, but not all, of the activities pursued by the city of Pasadena.

The city of Pasadena for some years adopted the strategy of the dominant player in a privileged group. From 1914 to 1923, for example, the city replenished the basin by capturing floodwaters and spreading them on the gravel areas located at the feet of the San Gabriel Mountains. The water that percolated into the basin was then available for capture by the city of Pasadena as well as by other groundwater producers. In the late 1920s, the city of Pasadena was a leading participant in the formation of the Metropolitan Water District of Southern California, which would eventually construct an aqueduct to bring water 250 miles to the Los Angeles area from the Colorado River.

During the 1930s, however, the city of Pasadena was no longer willing to undertake independent actions that were substantially benefiting others who were not contributing to the costs. The city tried unsuccessfully to negotiate a voluntary settlement with the other producers whereby all producers would jointly reduce the amounts of water they were withdrawing from the basin. In 1937 Pasadena initiated legal proceedings against the city of Alhambra and 30 other producers.[6] The case was referred to the Division of Water Resources of the California Department of Public Works for determination of the geologic structure of the basin, the safe yield of the basin, and whether or not there was a surplus.

That referral procedure was time-consuming and costly. The draft report of the referee was not completed until March of 1943 and cost about

111

$53,000. The referee found that the yearly withdrawals from the basin were 29,400 acre-feet, whereas the safe yield of the basin was 21,900, leading to an annual overdraft of 8,500 acre-feet per year. The referee recommended that the parties curtail their pumping to the safe yield of the basin.

The parties then shared a single, authoritative "image" of the problem they faced. They also would confront a new "default condition" (E. Ostrom 1986a) if they could not agree on their own solution. Prior to litigation, the failure to agree would simply mean a return to the pumping race. Once the court took jurisdiction, an absence of agreement would mean that the judge would decide which parties had to bear the brunt of the cutback. It was not at all clear what the judge would decide. The judge might, for example, assign preeminent rights to the overlying owners and then assign the remainder of the 21,900 acre-feet as a "surplus" to the appropriators to be apportioned according to their seniority. Or the judge might decide that there was no surplus. In that case, senior appropriators might be granted prescriptive rights, and overlying landowners would bear the major brunt of the cutback.

A simplified picture of the bargaining problem that the producers faced is shown in Figure 4.2. If we assume that the overlying owners were withdrawing 12,000 acre-feet and the appropriators (who might become prescriptors) were withdrawing 18,000 acre-feet, the total withdrawals prior to a decision would be 30,000 acre-feet. Everyone accepted the fact that a cutback to 22,000 acre-feet would occur. A worst-case analysis done by the overlying landowners would assume that the judge would declare that there had been no surplus for more than five years prior to litigation. Thus, the appropriators would be given superior rights to all that they had withdrawn. They would be assigned 18,000 acre-feet, leaving only 4,000 acre-feet for the overlying landowners. Point B marks the worst possible solution that the overlying owners could face.

Similarly, the appropriators could do a worst-case analysis and assume that the judge would assign firm rights of 12,000 acre-feet to the overlying landowners and then assign the "surplus" of 10,000 acre-feet to the appropriators according to their seniority. Point A is the worst possible solution from the perspective of the appropriators. For all participants, the range of variation between complete protection and major loss (the line connecting A and B) would be considerable. Further, a fully contested trial would last a long time, given the conflicting legal doctrines, and the costs of litigation would be extremely high.

At the instigation of the city of Pasadena, the parties held some serious negotiations in the shadow of the court. Within six months they had drafted a stipulated agreement signed by all but 2 of the 32 parties involved in the litigation. The negotiation process was furthered in that instance by the unusual fact that one attorney, Kenneth Wright, represented 16 of the parties. After another six months, one of the holdouts also agreed to the stipulation. The other – the California-Michigan Land and Water Company – never agreed to the stipulation and challenged the final court decision based on the stipulation.

The signatories agreed that the safe yield had been exceeded for a long time and that it was necessary to cut back to the safe yield of the basin. They stated that each producer's withdrawal of groundwater had been open, continuous, and notorious and was, because of the overdraft, adverse to the claims of all of the others. Thus, each producer had prescribed against all of the others. The term "mutual prescription" has been used to describe the concept used by these parties as the foundation for their negotiated settlement. The signatory parties agreed to *share the cutback proportionately* instead of pursuing further legal procedures to determine whose rights took precedence.[7] The proportional division of the cutback is represented by point D in Figure 4.2.[8] They further guaranteed each other's proportional shares of the safe yield (if it were to change in the future) and established an arrangement to enable those most adversely affected by the

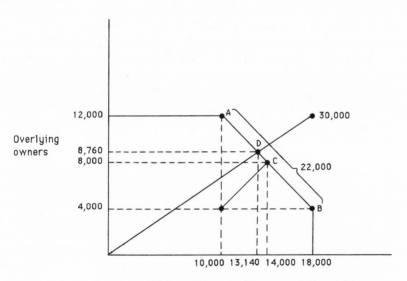

Figure 4.2. The bargaining situation faced by overlying owners and appropriators.

113

cutback to obtain exchange rights from others willing to sell their rights on an annual basis.

A short trial was held to hear the objections of the California-Michigan Land and Water Company and to assign the Division of Water Resources of the California Department of Public Works to serve as the watermaster– an official monitor – to supervise the agreement. Rather than imposing his own solution,[9] the judge, after considerable reflection, issued a final judgment on December 23, 1944,[10] based on the stipulated agreement. The final judgment declared all of the decreed rights to be of equal standing in any future dispute and enjoined all parties from taking more than their decreed rights. The judgment continued the role of the watermaster to enforce the provisions of the judgment and to supervise the exchange pool they had developed. In addition to the leasing arrangements of the exchange pool, decreed rights could be leased or sold outright so long as the transfers were recorded by the watermaster. Two-third of the costs of the watermaster were to be paid for by the parties, and the state of California would pay for the remaining costs of monitoring the agreement. The case was appealed to the California Supreme Court, and the decision was upheld.[11] The United States Supreme Court declined to review the case.

By negotiating their own agreement, the parties had ended the pumping race faster and at a lower cost than they could have through a court proceeding.[12] They also had gained firm and marketable rights to defined shares of the safe yield of the basin. A market for those water rights developed, and most of the smaller right-holders have sold their rights to the water companies, for whom the rights have a higher value. There are now 17 active producers from the basin, and they are almost all municipal or private water companies. Only three overlying landowners continue to produce water from the basin. The areas within the basin that did not have access to imported water formed a municipal water corporation in 1953 and started receiving imported water in 1955.

### The West Basin negotiations

West Basin, with a surface area of 170 square miles, is a much larger area than Raymond Basin. Located immediately adjacent to the ocean, it extends from the city of Inglewood to the Palos Verdes Peninsula. The situation in West Basin was not as favorable for negotiations as that facing the Raymond Basin producers. The major advantage for the West Basin producers was that their upland neighbors had already borne the costs of innovation and had developed a formula for reaching a negotiated settlement within the California legal environment that was considered to be fair

114

by many potential litigants. The disadvantages faced in West Basin included (1) a large number of producers (around 500 parties were named in the litigation), (2) the absence of a single dominant producer, and (3) considerable asymmetry in the risks regarding saltwater intrusion (those near the sea would lose their wells long before those pumping inland). The problem of the size of the group was offset to some extent by the concentrated nature of the groundwater production in the basin: 19 producers accounted for about 85% of the total quantity of water withdrawn from West Basin.[13]

The overdraft came a decade later to West Basin than to Raymond Basin. The heavy industrialization that occurred during World War II exacerbated the already growing overdraft, particularly because there were many oil companies located in the area whose water production had increased steadily. In the early 1940s, wells located along the coast began to show increasing salinity. Many water producers in the basin continued to believe, however, that the salinity in those wells was symptomatic of only a "local" problem immediately along the coast, not a more general problem that could affect their own situation in the future. During 1943, nine of the coastal municipalities met several times to discuss the importance of the increasing salinity of their wells. They agreed that more information was needed to gain a realistic and common image of the structure of the groundwater basin. Those cities signed a cooperative agreement with the United States Geological Survey and the Los Angeles County Flood Control District to undertake an initial study of the problem of groundwater supply in the basin.[14]

The report, completed in 1944, painted a grim picture. Wells all along the coast had been invaded by seawater. The investigators had found no natural barrier at any point in the basin to halt the advance of the sea. The entire basin was threatened with destruction. The report provided a common image of the general boundaries of the basin and the extent of the problem without providing an exact picture of the safe yield and current levels of water production. It was no longer possible, however, for producers to maintain that the salinity in the coastal wells was strictly a local problem.

In December of 1944, all of the major water producers met and established an ad hoc committee to consider what should be done next. That committee had three major recommendations:

1 that a permanent association be created of all interested water producers so that they could continue to discuss their mutual problems and possible joint actions,

2 that a technical survey be made of alternative sources of water for the area, and

3 that water producers consider initiating legal action similar to the action just completed in Raymond Basin to reduce total pumping and to ration the limited water supply in West Basin among all water producers (Ways and Means Committee 1945, p. 16).

All three recommendations were followed. The West Basin Water Association was created within a few months.[15] The association provided a continuous open forum[16] for discussion of all major steps taken in West Basin by producers and representatives of various local, regional, and state public agencies. The resources of the association frequently were used to obtain and make available the best possible technical information about the basin. Extensive minutes were kept for all West Basin Water Association meetings, as well as the meetings of the Executive Committee and most of the working committees of the association. Those files were open to all members, as well as to others interested in gaining information about past decisions, technical data, and studies of the benefits and costs of alternatives. A weekly newsletter was dispatched to all members from 1946 through 1954. The motto of the newsletter, according to its editor, was "let there be no surprises, either pleasant or unpleasant" (Fossette and Fossette 1986, p. 57). The practice of obtaining the best information available and disseminating it widely increased the degree of understanding and level of cooperation among the participants.

The first official act of the association, in March 1946, was to retain a renowned engineer, Harold Conkling, to examine the possibility of finding alternative sources of supplemental water for the basin. Conkling recommended the creation of a municipal water district to import water from the Metropolitan Water District of Southern California. Obtaining surface water eventually would mean that the groundwater basin would no longer serve as the major source of water for the area, but the question who would obtain rights to use the reservoir capacities of the basin had to be resolved.

Three appropriators initiated the West Basin litigation in October 1945: the California Water Service Company, the city of Torrance, and the Palos Verdes Water Company. Kenneth Wright, who had served as the attorney for the city of Pasadena in the Raymond Basin litigation, was the attorney for the California Water Service Company and had made several presentations to West Basin producers concerning the mutual-prescription concept used in the Raymond Basin case. Although the initiators of the litigation, and many other water producers in the basin, strongly supported the

116

concept of proportionate cutbacks by all water producers, several major water producers vigorously opposed such a plan.

The Dominguez Water Corporation, a senior appropriator with overlying rights as well, was one strong opponent. Because Dominguez was the largest producer from the basin,[17] it was unlikely that others would agree to a curtailment without the participation of the Dominguez Corporation. The city of Inglewood initially opposed the litigation and all of the actions proposed within the context of the West Basin Water Association. Inglewood's lawyers had advised city officials that its status as senior appropriator would protect it from having to cut back production. Inglewood's position changed, however, after the Raymond Basin decision had been sustained in the California Supreme Court.[18] Inglewood, which owned some wells near the sea, was to become an active participant in the effort to find solutions.

The city of Hawthorne, on the other hand, was located inland, and its people believed that their water supply was protected. Hawthorne adopted a hold-out strategy for many years. Thus, whereas the Raymond Basin case was a guiding model in the minds of the initiators of the litigation, it was not at all certain that the water producers of West Basin would achieve the high level of agreement needed to negotiate their own settlement. Once litigation had been initiated, however, the court could impose its own judgment if the water producers could not reach an agreement on their own. Thus, again the default rule had been changed by the initiation of litigation.

The case was referred to the Division of Water Resources of the California Department of Public Works. The difficult task of ascertaining the production levels for more than 500 producers and determining the geologic structure and inflow levels for a large and complex basin took four years. By the time the referee's report was completed, the decision of the trial court based on the stipulated agreement in the Raymond Basin case had been upheld by the California Supreme Court. Therefore, the West Basin water producers knew that the mutual-prescription concept could withstand a legal challenge by a private company.

The referee's findings and recommendations, however, came as a written bombshell. The referee found that overdrafts had been occurring since 1920 and that the safe yield of the basin was 30,000 acre-feet per year. The referee recommended a curtailment to the safe yield. By 1952, total groundwater withdrawals had reached 90,000 acre-feet per year. Even the supporters of mutual curtailment vigorously opposed a two-thirds reduction in groundwater production. Imported water had just begun to trickle

*Governing the commons*

into the basin. Many water suppliers would not be able to meet their customers' demands if they were to reduce the quantity of water pumped by two-thirds. Early experiments with injection wells provided some encouraging indications that the supply of water to the basin could be increased. An increase in the supply would reduce the necessity of cutting back to the safe yield. The default condition, however, had again been changed. If the water producers were unable to arrive at their own settlement, they could expect the court to order a two-thirds cutback.

The West Basin Water Association provided a forum for serious negotiations about a settlement. The association established a Legal Settlement Committee composed of six attorneys and five engineers. The creation of the Legal Settlement Committee within the association changed the structure of the bargaining situation in subtle but important ways. Although the 11 committee members continued to represent the interests of their own firms, they were accountable to the members of the association as well. The association charged the committee with the responsibility for achieving *timely* curtailment of water production. The committee had to report quarterly to the full membership. The committee members would be subject to public criticism by respected colleagues if they simply pursued recalcitrant strategies and failed to find sources of agreement on which progress toward settlement could be based.[19] The members of this committee were expected to achieve an agreement whereby *all* parties would curtail their withdrawals. The first question to be resolved concerned how much curtailment.

The negotiators had to find a method to reduce withdrawals below 90,000 acre-feet and above the 30,000 acre-feet recommended by the referee. If the negotiated settlement was not above the referee's recommendation, some litigants would prefer to contest the matter in court in the hope that a judge would give their claims precedence over those of others. The engineers on the committee were asked to determine the maximum cutback that the parties could undertake in the near future without grave economic damage. The engineers concluded that a reduction of 25% to 30% could occur without serious economic harm to any water producer, if an exchange pool similar to the one devised in Raymond Basin were established.

Next the committee searched for a particular formula, based on the concept of mutual prescription, that would enable them to achieve a proportional cutback of 25% to 30%. Because 340 additional parties had been added to the case in 1949, one possibility was to use 1949 for determining shares, rather than the 1944 water year that immediately preceded the initiation of litigation. Using the referee's historical findings, the committee

118

compiled estimates of each party's "prescriptive rights" based on the 1944 water year versus the 1949 water year.[20] Their estimates totaled 44,387 acre-feet for 1944 and 63,728 for 1949. The committee proposed to use the 1949 data as the basis for negotiating an *interim* agreement that the parties could ratify immediately in order to achieve an actual cutback within a short time. One member of the committee reasoned that

> with the present usage in the amount of 90,000 acre-feet and . . . with the historical usage of 1949 amounting to 63,000 acre-feet or one-half way back to where the Division wanted the curtailment to go, a cutback to 1949 might be more acceptable at the present time . . . . [T]he parties would have enough water left under this arrangement to meet peak demands and it would afford a period in which to adjust to curtailment and . . . no one would be giving up any prescriptive rights already acquired. (West Basin Water Association, Legal Settlement Committee minutes, February 25, 1953, p. 4)

The interim agreement was drafted as a contingent contract. In other words, a water producer who signed the agreement and thus promised to curtail production to his own "Prescriptive Rights, 1949" was not committed to curtail until producers representing at least 80% of the total "Prescriptive Rights, 1949" had signed and the agreement was presented to and approved by the court. A signatory was committed to undertaking this "cooperative action" only if most of the other large water producers were also committed to the action. Thus, no one would be a "sucker," and the joint impact of their curtailments would make a substantial difference. By November 1954, agencies representing 82.5% of the total "Prescriptive Rights, 1949" had signed the agreement, and it was filed with the court. The court appointed the referee to continue as the official watermaster to ensure that the provisions of the agreement were followed.

It had taken two full years of negotiations and the threat of court action[21] to achieve this interim agreement, but at last a major change in the basic rules affecting the use of West Basin had occurred. Water levels in the basin rose immediately and continued to rise for several years, except in a water trough underlying the city of Hawthorne, which refused to sign the agreement.

The interim agreement was used for seven years while the water producers pursued other strategies to enhance the local water supplies, to replenish the basin, and to try to convince nonsignatories to agree to the curtailment. Two major parties did not sign. The first was the California Water Service Company, which had been one of the three initiators of the litigation and had borne a large share of the cost of the litigation. That company had not increased its water production after 1944, presuming that the litigation had protected its interests and that it could afford to take an independent action to conserve water supplies. The choice of 1949, rather than 1944, as the date for determining rights meant that some of the water producers who had increased production during the four-year period gained somewhat proportionately, while California Water Service slipped behind a little in its proportionate share.[22]

Although it refused to sign the interim agreement, California Water Service Company voluntarily limited its own groundwater production. It did not pump any more water than allocated to it under the interim agreement. Consequently, the effect of the company's refusal to sign the interim agreement was to shift the burden of the cost of watermaster services back onto those who had gained proportionately more rights under the Agreement. The company's actions imposed no physical harm on others. Further, the company clearly did not plan to challenge efforts to make the interim agreement the basis for a final settlement.

On the other hand, the city of Hawthorne increased its withdrawals. By 1960, Hawthorne pumped more than 2,250 acre-feet in excess of its allocation under the interim agreement. During the period of the interim agreement, Hawthorne saved at least $100,000 by pumping more groundwater per year than it had been allotted. As Hawthorne's production increased, the pumping trough beneath the city continued to drop. The watermaster's report for 1960–1 (plate 4) shows that the 1961 water levels below Hawthorne averaged 30–40 feet below those for surrounding territories (California, State of, 1960–1). Nearby producers were harmed substantially.[23] The economic costs of Hawthorne's action were spread generally among all signatories who paid higher costs for imported water while Hawthorne continued to utilize the least expensive source of water.

From the perspective of Hawthorne's leaders, however, the problem seemed different. Instead of viewing the basin as something jointly owned by all water producers, Hawthorne viewed its needs to serve a municipality with water as superior to the needs of industry in the area. Hawthorne saw the interim agreement as favoring the industrial producers, an effort to take away water rights that should be devoted to public use. Hawthorne looked to other cities for support for its position. However, the beach communities had already suffered severe hardship because of saltwater intrusion. According to Hawthorne officials, those communities were willing to see any basis used to curtail production from the basin and slow down the saltwater intrusion. Hawthorne argued that the beach cities were giving away their rights.

During most of 1957 and 1958, the Legal Settlement Committee met weekly and sometimes biweekly trying to prepare a final agreement. The

## Analyzing institutional change

technical problems of tracing all water-rights transactions for such a large group delayed the process substantially. The substantive problems were also considerable. Some signatories of the interim agreement opposed any final agreement that would not achieve curtailment down to the safe yield. Others preferred to wait until experiments with the saltwater barrier could establish the feasibility of being protected against the sea. The lack of *total* agreement to the interim agreement disturbed many who feared that Hawthorne or others might appeal. Given the experience of a costly appeal to the California Supreme Court in the Raymond Basin case, negotiators hoped to avoid an appeal of their settlement. Because the interim agreement afforded partial physical protection, many signatories believed that they had time to work out an agreement satisfactory to all parties.

Envoys were sent to the city of Hawthorne to urge city officials to reconsider their previous stance in regard to the interim agreement.[24] In 1958, the association appointed the mayor of Hawthorne to its Executive Committee in the hope that he would be able to change the attitude of other city officials. However, the attempts to reach an agreement with Hawthorne were unsuccessful. A final draft of a proposed "Agreement and Stipulation for Judgment" was presented to a meeting of the West Basin Water Association (WBWA) in February 1960. The Dominguez Water Corporation, as the largest water producer from the basin, gave the final agreement its full support by bringing signed copies of the agreement to the meeting. The city of El Segundo and Chanslor-Canfield Midway Oil Company joined Dominguez in this effort to show immediate support (WBWA minutes, February 25, 1960, p. 8). Three months later, 20 parties representing 32.5% of the total adjudicated rights had signed the agreement (WBWA minutes, May 26, 1960, p. 15). Obtaining the remaining signatures took one more year. By early summer of 1961, producers holding 82% of the adjudicated rights had signed the agreement. The Legal Settlement Committee indicated that it was unlikely that further signatures could be gained.

On July 21, 1961, 16 years after the litigation was initiated, a short trial was held, and the proposed judgment was presented to the court. The judgment was entered in August of 1961 substantially as presented to the court. As of October 1, 1961, all entities included as parties in the case were "perpetually enjoined and restrained from pumping or otherwise extracting from the Basin any water in excess of said party's Adjudicated Rights" (Judgment, *California Water Service Company et al. v. City of Compton et al.*, Civil Case No. 506806, Superior Court of the State of California in and for the County of Los Angeles, Sec. 5). Ninety-nine parties were found to

121

have adjudicated rights of 64,065 acre-feet.[25] The city of Hawthorne, like all nonsignatories, was placed under legal order to reduce its groundwater production to that stipulated in the agreement.

At the association meeting following the trial court's decision, a city councilman from the city of Hawthorne rose to congratulate the group on their "victory," but he warned them that his city planned to fight the decision "through every court in the land." The city of Hawthorne backed up that threat by retaining a firm of highly respected attorneys specializing in water law. At first, the association assumed the financial responsibility for supporting the judgment against the Hawthorne appeal. In 1962, when a Replenishment District had been formed, as described later, the new district undertook financial responsibility for defending the judgment, while the association maintained direct relations with the attorneys. After hearing the Hawthorne appeal, the District Court of Appeals concluded that the trial court had acted properly and affirmed its decision. After the California Supreme Court declined to review the decision made by the District Court of Appeals, the California Water Service case closed 18 years after it had opened.

No one really knows the exact costs involved in the West Basin litigation, given the large number of parties and the length of time involved, but the best available estimate is $3 million (Blomquist 1987a, p. 39). On the one hand, that was 10 times as expensive as the Raymond Basin negotiations. On the other hand, it was one-tenth of costs that would be involved in replacing the short-term storage capacities of the basin when used in conjunction with a surface supply. Amortizing the costs of the litigation over a 50-year period (as one would do for the construction of a major physical facility), the adjudication in Raymond Basin amounted to an annualized cost of 50 cents per acre-foot of water rights allocated, whereas the adjudication costs in West Basin amounted to an annualized cost of $2.50 per acre-foot of water rights (Blomquist 1987a, p. 39). In 1985, the annual costs of monitoring these water rights were $3.00 per acre-foot in Raymond Basin and $2.40 per acre-foot in West Basin.[26]

Adjudicating the water rights in West Basin was only one of a long series of steps taken by water producers to regulate their basin. Some of the subsequent steps are discussed later. The Raymond Basin and West Basin experiences were closely watched by water producers located in Central Basin. These producers also used court litigation as the setting in which to negotiate settlements of their individual rights to water. Central Basin is larger and more diverse than West Basin. Considerable effort was expended there to learn from the difficulties of the West Basin case and to adopt the process so as to reduce both the length of time needed to achieve agreement and the high costs. The effort was successful on both counts. We now turn to a brief discussion of the Central Basin negotiation process.[27]

## The Central Basin litigation

Overdraft conditions in Central Basin occurred much later than they had in Raymond Basin and West Basin. Central Basin is quite large (277 square miles of surface area) and was being used by around 750 owners of wells in the 1950s. The overdraft in Central Basin began in 1942. Most of Central Basin is located inland, and it is protected from the ocean on its western border by its downstream neighbor, West Basin. Thus, water producers in Central Basin are able to draw down their water levels farther than are those in West Basin without immediate adverse consequences. On the other hand, Central Basin does have a small southern exposure to the sea, and saltwater intrusion did begin to occur along that boundary as early as 1950.

At the prodding of their downstream neighbors, Central Basin water producers formed the Central Basin Water Association in 1950 using an organizational structure similar to that of West Basin. The part-time executive director of the West Basin Water Association became the part-time executive director of the newly formed Central Basin Water Association.[28]Some West Basin water producers were also active in Central Basin. Discussions immediately focused on the importance of achieving a negotiated settlement of the water rights in Central Basin. Central Basin producers, however, wanted to avoid the long delay and high cost of using the court-ordered reference procedure and avoid involving all of the very small water producers in the basin.

Consequently, instead of moving immediately toward the initiation of a suit, the Central Basin Water Association employed the services of a private engineering firm, well known for its expertise in the area of groundwater basins, to conduct an initial survey of conditions in the basin and of past water use. Further, a considerable effort was made to achieve a general agreement about the type of negotiated settlement they would reach before they actually went to court in 1962. An interim agreement, signed by parties holding 79% of the water rights, was approved by the court just 10 months after the litigation was initiated. The producers agreed to cut back production on a proportional basis by 20% and to establish a set of working rules modeled on the West Basin agreement, but also reflecting the particular circumstance in Central Basin. Watermaster services were initiated in October 1962. A voluntary cutback of approximately 45,000 acrefeet was initiated immediately (Fossette and Fossette 1986, p. 182). The

123

final settlement, signed by parties holding over 75% of the rights, was approved by a judge in October 1965 and went into effect in October 1966 – four years after initiation. The estimated costs of the Central Basin litigation were $450,000.

The litigation and negotiation processes in these three basins involved different problems and followed different paths. In Raymond Basin, the number of pumpers was relatively small, and one participant – the city of Pasadena – was more dominant than was any participant in West Basin or Central Basin. Pasadena withdrew about one-half of all water obtained from the basin. The city could not ignore the action of the other pumpers, because their actions could adversely affect joint outcomes. However, Pasadena had such a large stake in seeing that the basin was preserved that the city was willing to invest heavily in achieving a settlement. After failing to obtain a voluntary agreement to curtail pumping, the city initiated legal action and bore more than its proportionate share of litigation costs. By initiating efforts to obtain an external water supply and to control pumping from the basin before pumpers had become accustomed to withdrawal far in excess of safe yield, it was physically possible for all pumpers to cut back their water withdrawals and still serve the growing urban population settling in the area. The major asymmetry of interest faced by the litigants in Raymond Basin was their legal status as overlying owners or appropriators. By devising a new legal concept of mutual prescription, the parties found a basis to share the costs of curtailing groundwater production equitably. All pumpers could continue to use the basin for peaking purposes or could sell water rights, which had been well defined, to those who placed a higher value on acquiring such rights.[29]

Negotiators in West Basin faced three disadvantages not faced in Raymond Basin: (1) the large number of parties involved, (2) the absence of a dominant party, and (3) the asymmetrical risks faced by inland pumpers versus coastal pumpers. The negotiation process took longer, was more expensive, and involved a major conflict between coastal and inland pumpers. By using mutual prescription as the basis for an agreement, the parties reduced other potential asymmetries of interest that could have exacerbated the conflict. Once a final judgment was reached, all parties shared proportionately in the cost of curtailment. The process took sufficient time, however, that it became difficult to cut back to the safe yield and still serve the urban population, which had increased in the years following World War II. As discussed later, water producers in the area had to turn to other mechanisms to increase the supply of water to the groundwater basins, because the control over demand that they achieved did not bring the basin into balance.

## Analyzing institutional change

Pumpers in Central Basin had several advantages in this process. Because the basin was very large and had only a small coastal section, pumpers could safely delay resolution of their water rights while they watched the process in the other basins. They were prodded into action by their downstream neighbors, who feared that lack of action in Central Basin might eventually negate the benefits of conservation in West Basin. By acting before it would be necessary to cut back much more than 20%, and using a private firm to gather much of the information before they went to court, Central Basin pumpers saved themselves considerable time and money in achieving a negotiated settlement based on the same principle that had been used in Raymond Basin and West Basin.

### Conformance of parties to negotiated settlements

Forty-five years have passed since the judgment was entered in the Raymond Basin case, and 35 and 27 years have passed since the interim agreements were signed in West Basin and in Central Basin. Thus, the parties to these three agreements have had many occasions to decide whether or not to comply. Given the value of groundwater, the temptation not to comply must have been relatively great for all producers at one time or another in the combined 107 years of water use that have elapsed. However, the level of infractions has been insignificant during that time.

The watermaster in each basin has extensive monitoring and sanctioning authority. Monitoring activities are obvious and public. Every year, each party reports total groundwater extractions and receives a report listing the groundwater extractions of all other parties (or anyone else who has started to pump). The reliability of these records is high. Several agencies cross-check the records. The watermaster is authorized to calibrate all meters, thereby reducing the probability of one form of cheating. Given the accuracy of the information and its ease of access, each pumper knows what everyone else is doing, and each knows that his or her own groundwater extractions will be known by all others. Thus, the information available to the parties closely approximates "common knowledge," so frequently a necessary assumption for solutions to iterated dilemma games (Aumann 1976).

Instead of perceiving itself as an active policing agency, the watermaster service tries to be a neutral, monitoring agency. Because anyone who possesses a legal water right can initiate a court action to enforce compliance to the judgments, the watermaster does not need to initiate punitive actions against nonconformers. As expressed by an official of the watermaster service in 1960,

125

it is our policy not to take any affirmative actions against any party since this would place us in the position of being an active party in the action. Our policy has been to inform the active parties of any infringements and leave affirmative action up to them. We want to stay as neutral as possible in order to gain as much voluntary cooperation as possible.[30]

In the early years of the West Basin agreement, for example, the Moneta Water Company began to withdraw more than its allocation. After a couple of years, it was obvious that the overextractions were not accidental. In addition to listing Moneta's annual withdrawals in the tabular material included in all reports, the watermaster devoted several pages in an annual report to the recent activities of the company. The company began to comply with the judgment soon after the publication of those facts. Other than a few isolated incidents, handled in the same manner, the original litigants have complied with the curtailments without formal sanctions being imposed. Even the city of Hawthorne has curtailed its withdrawals to the stipulated amounts of the final judgment. It has been necessary, however, to initiate legal action against new pumpers who have attempted to withdraw groundwater without first purchasing water rights. Charges have been filed and defendants enjoined from groundwater production other than under the rights they eventually acquired by purchase.[31]

The levels of quasi-voluntary compliance with the final judgments in all of these court decisions have been extremely high. Although each pumper might be tempted from time to time to withdraw more water than legally allowed, each pumper wants total withdrawals from the basin constrained so that access to the storage and flow values of the resource will be continued over the long run. Given the active, reliable, and neutral monitoring of the watermaster service, no pumper can expect to overextract without everyone else learning about any noncompliance at the end of the next water year. Because everyone is organized and communicating with one another about joint strategies, continued noncompliance is likely to bring legal sanctions, as well as loss of reputation and the application of informal sanctions. Because a pumper is constrained, and almost all pumpers voluntarily agreed to the initial allocation of rights, the basic system is perceived to be fair by most participants. Further, participants continue to have control over the monitoring system to ensure that it continues to be active, fair, and reliable. Two-thirds of the watermaster's budget is paid for by those possessing water rights, and they can petition the court to appoint a different watermaster if they are not satisfied with performance.[32]

# Analyzing institutional change

## THE ENTREPRENEURSHIP GAME

Immediately after the interim agreement was signed in West Basin, and before litigation was initiated in Central Basin, West Basin water producers recognized that litigation was not a sufficient means to achieve long-term regulation of their basin. They took steps that culminated five years later in the creation of a new public enterprise and a series of agreements with surrounding public enterprises to manage West Basin and Central Basin as interconnected basins. The process of problem-solving and negotiation involved in the establishment of this new district and the series of agreements with existing agencies illustrates how public entrepreneurship can be used as a strategy to transform the structure of incentives facing those jointly using a CPR. The process of putting together the necessary components of a new enterprise was immensely complicated. Only a sketch can be presented here, but I try to present the problems the water producers faced, as they saw them, and the steps they took to try to solve them in the political environment they faced.

The litigation had left several unresolved questions. First, producers had been unwilling to cut back production to the safe yield. Although the cutbacks immediately improved water conditions, they were insufficient to achieve a final regulation of the basins. Either the replenishment of both basins had to be accelerated or further cutbacks in production were needed. If the replenishment rate could be increased, then it would be possible to use the underground storage capacity in a manner somewhat analogous to the use of surface storage facilities, whereby one draws down and then refills the facility repeatedly.[33]

A second unresolved, and related, problem was the specific danger that saltwater intrusion posed along the long western border of West Basin and the short southern border of Central Basin. Early in the 1960s, water engineers from West Basin and the Los Angeles County Flood Control District began to experiment with the concept of building a freshwater barrier against the sea. An initial experiment, funded in part by local sources and in part by the state of California, proved that it was both technically and economically feasible to construct a series of wells along the coast that could be used to inject fresh water under pressure into a groundwater basin. The resulting cone of fresh water would prevent further saltwater intrusion. Most of the fresh water would then be available at a later juncture to be withdrawn when needed. If such a barrier could be constructed along the entire coastline, the artificial recharge of the basin would be greatly enhanced, and the threat of the sea would be eliminated. Once the technical and economic feasibility had been established, the

127

question of exactly who would pay for the barrier, and how, remained to be resolved.

A third delicate question centered on the relevant boundary for managing West Basin and Central Basin. That question had not arisen in regard to Raymond Basin, which was an upland basin and relatively self-contained. Once water producers in West Basin reduced their pumping levels, while water producers in Central Basin continued heavy production, water from West Basin began to flow eastward into Central Basin, instead of westward from Central Basin into West Basin. That change in the direction of the "natural" water flow led producers in both basins to recognize how closely interconnected their two basins were. A barrier erected along the coast would afford protection not only for West Basin but also for Central Basin. Further, an open porous area in Central Basin could be used to replenish far more efficiently than any area located in West Basin. Water spread at that location could raise water levels in Central Basin, which, combined with a cutback in production in Central Basin, would increase the flow of water into West Basin.

No existing public agency had the authority or the appropriate boundaries to address these questions. Water producers in West Basin and Central Basin were reluctant to turn to any of the large-scale agencies currently in existence for fear that they would lose control of the decisions being made and might end up worse off.[34] In the fall of 1954, the president of the West Basin Water Association suggested to the president of the Conservation Association of Southern California that there was a need for representatives from all segments of the California water industry to meet and discuss potential legislation for solving critical groundwater problems. As a result, 45 agencies were invited to meet in September of 1954 "to draft equitable and effective ground water legislation for introduction at the 1955 Legislature" (letter from W. S. Rosecrans to the Central Basin Water Association). From that group, the "Committee of Twelve" was formed to draft legislation.[35]

Discussion of the proposed legislation centered on two types of changes. The first was designed to expedite future groundwater adjudications. The referee in the West Basin case had taken seven years to prepare a report because of lack of information concerning the historical patterns of water use by a large number of the producers. To correct that situation for the future, the committee drafted legislation to require all those who produced at least 25 acre-feet of groundwater per year to file notices of their annual extraction with a state agency. That legislation could not expedite the West Basin case, but it did provide some of the information necessary for relatively rapid adjudications in Central Basin and San Gabriel Basin.

## Analyzing institutional change

The second area of concern in the proposed legislation involved the authorization of a new type of district empowered to undertake broad replenishment responsibilities financed primarily by a "pump tax" or an assessment on the groundwater production within the boundaries of a district. The legislation as finally drafted was different from what producers in either West Basin or Central Basin might have drafted on their own.[36] By taking into account the needs of other areas and existing water service agencies, West Basin and Central Basin producers were able to gain rapid approval of both pieces of legislation when they were submitted to the state legislature in 1955.

The new Water Replenishment District Act authorized citizens located in southern California to create a new district after they had (1) obtained signatures from at least 10% of the registered voters residing within the boundaries of the proposed district, (2) proposed specific limits on the taxing power of the new district, (3) received agreement from the Department of Water Resources that the area included within the boundaries of the district would be benefited by inclusion, and (4) received a majority of positive votes in a special election held to consider the creation of the new district. A district, once created, was given a wide diversity of powers to raise revenue through a pump tax and, to a limited extent, through a property tax and to undertake actions to replenish a groundwater basin. The organic legislation included a unique provision intended "to avoid duplication of similar operations by existing agencies and replenishment district" (*California Water Code*, sec. 60231). The provision stated that

in the event an existing agency has facilities available and adequate to accomplish any part of the purposes of a district . . . the district shall investigate and determine the cost of contracting for the accomplishment of such purposes through such existing agency. (*California Water Code*, sec. 60231)

In other words, a new replenishment agency would be expected to investigate the costs of contracting to have services provided, rather than immediately creating its own production staff for any activity it wanted to undertake.[37] The legislation provided a general "constitution" for a new district. Water producers in any specific area could then use that general framework to create a particular "constitution" for their own district. At first, West Basin producers presumed that they would go it alone and created a working committee within the association to draft a specific proposal to create a district.

The basic issues that had to be resolved in that constitutional process were (1) the source of water for the barrier, (2) the exact boundaries of the new district, (3) how the internal electoral boundaries would be drawn,

129

## Governing the commons

and (4) the extent of taxing powers to be authorized. West Basin water producers had hoped that it would be possible to purchase reclaimed water from the Hyperion water-treatment plant – a sewage-disposal facility operated by the city of Los Angeles – located on the coast. If that had proved technically feasible, they would have had a source of low-cost water and would not have had to negotiate with the powerful Metropolitan Water District of Southern California (MWD). After considerable experimentation, it proved technically infeasible to use the reclaimed water, at least in the short run. The committee had to start over again. Members of both associations were appointed "to approach the Metropolitan Water District . . . to see whether a firm commitment of a sufficient quantity of water could be obtained . . and to request a certain amount of engineering and costs estimates which would be needed" (report by Allan Harris, West Basin Water Association, minutes, March 22, 1956, p. 6).

Once West Basin producers realized that they would have to use MWD water for the barrier, they began more intensive talks with their Central Basin neighbors concerning the creation of one large district to include both basins. When the two associations first started discussions, the differences between the two basins were quite apparent. West Basin was smaller in area, population, and assessed valuation. In a joint district, it could be dominated by Central Basin. In 1955, West Basin producers had signed the interim agreement and had limited their production to 60,000 acre-feet per year, whereas Central Basin producers were pumping 110,000 acre-feet and still increasing their annual rates of withdrawal. At a meeting of the West Basin Water Association, the chairman of the committee devising the proposal outlined the reasons for and against forming a district to include both basins.

### Reasons for forming a district to include both basins

1 The purpose would be the same in both basins: replenishment of the groundwater supply.
2 Greater financial resources would be available; hence, the tax rate and amount of pumping assessment could be lower.
3 A large district would have greater political strength and would be more effective in dealing with the Upper San Gabriel Valley District and various state bodies.
4 The Long Beach harbor area offers a potential route for intrusion of seawater into West Basin and probably would be included. It is doubtful that any of Long Beach could be included in a district comprising only the West Basin.

5 The flow of groundwater across the fault from Central Basin to West Basin probably would be greater under the replenishment program of a larger district.
6 Administration costs would be less in a larger district.

### Reasons against forming a district to include both basins

1 The injection of replenishment water would be unique and necessary to West Basin. Central Basin would control that program in the West Basin if a large district were formed and might not want to continue the well-injection method along the coast.
2 Pumping was curtailed in West Basin, but not in Central Basin.
3 The degrees of ultimate curtailment might not be the same in the two basins.
4 Control of the local tax rate and amount of pumping assessment would be relinquished by West Basin.
5 A local district could initiate proceedings to ensure financial replenishment from Central Basin.[38]
6 Extensive recharge of Central Basin might contribute free water to West Basin (West Basin Water Association, minutes, November 17, 1955, pp. 9–10).

The West Basin water producers were physically disadvantaged because they were at the end of the groundwater "pipeline." They were concerned that their physical disadvantage could be exaggerated by the creation of a new public agency in which they would be politically dominated. The hopes and fears of West Basin producers were summarized in a letter written by the chairman of the West Basin committee to his committee:

In the event a water replenishment district to include both Basins is decided upon, it appears desirable that a statement of policy morally binding on the new district board of directors should be adopted. The policy should provide assurance of an effective salt water barrier program for West Basin, a curtailment of pumping in Central Basin to insure continued ground water flow into West Basin, and an arrangement of the five divisions of the new district so that territory of both Basins would be included in each such division to prevent West Basin versus Central Basin representation on the board of directors.
(letter from R. R. Thorburn to the Replenishment District Boundary Committee, October 27, 1955, p. 2)

Soon thereafter, members of both associations came to a working agreement that the benefits of a larger district would outweigh the costs. Assurances were given to West Basin producers that they would not be

131

dominated by their eastern neighbors. Next, a joint committee of both associations began a series of relatively tough negotiations with all of the public agencies that might eventually be involved in managing these two basins.[39]

The results of those negotiations were formalized in a seven-page proposal that the committee submitted to the two associations for approval in August of 1958. The proposal set forth the essential factors for constituting the new enterprise. The statement proposed that a new replenishment district would be formed to (1) repel saltwater intrusion, (2) recharge the groundwater basins, and (3) reduce pumping in the basins to safe limits (West Basin Water Association and Central Basin Water Association, "Proposal Submitted by the Joint Committee on Water Replenishment District," mimeograph, July 30, 1958, p. 1). The proposal stated that to accomplish those purposes, "the district will have responsibility for financing the purchase of water used in halting the intrusion of sea water and in replenishing the groundwater supply" (ibid., p. 3).

The proposal then clarified the future relationships of the replenishment district to all of the existing agencies that might consider the replenishment district to be a potential competitor. It then outlined the amount of water that would be purchased from MWD and spread or injected by the Los Angeles County Flood Control District. The proposal stated that the new district "would have no authority to purchase replenishment water with *ad valorem* tax derived funds, and the petition for the formation of the district will clearly set forth this limitation on its taxing power" (ibid., p. 6). It was estimated that a levy of $6.00 per acre-foot would be necessary to raise the necessary funds to purchase 165,000 acre-feet of water from MWD – an amount equal to the average annual overdraft. The proposal concluded by stating that the new district would be "an administrative agency operated by a five-member board of directors with a minimum staff" (ibid., p. 7).

The proposal was in effect a "constitution" for a multiple-agency management system to operate a coordinated program. Constitutional documents do not need to carry the formal name "constitution" to serve the purpose of determining the decision rules to be used for making future collective choices about some specified physical domain. The proposal was attached to the formal petitions presented to the Los Angeles County Board of Supervisors (to gain approval for the special election) and to the California Department of Water Resources (to gain approval for the boundaries), and in that way had formal recognition as a type of constitutional document. Once that constitution had been approved by the two private associations, all formal steps outlined within it were achieved within a few months, and the Central and West Basin Water Replenishment District was

132

*Analyzing institutional change*

supported in the election of November of 1959 by a vote of 4 to 1 (*Los Angeles Times*, November 18, 1959).

## THE POLYCENTRIC PUBLIC-ENTERPRISE GAME

The creation of the Central and West Basin Water Replenishment District in 1959 dramatically transformed the structure of incentives facing water producers and their representatives. It was an enterprise created by the water producers (and approved by the citizens living in the area), with public powers to tax, to sue, and to engage in the provision of collective goods. Whereas the replenishment district took over the *active* role of managing West Basin and Central Basin, the two private water associations continued to have strong input into all policy decisions.

Further, the replenishment district is only one public enterprise among a half dozen agencies that are actively involved in the management program. Thus, instead of one central governmental authority, a polycentric public-enterprise system has emerged to achieve a very sophisticated management system. This polycentric system has restored water levels throughout both basins, has completed a freshwater barrier along the exposed coasts of both basins, and is now engaged in focused efforts to eliminate pumping troughs and other physical impediments that inhibit the effective use of the basins in conjunction with a surface supply.

The overall costs of this system are quite low.[40] In Table 4.1, the amortized and annual costs (in constant dollars) of the management systems in these basins, as computed by Blomquist, are contrasted with the amortized costs of replacing the basins with surface storage. Total costs are substantially lower in each basin than they would be if the basins had been destroyed. Total costs would, of course, be lower if water producers had been able to negotiate a settlement of their water rights at an earlier juncture and had not had to pay the high costs of prolonged negotiations. The water producers of Central Basin, however, learned from the experiences of their colleagues in Raymond Basin and West Basin and thus were able to achieve a settlement at lower costs.

In this discussion I have tried to focus more on the origins of these institutions than on their current operations, because it is so difficult to find documentation about the origins of institutions. I do think it is important, however, to describe briefly the types of polycentric relationships that exist among the public enterprises that currently manage West Basin and Central Basin.

At the core of each of those relationships is the Central and West Basin Water Replenishment District. This district receives the funds assessed on

133

## Governing the commons

Table 4.1. *Basin management costs and savings per acre-foot resulting from basin management in the three basins (dollars)*

| Cost | Raymond | West | Central |
|------|---------|------|---------|
| Basin management cost per acre-foot of ground-water extraction, 1985 | 3.50 | 77.40 | 73.77 |
| Average cost of an acre-foot of water with basin management | 184.65 | 235.71 | 224.85 |
| Estimated cost of an acre-foot of water if all groundwater were replaced by imported water | 748.68 | 739.30 | 739.94 |

*Source*: Adapted from Blomquist (1987a, Figure 9).

all water pumped in the district and thus has the power to take collective action for both basins. To get the water into the basins, however, the replenishment district must relate to several other public districts. Until the late 1960s, the replenishment district depended on a monopoly supplier of water, the MWD, for its replenishment water. In 1966, MWD unilaterally announced a change in its pricing structure that would substantially increase the cost of replenishment water. The replenishsment district and both associations bargained hard, but unsuccessfully, for a reconsideration. The replenishment district then opened negotiations with the Los Angeles County Sanitation Districts to obtain a reliable supply of water at lower cost from a specially constructed reclamation plant.[41] Opening this alternative source of water supply has meant that the replenishment district has assured itself of a continuing supply, and at a cost well below that of imported water. In 1987, for example, the district was seeking approval from the relevant regulatory agencies to increase its purchase of reclaimed water from 30,000 acre-feet per year to 50,000 acre-feet per year, at an average cost of $8.00 per acre-foot, as compared with the $153 it has to pay MWD for replenishment water (Central and West Basin Water Replenishment District 1987, pp. 44–56).

In regard to the actual operation of the replenishment works, the replenishment district entered into an exchange agreement with the Los Angeles County Flood Control District (reorganized in 1987 to be the Los Angeles County Department of Public Works). Thus, the replenishment district has maintained only a skeletal staff (an executive director and a secretary), rather than employing its own engineering staff. The county cannot exert full monopoly power in its supply of replenishment services, because the replenishment district has access to several other potential suppliers and could always create its own staff to undertake the replenishment activities.[42] At one point when the replenishment district was particularly unhappy with the progress of some construction work undertaken by the county, the replenishment district was able to use its bargaining power to insist that a portion of the design for one of the barriers be contracted out to a private firm.

The watermaster service of the California Department of Water Resources performs an essential service for the replenishment district and the producers by monitoring the extractions by producers. Two-thirds of the cost of this service is paid for by the producers. If these costs become too high, the producers can petition the court to assign some other agency – public or private – to be their watermaster.[43] The replenishment district and the watermaster service have entered into cooperative agreements to reduce duplication in their activities. Records of withdrawals submitted by groundwater users to the replenishment district as the basis for taxation are also made available to the watermaster. Instead of relying strictly on hierarchical relations, as within a single firm, the management system is governed by negotiation and bargaining processes among many different actors in several different arenas. Strict majority-rule procedures are rarely used in any of the decision arenas governing this system.

In addition to the public districts, private water associations remain active in each of the basins. Public officials are asked to make frequent reports to the regular meetings of the water associations. The water engineers of the private and municipal agencies who attend these meetings tend to ask tough questions and want reasoned answers. They have access to independent information about conditions and are not satisfied by stylized responses that provide little information. Many of the individuals who are elected to office in the public districts have been active in the water associations for many years. Their tenure in public office tends to be long, and normally they are active in one or another public or private role for a quarter of a century.

This brief sketch of the patterns of relationships among public enterprises illustrates how a governance system can evolve to remain largely *in* the public sector without being a central regulator. Aspects of both private and governmental activities are involved in all of these basins. Some scholars have characterized the assignment of well-defined rights to the flow of a

135

CPR as "privatization." Given that the water rights held by water producers are now entirely separable from land and are well defined, a market for water rights has evolved in each of these basins, and rights are actively transferred. But that is only part of the story. No one "owns" the basins themselves. The basins are managed by a *polycentric set* of limited-purpose governmental enterprises whose governance includes active participation by private water companies and voluntary producer associations. This system is neither centrally owned nor centrally regulated.

Although the solution to the problems facing these groundwater producers did not involve either a central regulator or a private-property system, it did involve creating an institutional arrangement that incorporates the full set of design principles discussed in Chapter 3. Well-defined boundaries were achieved through litigation. Viewing this set of institutions together,[44] it can be seen that congruence between appropriation and provision rules and local conditions has been achieved. Collective-choice arrangements are provided by the voluntary associations and by the special districts so that most pumpers can actively participate in the modification of rules as needed. The court-appointed watermaster has considerable monitoring powers and issues annual reports that give all participants accurate information about rule compliance and water conditions. The informal sanctions that have been utilized to encourage rule conformance have, in the main, been modest. Formal sanctions are available for use if they are needed. The continuing jurisdiction of the court and the regular meetings of the voluntary water associations provide conflict-resolution mechanisms. The legal structure of the state of California recognizes the rights of pumpers and others to organize, and the organization units are nested within larger units. Given the stability that these institutions have demonstrated thus far, and their conformance with these design principles, I believe that these CPR institutions are robust and will survive for a long time to come.

## THE ANALYSIS OF INSTITUTIONAL SUPPLY

In this chapter I have described several efforts to solve second-order collective dilemmas. A pumping race is the first-order dilemma facing pumpers from a groundwater basin where legal rights to withdraw water are not limited. Each pumper has a dominant strategy to pump as much water as is privately profitable and to ignore the long-term consequences on water levels and quality. The experience in all of these groundwater basins illustrates how a pumping race can continue for many years, even though water levels fall (raising everyone's costs of lifting water) and salt water intrudes

## Analyzing institutional change

(threatening the long-run survival of the basin itself). Overdraft conditions continued for several decades in these basins. The best explanation for the actions and outcomes during that period is that individuals caught in a pumping race will select their dominant strategy to pump as much as is privately profitable and ignore the consequence for themselves and others.

Given the initial empirical support for this prediction, it is easy to see why theorists would also predict that individuals caught in such situations would refrain from investing resources in designing, negotiating, and supplying new institutions. If pumpers will not limit their groundwater production, why should they invest in the provision of new institutions? The effort to supply institutions is described as simply a second-order dilemma that is no more solvable than the first-order dilemma. The prediction that appropriators will not expend resources to supply new institutions is, however, not supported by these case studies.

These groundwater pumpers invested heavily in the supply of institutions. They created new private associations. They paid for costly litigation to allocate water rights. They drafted legislation, had it introduced to the state legislature, and gained sufficient support from other water enterprises to get the legislation passed. They created special districts to tax all the water they withdrew from the basins, as well as the property overlying the area. They spent seemingly endless hours informing themselves about the structures of their basins, the various concerns and intentions of all parties, and future possibilities.

### Incremental, sequential, and self-transforming institutional change in a facilitative political regime

The substantial investments that these groundwater pumpers made in providing new institutions occurred in an incremental and sequential process in the state of California – a home-rule state – where many statewide institutional facilities are provided to reduce the costs of local institutional supply. The investment in institutional change was not made in a single step. Rather, the process of institutional change in all basins involved many small steps that had low initial costs. Rarely was it necessary for participants to move simultaneously without knowing what others were doing. Because the process was incremental and sequential and early successes were achieved, intermediate benefits from the initial investments were realized before anyone needed to make larger investments. Each institutional change transformed the structure of incentives within which future strategic decisions would be made.

Further, because the appropriators from several neighboring basins were

137

all involved in similar problems, participants in one setting could learn from the experiences of those in similar settings. Sufficient overlap existed among participants across basins to ensure communication about results. Interbasin coordinating arenas were created at several junctures to enhance the ability to exchange information about agreements reached within and across basin boundaries.[45]

In each basin, a voluntary association was established to provide a forum for face-to-face discussions about joint problems and potential joint strategies. Given the uncertain legal structure, attorneys advising water companies and public utilities had consistently advised their clients to pump as much water as they could profitably use and worry about defending their water rights later. The provision of a forum for discussion transformed the structure of the situation from one in which decisions were made independently without knowing what others were doing to a situation in which individuals discussed their options with one another. Discussion by itself was not sufficient to change the pumping strategies of the participants, but discussion did lead to the initiation of litigation, which enabled the participants to reach an enforceable agreement to limit their water withdrawals.

Further, the voluntary associations provided a mechanism for obtaining information about the physical structure of the basins to be made available to all pumpers simultaneously. Prior to that investment in information, no one had a clear picture of the boundaries, demand patterns, and water levels throughout a basin. One knew only that the water levels in one's own wells were falling. No one knew the extent of saltwater intrusion or the total quantity of water withdrawn from the basin. The private associations provided a mechanism for sharing the costs and the results of expensive technical studies. By voluntarily sharing the costs of providing information – a public good – participants learned that it was possible to accomplish some joint objectives by voluntary, cooperative action. The membership dues for the associations were modest and were allocated in rough proportion to the amount of water an enterprise withdrew from a basin.[46] By spending time to attend meetings, members gained considerable information about the condition of their basins and the likelihood that others would commit themselves to follow different strategies in the future.

Whereas the voluntary associations provide a mechanism for sharing costs, the state of California provides facilities that help reduce the level of those costs. Maintaining a court system in which individuals have standing to initiate litigation in order to develop firm and transferable rights to a defined quantity of water is one such contribution. The state of California goes even further and subsidizes one-third of the cost of such litigation in

138

Analyzing institutional change

order to encourage full exploitation of water resources and settle disputes over water rights when necessary. The Department of Water Resources has provided technical assistance throughout the period, as has the U.S. Geological Survey.

The general home-rule tradition that is built into the state constitution and legislative practices in the state also helps reduce the costs of transforming existing rule systems. It is relatively easy for a group of individuals to introduce new organic legislation authorizing a new type of special district, but state legislators will rarely support such proposed legislation when there is substantial opposition to it in the state. But when individuals in one area have discussed such proposals with others who are likely to be affected, organic laws frequently are passed with close to unanimous support.

In other words, the rules for engaging in microconstitutional choice related to the control of groundwater have encouraged investments in self-organization and the supply of local institutions. A similar set of individuals facing similar problems in an entirely different type of political regime might not be able to supply themselves with transformed microinstitutions. The difference between an active effort by a central government to regulate appropriation and provision activities and an effort to provide arenas and rules for microinstitutional change is frequently blurred.

*Reformulating the analysis of institutional change*

Trying to understand the incremental, sequential, and self-transforming process of institutional change in these groundwater basins leads me to suggest that institutional analysts should reconsider the ways in which they conceptualize the problem of supplying institutions. Such a formulation should involve several subtle but important changes in the way analysts think about institutional rules, their origin, and their changes. An important step is to assume that all recurring situations are shaped by a set of institutional rules. Institutional rules are prescriptive statements that forbid, require, or permit some action or outcome (E. Ostrom 1986a). One of the three deontic operators – forbid, require, permit – must be contained in a statement for it to be considered a rule.[47] All three deontic operators are used in this definition of rules.[48]

Some analysts limit their conception of rules to prescriptive statements containing only required or forbidden actions and outcomes.[49] With that limited conception, some recurring situations are rule-governed, and others are not. By including all three deontic operators in a definition of a rule, it is always possible to identify the set of rules that constitute a situation.

139

One needs to ask only two questions concerning the actions and outcomes of relevance to this situation: (1) Is this action or outcome (or its negation) required? (2) Is this action or outcome (or its negation) forbidden? Any action or outcome (or its negation) that is not required nor forbidden is permitted. Consequently, the absence of a rule forbidding or requiring an action is logically equivalent to the presence of a rule that permits an action. Hobbes's state of nature is a situation in which no rules requiring or forbidding any actions or outcomes are present. The Hobbesian state of nature is logically equivalent to a situation in which rules exist permitting anyone to take any and all desired actions, regardless of the effects on others.

Usually it is possible to answer the two foregoing questions regarding any recurring situation that is sufficiently structured that one can analyze it. Consequently, for any such situation, one can identify a set of status quo rules related to the situation. Status quo rules continue in effect until changed. The status quo rules in a Hobbesian situation can be viewed as a set of default rules by which everything is permitted (Gardner and E. Ostrom 1990). Similarly, a CPR situation in which no one is forbidden or required to take any action is logically equivalent to a CPR situation in which everyone is permitted to take any and all actions. The rules governing such a situation are all default rules.

Once one assumes that all recurring situations are characterized by a set of status quo rules, then it is possible to broaden the concept of institutional supply to include both what can be called the "origin" of new institutions and the changing of existing institutions. The origins of institutions and changes in institutions frequently are considered to be fundamentally different.[50] In this view, origin is characterized as a situation in which individuals move from having no rules to having a set of rules. In such a view, the origin of institutions is thought of as a major, one-step transformation, whereas institutional change is viewed as involving incremental changes in existing rules.[51] Supplying new institutions is consequently viewed as nonincremental and costly, whereas changing existing institutions is viewed as incremental and not as costly.

Both origins and changes in institutions can be analyzed using the same theory when both are viewed as alterations of at least one status quo rule.[52] A change in any rule affecting the set of participants, the set of strategies available to participants, the control they have over outcomes, the information they have, or the payoffs (E. Ostrom 1986a) is an institutional change. The costs of changing the rules vary substantially from one rule to another, from one political regime to another, and from one level of analysis to another, and they also vary over time as participants and conditions change. Whether or not it will be costly to achieve any institutional change will depend on many variables (to be discussed in Chapter 6), not simply on whether or not a new institutional arrangement is being created.

The creation of a new institutional arrangement can sometimes be quite easy and involve little cost. In the cases discussed earlier, for example, creating new voluntary associations to discuss common problems did not involve major investments by any of the participants. On the other hand, creating the Central and West Basin Water Replenishment District involved major investments in time and money. Transforming existing rules can also be very costly. Changing the water rights for overlying and appropriative water producers, for example, involved many years of costly litigation. All of these rule changes were crucial aspects of the process of institutional supply in these cases. Each built on the base of prior rules. That some rule changes could be undertaken with low transformation costs enabled the participants to gain some advantages of collective action before they were faced with more costly alternatives. All of these transformation costs are affected by the surrounding political regime. After several decades of institutional change, the resulting institutional infrastructure that had been created represented a major investment that dramatically changed the incentives and behaviors of participants and the resulting outcomes. Each institutional change became the foundation for the next change.

What is presumed to be a second-order dilemma, in which institutional change is viewed as one large step, may or may not have the structure of a dilemma when institutional change is viewed as a sequential and incremental process. The net payoffs of solving a small part of a large second- or third-order problem may be sufficiently high and distributed in such a manner that some participants will voluntarily provide initial second-order collective benefits, whereas they are unwilling to provide first-order solutions on their own. Solving some initial second-and third-order problems can help participants move toward solving first-order problems, as well as the more difficult second- and third-order problems.

With these conceptual revisions, it is possible to move toward the development of a single theory of institutional change, rather than one theory about origins and another theory about reform. Both constitutional-choice and collective-choice processes produce rules affecting the behavior of actors in linked situations (see Figure 2.2). Both constitutional-choice and collective-choice processes are themselves structured by rules. In a constitutional-choice situation, individuals decide whether or not to change a set of status quo rules that determine who is eligible and how future collective-choice decisions are to be made. Similarly, in a collective-choice situation, individuals decide whether or not to change a set of status quo rules that determine who is eligible and how future operational choices are to be made.

The outcome of a collective-choice process frequently is conceptualized as a "policy space," leaving unspecified what is contained in that policy space. When a budget is to be determined in a collective-choice arena, the policy space can be thought of as a set of rules concerning who is required, forbidden, or allowed to spend how much money for what purpose during what time frame. When a regulation is to be determined, the policy space can be thought of as a set of rules concerning who is required, forbidden, or allowed to take what action or affect what outcomes related to a specific domain.

In both processes, individuals compare the net flows of expected benefits and costs to be produced by the set of status quo rules, as compared with an altered set of rules. To explain institutional change, it is therefore necessary to examine how those participating in the arenas in which rule changes are proposed will view and weight the net return of staying with the status quo rules versus some type of change. In Chapter 6, I shall develop these ideas further and present the rudiments of a theory of institutional change applicable to the changing of rules that structure collective-choice or operational-choice situations. Before I do that, however, it is important to examine the failure cases discussed in Chapter 5 so that these conjectures can also build on information from situations in which participants were not successful in changing their institutions.

# 5

## Analyzing institutional failures and fragilities

The empirical cases presented so far have been success stories. Given the presumption of failure that characterizes so much of the policy literature, it is important to present examples of success. Now the time has come to examine several cases of outright failure and cases in which the institutions designed by appropriators are in a fragile condition.

Near Alanya, Turkey, where fishers were able to establish their own set of rules for regulating inshore fisheries, there are two other fishing areas whose fishers have failed to establish effective rule systems – Bodrum and the Bay of Izmir. Both suffer severe problems of overcrowding and rent dissipation. In San Bernardino County, California, groundwater pumpers are still facing overdraft conditions even after they initiated litigation and created a special district. The institutional arrangements described in Chapter 4 that helped nearby basins solve CPR problems did not work as effectively when applied to a region rather than to a basin.

In another part of the world, Sri Lankan fishers, who had devised an ingenious system for rotating access to an inshore fishery, found themselves unable to enforce an additional rule to prevent the entry of new appropriators. The rotation system continues to spread the risk involved in an uncertain environment across all participants. With too many appropriators, however, the profits obtained by local fishers have steadily declined as rents have been dissipated.[1]

In the interior of Sri Lanka, central-government authorities and donor countries have invested large sums in the reconstruction of major irrigation systems. To work successfully, these systems need the active cooperation of the farmers to schedule and manage water use so as to minimize wastage. National officials have altered the administrative structures of these systems several times without succeeding in obtaining farmer cooperation in

143

implementing rules to allocate water to minimize overuse. The Sri Lankan experience with the reluctance of farmers to invest time and effort to enhance the productivity of a centrally managed system has been repeated in many diverse forms throughout South and Southeast Asia. In some cases, centralized efforts to reform the structure of a system have led to worse problems. However, an experimental project to organize farmers from the ground up, without an organizational blueprint, has produced a reversal of that problem in one large Sri Lankan irrigation system.

The last case to be considered, not yet a failure, is an instance of locally developed rules to regulate access and use of an inshore fishery, but they are not recognized as legitimate or effective by national authorities. In both Nova Scotia and Newfoundland, many local villages have devised their own rules to determine who can use local fisheries and how resources are to be harvested. Recently, the Canadian national government has taken a more active role in fishery regulation along its eastern coast. The national government is attempting to develop uniform policies for the entire coast. There are, however, two quite different types of fisheries on this coast: (1) the deep-sea fisheries, which are open-access CPRs, and (2) the inshore fisheries, in which local fishers have established informal rules controlling access and use. The need for a large-scale governmental agency that can restrict access to the deep-sea fishery is well established. But the unwillingness of the national authorities to develop a nested system of rules, drawing on the experience of many generations of fishers who intimately know their own fisheries, may destroy one set of effective CPR institutions without necessarily developing effective alternatives.

## TWO TURKISH INSHORE FISHERIES WITH CONTINUING CPR PROBLEMS

Bodrum is located about 400 kilometers west of Alanya on the Aegean Sea. The number of fishers appropriating from the Bodrum fishery is substantially larger than the number of fishers in Alanya. In the Bodrum fishery in 1983, there were 100 small boats with inboard power, 11 trawlers, 2 purse seiners, and 9 bottom seiners, operated by approximately 400 fishers (Berkes 1986b, p. 68). Until the 1970s, Bodrum had been the site of a successful inshore fishery. Fikret Berkes reports that in the 1970s the government of Turkey had encouraged some Bodrum fishers to construct larger trawling vessels and "had rarely enforced the three-mile limit, much to the anger of the small fishermen" (Berkes 1986b, p. 79).[2]

The early financial success of the trawlers lured others to enter the local fishery, until the revenues from the fleet as a whole were less than the costs

144

of fishing in the area. As Berkes indicates, Bodrum was a "textbook example of rent dissipation in a fishery" (1986b, p. 79). Although the total annual yield of fish remained approximately the same, the catch per unit of effort sharply declined. The larger vessels operating out of Bodrum could no longer make a living there and began to travel to the shrimp grounds near Mersin. A booming tourist trade lured many part-time fishers and charter fishing boats into the fishery.

A local fishing cooperative struggled unsuccessfully during the 1970s to mediate the conflicts among the small-boat fishers, the new entrants, and the trawlers. That cooperative had disappeared by 1983. Six groups of fishers with distinct interests now compete to appropriate from the same fishery:

(1) small-scale coastal fishermen, (2) larger-scale operators including trawlers and beachseiners, (3) semiprofessionals who obtain their own fish and sell the occasional surplus, (4) large numbers of unskilled sport fishermen, (5) spear-fishermen licensed as sponge fishermen but who sell fish on the open market, and (6) charter boat operators who fish to feed their clients and occasionally sell the surplus. (Berkes, 1986b, p. 74)

A similar problem exists in the larger fishery of the Bay of Izmir, located farther north on the Aegean coast. In 1983, 1,800 fishers lived in the area and used 700 small boats with inboard power, 30 bottom seiners, and 27 purse seiners. The subgroup structure seen in Bodrum is similar to that in Izmir, where it is complicated by the fact that Izmir is a large urban center (a metropolitan area with a population of over 1 million) with a high demand for fresh fish. The result is an overcapitalized fishery, with too many fishers chasing too few fish.

The trawlers were not the problem in Izmir. It is difficult for trawlers to operate in such a crowded environment, and the Turkish coast guard actively patrols a major harbor. This CPR problem has been produced by a number of factors: the opportunities for quick economic gain, the large number of fishers, the internal division of the fishers into distinct subgroups with conflicting interests, and the lack of an overarching institutional mechanism in which local rules and conflict-resolution mechanisms could be designed. Two large fishing cooperatives are based at Izmir, but they represent distinct subgroups of fishers. Several other fishing cooperatives operate nearby, but also represent distinct subgroups. Each group had conflicts "with at least one other group, and in some instances, with more than one." Consequently, there were "no operational rules in place to allocate the fish, to reduce the conflicts, or to limit crowding" (Berkes 1986b, p. 75).

The general institutional setting within Turkey could be called "benign

145

neglect." National legislation required fishers to be licensed, but did not limit the number of licenses. Restrictions were placed on fishing during the spawning season and on the equipment that could be used. An effort had been made to segregate inshore fisheries from offshore fisheries by forbidding trawlers to fish within a three-mile offshore zone and within bays. The agency responsible for fishery rules (the Ministry of Agriculture) employed no agents to enforce those rules. The coast guard, the rural police, and the Ministry of the Interior were supposed to enforce the rules. Nonenforcement of the three-mile zone (other than in the large bays) and the financing and encouragement of new trawlers were thus sources of the failure in Bodrum.

The failure of the fishers in the Bay of Izmir and Bodrum to organize themselves to prevent rent dissipation cannot be attributed to a single cause. Internally, these were large groups that were characterized by severe heterogeneity of interests and of relevant time horizons. Given the different technologies in use, any rules that were defined to limit use would tend to benefit one subgroup over another, rather than benefit all in a similar manner. The costs of overcoming size differences and heterogeneity are substantial. In a political regime that does not provide arenas in which low-cost, enforceable agreements can be reached, it is very difficult to meet the potentially high costs of self-organization.

## CALIFORNIA GROUNDWATER BASINS WITH CONTINUING CPR PROBLEMS

Although the groundwater pumpers in most of southern California have resolved their conflicts over limited water supplies and have protected their groundwater basins against continuing overdraft conditions, that experience has not been universal. The groundwater basins located in San Bernardino County, northeast of the basins described in Chapter 4, continue in overdraft condition, even though efforts have been made to allocate water rights through litigation and the creation of water districts. Why is it that individuals who have adopted strategies of institutional change that appear to be quite similar to those described in Chapter 4 have not succeeded in devising a workable set of institutional arrangements to manage their basins?

Obvious differences have to do with size and complexity. San Bernardino is the largest county in the United States, and there are nine states that are not as large as San Bernardino County. The combined areas of New Jersey, Hawaii, Connecticut, Delaware, and Rhode Island would fit into this one county (Blomquist 1989, p. 2). Approximately 83% of the county

146

is part of the Mojave Desert. Fifteen different groundwater basins – some interconnected and some totally independent – underlie the area. Some of these basins are fed by the Mojave River, which flows largely underground through a substantial portion of the county. Other basins are replenished only by local precipitation. The region was sparsely populated before World War II, but its population has grown dramatically in the postwar era.

Overdraft conditions were reported in some of the basins during the 1950s. During the late 1950s, the California Department of Water Resources began to plan the Feather River Project to bring water from the water-rich northern region of the state to the water-poor southern region. Areas desiring this water were encouraged to form water agencies in order to contract with the state for future deliveries of this water. The Mojave Water Agency was created, first by state law, and then by a special election in 1960, in order to levy a land tax to pay its share of the capital costs of constructing the aqueduct. After helping to pay for construction of the aqueduct, residents living in the area served by the Mojave Water Agency would eventually be able to claim 50,800 acre-feet of imported surface water per year, provided they paid for the marginal costs of a delivery system and the water itself.

Some of those who had been involved in establishing the Mojave Water Agency thought of it as a water wholesaler, similar to the Metropolitan Water District of Southern California, and as an insurance strategy for a growing area that lacked a local water supply. As a wholesaler, the agency could play an important role in obtaining water for the region, but not in managing the many hydrologic subareas of this vast terrain. As an insurance strategy, the primary activity of the agency would be to collect taxes to ensure that the area would eventually be entitled to a flow of imported water. If that view had predominated, the next steps after the creation of the Mojave Water Agency would have been the development of a diversity of smaller-scale private and public enterprises to resolve water-rights issues, devise management plans within subareas, and develop a polycentric system similar to the one that emerged in Los Angeles County.

Others saw the agency as the primary water-management institution for the entire area. That group included most of the officials who were initially elected to serve on the agency's council. Within a short time of its formation, the agency hired a distinguished water-rights attorney, James Krieger, who had been involved in the West Basin and Central Basin litigations, to initiate legal action to settle water rights for the entire region. In 1966, when litigation was initiated in the Superior Court of San Bernardino County, no consensus had developed concerning several key issues:

147

1 Could the region best be described as one region with a single under-ground river, as a series of interconnected groundwater basins, or as some combination of a river system, interconnected groundwater basins, and independent groundwater basins?

2 Were all parts of the region, or only localized areas, suffering from overdraft problems?

3 Should all groundwater pumpers be treated as coequal in status, or did some pumpers have prior rights that should be given preferential treatment?

4 Should an administrative settlement be worked out by the agency staff working primarily with the larger pumpers, most of whom were located in the upper reaches of the area, or should it involve the vast number of small pumpers, most of whom were located in the lower portions of the area?

5 Should water rights be separated from land ownership in a region that had not yet been developed?

Coherent arguments could be advanced for the opposing positions on each of these issues. Krieger and the staff members of the Mojave Water Agency, however, approached the situation as if there were only one legitimate answer to each of those questions. They viewed the entire region as if it were a single underground basin with a well-documented history of overdraft conditions. They treated all groundwater pumpers as having coequal rights and attempted to reach a stipulated settlement – to separate water rights from the land as rapidly as possible – with those who had been pumping 500 acre-feet or more per year. Their view of the issues, however, was not widely shared. In 1964, for example, the California Department of Water Resources published a report that denied the existence of over-draft conditions in two of the large subbasins included within the region under adjudication. On the other hand, the Mojave Water Agency had declared in the same year that overdraft of the Mojave River basins was an "unquestionable fact" (Blomquist 1989, pp. 63, 113).

No voluntary water associations were created to facilitate discussion of these issues, and no consensus emerged over time about any of them. Conflicts emerged between the large and small water pumpers, between advocates for development and advocates for no-growth policies, between industry and agriculture, between locals and "external experts," and be-tween appointed personnel and elected officials. The lack of fundamental agreement led to acrimonious political conflict, including several recall elections, front-page stories in the local papers that pushed aside stories on the Watergate scandal, and finally the suspension of the litigation in 1974

148

(Blomquist 1989, pp. 57–77). No action has since been taken to limit groundwater pumping.

During the past decade the region has undergone massive development, and overdraft conditions have now been documented by all agencies. No one has yet found an effective means for resolving the problem of water-rights allocation or even the problem of purchasing surface-water supplies. The 50,800 acre-feet of Feather River water to which the Mojave Water Agency is entitled flows by each year to be used by others in the southern California region who have organized themselves to purchase water for immediate use or to store as part of a groundwater-management plan. No one has yet found an acceptable plan for building a distribution system and a means of financing that would enable residents of this area to pay for the marginal costs of obtaining the water to which they have an entitlement.

Attempts to solve the difficult problems of this large and complex region primarily on a regional scale using one instrumentality did not enable those involved to devise effective institutional arrangements to address the diverse problems they faced. Unlike the larger-scale fisheries in Bodrum and the Bay of Izmir, individuals in the Mojave area were able to initiate major changes in institutional arrangements. The changes they made, however, did not give them effective tools for dealing simultaneously with the diversity of problems involved. Even when individuals have considerable capabilities to engage in self-governance, there is no guarantee that solutions to all problems will be achieved. Individuals who do not have similar images of the problems they face, who do not work out mechanisms to disaggregate complex problems into subparts, and who do not recognize the legitimacy of diverse interests are unlikely to solve their problems even when the institutional means to do so are available to them.[3]

## A SRI LANKAN FISHERY

At the southern tip of Sri Lanka lies the fishing village of Mawelle, as described by Paul Alexander (1977, 1982). Approximately 300 Sinhalese fishers live in the village and engage in three distinct types of fishing technologies: (1) large beach seines used to catch shoals of anchovies and similar species, (2) small traditional craft that use "bible" nets and fishing lines to obtain anchovies, squid, and rockfish, and (3) deep-sea fishing for tuna off the continental shelf. Most of the fishers in Mawelle come from the Karave caste[4] and are beach-seiners. We shall focus on this aspect of the local fishery.

Beach seines (called *madella* or "big net") are half-mile-long nets that may harvest a ton of fish at one time during the prime period when many

149

fish are available. The peak period occurs sometime during September or October and can constitute as much as one-third of the catch for an entire year (Alexander 1982, p. 134). A beach seine lasts for about five years before it must be replaced, at a cost of about three times the average household's annual income. Beach seines can be used only on beaches with relatively hard sand. On the Mawelle beach, there is room for only two nets to be used simultaneously. If the Mawelle fishers owned only 20 to 30 nets, they could make optimal use of most of their nets;[5] however, they own 100 beach seines, and the average net was in use only seven times during 1971 – strong evidence of severe overcapitalization.

Mawelle is another classic case of rent dissipation. This case has, however, an important twist. Whereas the fishers in Bodrum and the Bay of Izmir were unable to develop any effective rules to limit entry or the use of their local fishery, the fishers in Mawelle had devised quite elaborate rules regulating access to the beach and the use of the beach seines, but they were not able to sustain an entry rule controlling the number of nets to be used. When some of the fishers tried to get officials to enforce a provision in the national legislation that limited the number of nets to be used, others were able to convince national public officials not to enforce that provision. But before we discuss this problem concerning the enforcement of entry rules, let us examine the system of appropriation rules that Mawelle fishers had devised.

The appropriation rules in operation in Mawelle involve naming all the nets and placing them into a sequence. Each net owner is aware of the sequence of nets immediately preceding and following his net. The beach is divided into two launching sites, one on the harbor side and one on the rock side (Figure 5.1). A net may first be deployed on the harbor side anytime during the day after the net preceding it has been used. As illustrated on Table 5.1, once a net has worked its way up in the sequence so as to have had a dawn run on the harbor side, the net is next eligible for the dawn run on the rock side. "Subsequently, it may be used on the rock side at any time of the day once the net immediately following it in the sequence has been used" (Alexander 1982, p. 145).

The Mawelle fishers provide a coherent explanation for why they use this complex set of authority rules, rather than a simple rotation system, to equalize the opportunity to make a big catch. Four environmental or technological considerations affect the problem of equalizing access: (1) The harbor side produces the really big catches, but the rock side is more consistently productive when there are fewer fish. (2) The first catch of the morning is most likely to be the biggest catch of the day, and prices are highest in the morning. (3) The weather affects the number of hauls that

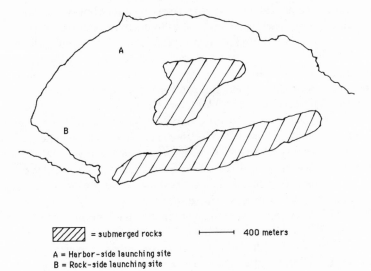

= submerged rocks    ⊢———⊣ 400 meters

A = Harbor-side launching site
B = Rock-side launching site

Figure 5.1. Harbor at Mawelle. (Adapted from Alexander 1982, p. 17.)

Table 5.1. *Net sequencing at Mawelle*

| Day of week | Harbor side | | | | Rock side | | | |
|---|---|---|---|---|---|---|---|---|
| | Dawn → | | | | Dawn → | | | |
| Monday | B | C | D | E | A | Z | Y | X |
| Tuesday | C | D | E | F | B | A | Z | Y |
| Wednesday | D | E | F | G | C | B | A | Z |
| Thursday | E | F | G | H | D | C | B | A |
| Friday | F | G | H | I | E | D | C | B |

*Note:* This is a stylized representation of how the first four nets (using letters of the alphabet to symbolize a net) would be launched daily at each site, based on Table 7.1 of Alexander (1982). In practice, the number of nets in use varies from day to day, and the same number of nets may not be launched from both sites.

151

*Governing the commons*

can be made in a day, and any system assigning a set hour of the day would be inefficient. (4) Beach-seining involves high labor inputs to prepare a net for use and to restack it afterward, and simple rotation systems allowing all nets to be used only once per rotation would involve higher labor costs (Alexander 1982, p. 146).

Disputes about this sequencing are rare, except when the rules themselves are challenged, as described later. During the two years that Alexander spent in Mawelle, he never observed a dispute about the sequence in which nets would be beached. The absence of conflict over the authority rules in the fishery contrasts sharply with that society's high levels of violence, in Mawelle as well as similar fishing villages. During Alexander's stay, "three men were murdered and seventeen other assaults resulted in serious injuries" (Alexander 1982, p. 8).

The rotation system evolved in an era in which the number of nets varied around 20. With that number of nets, the system produced relatively equal and profitable incomes for all net owners. Because nets were so expensive and because at least eight men were needed to haul in a net, a net was divided into eight ownership shares. Until recent times, each owner did his share of the work, and they divided the value of the net's haul equally. Shares were bought and sold among village residents:

> Shares may be freely bought, sold, and used as security for various forms of mortgage. In former years they were often the most valuable item inherited, and, less frequently, were included in dowry payments. Although shares are freely transferable, in the sense that the other shareholders in the net do not have a legal veto over a prospective sale, the other shareholders do have a strong practical veto. Shareholders must work closely together and few men would buy a share in a net where the other shareholders strongly objected to the sale.
>
> (Alexander 1982, p. 143)

Until the late 1930s, fishing in Mawelle was largely for subsistence and to produce dried fish for a winter market. The returns from selling dried fish were relatively low. But demographic pressure, market opportunities, and the relationship between internal rules and external rules together changed that situation markedly.

The population of Mawelle grew by 70% between 1901 and 1931, with a disproportionate amount of the growth occurring among beach-seining families (Alexander 1982, p. 204). That disproportionate growth was due to an earlier labor shortage that had led the heads of beach-seining families to encourage their sons-in-law to live in Mawelle and invest in one of the eight shares of a family net. By 1931, the second generation of this in-migration began to marry and wanted access to the harvest. Given that access was tied to the eight-share system, sons had great motivation to

152

attempt to acquire a share in a new net. Alexander illustrates the logic of the situation clearly:

If there are twenty nets, a man with one share will receive 1/160th of the annual catch. But if after his death his two sons take joint ownership of his share, they each receive only 1/320th of the catch, whereas if one joins in the construction of a new net they each receive 1/168th. (Alexander 1982, p. 204)

In 1933, legislation was enacted requiring the registration of beach-seines throughout the country. Along the southern coast, where share systems were the dominant forms of ownership, the "government limited the number of nets at any site to those in use in 1933 and codified the criteria for allocating access to the water" (Alexander 1982, p. 206). Thirty-two nets were registered in 1933. The registry reveals that almost all fishers owned a single share in one net. The legislation allowed in-dividuals who did not inherit access rights to the fishery to purchase shares in established nets. That opened access to the fishery to persons outside the limited number of families that previously had shared access to the use of beach seines on the Mawelle beach. Opening access outside the original kinship groups would not have affected the number of nets competing for access if the provision limiting the number of nets to the number in use in 1933 had been enforced. Unfortunately, the limit on nets was not enforced, as we shall see.

During the early 1940s, the construction of a new road linking Mawelle to marketing centers, the construction of an ice factory nearby, and the marketing efforts of the Fish Sales Union greatly increased the demand for and market value of fresh fish. Prices for fish increased fourfold between 1938 and 1941 (Alexander 1982, p. 210). Then the pressure to introduce new nets really gained momentum. By 1945, 71 nets were in operation. At first, the operation of that many nets was highly profitable, even though the marginal product of each additional share was negative.[6] The average price of a share had risen substantially from 1935 to 1945 and was to continue to rise for another two decades, before dropping to a lower level again (Alexander 1982, p. 227).

New entrepreneurs began to buy shares in more than one net and to hire wage laborers to work their shares. By purchasing shares in nets well separated in the sequence, profitable returns could be made during each year. On the other hand, a poor fisher, who owned only a single share, received a profit only in those years when his net operated during the limited flush season. In earlier times, everyone had operated a net during the high-yield season. By 1971, however, that occurred, on the average, every three years. In the other two years, the income earned from a single share was less than a subsistence-level income. Poorer owners of single shares began to sell their shares to others. A fisher who owned one share in each of five nets appropriately spaced throughout the sequence could make a modest profit each year, but he would have to make a substantial capital investment to spread his risk appropriately. Alexander computed the optimal number of shares for a person who intends to work his own shares to be 6.5 shares. In 1971, 95 of the fishers (58%) owned 5 shares or less.

Thus, the ownership patterns were shifting at the same time that the number of nets was greatly increasing. In the earlier system, those who owned shares had been long-term residents of the village, had belonged to the same kinship group, had owned only a single share each, and had worked that share. By 1971, many of the owners were not members of the same kinship group, owned shares in multiple nets, and hired wage laborers to work their shares. Further, the heads of several factions in the village purchased shares both for the economic return they could obtain and as a means of providing work for their loyal followers.

During that time, several efforts had been made to enforce the net-limiting provision in the 1933 legislation. After petitions had been submitted to the government agent in Hambantota in 1940, 1942, and 1945, a petition submitted in 1946 was accepted by the government agent, who agreed that the number of nets to be used in the future would be limited to the 77 nets then registered (Alexander 1982, p. 213). The 1946 petition was supported not only by the fishers who owned single shares and had actively supported the earlier efforts but also by the three largest shareholders in the village, who had earlier opposed such restrictions.

The government agent's decision substantially slowed, but did not completely stop, the construction of new nets. Entrepreneurs who offered sufficient inducements to government authorities were able to add a new net from time to time. Seven new nets were added in the next two decades, as compared with the 39 nets that had been added in the prior decade. That temporary brake on new entrants was to be completely destroyed in 1964 by the entry of a new entrepreneur – David Mahattea – into beach-seining. Finding it difficult to buy shares in current nets, Mahattea approached the local member of parliament (MP), a member of the Sri Lankan Freedom Party, and argued for permission to construct additional nets. The MP asked the district revenue officer to consider the proposal. The district revenue officer refused at first, arguing that there were too many nets. When the day came for the annual registering of nets, four members of Mahattea's faction appeared with nets borrowed from a nearby village. After considerable conflict in the village, the district revenue officer ordered those nets to be registered. Further nets were added when another faction leader supported a candidate from the opposition party and he won at the next election, after agreeing that additional nets could be registered in 1965. Between the two faction leaders, 24 new nets were constructed and added to the 84 nets then in operation.

At first, the other fishers were successful in excluding these new nets by devising a well-planned maneuver. The objective was to preclude the launching of the newly registered net 85. Once that net was launched, 23 more nets would follow. Fortuitously, one family owned shares in both net 1 and net 84. After net 83 was launched, that family refrained from launching net 84, and instead launched net 1. Thus, they started a new sequence, excluding one of their own nets (84) and all of the newly registered nets (85–108). That strategy was widely supported by all those who owned limited numbers of shares and by a faction leader who had not participated in the effort to bring in new nets. "As fishing was poor at the time the owners of the new nets did not protest very vigorously, but when the stratagem was repeated in the next cycle, [they] made it clear that they would resist future attempts" (Alexander 1982, p. 225).

That challenge came in 1966, when the net cycle reached net 83. Both net 1 and net 85 were launched at the same time, and fishers engaged in a brawl at sea. The boat carrying net 1 overturned. "Members of all three factions had gathered on the beach, and only the arrival of three jeep-loads of armed police, whom David [Mahattea] had warned in advance, prevented a riot" (Alexander 1982, pp. 225–6). The police stayed on for weeks to ensure that the 24 new nets were added to the sequence. The national government then issued regulations freezing the number of nets at 108. No nets were added to the official list between 1966 and 1971, when Alexander conducted his study. Alexander reports that the actual number of nets in use had dropped to 99 because of the burning of some nets in interfactional conflicts.

I have described this case in some detail because Alexander provides such an excellent record of the key steps in this process of rent dissipation. This was not a problem of ignorance. The fishers involved were aware of the consequences of adding nets. It was not a case of individuals being incapable of devising and enforcing rules well tailored to their local circumstances. The sequencing rules had been practiced successfully for many years. It does illustrate what happens in a *dynamic* local setting when appropriators do not have autonomy to make and enforce new rules.[7]

Before independence in 1948, the British had recognized the position of village headman (*vidāna arrachi*) and an official responsible for all aspects of fishing (*patabāndi arrachi*). The village headmen were responsible for a wide variety of activities in a local village, usually were appointed from among the local landowners, and frequently increased their wealth substantially as a result of holding office. They did have some real representation functions for a village. The duties of that position were abolished in 1965, and a new position was created in the civil service to handle village administrative matters. The occupants of the new offices were in an extremely weak position. They came from other locations and were subject to transfer out of an assignment if local residents with political contacts raised objections. During the year of Alexander's fieldwork in Mawelle, four men were successively appointed to that position, none staying for more than one month. The position of *patabändi arrachi* has continued in existence, but virtually the only task for the incumbent in recent times has been the annual registration of nets.

Sri Lanka has an extensive system of income-redistribution policies that bring central officials into direct contact with citizens on a frequent basis. Even though Mawelle is a relatively isolated village, villagers find themselves having to seek permission from central authorities located in Hambantota for many aspects of daily life:

They must visit the District Revenue Office to obtain a rice ration book and the Police for a license to tap toddy. Chits to buy a variety of goods ranging from cement to extra food for a daughter's wedding are issued by the Government Agent. The Fisheries Department controls the sale of fishing gear and engine parts, while a number of consumer staples including rice, condiments, textiles and kerosene are sold through state run co-operative stores. In every case the villager is confronted by a shortage of goods, long slow-moving queues, and supercilious clerks. Yet despite the centralised control of goods and services, government agencies have few direct contacts with the village.     (Alexander 1982, p. 31)

Political relationships between elected officials and local villagers revolve around patronage positions given to faction leaders in return for electoral support. Relationships inside the village are strongly affected by efforts to obtain private returns from the public treasury.

No arenas were provided by either the British or the Sri Lankan government for local discussion or local decision making at a constitutional-choice or collective-choice level. The villagers' own rotation system was codified in 1933, prior to the dramatic economic changes that would alter the incentives for all participants, and the villagers lost their right to change their own rules to adjust to the rapid change in the value of fish. National officials had promulgated a law that limited entry, but they failed to enforce it. Instead of enforcing entry rules limiting the number of nets, national officials could be convinced with promises of votes (and perhaps even bribes) to intervene and prevent the enforcement of a national rule

## Analyzing institutional failures and fragilities

considered desirable by most local fishers. In any effort to close entry to a resource, some participants, or potential participants, are strongly motivated to ride free on the restrictions imposed on others. If these participants are able to make an "end-run" around local authorities, rule enforcement can be disrupted even when most appropriators strongly prefer tight enforcement.

Most of the beach-seining operations along the southern shore of Sri Lanka originally used share systems similar to the one described here. Villages that were located in closer proximity to marketing centers succumbed at an earlier date to the problem of rent dissipation. In most of those villages, a single entrepreneur bought up the shares to the local beach-seines and operated the beach-seines as a single firm. The owner hired wage laborers and captured the residual claims to profits. In villages where there were many employers of labor, such systems should have operated efficiently. Where the beach-seine operator held a monopsony position in regard to labor and the supply of labor was abundant, one would expect that the owner would keep wages as low as possible. The distributional consequences of that system frequently were undesirable. Private ownership may have been the only viable institutional arrangement along this coast, not because it was "the only way" but because the external regime was unwilling to allow local rule determination and enforcement. External intervention to prevent rule enforcement against political favorites undermines the viability of common-property arrangements.

### IRRIGATION DEVELOPMENT PROJECTS IN SRI LANKA

Millions of dollars have been poured into the development of irrigation works in the dry zone of Sri Lanka. Extensive irrigation works had been developed in that area before the Christian era and had flourished until the twelfth century, when the population dependent on those systems began, for unknown reasons, to migrate to other parts of the island. In the nineteenth century, the British first began to restore the ruins of the bunds (embankments) that had created small and large reservoirs – called tanks in that part of the world – and the long, ribbonlike canal systems that stretched for great distances below the tanks. After independence, the government of Sri Lanka, assisted by foreign donor agencies, continued to invest heavily in irrigation projects.

The quantity of paddy rice produced in Sri Lanka has grown steadily in recent decades, particularly since the 1950s. The introduction of higher-yield varieties of rice has contributed to this growth,[8] but the amount of land under irrigation is the single most important factor affecting the

157

## Governing the commons

quantity of rice produced (Madduma Bandara 1984, pp. 298–301).[9] Although the quantity of rice produced has steadily increased, the output is substantially short of the expectations of project planners. In few of these projects has the amount of land actually irrigated approached the projections. Few systematic final evaluations of those projects have been conducted, but the detailed cost–benefit evaluation of the original Gal Oya project showed that discounted costs exceeded discounted benefits by 277 million rupees (Harriss 1984, p. 318). The area actually irrigated in another major project – Uda Walawe – was one-third of that planned when the project was funded. Much of the land that the planners presumed would produce two crops per year produced only a single crop after project water was made available.

One source of the disappointing effects on rice production is the discrepancy between project plans and project performance in terms of the amount of water that Sri Lankan farmers actually apply to their paddy lands. To understand this discrepancy, one needs to examine the relation between the quantity of water applied and the yield of paddy rice. Obtaining a high yield is dependent on receiving a substantial and reliable supply of water throughout the growing season. Farmers are strongly motivated to irrigate their fields as often as possible during the growing season. The yield for most varieties of paddy rice, in contrast to grains such as wheat, is highly sensitive to a scarcity of water and relatively insensitive to an overabundance of water (Levin 1980, pp. 52–3). Keeping fields flooded for long periods of time reduces the amount of backbreaking weeding that a farmer must do. A farmer has every reason to take almost any quantity of water that can be obtained through legal or illegal means, and very little reason to conserve water at all.

On the other hand, water is a scarce and costly factor of production. Farmers are rarely required to pay the full costs or even any costs at all for the water they receive. Further, diverting water from areas in the upper reaches of a system, when taken in excess of crop requirements, to be used in downstream areas will not reduce the yields upstream. Such a reallocation will greatly increase the rice yields in the lower reaches. Thus, if farmers are able to follow their own unconstrained preferences, they will apply far more water than is economically justified, in order to reduce their own personal labor input (even in areas where there is an abundance of labor), with the result that the total agricultural yield of the system will be substantially less than the projections made by irrigation engineers based on formulas of "optimal water-usage patterns."

A realistic estimate of actual water use in the major project areas of Sri Lanka is 12–15 feet of water applied to each hectare of paddy fields: 5–6

158

feet for the major (*maha*) growing season, when precipitation augments irrigation, and 7–9 feet for the minor (*yala*) growing season, when there is little or no precipitation. The most effective use of water to be recorded was in a small pilot project run by the Irrigation Department, with tight controls: a total water use between 8.4 and 10.2 feet. The 1969 project-planning document for the Mahaweli Development Programme – the largest of all the Sri Lankan projects – estimated the amount of land to be irrigated based on a presumption that 8.3 feet of water would be applied to yield two crops of paddy rice. When the project was evaluated again in 1977, planners reestimated the amount of land that could be irrigated assuming that about 7.5 feet of water would be applied over the entire project area to produce two crops of paddy rice (Harriss 1984, p. 319). Thus, the engineering plans were based on the presumption that water would be treated as a scarce good and that strict allocation rules would be enforced. Neither presumption was appropriate (Ascher and Healy 1990; Lundqvist 1986).

Bringing water use close to the figures used in project-planning documents would require a high level of organization by the farmers themselves to allocate water in the channels serving their fields according to strict self-discipline. Central-government efforts to achieve such a level of organization have not changed the fundamental incentives facing participants or their behavior. The dominant pattern of their behavior is to take as much water as their paddy fields will hold whenever they can legally or illegally obtain it and to refrain from active participation in efforts that would require them to accept any limits on their water use. The contemporary structure of incentives facing many farmers reinforces a short-term, "individualistic" strategy and discourages efforts devoted to longer-term investments in the organizational structure needed to achieve collective action. In this system, not only do the upstream irrigators seriously harm the downstream irrigators, but the general lack of reliable rules greatly increases the production and transactions costs for all irrigators.

To illustrate this problem, I shall describe the patterns of incentives and behaviors that evolved in the Kirindi Oya project, a project completed in 1920 under British colonial rule. After describing some of the vicious circles that evolved in that project, I shall then show how similar patterns of incentives have been generated in some other projects. The collective welfare of the impoverished farmers in the dry zone is dependent on their obtaining the additional food and income that would result from the design of an effective and enforceable set of rules for managing irrigation systems to increase their yields. But the farmers in that system are indeed caught in a system that is unlikely to facilitate their achieving an improved system of

159

rule-ordered relationships without outside help. And officials of the central government are equally trapped – given the current setting – and are also unable to break the vicious circles encompassing them and the farmers they are supposed to be serving.[10]

In 1876, the remnants of a bund located at Ellagala, on the left bank of the Kirindi Oya River, were restored, and a new settlement area was opened up. Thirty years later, a similar scheme was developed to restore a bund on the right bank of the river, using the same diversion works to fill the tank, thus opening up more land for resettlement. The construction phase was completed in 1920. Approximately 2,500 acres are served by this irrigation system. Most of the irrigators served by this system are poor tenants who are dependent on those who own large parcels of land in the area. Many of the major owners of land live elsewhere and are not dependent on local support (Fladby 1983).

The rainfall in the dry zone is 50–75 inches per year, which is a substantial amount when compared with the average for Valencia, Spain, of 10 inches and that for the Los Angeles metropolitan area of 14 inches per year. However, compared with other tropical areas, 50–75 inches is low. More important, it is highly concentrated in the October-to-December period, when dry steambeds are turned into torrential rivers. But everything will be dry a few days later (Gunasekera 1981). There is a minor rainy season in April and May. The irrigation systems restored by the British were relatively primitive structures, with few regulatory sluices or gates. Rainfall was retained behind a bund until the rainy season ended. The amount of water available in the reservoir determined the amount of land that could safely be placed under cultivation for the next growing season. For the smaller tanks, the land area covered by water just about equaled the land area that could be irrigated.

The administrative structure established by the British was designed to run a system that involved the release of water from shallow bunds in short bursts after water had been captured during one of the rainy seasons. Water would then accumulate behind the bund during the next rainy season, later to be released again. Farmers along the entire system had to be prepared to use the water during a brief period of time, or they would miss the opportunity to plant a crop for that season.[11] Under the British, the Irrigation Department named fixed dates for the release of water; the dates were supposed to be invariable each year to ensure time for two crops and for maintenance work on the bund and the channels. The notion of fixed dates was related to "a general view of British irrigation authorities that schemes should operate according to standard programmes so as to be subject to as little influence from events and personalities as possible" (Harriss 1977, p. 367).

From 1920 to 1958, the Kirindi Oya system was managed by a dual executive structure. In principle, the responsibility for maintenance of the tank and the main canal and for allocation of water to the tank from the river was under the jurisdiction of the Irrigation Department. A subdivisional officer responsible to the director of irrigation engineering was the only person with the power to instruct an irrigation overseer to release water from the tank into the 10-mile-long main channel. Two "watchers" or "water-issue laborers" were then responsible for opening or closing the headgates, composed of simple planks, into the 11 main subchannels and for reporting on the condition of the main channels. All of these officials were paid fixed salaries by the Irrigation Department.

A different line of responsibility started at the level of the farmers' fields. There the lowest official was the *vel vidane*. In an earlier era of British colonial rule, that position was appointive and carried considerable power and prestige.[12] Because many cultivators were tenants, they did not participate in the selection of the *vel vidanes*, who were beholden primarily to the larger landowners for their positions. The *vel vidanes* were responsible for reporting on the progress made in cultivation and could enforce sanctions on cultivators who did not use water according to the rules agreed to by the landowners. They were paid a share of the yield by the cultivators. "In theory the Vel Vidanes were the instrument of swift discipline, empowered to ensure water conservation by the application of a code which laid down automatic punishments for any practices which would waste water, such as poor levelling of fields" (Harriss 1977, p. 369). However, practices varied greatly from one system to another. Some *vel vidanes* were subject "to influence by the big land controllers, so that performance of their duties was often slack and subject to bias" (Harriss 1977, p. 369). Some *vel vidanes* were known for their vigorous efforts to impose rigorous and fair discipline. Although elected locally, the *vel vidanes* were responsible to an assistant government agent (AGA) employed by the Revenue Department. Information about the status of the crops was reported upward from the *vel vidanes* to the AGA.

Water shortages occurred rather frequently. Considerable conflict was engendered between the Revenue Department, which wanted to save crops, and the Irrigation Department, which wanted a regular schedule and a set time to maintain the bund and channels. The AGAs from the Revenue Department regularly requested delays in the timing of water releases in order to prevent destruction of the first crop, which would lead to a lower

161

tax yield on the land. The effects of such delays were failure of the second crop in many years and a cumulative deterioration in the maintenance of the system. Further, the conflict between the two agencies could be manipulated by the larger landowners, who played on the concern of the AGAs for cultivation, rather than irrigation maintenance, and the somewhat more participatory orientation of the Revenue Department.

John Harriss reports that it was possible to make this system work when a strong AGA considered cultivation a priority. One AGA in the early 1920s was quite successful:

He was able to resist the pressures of the powerful landowners and to exercise his power ruthlessly with regard to late cultivation, but also to manipulate the Vel Vidane system to make optimum use of available water and offer positive inducements to timely cultivation. For the system did provide for a kind of monitoring organisation throughout the tract. (Harriss 1977, p. 369)[13]

The *vel vidanes* were paid a proportion of the resulting crop, rather than a fixed income. Therefore, when coordination at the tract level was matched by predictability in water releases, there were strong motivations to enforce a discipline on the farmers that would ensure that two crops would be brought through to a successful harvest.

The British system was left substantially intact for the first decade of independence. In 1958 the system was changed by the national government in an effort to make it more democratic. The Revenue Department was removed from any responsibility for cultivation and eventually was replaced by a Department of Agrarian Services, which had no direct supervisory role in irrigation management in large projects, though it was responsible for overseeing and assisting small projects. The *vel vidanes* were replaced by the administrative secretaries (*govimandala sewakas*) of newly created Cultivation Committees. Initially, the "water meetings" held in each tract were attended by all registered cultivators, instead of just the owners of land, and elected a Cultivation Committee for a period of three years. Each Cultivation Committee met separately to set its own cultivation dates for each cultivation season of the year.[14] That arrangement greatly enhanced the flexibility of the system, but reduced the level of coordination across irrigation canals that had been possible when the Revenue Department had responsibility for cultivation matters throughout entire systems. Because most canals were unlined, water releases scheduled frequently throughout a long season, rather than at a few brief periods, would increase the amount of water lost to seepage.

The administrative secretary was responsible for enforcing compliance with the rules for water use, but he had fewer enforcement powers than

## Analyzing institutional failures and fragilities

had the *vel vidanes*. The administrative secretary was paid from a fixed cash assessment levied per acre of land in each tract, whether or not the land was cultivated. Thus, the incentives of the administrative secretary were different from those of the *vel vidane*: The administrative secretary was no longer formally beholden to a small group of large landowners for his position; he had fewer powers than the *vel vidane* had had, and he was paid a set amount no matter how inefficiently water was distributed and used. On the other hand, he was dependent on satisfying farmers in his unit, to some extent, or he could not be reelected. Also, he was no longer directly accountable to external agencies for his work activity or for providing information about the condition of the crops or the condition of the irrigation works.

Large landowners frequently captured the major positions on some of the Cultivation Committees for Kirindi Oya and obtained special privileges related to water distribution through internal influence or by seeking external political intervention. In the Irrigation Department, one technical assistant became responsible for both the right side and the left side of the Kirindi Oya development. He had one maintenance overseer and two water-issue laborers assigned to him – hardly a sufficient work force to supervise 11 major outlets, many minor ones, and irrigation activities in over 2,500 acres of land (Harriss 1977, p. 371).

Effectively, the system had to operate without the services of coordinators at the tract level. The water-issue laborers were expected only to open and close gates and report damage. In any case, they could not physically limit the amount of water that any group of farmers obtained. Farmers blocked channels easily and forced water to back up into their fields. Disputes among irrigators were sometimes resolved in a violent manner. Farmers who benefited from unofficial channel blockage were not censored by their neighbors who were adversely affected (Harriss 1977, p. 374).

From 1973 to 1977, the members of the Cultivation Committee were appointed by the minister of agriculture, which meant that the local MP effectively controlled the appointment (Fladby 1983; N. T. Uphoff, personal communication). By the mid-1970s, control over water theft was "virtually nonexistent." Although 200 reports of water poaching had been submitted, none had been officially pursued. In the lower portions of the system, "about 80 acres of paddy are irrigated by means of an unofficial channel which blatantly taps the main channel, and disrupts cultivation in the last yaya (tract) irrigated. . . . This has been going on for about fifteen years" (Harriss 1977, p. 372). Those who irrigated at the tail end of this system, as in many systems, had the most unreliable supplies.[15]

163

# Governing the commons

Several administrative secretaries indicated when interviewed that they did not file official actions against irrigators for water poaching even though they "regularly file cases in the event of non-payment of the acreage taxes upon which they depend for their remuneration" (Harriss 1977, pp. 372–3). Irrigation rates had not been assessed since 1958. The chief engineer of the system concluded that "there is no law now" (Harriss 1977, p. 373).

The Cultivation Committees were abolished altogether in 1977, and their functions were given to appointed cultivation officers, thus replacing a system that had had at least some communal input, and bringing in an entirely centralized system. A modest change was made in 1980 to create an elected track leader (*yaya nayakaya*), but the position is quite anomalous. Although chosen and paid by the farmers, track leaders are supposed to follow the orders of the cultivation officers. As a result, no one other than the farmers themselves can allocate water or attempt to coordinate actions, at least in some villages (Fladby 1983, pp. 102, 191–5).

None of the participants in the Kirindi Oya project is motivated to do anything but follow dominant strategies. For the individual farmers, the only reasonable strategy to follow in a system in which others steal water with impunity (and use it for weed control) is to flood their own fields as much as possible, using whatever means are necessary to do so.[16] For the large landowners, keeping active political contacts with national leaders is one method of ensuring some protection for illegal practices. Politicians, for their part, interfere with irrigation procedures in order to provide "spoils" for those who support them.[17]

Because of the general personnel structure for Sri Lankan public officials – and especially irrigation engineers – few incentives exist for Irrigation Department staff to devote much time and energy to an attempt to enhance the operation and maintenance of canal systems such as the Kirindi Oya project. Recruitment is based primarily on educational qualifications and passing scores on examinations. Promotion and advancement are based almost entirely on seniority, with little crossing-over between nonprofessional and professional ranks. Irrigation engineers strongly identify with the civil-engineering profession, in which esteem derives largely from designing and constructing public works, rather than operating and maintaining them. Engineers make more money when they are assigned to construction projects than they do when assigned to operation and maintenance duties.

After a detailed analysis of this personnel system, Michael Moore concludes that it impedes efficient water management in several ways: (1) Recruitment patterns "impede effective social interaction between public

*Analyzing institutional failures and fragilities*

servants and cultivators," as well as "internal communication and working relationships which are especially important for water management." (2) Performance in written examinations is not associated with good work performance. (3) "There are in general few incentives for good work performance." (4) The way the bureaucracy is organized "consistently if unwittingly results in the devaluation of performance" (M. Moore 1979, p. 103). These factors lead "to poor work performance in general" and specifically to a lack of "good performance in the operation and maintenance of canal systems" (M. Moore 1979, p. 103). On top of all that, Irrigation Department officials are overworked and underpaid.

Tragically, it appears that similar problems afflict some of the other projects undertaken in Sri Lanka, as well as in other parts of Asia and the Third World.[18] Recently constructed irrigation works in Sri Lanka still are characterized by long distributory canals and few control structures. Measuring the amount of water that is allocated to different canals is extremely difficult, as is simply getting water to the tail ends of irrigation channels (M. Moore 1980, pp. 3–4). Further, the few existing control structures are easily tampered with. After reviewing recent developments, Harriss (1984, p. 322) indicates that "gates are missing, structures damaged, channels tapped by encroachers and others." When asked why they did not prevent some of the more blatant offenses, two young technical assistants replied "that they were afraid to because of the fear of being assaulted" (Harriss 1984, p. 322). Even a brave technical assistant must feel that such actions are futile, given the low probability of actually punishing an offender:

Prosecutions have to be carried out by the police, who have usually treated water offenses as trivial, and who do not have the same incentives to tackle them as in other cases. Further, delays over court proceedings and the very light fines which have been imposed on those who have been found guilty of irrigation offenses, have made the legal sanctions ineffectual.                                        (Harriss 1984, p. 322)

Irrigators with the appropriate connections to party officials may never be prosecuted at all.

Many settlements are heterogeneous, composed of individuals coming from different regions, castes, and kinship groupings, all of whom are initially poor and dependent on the irrigation projects for housing, initial income supplements, and provision of social services. The way in which settlers have been recruited and selected has also compounded the problem of farmer organization. The major selection criteria have been (1) being landless and (2) having a large family to enhance the labor supply (Harriss 1984, p. 325). At the same time, land allotments distributed to new settlers are supposed (by law) to be passed along intact from one generation to the

165

next. Although one can understand that attempt to avoid extreme fragmentation of landholdings, the result has been to exacerbate sibling rivalries within families and encourage young men to seek opportunities elsewhere. For some projects, the proportion of young men remaining to work on the family farm has fallen as low as 10% to 15% (Harriss 1984, p. 328). Paddy rice cultivation has always been a labor-intensive business. Given a shortage of family labor, the use of water for weed control to reduce the demands for labor in cultivation seems to make good economic sense for individual families, even though the subsidized water is actually more expensive than would be the marginal costs of an underemployed labor force. It makes little economic sense for a developing country with an underutilized labor supply to subsidize expensive irrigation water and have it allocated in this fashion.

The failure of the Kirindi Oya farmers to develop an effective set of rules for organizing their irrigation system is not unusual for large-scale, donor-funded irrigation systems in Third World settings. The lack of capacity to achieve self-governance appears to stem from internal factors related to the situation of the farmers and external factors related to the regime structure under which they live. Among the internal factors, I would include the following:

1 the very large number of farmers involved,
2 the fact that most farmers are poor settlers who have recently been recruited to the project and have little attachment to their land or to one another,
3 the extreme diversity of ethnic and cultural backgrounds,
4 the opportunity for wealthier farmers to control water through illegal or questionable strategies (potential leaders thus being able to take care of themselves without having to exert leadership to solve larger communal problems), and
5 the lack of physical control structures in the irrigation system itself.

These are difficult problems to overcome. They are exacerbated by the spoils politics of a central regime unwilling to enforce rules impartially, no matter whose rules they are. Those appropriators who want to avoid rule enforcement have considerable opportunity and means to obtain the help of central officials in obstructing such enforcement, thus undermining any effort to supply new local institutions.

The situation facing appropriators in such systems is one of inexorable tragedy. Or is it? Are the farmers on large Sri Lankan irrigation settlements (or similar projects elsewhere) doomed to eternal conflict and lack of cooperation? Unless there are major changes in local institutions, a firm yes is the only answer. But then the key question is whether or not it is possible to change local institutions and thus the incentives and behaviors of the farmers. A recent experiment in the development of new organizations to enlist the cooperation of farmer-irrigators in one Sri Lankan irrigation system (International Irrigation Management Institute 1986; de Silva 1981) leads me to give a qualified affirmative answer to this second question. The situation is grim, but not hopeless.

A dramatic turnaround story has occurred on the left bank of the Gal Oya irrigation project (Perera 1986; Uphoff 1985a–c). The Gal Oya irrigation system is the largest irrigation-based settlement project in Sri Lanka. The system was completed in 1950. The system has three major divisions: the river division, the right bank, and the left bank. The left-bank division was designed to irrigate about 65,000 acres of land and is composed of "nearly 32 miles of main channels, 150 miles of major distributaries, and about 600 miles of field channels" (Perera 1986, p. 88). By the late 1970s, Norman Uphoff described the Gal Oya left bank (GOLB) as a "hydrological nightmare" (Perera 1986, p. 88). Channels had not been maintained, and their banks were broken and silted. Control structures had been destroyed, and the system was providing water to a much smaller area than originally planned. Further, lack of trust among farmers and between farmers and the officials of the Irrigation Department (ID) was endemic:

Cooperation among farmers was minimal. Social relations among settlers, who came from different areas of the country, were often strained.... Relations between farmers and ID officials were marked by mistrust and recriminations. Farmers had no confidence in the competence or the trustworthiness of the ID's staff.... Many field-level officials ... were notorious for their corruption and thuggery. The main obstacle to efficient water management, from the farmers' view point, was the local-level officials, who had political and bureaucratic power behind them.

On the other hand, the ID officials, especially irrigation engineers, believed that farmers could not use water responsibility and carefully. Therefore, they argued that it was necessary to organize, educate, and discipline the farmers to do what the ID asked them to do. Thus farmers were considered a part of the problem while the latter constitute the solution. (Perera 1986, pp. 89–91)[19]

The entire situation was made even more difficult and tense because "most of the cultivators in the tail areas were Tamil speakers settled from nearby coastal areas while most of the upstream cultivators were resettled Sinhalese" (Uphoff 1986a, p. 202).

The original project design called for regimentation of the farmers and increased law enforcement. That approach was modified to some degree in the final proposal, which called for the organization of farmers throughout GOLB to ensure that farmers would contribute free labor to rehabilitate and then maintain the channels that served their fields in order to increase efficient use of water. The final project assigned certain funds and responsibility to the Agrarian Research and Training Institute (ARTI) for farmer organization. ARTI was assisted by the Rural Development Committee at Cornell University.

The ARTI/Cornell team, on consideration, rejected the goal stated in the project plan to devise and test a single model of "farmer organization" for all 19,000 farmers served by GOLB within a four-year period. Instead, the ARTI-Cornell team chose to introduce "catalysts" into the situation of mutual distrust and unpredictability – institutional organizers (IOs), as they were called. The IOs could be college graduates, because Sri Lanka has one of the highest educational levels among less-developed countries (LDCs), and many college graduates there were unemployed. As college graduates, they would be able to grasp organizing principles rapidly and would have the status needed to deal effectively with ID officials. To ensure that the IOs were also able to work with the farmers, applicants were recruited who had farm backgrounds – if possible, from large settlements like Gal Oya. IOs also had to be willing to live in the remote project area.[20] The ARTI/Cornell team started development of IOs in a 5,000-acre pilot area near the head of the system, where rehabilitation was to occur first. It has been expanded to 25,000 acres, but does not yet cover the entire system.

The IOs received about six weeks of training in how to approach and motivate farmers and in technical subjects related to agriculture and irrigation. They were divided into small groups of four or five, each group responsible for the area served by one distributory canal. Each team divided its area into smaller units using field canals as the primary basis for division. Each group of IOs met weekly in order to learn from each other's experiences and bolster morale when necessary. IOs also filled in for one another in times of sickness or when one left.

An IO was expected, first, to meet each farmer sharing water from a field canal to discuss the types of agricultural and irrigation problems they faced and to complete a survey of relevant information about the area.[21] After becoming familiar with the farmers and their problems, the IO was expected to meet informally with small groups of farmers sharing the same field channel to plan self-help strategies. Instead of establishing a predefined organization, the IO tried to form a working committee to solve particular problems, such as repairing a broken control gate or desilting a field channel. Further, IOs identified problems beyond those that could be solved by the farmers working together, problems that needed to be articulated to ID officials and others. Once farmers were used to working together and had achieved benefits from group action, the IO would then help form a local organization and select, through consensus, a farmer-representative. This representative could articulate the interests of the other farmers on his field channel at larger meetings and report back to the others what had happened in larger arenas.

The ARTI/Cornell team tried to get these bottom-up organizations in place before physical rehabilitation started, so as to provide an arena for discussions between the farmers and engineers about the plans for local rehabilitation. In discussions with ID officials, the ARTI/Cornell team used the fact that the farmers were expected to contribute considerable amounts of labor to rehabilitation and maintenance to convince the engineers that high levels of labor contribution were far more likely if the farmers were consulted during the design stages of the rehabilitation. By the time the design phase was initiated, the farmers had already begun to work together and had good ideas about how to rehabilitate their field channels. As a result, irrigation officials began to change their fundamental orientation toward the farmers.

The "field channel organization" (FCO) was the basic organizational building block for the Gal Oya project. FCOs were uniformly small, around 12 to 15 farmers. FCOs were problem-solving units that operated often without regular meeting times, agendas, or written records. A second tier of organization was built on top of the FCO at the level of the distributory channel, the "distributory channel organization" (DCO), involving 200 to 800 acres and around 100 to 300 farmers. Each farmer was thus a member of both an FCO and a DCO. Each DCO developed its own organizational arrangements, which generally involved a general assembly encompassing all farmers and committees made up of the farmer-representatives from the FCOs. Officials were selected by consensus and were nonpartisan.[22]

The third tier of organization, at the branch-canal or area level, was to follow after FCOs and DCOs had been established and linked.[23] There are four major areas in GOLB, and each eventually was represented by an "area council." All of the farmer-representatives within the area served by a branch canal were eligible to attend the general assembly of the area council. The fourth tier of organization – a project-level committee – was initiated by the farmer-representatives and the IOs. The Project Committee provides a forum in which farmers can directly participate in policy discussions. Farmers have seen real changes in the attitudes and behavior of irrigation officials toward them and in the policies adopted by the ID.[24]

Farmer behavior has changed markedly since the evolution of new institutions for collective action. In those areas where FCOs and DCOs have been established, water rotation procedures are quite generally practiced.

## Governing the commons

In a recent survey, 98% of the field representatives "felt that water rotation leads to equity in water distribution and 79 percent of the farmers felt that they would themselves be assured of adequate water under rotation" (Kasyanathan 1986; Perera 1986, p. 103). Rotations have frequently involved deliberate efforts by those located higher in the system to make water available to tail-enders. That is all the more noteworthy given that head-enders tend to be Sinhalese, and tail-enders tend to be Tamils. On one distributory channel, for example, which straddled the Sinhalese and Tamil areas, little channel maintenance had been undertaken for years. Water deliveries had been extremely unreliable, and farmers talked about previous murders over water disputes (Uphoff 1986a, p. 207). Within a few months of the creation of an FCO, Sinhalese and Tamil farmers began to work on clearing out the channels. Uphoff (1986a, pp. 207–8) described the changes:

During my visit in January 1983, I observed fifteen Tamil and twelve Sinhalese farmers finishing the cleaning of [the channel]. The thickness of the tree root that had grown through the channel and which the farmers were chopping out by hand was mute evidence that water had not reached the tail in some twenty years. The farmers worked together for three days to get the channel cleaned, just in time for arrival of the season's first water delivery.

The result of that effort was an additional 1,000 acres brought under cultivation, benefitting 300 families who harvested two crops of rice that year (Uphoff 1986a, p. 208). Farmers have regularly participated in group projects organized by their own FCOs to clear the field channels serving their own land and even, at times, to clear distributory channels that were not cleared by officials because of lack of funding. Whereas 80% of the farmers indicated that the record for channel clearing had been poor prior to the establishment of FCOs, only 6% indicated that it was poor in 1986 (Kasyanathan 1986; Perera 1986, p. 104).

The level of conflict among farmers has also declined. "Now with the assured water supply and the availability of a forum, i.e., the FCO, to discuss and settle disputes at the [FCO] level, the frequency and the seriousness of conflicts have been greatly reduced in FCO areas" (Perera 1986, p. 104). During 1985, 77% of the farmers reported that not a single conflict occurred in their field channels over water distribution (Kasyanathan 1986; Perera 1986, p. 104). Because of the nonpartisan nature of the organizations and the bypassing of those who had been the elite, many powerful farmers in the area had originally opposed the organization of farmers at GOLB. By 1983, the opposition from such groups had disappeared, and some politicians had spoken publicly to praise the non-

170

partisanship of the FCOs and DCOs. Although keeping the organizations nonpartisan appeared to be difficult at the beginning, it was not unusual to find farmers from all parties holding offices in FCOs and DCOs and working well together.

The attitudes of farmers toward the officials of the Irrigation Department changed, as did the attitudes of officials toward the farmers. Officials were perceived as being far more responsive to farmers' needs, and farmers could document specific incidents in which policies had been changed in response to requests made by farmer groups. Over 70% of the GOLB officials believed that official–farmer relationships had improved and that FCOs had facilitated more communication, better understanding, and mutual trust (Kasyanathan 1986; Perera 1986, p. 103). The increased trust crossed ethnic lines. The extent of that mutual respect was demonstrated in 1981 when communal violence broke out in the district, with some roving bands of Sinhalese youths burning Tamil shops in the marketplace: The reaction of the Sinhalese farmer-representatives was to go to the homes of the Tamil Irrigation Department officials in order to protect them from violence (Uphoff 1986a, p. 206).

The major weakness of the Gal Oya organization program was that farmers were expected to undertake construction at the field-channel level without pay. Somewhere between 30% and 60% of the field channels were completed (N. T. Uphoff, personal communication). It probably was an unrealistic hope on the part of the planners to expect farmers to do hard physical work, with little immediate payoff, based simply on a nascent community spirit at the same time that private contractors were making substantial, often lucrative, profits for undertaking the same type of work. The Irrigation Department itself was not able to keep to its planned schedule, complicating still further the task of trying to motivate farmers to do those tasks on time.

No one would argue – least of all the ARTI/Cornell team – that the Gal Oya project operated without minor problems, and sometimes major problems. They faced high turnover (95%) among the IOs, who would leave their temporary jobs when permanent positions opened in the Ministry of Education or elsewhere. Some IOs were fielded with inadequate training. The supervision given to the program was thin on the ground. Some Irrigation Department officials and some farmers were not as responsive as others. But, overall, the modest cost of the program was more than offset by the increased yields resulting from successful introduction of water rotation procedures (Perera 1986, p. 105).

On balance, the Gal Oya project represents a dramatic turnaround in a system in which there once was little hope of gaining farmer cooperation

171

Governing the commons

in the use of water and maintenance of field canals. Beyond gaining the coordinated effort needed to maintain the field channels and equitably distribute water, thus enhancing the efficiency of the system, the project has left organizations in place that can continue to develop new skills and new problem-solving abilities.

Given the perverse incentives that beset all of the participants in Gal Oya prior to the project, it seems unlikely that the farmers or the officials by themselves would have overcome the structure of the situations they faced without external intervention. The type of intervention adopted in the Gal Oya project, however, was not that of a central agency regimenting the farmers by enforcing rules designed by others, although that had been the conception of the intervention in the initial project documents. The ARTI/Cornell team specifically rejected that model of external regimentation. Instead, they chose to facilitate the problem-solving capabilities of local farmers and officials by introducing "human catalysts" who were to work directly with farmers and officials at the field-channel level trying to solve problems. Only after some initial success in getting farmers to undertake collective actions that required some working together did any movement toward more formal organization take place, and even then the field organizations were deliberately kept simple and oriented toward problem-solving. Farmer-representatives were selected through consensus, rather than having "leaders" elected by majority vote. Consensus was the dominant rule used in making decisions at all tiers. Given the spoils systems that had evolved in Sri Lanka, the fact that the day-to-day problem-solving regarding irrigation and agricultural problems could be taken away from politicized channels was an extremely important step.

Mutual trust and reciprocity were nourished on a face-to-face basis prior to attempts to organize farmers into larger groups. At the distributory-channel level, formal organizations were developed by the farmers without following a single, externally authorized model. Eventually, farmers were organized on four mutually reinforcing levels and were given recognition and encouragement. Most important, farmers saw that their own proposals were treated seriously, for the first time, by irrigation officials, and they saw definite results.

The Gal Oya project demonstrates how external agents may help appropriators overcome perverse incentives that lead to suboptimal outcomes, even when traditions of mutual distrust and animosity have been reproduced over several generations. Such problems may be intractable from "inside" the situation unless the major participants holding diverse positions can simultaneously be shown the necessity for major changes in the incentive structure facing them all.[25] The amount of external intervention

172

*Analyzing institutional failures and fragilities*

need not be large nor expensive. Nor is it necessary to maintain large numbers of catalysts in the field for a long time. For a program such as this to be successful, it is necessary that both farmers and irrigation officials come to view the resulting farmer organizations as legitimate and permanent tools for coping with the long-term problems involved in the governance and management of any complex irrigation system.[26]

## THE FRAGILITY OF NOVA SCOTIAN INSHORE FISHERIES

The cases discussed earlier have illustrated some of the problems that make it difficult for CPR appropriators to develop effective rules for limiting entry and use patterns. Now I wish to turn to a different type of problem – that of fragile CPR institutions. Some fragile institutions devised by CPR appropriators are still in use and effective. These institutions exist, however, in a broader setting that renders doubtful their continued use and effectiveness.

The eastern coast of Canada is dotted with small fishing villages where fishing has been the major economic activity for generations. The fishers in many of these villages, particularly those located in Nova Scotia and Newfoundland, have developed their own rules governing the use of nearby fisheries. These local rule systems control who can enter the fishery and how local fishing grounds are divided among fishers using different technologies. In some cases the fishers have established lottery systems to allocate the best locations for setting traps or nets.[27] The local rules that have evolved for one Nova Scotian village are described in considerable detail by Anthony Davis (1984) for a village he calls "Port Lameron Harbour."

Almost all of the 99 fishers currently using Port Lameron Harbour are descendants of fishers who settled in the area during the last decades of the eighteenth century. They all fish from relatively small boats, even though 10 of the 52 boats fish in the offshore waters. Most inshore boats cost less than $30,000, whereas offshore boats tend to cost around $50,000. The average crew size on the inshore boats is 1.8, and on the offshore boats 2.5 (A. Davis 1984, p. 135).

The fishers engaged in the offshore fishery are on the water throughout the entire year, repairing their boats from time to time as needed. The inshore fishery is conducted from the end of March through December, when the boats are hauled up on the shore for repair and refitting. Both types of crews use a diversity of fishing technologies and seek out various species (cod, halibut, herring, mackerel, lobster), depending on the time of year. There are differences in value, size, and technologies between the

173

inshore and offshore fishing boats, but they are not as substantial as the difference between the various types of fishers in Bodrum and the Bay of Izmir described earlier.

Most of the fishing villages along the southwestern coast of Nova Scotia have broadly defined fishing territories.[28] The Port Lameron Harbour inshore fishery zone extends outward for about 25 kilometers and along the coast for about 20 kilometers. The offshore boats use the outer portion of that fishing ground and also go considerably farther to sea. The territory used primarily by Port Lameron fishers is divided into several subzones, each devoted to a particular type of technology. Herring and mackeral gill nets are set in a rectangular area beyond the harbor but close to shore. If they were set farther inshore, they would restrict travel in and out of the harbor, and if set farther to sea they could be destroyed by the strong currents. Similar areas are set aside for lobstering, when it is in season, and for various potentially conflicting technologies used to obtain cod and halibut.

Basically, the Port Lameron fishers have divided their territory on pragmatic grounds: which microenvironments are best suited for which technologies at particular seasons of the year. These use patterns "reflect practical and informal resource management strategies developed by a community of fishermen through years of experience" (A. Davis 1984, p. 145). Not all technologies are mutually compatible in this environment. Four of the captains of offshore boats, for example, purchased offshore groundfish gill nets in 1975 when substantial federal subsidies were offered for such purposes. Their use, however, substantially interfered with the operations of the other inshore and offshore boats. As a result of the intraharbor opposition to the use of those gill nets, all four captains had disposed of that gear by 1980.[29] The division of the territory into zones to be used by fishers using particular technologies not only reduces the externalities that the use of one technology may impose on others but also constitutes a low-cost system for apportioning a reasonable yield to all participants. The cost of monitoring an apportioning scheme based on an easily observable factor – what technology a boat is using – is much lower than the cost for one based on the quantity of fish harvested.

The claim of Port Lameron fishers to the use of their fishing grounds is based on tenure: For generations, they and their families have fished and jointly managed this resource. As expressed by a local fisher,

I've fished here all my life. So did my father and his father. Men in my family have been fishin' here for a long time. If anyone's got a right to fish here it's me and I'm no different than most of the fellas fish'n here.        (A. Davis 1984, p. 145)

174

## Analyzing institutional failures and fragilities

They see themselves as having exclusive rights to their lobster territory, which can yield up to 40% of a fisher's yearly income. In addition, they exercise the right of first access (and the right to refuse access in years of scarcity) to the remaining zone. Although some fishing by neighboring fishers is tolerated in good years, the property lines are drawn tight when the fish are scarce. The years of scarcity are, of course, exactly the years when conflict over territory can erupt. Policing their boundaries is something that all fishers do. The burden of enforcement must be borne by the local fishers, as they cannot call on external authorities to enforce their local rules of access. Davis illustrates how this enforcement is done:

For example, a Port Lameron Harbour fisherman, after setting his longline gear, watched a fisherman from a neighboring harbour set his gear close to and, on occasion, across his line. Subsequently, the Port Lameron Harbour fisherman contacted the "transgressor" on the citizen band radio to complain about this behaviour. Other Port Lameron Harbour fishermen who were "listenin' in" on the exchange demonstrated support for their compatriot by adding approving remarks once the original conversation had ended. The weight of this support, coupled with the implied threat of action, i.e., "cutten' off" the offender's gear, compelled the erring fisherman to offer his apologies. (A. Davis 1984, p. 147)

This rule system is fragile because it is not recognized by federal authorities in Canada, particularly the Department of Fisheries and Oceans (DFO). Fishery policies in Canada have undergone substantial changes over the years. At an earlier date, the provinces played a much more important role in the regulation of inshore fisheries. That was particularly the case in Newfoundland, which was not included as part of the confederation until 1949. The regulatory stance taken by Newfoundland authorities was to provide arenas in which conflict between fishers using different territories and different technologies could be resolved. The Newfoundland fisheries regulations basically codified into law the fishing rules devised in local settings (K. Martin 1979).

The federal stance toward local rules has been exactly the opposite. Current Canadian policy gives "little credence to the ability of local customary regulations to adequately police the fishery" (Matthews 1988, p. 6). Federal officials presume that the entire eastern coast is an open-access fishery.[30] They have adopted the dominant policy orientation described in Chapter 1, namely, that there are only two options available: private property rights and government regulation. Ruling out private property leads to an official policy of federal-government regulation:

The federal government . . . carries the jurisdictional responsibility for conserving fisheries resources . . . and for allocating the distribution of these resources among

175

# Governing the commons

competing users. Since the establishment of private-property rights in fishery resources is impracticable in the great majority of cases, the state's responsibility for resource conservation and allocation cannot be delegated.

(Government of Canada 1976, p. 20)

The deep-sea fishery off the eastern coast has long been an open-access fishery, as most offshore fisheries are. The competition from foreign fleets for these productive fishing grounds led to severe stock depletion in many instances prior to 1976, when Canada claimed jurisdiction over a 200-mile extension beyond its coastline under the "Law of the Sea Convention." That extension of Canadian authority enabled Canadian officials to begin to cope with the open-access nature of the far-offshore fisheries. That extension of authority also led Canadian fishery planners to believe that they were then "in a position to 'rationalize' all aspects of the fishing industry including the inshore and processing sectors" (Matthews 1988, p. 8).

Many of the government's initial steps have been related to efforts to license fishing vessels, as well as the fishing activities of different sorts. Given that many full-time and part-time fishers fear that licensing is only the beginning of an effort to reduce the number of fishers in the industry in general, many individuals who were not currently active in fishing obtained commercial fishing licenses so as to ensure that they would already have licenses if limits were later imposed. Further, given the variety of fishing technologies used by Port Lameron fishers, the immediate response of fishers in that community was to obtain licenses for technologies they were not using in case they might need them in the future. Similar practices were undertaken in other regions. Parzival Copes (1983, pp. 16–17) reported that the number of fishers registered in Newfoundland rose from 15,351 in 1974 to 35,080 in 1980, and he estimated that there were only 21,297 persons actually fishing.

The importance of such "defensive" licensing practices was brought home to Port Lameron fishers who had not obtained licenses to set gill nets to obtain herring for their bait. When federal officials then froze the number of licenses available, without prior notice, and threatened sanctions against those found using gill nets illegally, conflict exploded in the community:

Several fishermen reacted angrily when told that they could not obtain a license unless they currently held one and that fisheries officers would confiscate the unlicensed set nets. One man exclaimed that: "If they touch my nets they'll get a surprise!"

(A. Davis 1984, p. 157)

Protest meetings were held along the entire coast, leading federal officials to back off long enough to allow fishers to obtain herring licenses whether or not they intended to sell herring. The entire experience reinforced local feelings that federal officials would tend to act arbitrarily without consultation and devise regulations that were not well tailored to the local circumstance:

What do they know about what we do? Fisheries Officers are only around here now and then. How do they know what's best for us? We've fished here for a long time and we know what's best for our ground. We know what it can take.

(A. Davis 1984, p. 156)

Instead of finding means for strengthening locally evolved rules systems to ensure that access and use patterns would continue to be controlled in those territories where effective rule systems had already been devised to match local environmental and technological systems, Canadian policy has been to develop one standard set of regulations for the entire coast. If future Canadian policies produce still further counterproductive reactions on the part of the fishers, they may fail to gain control of the open-access deep-sea fishery and lose control of some inshore fisheries previously subject to entry control.

It is difficult to tell exactly what the future holds for fisheries like that offshore of Port Lameron Harbour. If national policies were to change, and officials were to try to develop a set of nested rules that would help enforce the local regulations that have been developed over the years, while focusing most of the new regulatory effort on the far-offshore fisheries that are indeed open-access, then this fragile rule system could survive, adapt, and enable fishers to make effective use of this local resource indefinitely into the future.[31] However, if Canadian authorities continue to try to develop a single policy for all fisheries along the entire eastern coast, then eventual deterioration of the locally evolved system seems probable. Further, it is doubtful that any national agency can ever have the extensive time-and-place information needed to tailor a set of rules to the particulars of local situations.

Federal officials in Canada are not the only officials who have presumed an absence of local institutions for regulating CPRs and have taken actions that have either threatened or destroyed existing institutions. Cordell and McKean (1986) describe a form of sea tenure developed by poor, black raft fishers living along the coast of Bahia in Brazil – tenure that is not recognized by national, regional, or local governments in Brazil. Further, the official policy of the Brazilian government is open access, rather than the limited-access system of the raft fishers. Brazilian national fishing codes

177

*Governing the commons*

define all Brazilian territorial waters as public waters *open to any Brazilian boat* registered in a Brazilian port.

Several scholars have documented what occurred when the government of Nepal passed the "Private Forests Nationalization Act" (Arnold and Campbell 1986; Bromley and Chapagain 1984; Chapagain 1984; Messerschmidt 1986). Whereas the law was officially proclaimed to "protect, manage, and conserve the forest for the benefit of the entire country," it actually disrupted previously established communal control over local forests. Messerschmidt (1986, p. 458) reports what happened immediately after the law came into effect:

Nepalese villagers began free riding – systematically overexploiting their forest resources on a large scale. The usual explanations for this free riding are that the villagers felt they had lost control of their forests, and they were distrustful of government control and national resources policy.

In 1978, the government of Nepal reversed its policy and began to encourage the transfer of forest land back to village control, with quite encouraging results in regard to forestation efforts (Arnold and Campbell 1986). Similar stories of disruption of fragile CPR situations, when central-government officials have presumed an absence of local institutions, can be told for many other parts of the world.

LESSONS TO BE LEARNED FROM COMPARING THE CASES
IN THIS STUDY

The purpose of presenting these instances of success, failure, and fragility is to determine what these cases have in common. Now that the cases have been described, I shall use them for two types of analysis. First, I shall compare the extant institutions using the design principles described in Chapter 3: Which of the design principles derived from the robust institutions described in Chapter 3 characterize the other cases? If the cases of institutional failure and fragility are characterized by design principles similar to those of the robust institutions, then perhaps those principles should be rejected as not helping to distinguish among robust, fragile, and failed institutions. Second, I shall analyze the situational and regime characteristics that appear to affect the capacities of individuals to change their institutions (as described in Chapter 4 and, for cases dating from earlier times, in Chapter 3), as well as factors that appear to limit the capacities of individuals to change their own institutions (or prevent external changes being imposed on them), as described in this chapter. The first analysis is

178

the topic of this concluding section. The second analysis is addressed in Chapter 6.

As a first step toward assessing the validity of the proposed design principles, I have arrayed all of the cases discussed in this study in Table 5.2. For each case, I have indicated which of the design principles clearly apply, which apply in a weak form, and which clearly do not apply. The long-enduring cases presented in Chapter 3 obviously are characterized by these principles, because the principles were devised to summarize factors common to these cases. The institutions developed in Raymond Basin, West Basin, and Central Basin to prevent their destruction are also characterized by these design principles. Those institutions have already shown themselves capable of surviving for 30 or 40 years. I am willing to presume they are robust.

These principles also clearly differentiate between the success and failure cases. Turning to the failure cases, none of the principles characterize the two Turkish fisheries (Bay of Izmir and Bodrum), where severe rent-dissipation problems continue unabated. Only one of the principles characterizes the Kirindi Oya irrigation project in Sri Lanka (clear boundaries); two characterized the Mawelle fishery after 1938, when rent dissipation became a severe problem (congruent rules and monitoring); two characterized Raymond, West, and Central basins prior to the institutional changes initiated there (conflict-resolution mechanisms and recognized rights to organize); three characterized the Mojave case (collective-choice arenas, conflict-resolution mechanisms, and recognized rights to organize). Thus, no more than three of the design principles characterized any of the cases in which CPR appropriators were clearly unable to solve the problems they faced.

In this chapter, I characterize the CPR institutions in Port Lameron, Canada, as fragile. I also consider the institutions devised in Alanya, Turkey – though ingenious – to be fragile, as well as those devised for the Gal Oya project in Sri Lanka. Let me explain why. Although the rules devised in Alanya provide an elegant way to solve an assignment problem, they do not address the problem of limiting access to the local fishery. At the current time, the number of fishers desiring to fish in Alanya does not threaten the viability of the fishery. But if more individuals were to want access to the fishery, the problem of rent dissipation that characterized Mawelle could well arise in Alanya. In the past, collective choices were made partly through the facilities of a local co-op and partly through discussions in the local coffeehouse. Without a regular arena for collective choice, it would be difficult for the Alanya fishers to adjust their rules in the future if conditions were to change.

179

Table 5.2. Design principles and institutional performances

| Site | Clear boundaries & memberships | Congruent rules | Collective-choice arenas | Monitoring | Graduated sanctions | Conflict-resolution mechanisms | Recognized rights to organize | Nested units | Institutional performance |
|---|---|---|---|---|---|---|---|---|---|
| Törbel, Switzerland | yes | yes | yes | yes | yes | yes | yes | NR[a] | robust |
| Japanese mountain villages | yes | yes | yes | yes | yes | yes | yes | NR | robust |
| Valencia, Murcia, & Orihuela, Spain | yes | yes | yes | yes | yes | yes | yes | yes | robust |
| Raymond, West, & Central basins (current) | yes | yes | yes | yes | yes | yes | yes | yes | robust |
| Alicante, Spain | yes | yes | yes | yes | yes | yes | yes[b] | yes | robust |
| Bacarra-Vintar, Philippines | yes | yes | yes | yes | yes | yes | yes | yes | robust |
| Alanya, Turkey | no | yes | weak | yes | [c] | weak | weak | NR | fragile |
| Gal Oya, Sri Lanka | yes | yes | yes | yes | yes | weak | weak | yes | fragile |
| Port Lameron, Canada | yes | yes | weak | yes | yes | yes | no | no | fragile |
| Bay of Izmir & Bodrum, Turkey | no | no | no | no | no | no | weak | no | failure |
| Mawelle, Sri Lanka | no | yes | no | yes | yes | no | no | no | failure |
| Kirindi Oya, Sri Lanka | yes | no | no | no | no | no | no | no | failure |
| Raymond, West, & Central basins (earlier) | no | no | no | no | no | yes | yes | no | failure |
| Mojave groundwater basins | no | no | yes | no | no | yes | yes | no | failure |

[a]NR = not relevant.
[b]With two major exceptions, from 1739 to 1840 and 1930 to 1950.
[c]Missing information.

## Analyzing institutional failures and fragilities

In regard to Gal Oya, boundaries and membership have been clearly designated, congruent rules have been devised and monitored, and collective-choice arenas have been set up. Until the rights of farmers are clearly recognized and guaranteed and conflict-resolution mechanisms are in place, however, I am unwilling to assume that these are robust institutions. Given the long history of central control, it would be difficult for farmers in Gal Oya to continue their organized efforts if a major change in the Irrigation Department were to place in office engineers who presumed that local farmers had little to offer. The fragile cases stand as intermediate cases in terms of the design principles. Enough of the principles are in use to enable appropriators to solve some of their immediate CPR problems, but one would be hesitant to predict institutional endurance unless further institutional development occurs and the arrangements come closer to meeting the full set of design principles.

The cases discussed in this volume compose a limited set. Further empirical and theoretical work is needed before one can have a high degree of confidence that this set of design principles is the best way to distinguish among robust, fragile, and failed institutions. Several colleagues and I currently are collecting information on a large set of empirical cases to determine if the pattern of relationships shown on Table 5.2 is replicated. An initial explanation of why these design principles would be associated with robust institutions was presented in Chapter 3. Sufficient support for those initial theoretical speculations is presented in Table 5.2 that further theoretical and empirical analyses appear warranted.

# 6

## A framework for analysis of self-organizing and self-governing CPRs

In Chapter 1, I discussed three models that are used to justify the policy recommendation that external governmental authorities should impose solutions on individuals who jointly use CPRs: Hardin's tragedy of the commons, the prisoner's dilemma game, and Mancur Olson's logic of collective action. All three models lead to the prediction that those using such resources will not cooperate so as to achieve collective benefits. Further, individuals are perceived as being trapped in a static situation, unable to change the rules affecting their incentives.

The cases presented in this study are from a universe of relatively small scale CPRs (the largest involves about 15,000 appropriators), each located within a single country. The appropriators in these cases are heavily dependent on a flow of scarce resource units for economic returns. The cases illustrate that some, but not all, appropriators in these settings solve what are thought to be second-order dilemmas to provide their own institutions. Various institutional arrangements are devised to accomplish these results. Marketable rights to the flow of resource units were developed in Alicante and in three of the California groundwater cases, but the resource systems themselves did not become private property. Forms of public instrumentalities were also used in the California groundwater cases and several other cases, but none of the success cases involved direct regulation by a centralized authority.

Most of the institutional arrangements used in the success stories were rich mixtures of public and private instrumentalities. If this study does nothing more than shatter the convictions of many policy analysts that the *only* way to solve CPR problems is for external authorities to impose full private property rights or centralized regulation, it will have accomplished one major purpose. At the same time, no claim is made that institutional

182

arrangements supplied by appropriators, rather than by external authorities, will achieve optimal solutions. The Mojave case clearly illustrates this point. But the survival, over long periods of time, of the resources described in Chapters 3 and 4, as well as the institutions for governing those resources, is testimony to the achievement of at least a minimal level of "solution."

This study has an additional purpose beyond challenging the presumption that universal institutional panaceas must be imposd by external authorities to solve smaller-scale, but still complex, uncertain, and difficult, problems. The observation that the world is more complex than it is presented in these models is obvious, and not useful by itself. What is needed is further theoretical development that can help identify variables that must be included in any effort to explain and predict when appropriators using smaller-scale CPRs are more likely to self-organize and effectively govern their own CPRs, and when they are more likely to fail. Such theoretical development not only should provide more useful models but also, and more important, should give us a general framework that can help to direct analysts' attention to important variables to be taken into account in empirical and theoretical work.

The models described in Chapter 1 are not wrong. When conditions in the world approximate the conditions assumed in the models, observed behaviors and outcomes can be expected to approximate predicted behaviors and outcomes. When individuals who have high discount rates and little mutual trust act independently, without the capacity to communicate, to enter into binding agreements, and to arrange for monitoring and enforcing mechanisms, they are not likely to choose jointly beneficial strategies unless such strategies happen to be their dominant strategies. The collapse of the Pacific sardine fishery (McHugh 1972) and the collapse of the Antarctic blue whale fishery (Clark 1977) are tragic testimony to the capacity of these models to predict outcomes in empirical situations approximating the theoretical conditions.

Instead of being wrong, these are special models that utilize extreme assumptions rather than general theories. These models can successfully predict strategies and outcomes in fixed situations approximating the initial conditions of the models, but they cannot predict outcomes outside that range. They are useful for predicting behavior in large-scale CPRs in which no one communicates, everyone acts independently, no attention is paid to the effects of one's actions, and the costs of trying to change the structure of the situation are high. They are far less useful for characterizing the behavior of appropriators in the smaller-scale CPRs that are the focus of this inquiry. In such situations, individuals repeatedly communi-

183

Governing the commons

cate and interact with one another in a localized physical setting. Thus, it is possible that they can learn whom to trust, what effects their actions will have on each other and on the CPR, and how to organize themselves to gain benefits and avoid harm. When individuals have lived in such situations for a substantial time and have developed shared norms and patterns of reciprocity, they possess social capital with which they can build institutional arrangements for resolving CPR dilemmas.

When models that assume no communication and no capacity to change the rules are applied to the smaller-scale CPRs, they are applied out of their range. Applying models out of range can produce more harm than good. Public policies based on the notion that all CPR appropriators are helpless and must have rules imposed on them can destroy institutional capital that has been accumulated during years of experience in particular locations, as illustrated by the Nova Scotian fishery cases.

That models are used metaphorically in applications to a wide diversity of situations, rather than to a limited set of conditions, should not be blamed entirely on policy analysts and public officials. Fads and fashions sweep through academia as well as elsewhere. Among many academics there are strong preferences for tight analytical models that will yield clear predictions. To make a model tractable, theorists must make simplifying assumptions. Many of these assumptions are equivalent to setting a parameter (e.g., the amount of information available to participants, or the extent of communication) equal to a constant (e.g., complete information, or no communication). Because the resulting model appears to be relatively simple, with only a few "moving parts," it may be considered by some to be general, rather than the special model that it is. Apparent simplicity and generality are not, however, equivalent. Setting a variable equal to a constant usually narrows, rather than broadens, the range of applicability of a model.

Further, policies based on models that represent the structures of situations as unchanging or exogenously fixed, even if repeated, lead to policy recommendations that someone external to the situation must change the structure. The analyst attempting to make a clear prediction about equilibria must hold some variables constant (and thus exogenous) while exploring the effects of a limited number of endogenous variables conceived to be under the control of those in the situation. These models demonstrate what individuals will do when they are in a situation that they cannot change. We do not learn from these models what individuals will do when they have autonomy to craft their own institutions and can affect each other's norms and perceived benefits. Nor do we learn how the capacity of innovators to develop institutions that can lead them toward better, rather than worse, outcomes for themselves and for others might be enhanced or inhibited by the structures of the institutional arrangements of the surrounding political regime. It would, of course, be possible to develop models to describe how individuals can change the structure of the situation they face over time, but current policy analyses are based on the static models discussed in Chapter 1.

Analyzing the in-depth case studies can deepen one's appreciation of human artisanship in shaping and reshaping the very situations within which individuals must make decisions and bear the consequences of actions taken on a day-to-day basis. The appropriators in Alanya, Törbel, the Japanese mountain villages, Valencia, Ilocos Norte, the California groundwater basins, and even Mawelle all transformed the structures they faced, moving from a structure in which a set of unorganized individuals made independent decisions about using a CPR that yielded scarce resource units to a structure in which a set of organized individuals made decisions in a sequential, contingent, or frequency-dependent manner. The Sri Lankan farmers living on the large settlements were not able to transform the structure of incentives that they faced until external agents initiated small-scale changes that eventually were used as the foundation for major institutional changes. The fishers of Bodrum and the Bay of Izmir continue to experieince rent dissipation and appear unable to change the structure of the situation they face. The desert dwellers of Mojave may mine their underground basin dry, even though they tried to solve appropriation and provision problems by devising new, but inappropriate, institutions.

## THE PROBLEMS OF SUPPLY, CREDIBLE COMMITMENT, AND MUTUAL MONITORING

Why is it that some appropriators can supply themselves with new rules, gain quasi-voluntary compliance with those rules, and monitor each other's conformance to the rules, whereas others cannot? As discussed in Chapter 2, institutional supply, credible commitment, and mutual monitoring are not easily explained using current institutional theories. In Chapter 3, I offered an initial explanation for credible commitments and mutual monitoring in which CPR rules conform to a set of design principles. The explanation also draws heavily on the assumptions made in Chapter 2 about fallible, norm-adopting individuals who pursue contingent strategies in complex and uncertain environments. Such individuals can be expected to make contingent commitments to follow rules that

- define a set of appropriators who are authorized to use a CPR (design principle 1),

185

- relate to the specific attributes of the CPR and the community of appropriators using the CPR (design principle 2),
- are designed, at least in part, by local appropriators (design principle 3),
- are monitored by individuals accountable to local appropriators (design principle 4), and
- are sanctioned using graduated punishments (design principle 5).

When individuals are presented with rules meeting these criteria, a safe, advantageous, and credible commitment can be made. The commitment is to follow the rules so long as (1) most similarly situated individuals adopt the same commitment and (2) the long-term expected net benefits to be achieved by this strategy are greater than the long-term expected net benefits for individuals following short-term, dominant strategies.

This is an advantageous strategy, because if most individuals follow it, they will be better off than they would be following short-term, dominant strategies. It is safe in that individuals following it cannot be exploited for long by others who break their commitments. If more than a minimal level of rule-breaking occurs, any individual following this contingent strategy can adjust his or her rate of rule conformance downward until the rule-following behavior of others returns to an acceptable level. An announced self-commitment to follow such a strategy – "I will if you will" – is credible when there is monitoring, because each person knows that unprovoked deviations are likely to be discovered. When an individual's rule infractions are discovered, the probability increases that others will reduce their rates of rule conformance to the detriment of that individual.

Because sanctions are graduated, individuals who commit themselves to a contingent strategy also know that if an emergency were to occur, in which following the rules would be disastrous, an occasional deviation would be subjected to only a small fine or other punishment. Similarly, an individual who makes an occasional error will face moderate sanctions. The imposition of some sanctions reassures the rule-breaker that deviations by others are also likely to be discovered. The way in which rules are enforced is forgiving of occasional lapses or errors and allows appropriators to avoid the high costs that can result from rigid application of uniform rules in a changing and uncertain environment. Continued rule infractions, however, will lead to an increase in the severity of sanctions.

If occasional rule infractions are not discovered, the rule-breaker is even better off in the short run. However, if one were to break the rules several times without discovery, one might revise one's estimate of the efficacy of the current monitoring system in deterring others from similar infractions. That would lead an occasional rule-breaker to adopt a higher rate of rule-breaking behavior. Obviously, as undetected rule infractions become more frequent and CPR conditions become worse, the higher will be the probability that other individuals will increase their rates of rule-breaking behavior. Unless monitoring efforts are increased to reverse this trend, rule compliance will cascade downward. Thus, monitoring and graduated sanctions are necessary to keep the rate of rule-following high enough to avoid triggering a process in which higher rates of rule infractions fuel subsequent increases in rates of rule infractions.

Making a contingent rule-following commitment requires that individuals obtain information about the rates of rule conformance adopted by others. Otherwise, an individual cannot wisely pursue this contingent strategy. One way to obtain this information is to serve as a monitor from time to time. When the rules in use conform to the design principles discussed in Chapter 3 (enabling individuals to design rules that will keep monitoring costs low) and individuals adopt contingent strategies, individuals are also motivated to monitor each other to obtain the information they need to pursue this contingent strategy. Similarly, if individuals begin monitoring others and learn that others comply most of the time with a set of rules, they are more likely to be willing to adopt and/or continue contingent strategies.

Adopting contingent strategies enhances the likelihood of monitoring. Monitoring enhances the probability of adopting contingent strategies. Adding the capacity to use graduated sanctions initially for their informational value and eventually for their deterrence value, one can begin to understand how a complex configuration of rules used by strategic individuals helps to solve both the problems of commitment and the problems of mutual monitoring. The weight of the explanation does not fall on a single variable. Where individuals follow rules and engage in mutual monitoring, reinforcing institutional arrangements and individual strategies bolster one another so as to maintain enduring patterns of consistent, but not perfect, rule-following behavior.

What remains unexplained is how some appropriators overcome, and others do not overcome, the problems associated with collective provision of delicately calibrated institutions that create situations in which individuals find it advantageous, credible, and safe to pursue contingent commitments to rule compliance and mutual monitoring. Initial aspects of an explanation for institutional supply were presented at the end of Chapter 4, where the incremental, sequential, and self-transforming nature of institutional supply was analyzed in the context of a facilitative political regime. Most of the failure cases presented in Chapter 5 showed a different picture in which individuals were unable, because of internal and external variables, to overcome the problems of collective provision of new rules.

Recent efforts to modify the theory of collective action to explain the achievement of collective benefits by individuals acting independently have focused almost entirely on variables that are internal to the situation. One or more of the following variables are consistently shown to influence outcomes:

1 the total number of decision makers,
2 the number of participants minimally necessary to achieve the collective benefit,
3 the discount rate in use,
4 similarities of interests, and
5 the presence of participants with substantial leadership or other assets.

These same variables are relevant to an explanation of the supply of institutions, because this is clearly a problem of collective action. Several of the cases can be explained using this set of variables alone. In Alanya, a relatively small number of fishers (100) who planned to live and fish in Alanya for many years (low discount rate) and who had very similar interests (all used the same technology) were able to organize and devise new rules, even though no one had substantial assets. In Bodrum and the Bay of Izmir, larger numbers of fishers (400 and 1,700), some of whom lived locally and some of whom came from some distance to fish there (disparate discount rates), and who had dissimilar interests (many different types of technologies in use, and four to six subgroups in each), were not able to organize and devise new rules, even though some of them had substantial assets.

But several anomalies exist.[1] The numbers of appropriators in two of the successful groundwater basins were quite large (700 and 750), the disparity of interests was substantial, and discount rates were relatively high, given all of the alternative opportunities available to entrepreneurs. The numbers of irrigators in the Spanish *huertas* were even larger (2,400, 4,800, 13,300, and 13,500), and the systems were large enough that upstream and downstream differences were substantial. Although the number of major groundwater producers who together could have made a substantial difference in groundwater conditions was less than the total number of pumpers, a similar relationship did not hold in the Spanish *huertas*. At the other extreme, the number of fishers in Mawelle was just over 200, and all had similar interests and low discount rates. Neither leadership nor the type of production function helps to account for the differences in results.

The most frequently used theories of collective action are too sparse and too difficult to interpret to be fully satisfactory as foundations for effective policy analysis of institutional change. By "too sparse," I mean that key internal and external variables needed to explain self-organization are missing from the consideration. By "difficult to interpret," I mean that the theories do not yield clear implications for recommending public policies. What policy implications should one draw, for example, from knowing that the size of a group increases the difficulty of organizing collective action? Should one simply presume that small groups will take care of themselves, and that external authorities will have to govern and manage the CPRs used by larger groups? The anomalous cases illustrate that this is an inappropriate implication.

Let us take another look at the larger CPRs (within the universe of cases considered) and how those that have succeeded in solving problems of collective action have done so. All of these are characterized by design principle 8: the use of nested enterprises. The larger organizational units in these systems are built on previously organized smaller units. In the Spanish *huertas*, the fundamental organizational unit is the tertiary canal. The cost of organizing a group of farmers living near to one another and appropriating directly from the same canal is considerably less than the cost of organizing a large group of farmers many of whom never come into direct contact with one another. But once the smaller units are organized, the marginal cost of building on that organizational base is substantially less than the cost of starting with no prior base. Several of the Spanish *huertas* are three or four layers deep.

In the Philippine federation of *zanjeras*, the smallest unit is a work team of 5 to 10 members. Each of the individual *zanjeras*, comprising 20 to 75 members, is organized independently. Only after these units were in place did they federate into a larger unit. In the very large agricultural settlements in Sri Lanka, efforts to organize the farmers failed until the ARTI/Cornell team started to organize small, face-to-face groups of farmers to solve small problems that could be tackled effectively through ad hoc cooperation. Only after those first efforts to organize small, ad hoc groups of neighboring farmers were successful did they move to establish formal organizations of the farmers sharing field canals. Eventually the system that evolved in Gal Oya was four layers deep.

In the Raymond, West, and Central basins, the first step was the creation of a small, voluntary private association that enabled producers to obtain and disseminate accurate information about the condition of their resource. From there, several further enterprises were established, each built on the substructure that had already been created. Pumpers were able to call on public facilities – courts, a state department of natural resources, legislatures, special elections – to obtain information and to engage in constitutional decision making that would be considered legitimate and enforceable. In Mojave, by contrast, the approach was to organize a very large unit and attempt to assign, all at one time, water rights for 15 different basins and an underground river system.

Success in starting small-scale initial institutions enables a group of individuals to build on the social capital thus created to solve larger problems with larger and more complex institutional arrangements. Current theories of collective action do not stress the process of accretion of institutional capital. Thus, one problem in using them as foundations for policy analysis is that they do not focus on the incremental self-transformations that frequently are involved in the process of supplying institutions. Learning is an incremental, self-transforming process.

If we now look at the smaller systems in which appropriators were not able to organize, we learn a second lesson. In Mawelle, a small group of 200 was not able to enforce its own prior rules basing entry to the CPR on family membership, nor was it able to induce government officials to enforce the national rule excluding new entrants. A small group of appropriators was able to influence national officials to prevent formal rules from being enforced. How the activities and policies of external political regimes can affect the level and type of self-organization to achieve collective benefits is not one of the five variables (see the foregoing list) included in current theoretical explanations of collective action. In Newfoundland, small groups of local fishers had been able to devise and maintain their own rules, but those CPR institutions were rendered frail when national authorities refused to recognize their existence.

On the basis of the case studies, I would argue that the activities of external political regimes were positive factors in helping most of the groundwater producers in southern California to self-organize, but such activities were negative factors in preventing continued self-organization in Mawelle and threatening it in Newfoundland. A theory of self-organization and self-governance of smaller units within larger political systems must overtly take the activities of surrounding political systems into account in explaining behavior and outcomes. To distinguish between the successful and unsuccessful instances of self-organization to solve CPR problems, one must take account of how the strategies of external actors affect the costs and benefits of CPR appropriators.

A third problem with current theories relates to the way that information and transactions costs are assumed away. To assume that complete information is freely available and that transactions costs can be ignored does not generate theoretical explanations that can be used in a setting where information is scant, potentially biased, and expensive to obtain and where most transactions are costly.[2] Why individuals monitor each other's rule conformance would be difficult to explain using the assumption of complete information.

To summarize the foregoing discussion, there are three problems with the current theories of collective action that reduce their usefulness for providing a foundation for policy analysis of institutional change in smaller-scale CPRs. Current theories do not take into account

1 the need to reflect the incremental, self-transforming nature of institutional change,
2 the importance of the characteristics of external political regimes in an analysis of how internal variables affect levels of collective provision of rules, and
3 the need to include information and transaction costs.

Having recognized these problems, we can next ask how to start bridging the gap between current theories of collective action and empirical instances of collective action in CPR situations so as to move toward the development of more relevant theories of institutional change for policy analysis.

What is needed in the development of useful theory for the analysis of CPR situations – as well as many other important policy questions – is a somewhat different orientation toward the theoretical endeavor related to policy analysis. Clear analytical models provide an important part of the theoretical foundation for good policy analysis, but not the entire foundation. To get clear results from a model, some variables are omitted or consciously or unconsciously held constant. Models suggest to the analyst likely behaviors and outcomes in a situation with a *particular* structure. They do not tell the analyst how to discover the structure of the situation in order to conduct an analysis. Models that use assumptions such as complete information, independent action, perfect symmetry, no human errors, no norms of acceptable behavior, zero monitoring and enforcement costs, and no capacity to change the structure of the situation itself help the analyst derive precise predictions.

Models that make such assumptions do not, however, direct the attention of the policy analyst to some of the problematic variables of the situation that affect the incentives and behaviors of individuals. Assuming complete information about participant behavior does not push the analyst to examine how individuals in field settings obtain information, who has what information, and whether or not information is biased. Assuming independent action does not push the analyst to ask if individuals take into account the effects of their actions on the choices made by others. Assum-

191

Governing the commons

ing zero-cost monitoring does not push the analyst to examine cost and effectiveness for various monitoring rules. Assuming fixed structure does not push the analyst to examine whether or not and how individuals change their own rules and how the surrounding political regime enhances or inhibits institutional change.

Frameworks that relate whole families of models together also provide an important part of the theoretical foundation for policy analysis, because they point to the set of variables and the types of relationships among variables that need to be examined in conducting *any* theoretical or empirical study of a particular type of phenomenon. From a framework, one does not derive a precise prediction. From a framework, one derives the questions that need to be asked to clarify the structure of a situation and the incentives facing individuals. Once the incentives are clarified, the theorist can analyze a situation and predict likely behavior in terms of choice of strategy and the consequences that are likely to result.

Consequently, instead of building a specific model of institutional supply, I shall develop a framework to summarize the lessons to be learned from examining successful and unsuccessful efforts by CPR appropriators to change their institutions. The framework identifies sets of variables that are most likely to affect decisions about continuing or changing rules. The framework can be used by theorists to develop more precise theories, and models of theories, of institutional choice. It can also be used to organize further empirical research to generate findings about the relative importance of particular variables in the context of other configurations of variables.

A FRAMEWORK FOR ANALYZING INSTITUTIONAL
CHOICE

Institutional-choice situations, both constitutional-choice and collective-choice situations, as defined in Chapter 2, affect the rules used in operational situations. Decisions made in collective-choice situations *directly* affect operational situations. Decisions made in constitutional-choice situations *indirectly* affect operational situations by creating and limiting the powers that can be exercised within collective-choice arrangements (creating legislative and judicial bodies, protecting rights of free speech and property, etc.) and by affecting the decision regarding who is represented and with what weight in collective-choice decisions. Rather than examining constitutional-choice and collective-choice processes separately, I refer to both when I use the term "institutional-choice situation."

To analyze an institutional-choice situation, one needs to view it from

192

the perspective of the individuals making choices about future operational rules. Individuals who make institutional choices also make operational choices. When individuals face the question whether to retain or change status quo rules, the situation changes, but the individuals remain the same. Thus, one should use a similar conception of the individual when thinking about operational and institutional choices. In Chapter 2, I use a general conception of rational action involving four internal variables – expected benefits, expected costs, internalized norms, and discount rates – that affect individual choices of strategies in any situation. Individuals are perceived as weighing expected benefits and costs in making decisions as these are affected by internal norms and discount rates. Using this concept of rational action, one predicts that individuals will select strategies whose expected benefits will exceed expected costs. Without knowledge of the situational variables that affect benefits and costs, such a prediction is vacuous. This general conception of rational action places most of the explanatory weight on situational variables, rather than on assumptions made about the internal calculation process.[3]

In an institutional-choice situation, as shown in Figure 6.1, the basic alternatives available to an individual are (1) to support the continuance of the status quo rules or (2) to support a change in one or more of the status quo rules. Although more than one alternative may be considered at a time, the ultimate decision is between an alternative set of rules and the status

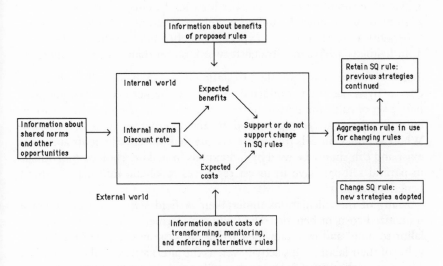

Figure 6.1. Summary of variables affecting institutional choice.

193

quo set of rules.[4] The strategies available to an individual are "to support" rather than "to choose" because no single individual makes institutional choices in other than totally monocratic systems. Whether or not a change in rules will be accomplished will depend on the level of support for the change and the aggregation rule used in the institutional-choice situation.

How an individual evaluates expected benefits in an institutional-choice situation depends on the information available to the individual concerning the benefits (or harm) likely to flow from an alternative set of rules as compared with the benefits (or harm) likely to flow from continued use of status quo rules.[5] How an individual evaluates expected costs depends on the information available to the individual concerning (1) the up-front costs involved in transforming status quo rules to an alternative set and (2) the net costs of monitoring and enforcement involved if one changes to an alternative rule configuration. Similarly, internal norms and discount rates are affected by the information that individuals have concerning the norms shared by other relevant individuals and concerning the range of opportunities that may or may not be available to them outside a particular situation. Data concerning *benefits, costs, shared norms,* and *opportunities* are *summary variables* that affect an individual's decision to support or not support a change in the status quo rules.

If the following three conditions are met, the institutional analyst need only ascertain the values of the summary variables to predict individual strategies:

1 Accurate summary measures exist for each summary variable.
2 Individuals completely and accurately translate information about net benefits and net costs into expected benefits and expected costs.
3 Individuals behave in a straightforward, rather than a strategic, manner.

The first condition is equivalent to stating that a valid and reliable benefit–cost analysis has been conducted to identify the net benefits of an alternative set of rules and that all of the net costs of transforming, monitoring, enforcing, and governing related to the alternative rules are known. Whereas policy models frequently assume that objective benefits and costs exist and can simply be used by individuals in making choices, individuals in natural settings have to invest resources to obtain information about benefits and costs.

Many of the calculations undertaken in field settings do not involve monetized costs or benefits. The Philippine farmers who invest their own labor to build and maintain their irrigation systems are able to judge the value of their labor in this activity versus the alternatives available to them. The costs of devoting 50 days to the *zanjera* are poignantly apparent to any

194

farmer trying to support a family. Further, it is also quite apparent how his agricultural yield responds to communal irrigation. The amount of labor contributed by each farmer is recorded in an attendance book kept by the *zanjera* secretary, but because they are not paid for this labor, it is not recorded elsewhere. Nor is the food produced for consumption recorded in market transactions. Individuals who are closely involved in such situations can make accurate judgments about the costs and benefits of alternative rules systems, taking into account a variety of monetized and nonmonetized benefits and costs. Individuals located in an administrative center will find it far more difficult to make good judgments about relative benefits and costs of alternative rules, because many of these costs and benefits are not recorded and summarized in the information available to those external to the situation.

The second condition is equivalent to stating that individuals are attentive to all available information and know how to weight that information in an unbiased manner. If both the first and second conditions were met, subjective benefits and costs would closely approximate objective benefits and costs. The third condition is equivalent to stating that individuals do not behave opportunistically in order to try to obtain benefits greater than those obtainable through straightforward behavior. This condition implies that individuals reveal their evaluations honestly, contribute to collective benefits whenever formulas exist for equitably assigning costs, and are willing to invest time and resources in finding solutions to joint problems. If this condition were met, some of the strategic behavior posited to occur in all social dilemmas would disappear.

Unfortunately for the analyst, few field settings are characterized by these three conditions, or even one or two of them. Variables such as the benefits of using an alternative set of rules or the costs of monitoring and enforcing a set of rules are rarely recorded in a form that an analyst (or the individuals making institutional choices) can resolve by simple computation. Consequently, one must go beyond the *summary variables* in analyses intended to be used in policy settings to the *situational variables* that affect them.

### Evaluating benefits

Let me illustrate this process by discussing the situational variables that affect the summary variable "information about net benefits of alternative rules." For a participant or an analyst to develop a measure of the net benefits of an alternative set of rules, questions such as the following need answers:

1 What are the predicted average flows and the predicted values of re-source units in the future under a proposed set of rules, as compared with the status quo rules?
2 How variable is the flow of resource units expected to be under a proposed set of rules, as compared with the status quo rules?
3 What quality differences will occur under a proposed set of rules, as compared with the status quo rules?
4 How long is the resource itself likely to generate resource units under a proposed set of rules, as compared with the status quo rules?
5 Will conflict be reduced, stay the same, or increase under a proposed set of rules, as compared with the status quo rules?

The ease or difficulty of answering these questions, as well as the specific answers to be obtained, will depend on a number of situational variables, including (1) the number of appropriators, (2) the size of the resource system, (3) the variability of resource units over time and space, (4) the current condition of the resource system, (5) market conditions, (6) the amount and type of conflict that has existed in the past, (7) the availability of recorded data on current conditions and historical appropriation patterns, (8) the particular status quo rules, and (9) the particular proposed rules (Figure 6.2). The first variable in this list – the number of appropriators – is included in most theories of collective action. The remaining situational variables are rarely considered.[6]

The larger the resource system and/or the number of appropriators, and the more unpredictable the flow of resource units and the market prices for these units, the more difficult and costly it is for anyone to obtain accurate information about the condition of the resource itself and the likely value of the flow of resource units under any set of rules. This can be offset, to some extent, if data on resource conditions, resource-unit quality, prices, and appropriation levels are recorded regularly. Prices and appropriation levels may be recorded for an inshore fishery, for example, if fishers bring all the fish they have caught to a single port to be sold. If fish are purchased by one or a few buyers, records of fish landings may be kept, and the purchaser may have a good picture of the harvesting patterns in these grounds. If the purchaser is motivated to share this information with the fishers, such as when the fishers create a marketing cooperative, the fishers may also gain accurate information about their prior catches and variations in the value of the catch over time. But if the purchaser is a monopolist, who has strategic reasons for withholding information, the purchaser may know much more than the fishers know about overall harvesting patterns.

The establishment of an official monitor (such as the watermaster in the

196

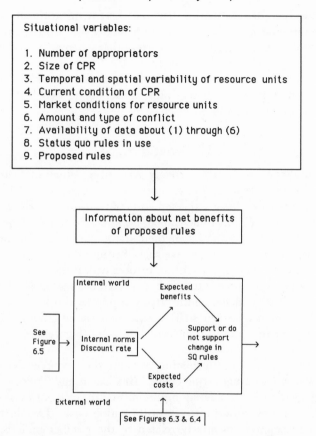

Situational variables:

1. Number of appropriators
2. Size of CPR
3. Temporal and spatial variability of resource units
4. Current condition of CPR
5. Market conditions for resource units
6. Amount and type of conflict
7. Availability of data about (1) through (6)
8. Status quo rules in use
9. Proposed rules

Information about net benefits
of proposed rules

Internal world

Expected benefits

See Figure 6.5

Internal norms
Discount rate

Support or do not support change in SQ rules

Expected costs

External world

See Figures 6.3 & 6.4

Figure 6.2. Situational variables affecting judgment about the benefits of an institutional choice.

groundwater cases and the local officials in the Swiss and Japanese mountain commons) provides information to appropriators that they would not otherwise obtain, information about appropriation levels and the condition of the resource system itself. The presence of appropriator organizations, such as cooperatives or voluntary associations, usually will increase the amount of information obtained and disseminated among appropriators concerning the variables that will affect whether or not a change in rules will produce a net benefit.

Thus, whether or not an individual perceives any benefits to be derived from a change in rules will depend on (1) the objective conditions of the

197

## Governing the commons

CPR, (2) the type of information that the current institutional arrangements generate and make available to individuals, and (3) the rules proposed as alternatives. It should now be clear that whether or not benefits can be obtained by changing rules is not a "fact" that simply exists in the world to be used by anyone – appropriators, analysts, or public officials – who wants to improve welfare. Information about benefits must be searched for, organized, and analyzed.

### Evaluating costs

Information about costs is also strongly affected by situational variables. Two major costs affect institutional choice. First are the up-front costs of transforming the rules. If the expected costs of transforming the rules are higher than the net benefits to be gained, no further cost calculations will be made. Appropriators will retain their status quo rules that produce fewer benefits than would alternative rules, because the costs of changing the rules are higher than the benefits to be obtained. If the ex ante costs of transforming the rules are not too high, expected changes in ex post costs will also be evaluated, including the effects of proposed rules on monitoring and enforcement costs. We shall first examine the situational variables that affect information about transformation costs (Figure 6.3).

*Transformation costs.* Transformation costs are the resources devoted to the process of considering a rule change (Buchanan and Tullock 1962). Many of the variables considered important in current theories of collective action, as listed earlier, affect transformation costs. Transformation costs are, for example, positively related to the number of individuals making institutional choices, the heterogeneity of interests at stake, and the proportion of individuals minimally necessary to achieve a change in status quo rules (set by the rules that govern the process of changing the rules). Transformation costs are lower when skillful leaders are involved. Because transformation costs are up-front costs, they are less likely to be affected by the discount rates used by participants. The sum of transformation costs is not affected by the presence of individuals who have substantial assets at stake, but the likelihood that these costs will be paid is positively related to the presence of individuals who will derive substantial benefits from a change in rules.[7]

Several variables affecting transformation costs are not included in the list cited earlier, however. The type of proposed rule, for example, affects transformation costs. The transformation costs of setting up a strictly private association of appropriators to discuss common problems are con-

## A framework for analysis of CPRs

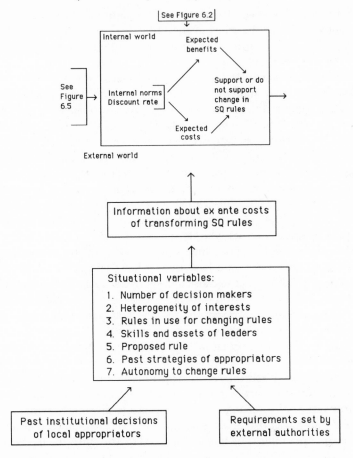

Figure 6.3. Situational variables affecting judgement about the costs of transforming status-quo rules.

siderably less than the transformation costs of creating a local public jurisdiction that can impose taxes on all citizens living in its boundaries. Rules are normally changed sequentially. Proposed rules with positive expected benefits and low transformation costs are likely to be adopted before rules with high transformation costs. If appropriators start with low-cost changes, they can gain experience concerning the costs of changing the rules in their setting before attempting changes that will require substantial transformation costs. If the transformation costs for changing some rules are low enough, one or two individuals may receive sufficiently

199

high benefits from the change to pay the entire costs themselves. Consequently, some of the steps in the process of institutional development may not be second-order dilemmas, even though others may have this structure. Further, achieving the benefits of small rule changes will transform the calculus involved in evaluating larger changes.

The norms that individuals share concerning appropriate strategies when engaging in collective choice will affect transformation costs directly and indirectly. When individuals adopt confrontational strategies, for example, transformation costs rise sharply (Scharpf 1989). When some individuals fear that others will attempt to organize minimal winning coalitions to impose costs on losers, that will affect their willingness to adopt changes that would reduce the inclusiveness of the rules to be used in the future. Thus, appropriators who share norms that restrain opportunistic behavior can adopt rules that are less costly to operate than are the rules adopted by appropriators who do not share such norms.

The rules instituted at one time will also affect the transformation costs (or costs of governing) at a later time. Changes in operational rules will affect benefit levels and their distribution to appropriators. Major changes in the level and distribution of benefits can increase or decrease the level of conflict among appropriators and the consequent difficulty that individuals will have in achieving future agreements.[8]

Whether or not appropriators have substantial autonomy to change their own rules will also affect the costs of transformation. Highly centralized regimes attempt to rely on the same operational rules in all locations within their territory.[9] If that is the case, local appropriators must convince a central authority to change the rules in use in all similar settings or convince the authority that an exception can be made in their case. In an honest regime, considerable time must be devoted to any effort to change rules set by central authorities. Time is spent in bureaucratic offices explaining the problem and what is wanted and consulting with others who will be affected by a change, in order to forestall their opposition. Time is spent waiting for an answer. If the request is turned down, time may be spent in appeal processes. In a corrupt regime, bribes may be sufficient to get officials to authorize a rule change or to ignore the fact that local appropriators are using a set of internal rules different from those legally required.[10] Also, in a corrupt regime, an influential person may be able to prevent a rule change by bribing an official.

In a regime that allows substantial local autonomy to engage in constitutional and collective choices, appropriators may be authorized to select their own rules so long as they follow certain procedures. The required procedures may vary from informal mechanisms that will ensure consultation to formal mechanisms including signed petitions, special elections, legislation, and court proceedings. The aggregation rule to be used frequently is specified in these procedures. The more inclusive the aggregation rule that must be used in making constitutional- or collective-choice decisions, the higher the costs of decision making, and the lower the losses that will be suffered by those protected by status quo rules (Buchanan and Tullock 1962).

Where regular procedures exist for transforming rules, appropriators may be able to estimate transformation costs precisely. If a charter of association is required before setting up private associations or cooperatives, a lawyer can provide a close estimate of the cost of drafting such a charter. If calling a special election to create a district requires 1,000 signatures on a petition, experienced organizers can provide a relatively good estimate of the cost that will be involved in obtaining those signatures.

Where appropriators face officials who have considerable discretion whether or not to allow them to change the rules, estimating transformation costs may be difficult. If such permission has required substantial legal or illegal payments in the past, appropriators may not attempt to change the rules for fear that the costs will be far greater than the benefits to be obtained. One would thus expect less rule innovation and change by appropriators living under political regimes that give regional and national officials considerable discretion whether or not to authorize changes in the rules governing access and use of a CPR, as compared with a jurisdiction in which more autonomy is allowed.

The autonomy of individuals to change their rules will be affected by the location of their CPR and the effectiveness of the political regime under which they live. Autonomy may not be formally extended, but may result primarily because of the distance between a CPR and the nearest administrative or political officials. Appropriators living in remote CPRs usually have more autonomy than those located near governance centers. Whether or not a particular CPR is remote obviously is also affected by the number of officials the political regime employs, the effectiveness of the administrative and political apparatus of the political regime, and the extent of the communication and transportation facilities involved.

The situational variables that affect information about transformation costs are themselves affected by the institutional requirements set by external authorities and the past institutional decisions made by local appropriators. The autonomy of a set of local appropriators to make their own rules is, of course, strongly dependent on what is allowed or forbidden by central authorities, modified by distance and the capacity of the external

*Governing the commons*

authorities to enforce their rules. The rules that govern the process of changing the rules, the number of decision makers who must be involved, and the resultant heterogeneity of represented interests are affected by the past decisions made by external authorities or local appropriators or both.

Once decisions of a particular type have been made, future options will be strongly affected. To understand institutional-choice processes, one must view them as historical processes whereby current decisions are built on past decisions. Prior decisions may open up some future options for development, and close out others.[11] The groundwater pumpers of Raymond Basin did not necessarily recognize that as soon as they allocated a defined quantity of water to each and every pumper, a market in water rights would emerge, but that is what happened. Similar markets appeared in West Basin and Central Basin. Once a watermaster had been appointed to monitor the usage patterns of all pumpers, the cost of administering a pump tax on withdrawals was substantially less than it would have been if a different type of legal settlement had been adopted. On the other hand, once water rights were assigned on a proportional basis, any future rules that might have protected the rights of municipal water companies above the rights of others using those basins were precluded from further consideration.

Thus, the past exerts its influence on institutional choices in several ways. Current operational rules – the status quo rules – are the results of past decisions. Status quo operational rules always protect some individuals and expose others. A proposed change in these rules must be supported by a set of individuals large enough to have the authority to change them, given status quo collective-choice or constitutional-choice rules for changing the rules. In almost all procedures used in a given collective-choice or constitutional-choice arena, the status quo rules will have a privileged procedural position. Past institutional choices open up some paths and foreclose others to future development.

*Monitoring and enforcement costs.* When appropriators contemplate changing their rules, part of the calculation has to do with the costs of monitoring and enforcing the new rules. Observing the activities of a diverse set of individuals and assessing whether or not their actions or the outcomes they produce are permitted by a set of rules involves the use of time and other resources that could be devoted to other activities. Monitoring activities frequently are undertaken by the appropriators themselves, either as they go about their normal activities (such as fishers who watch for boats owned by outsiders) or as a special job into which they rotate

202

(such as irrigators, each of whom is responsible for inspecting an irrigation canal for a specified period of time). Maintaining courts, police, and detention facilities to enforce rules also involves the use of resources that could be utilized productively for other purposes.

Monitoring costs are affected by the physical attributes of the resource itself, the technology available for exclusion and appropriation, marketing arrangements, the proposed rules, and the legitimacy bestowed by external authorities on the results of institutional choices (Figure 6.4). The larger the resource, the greater the costs of "fencing" and/or patrolling the boundaries to ensure that no outsider appropriates. For many natural resources, such as fisheries, fencing is physically impossible. Even maintaining effective markers may be costly. Inshore fisheries, particularly those located in lagoons or bays, involve lower exclusion costs than do offshore

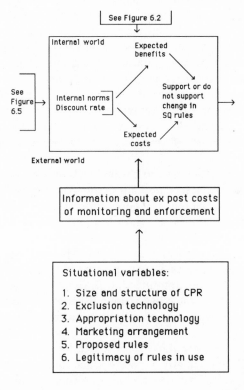

Figure 6.4. Situational variables affecting judgments about monitoring and enforcement costs.

## Governing the commons

fisheries. For resources such as groundwater basins or oil pools, the resource units move underground to the area that is most heavily pumped. Even determining the physical boundaries of such resources requires expensive geologic studies. Once the boundaries are well established, however, the presence of a renegade well may be difficult to disguise. The primary cost of exclusion may then be the legal action required to stop an unauthorized user from continuing to use a resource.

Factors that enhance the capacity of users to see or hear one another as they are engaged in appropriation activities tend to lower monitoring and enforcement costs. Alternatively, if appropriators all return to the same location at the end of their activities, so that the quantity of resource units each has acquired is open for casual inspection, monitoring costs will be low. The presence of a shared norm that rules decided on by the appropriators themselves should be followed will offset many physical disadvantages in monitoring a particular resource. Shared norms related to the legitimacy of the rules and the imperative that they be followed will reduce the costs of monitoring, and their absence will increase those costs. The availability of low-cost facilities for recording and disseminating information about regulated activities will also decrease monitoring costs.

Rules themselves vary in terms of monitoring and enforcement costs. The more frequent the required monitoring, the greater the resources devoted to measurement. Rules that unambiguously state that some action – no matter who undertakes it – is proscribed are less costly to monitor than are rules that require more information about who is pursuing a particular behavior and why.

Rules specifying the opening and closing dates of seasons, such as those used in Swiss and Japanese mountain commons, are far less costly to monitor than are rules that specify a quota for every appropriator in regard to a quantity of appropriation activities (e.g., acre-feet of water pumped, or tons of fish caught). Anyone found appropriating from the resource before or after the official season is unambiguously breaking the rules. Any appropriator can challenge such unauthorized use without fear that the charge will later be declared unfounded. Rules limiting harvesting technology, such as those used in the Nova Scotian fisheries, are also less costly to enforce, as compared with rules specifying a quantity of a resource to be withdrawn.

Rules that bring together those who would be tempted to cheat and those who would be particularly harmed by such cheating are also easier to monitor than are rules that depend on accidental discovery of a rule-breaker by someone who may be only indirectly harmed by the infraction. When irrigators using a canal are assigned particular time slots, as in

Murcia and Orihuela, each is motivated to be sure to receive his full time slot of water and to be sure that the next irrigator does not try to take water too soon. At the time of a switch from one irrigator to the next, both are likely to be present. They ensure by their presence that the rules are being followed. Monitoring the rules devised in the Alanya fishery involves minimal costs, for similar reasons.

Rules that place a limit on the quantity of resource units that can be produced during an entire season or year are more costly to enforce. Whether or not it is economically feasible to use quotas (which may be marketable) will depend on the regularity of the flow, the amount of storage in the CPR, the types of records that can be kept routinely, and the value of the resource units themselves.

In addition to the physical attributes of the resource and the specific rules contemplated, another factor affecting monitoring and enforcement costs is whether or not the authorities of the surrounding jurisdiction recognize the legitimacy of local rules. The Mawelle case documents clearly that when external authorities refuse to enforce a local rule excluding participants, or even their own rule, local appropriators may not be able to keep new entrants out, even though they strongly desire to do so. In some areas of the world, regional or national governments are supportive of locally developed property systems, and local appropriators are able to count on the help of government officials, at relatively low cost, to exclude outside appropriators if the threats of local appropriators are not sufficient.

In those areas where national governments fail to respect the property rights that local appropriators have developed for themselves (such as Nova Scotia and Newfoundland), exclusion costs can become very high (Cordell and McKean 1986; A. Davis, 1984; Matthews and Phyne 1988). In fact, indigenous institutions that have evolved in remote locations may become untenable at later junctures if those areas become attractive to external users who have the backing of a regional or national government. Some national governments have provided considerable economic support for the development of modern fishing fleets that have then successfully invaded inshore fisheries that previously were "owned" by local fishers. Without the advantage of being considered legitimate, a small group of local appropriators can face high costs in trying to exclude well-financed, government-supported users who do not have local property rights.

### Evaluating shared norms and other opportunities

How individuals weight their own assessments of benefits and costs will depend on the norms that they internalize and the discount rates that they

205

utilize. Coleman (1987a) distinguishes between norms that are internalized by individuals, where the sanctioning for nonconformity is an internal cost (e.g., guilt, anxiety, lowered conception of self-worth), and shared norms, where the sanctioning for nonconformity comes from others who are part of the same group and exhibit social displeasure if a norm is broken. Individuals frequently internalize a shared norm, in which case lack of conformity involves both internal psychic and external social costs.

Appropriators who live near the CPR from which they appropriate and who interact with each other in many situations other than the sharing of their CPR are apt to develop strong norms of acceptable behavior and to convey their mutual expectations to one another in many reinforcing encounters (Figure 6.5). The reason for the general hostility of inshore, small-boat fishers toward large-scale trawlers is not simply that the appropriation technology used by the trawlers is so much more powerful than theirs. Often the operators of trawlers live elsewhere, belong to different ethnic or racial groups, and share few of the local norms of behavior. They do not drink in the same bars, their families do not live in the nearby fishing villages, and they are not involved in the network of relationships that depend on the establishment of a reputation for keeping promises and accepting the norms of the local community regarding behavior.

Appropriators who are involved in activities that take them away from their CPR and into an economy in which other opportunities exist are most likely to adopt a high discount rate than are appropriators who presume that they and their children are dependent on the local CPR for major economic returns. It is also the case that shared norms can affect discount rates as much as can information about other opportunities. Individuals

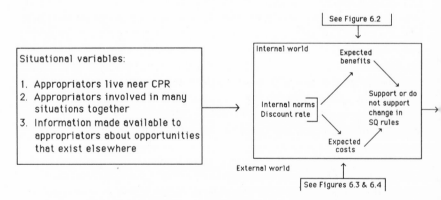

Figure 6.5. Situational variables affecting internal norms and discount rate.

206

living in a community where disregard for the future is censured by others will have a lower discount rate than will individuals living in a community where no opprobrium is attached to seeking short-term gain in preference to long-term benefit.[12]

## The process of institutional change

One can predict that in a highly competitive environment, those who do not search for and select alternative rules that can enhance net benefits will lose out to those who are successful in adopting better rules. It is the operation of firms in competitive, or at least contestable, markets that enables theorists to predict that surviving firms will choose strategies that will maximize profits (Alchian 1950). Theoretical equilibria exist in market models after all of the inefficient or non-profit-maximizing firms have been eliminated. The process of getting to equilibrium is not the focus of these models; rather, they focus on the characteristics of the market and the firms in the market at theoretical equilibrium. That many firms do not maximize profits prior to equilibrium is unimportant when the theoretical question of interest concerns the characteristics of actors who are present at equilibrium. The institutional arrangement of an open market and the theoretical interest in static equilibria enable theorists to posit maximization of a single variable – profits – as an internal decision rule for rational individuals in a market situation. Further, price is a sufficient statistic for summarizing an incredible amount of specific information of value to an entrepreneur. Profit maximization is a useful theoretical tool for predicting behavior in static market situations; it does not enable a theorist to predict which firms are most likely to survive or to predict innovative technological or institutional changes.[13]

CPR situations are rarely as powerful in driving participants – even survivors – toward efficiency as are competitive markets. Nor is there any single variable, such as market price, that can be used as the foundation for making rational choices in a CPR environment. Simply following short-term profit maximization in response to the market price for a resource unit may, in a CPR environment, be exactly the strategy that will destroy the CPR, leaving everyone worse off. Nonmonetized relationships may be of importance. It is thus not a judicious theoretical strategy to presume that choices about rules are made to maximize some single observable variable. The level of uncertainty when selecting new rules is far greater than the level of uncertainty when selecting pricing strategies when demand and supply are fixed. The intended outcomes of using new rules are not automatically achieved. They depend on many future choices to be made by many different individuals as to how they interpret the meaning of the rules and whether or not they will follow the rules, monitor each other, and impose sanctions on nonconformance.[14]

Instead of viewing decisions about changes in rules as mechanical calculation processes, a better theoretical stance is to view institutional choices as processes of making informed judgments about uncertain benefits and costs. It is then possible to draw on the empirically supported theoretical work of social psychologists concerning the processes of human judgment in an effort to characterize the institutional-choice process.[15] All human judgment in uncertain and complex environments is subject to several known biases.

Individuals weight, for example, potential losses more heavily than potential gains (Hardin 1982; Kahneman and Tversky 1979). Consequently, individuals will differentially weight the expected benefits of avoiding future harms more heavily than the benefits of producing future goods. From this, one can derive several general predictions about situational variables that are apt to lead individuals to adopt new rules to protect CPR resources. The propensity of political leaders to discuss CPR problems in terms of "crises" is far more understandable once one takes into account that individuals weight perceived harms more heavily than perceived benefits of the same quantity. Further, one should expect that resource systems that can be rapidly destroyed (such as fish populations that cluster together rather than disperse) are far more difficult to govern by appropriators, or anyone else, than are CPRs that are somewhat more resilient following damage.

One should expect individuals to be willing to adopt new rules that will restrict their appropriation activities when there are clear indicators of resource degradation, generally perceived to be accurate predictors of future harm, or when leaders are able to convince others that a "crisis" is impending. Gilles and Jamtgaard (1981), for example, argue from several empirical studies that whether grazing areas are used to produce milk or wool or meat can affect the ability of the appropriators to learn more rapidly about adverse conditions, should they arise. Milking occurs daily, and variations in yield are rapidly apparent to the herders. Wool is sheared less frequently, but the quality of wool is immediately apparent to those who herd sheep. The quality of meat produced for market is monitored less frequently and may not even be known by herders. Consequently, the quality and timeliness of the information that CPR appropriators obtain about their resource vary according to how a resource unit is used, as well as across resource types. The problems of groundwater pumpers in obtaining accurate and valid information about the condition of their CPR are more daunting than those of herders, regardless of the final products of herding activities.

As compared with uncertain benefits and costs extending over time, up-front transformation costs are easier to calculate and sometimes are substantial. All appropriators pay more attention to immediate costs than to benefits that will be strung out over the future. Given the tendency of decision makers to weight prospective losses more heavily than possible gains, transformation costs take on added importance in the judgments made by appropriators in regard to changing their rules. It is highly unlikely that CPR appropriators will pay immediate transformation costs to change their rules if the discounted net benefits of a rule change are not expected to be large.

The capacity of individuals to make accurate estimates of frequency-based probabilities is also quite limited. Individuals are apt to weight recent events more heavily than events more distant in a long history of experience. One should expect rule changes to be made after a series of relatively bad yields from a CPR, but not to be made after a series of relatively good years. Proponents of new institutions related to water supply problems pray for dry weather immediately preceding special elections or other decision points affecting institutional choice.[16] When the quantity of resource units varies wildly from season to season, it is particularly difficult for appropriators to obtain accurate estimates of average yields and to make reasoned judgments about the meaning of low yields. It is easy to argue that the resource has had low yields in the past and has recovered, when that has been the shared experience. It is far more costly to keep accurate records over a long period of time and to gain sufficient technical expertise to make accurate predictions about the future.

The particular set of rules that appropriators, or others, contemplate rarely contains all possible rules that might be used to govern an operational situation. The rules that are proposed are likely to be in a repertoire of rules already familiar to those who propose them. Given the substantial uncertainty associated with any change in rules, individuals are less likely to adopt unfamiliar rules than they are to adopt rules used by others in similar circumstances that have been known to work relatively well. In a setting in which considerable experimentation has occurred with diverse rules, appropriators learn about the effects of different rules by analyzing the experiences of appropriators using similar CPRs with different rules.

In southern California, for example, groundwater pumpers in West Basin and Central Basin were able to learn from the experience of those in Raymond Basin before they adopted variants of the rules used in Raymond Basin. Institutional arrangements that encourage communication among

209

individuals facing similar problems, such as regionwide associations, increase the knowledge base about how different rules work in practice. The wrong lessons can also be learned. Some of the water users in the Mojave Desert presumed that they could apply the strategy of litigation and formation of special districts, as used in Raymond, West, and Central Basins. Instead of applying the lesson by starting with small incremental changes at the basin level before attempting to build interbasin institutions, they went to the interbasin level first, before designing intrabasin institutions. What worked as an incremental bottom-up strategy at the basin level did not work when attempted at a regional level.

So far, I have not addressed the individual differences that may exist among individuals involved in an institutional-choice situation. The benefits to be derived from status quo rules or alternative rules may not be perceived similarly by all appropriators from a given CPR. If a current set of rules protects one subset of appropriators, while leaving others exposed to future harm, the two groups will evaluate the status quo rules differently. Some appropriators may be protected by their physical location (rather than by the rules in use) so as to be less exposed than others. Upstream appropriators (such as the city of Hawthorne in West Basin) may view proposed rule changes to restrict appropriation rates as providing few benefits to them. Because of their physical location, they will derive benefits from access to the CPR long after others have been eliminated. Proposed rules are apt to have strong distributional effects (Libecap 1989).

### Predicting institutional change

Clearly, we can reject the notion that appropriators are incapable of supplying their own institutions to solve CPR problems, but we cannot replace it with a presumption that appropriators will adopt new rules whenever the net benefits of a rule change will exceed net costs. Net benefits and costs from a change in the operational rules related to a CPR do not exist in the world as independent variables easily available to CPR appropriators or officials of external regimes to use in a simple maximization calculation. Benefits and costs have to be discovered and weighed by individuals using human judgment in highly uncertain and complex situations that are made even more complex to the extent that others behave strategically.

Designing and adopting new institutions to solve CPR problems are difficult tasks, no matter how homogeneous the group, how well informed the members are about the conditions of their CPR, and how deeply ingrained are the generalized norms of reciprocity. Given the strong temptations to shirk, free-ride, and generally act opportunistically that usually are present when individuals face CPR problems, overcoming such problems can never be assured. No strong external pressures drive individuals toward positive solutions to such problems. To the extent that there are strong pressures toward unique outcomes, they are more likely to be the deficient equilibria posited in the three models discussed in Chapter 1. We know that it is possible for individuals to use their capacities for self-reflection, communication, and self-commitment to design new rules to solve CPR problems, but we cannot assert necessity. Further, if individuals find rules that work relatively well, they may have little motivation to continue the costly process of searching for rules that will work even better. "If it ain't broke, don't fix it" applies as much to institutional capital as to physical capital.

Having stressed the importance of specific situational variables as they affect human judgments about the benefits and costs of institutional changes, I shall now summarize what I think can be said about predicting institutional change. To do this, it is essential to consider not only the variables that characterize a particular CPR situation but also the type of external political regime under which the CPR is operated.

To start this examination, let us consider a CPR in which appropriators face problems in a remote location under a political regime that is basically indifferent to what happens with regard to CPRs of this type. This is a "zero condition" in regard to the role of an external regime in affecting internal choices. In such a setting, the likelihood of CPR appropriators adopting a series of incremental changes in operational rules to improve joint welfare will be positively related to the following internal characteristics:

1  Most appropriators share a common judgment that they will be harmed if they do not adopt an alternative rule.
2  Most appropriators will be affected in similar ways by the proposed rule changes.
3  Most appropriators highly value the continuation activities from this CPR; in other words, they have low discount rates.
4  Appropriators face relatively low information, transformation, and enforcement costs.
5  Most appropriators share generalized norms of reciprocity and trust that can be used as initial social capital.
6  The group appropriating from the CPR is relatively small and stable.

These variables are weakly ordered, beginning with those that I think are most important in affecting the likelihood of individuals agreeing to new rules that will improve welfare, and ending with those that I think are somewhat less important. Although considerable emphasis has been placed on the size of the group involved in collective-action problems, I consider the first five variables to be more important than the number of persons involved.[17]

Most CPRs in the modern world are not found in isolated settings. The closer the CPR is to other centers of economic activity, the more likely it is that the population of the area, the value of the resource unit, and the activities of appropriators in nearby CPRs will change in ways that will adversely affect the outcomes achieved in the subject CPR. In nonremote locations, the orientation of the ruling political regime can make a substantial difference in whether local appropriators supply their own institutions or are dependent on external authorities to solve their problems.

Individuals who are not able to supply new rules in an indifferent setting may succeed in adopting new rules under a political regime that allows substantial local autonomy, invests in enforcement agencies, and provides generalized institutional-choice and conflict-resolution arenas. In other words, regional and national governments can play a positive role in providing facilities to enhance the ability of local appropriators to engage in effective institutional design. This positive role is quite different from the one envisioned in proposals to centralize control of natural resources. I illustrated this difference in Chapter 1 with the analysis based on Games 2, 3, and 4, on the one hand, and Game 5, on the other. The difference is also illustrated in the cases by the strategies adopted by the Department of Water Resources in California, as compared with the Canadian Department of Fisheries and Oceans in Newfoundland. I strongly doubt that the groundwater pumpers of Raymond, West, and Central basins would have been able to craft the institutional innovations that they devised had it not been for the professional informational services provided by the U.S. Geological Survey and the California Department of Natural Resources. Although the appropriators paid a share of the costs of the technical studies performed, they did not have to cover the full costs, and the governmental agencies already had substantial information about the geologic structure of southern California in hand.

Further, if they had not been able to use an equity court proceeding, it would have been extremely difficult to arrive at a negotiated settlement of water rights that would have been considered legitimate by all participants. Again, the participants paid a share of these costs, as did the state of California. Other generalized institutional facilities were used when local appropriators drafted state legislation and negotiated with others across the state to take their interests into account. This proposed legislation was then enacted by the state legislature, and it provided the foundation for organizing several special-purpose districts and interdistrict arrangements. The role of the surrounding political institutions in the California groundwater cases did not stop simply with providing generalized facilities. State and local officials also have oversight responsibilities. When special districts were considered, the proposed boundaries of new districts had to be reviewed to ensure that nonbeneficiaries, who would receive nothing for the taxes they contributed, would be excluded. Although the court was willing to agree to a negotiated settlement drawing on a new concept negotiated around a bargaining table, the participants would not have received similar approval for any negotiated settlement that would have taken water rights from some participants and given them to others. The oversight of local and state officials to ensure equitable solutions was an important factor in reaching those solutions. Given the heterogeneity of interests, the lack of accurate information about the groundwater basins, the large number of participants, the relatively high discount rates, the unwillingness of participants to rely on voluntary reciprocity, and the high transformation costs, it is highly doubtful that had these CPR appropriators faced an indifferent political regime they would have been able to supply new institutions to solve the difficult problems facing pumpers in Raymond, West, and Central basins. The failure of the Mojave pumpers to achieve similar success helps to illustrate that even given such a political regime, successful resolutions of difficult problems are not guaranteed.

Having considered the effects that indifferent and facilitative regimes can have on the likelihood that appropriators will adopt new rules that will enhance joint outcomes, let us turn to what can be expected from a regime whose officials presume that they, rather than the appropriators, must solve CPR problems. Let us first posit honest officials, who are seriously interested in helping to solve CPR problems. Once national or regional governmental officials indicate that they consider it their responsibility to solve CPR problems, one can expect local appropriators who do not already have local institutions in place to wait for the government to handle their problems.[18] If someone else agrees to pay the costs of supplying new institutions, it is difficult to overcome the temptation to free-ride. Then the problem for some appropriators is how to present the "facts" of the local situation in such a way that officials who may not know the local circumstances well will be led to create institutions that will leave some individuals better off than others.[19] Those individuals who have the resources to enable them to make the best case to external officials are most likely to gain rules (or exceptions to rules) that will advantage them the most.

One can expect that honest, hard-working regional or national officials may well supply new CPR institutions well adapted to local circumstances

213

in some of the CPRs under their jurisdiction. But the tendency to try to impose uniform rules throughout a jurisdiction, rather than specialized rules that apply to localities within a jurisdiction, makes it extremely difficult for such officials to set up and enforce rules that will seem effective and fair to local appropriators. Trying to get local appropriators to commit themselves to follow rules that are perceived to be ineffective and inequitable is difficult, and the costs of monitoring and enforcing such rules are bound to be higher than for rules crafted by participants to fit local circumstances.

If, instead of honest officials, one posits corrupt centralized regimes, the problems involved in institutional supply become more difficult. It may be possible for local appropriators to create their own local institutions outside the legal framework. One would expect, however, that any set of local appropriators capable of accomplishing that difficult task would be very homogeneous, would have good information about their CPR and about the behaviors of their peers, would have very low discount rates, and generally would exhibit all of the desirable characteristics listed earlier in the extreme. A more probable result would be that experienced by the settlers in the Kirindi Oya irrigation system in Sri Lanka, where no one cooperated with anyone else, and all lived in a hydrologic nightmare.

## A CHALLENGE TO SCHOLARSHIP IN THE SOCIAL SCIENCES

This framework for analyzing problems of institutional choice illustrates the complex configurations of variables that must be addressed when individuals in field settings attempt to fashion rules to improve their individual and joint outcomes. The reason for presenting this complex array of variables as a framework rather than as a model is precisely because one cannot encompass (at least with current methods) this degree of complexity within a single model. When one chooses to model relationships, one can include only a subset of variables, and even then it is usually necessary to set some of these equal to zero or to an absolute value. The typical assumptions of complete information, independent action, perfect symmetry of interests, no human error, no norms of reciprocity, zero monitoring and enforcement costs, and no capacity to transform the situation itself will lead to highly particularized models, not universal theories. It is as essential to map the terrain for a family of models as it is to develop specific models. If the social sciences are to be relevant for analyses of policy problems, the challenge will be to integrate efforts to map the broad terrain and efforts to develop tractable models for particular niches in that terrain. Each CPR can be viewed as a niche in an empirical terrain.

The intellectual trap in relying entirely on models to provide the foundation for policy analysis is that scholars then presume that they are omniscient observers able to comprehend the essentials of how complex, dynamic systems work by creating stylized descriptions of some aspects of those systems. With the false confidence of presumed omniscience, scholars feel perfectly comfortable in addressing proposals to governments that are conceived in their models as omnicompetent powers able to rectify the imperfections that exist in all field settings.

In contemporary conceptions of social order, "the government" often is seen as an external agent whose behavior is exogenous to the situation being modeled. Sugden argues that policy analysts taking this view see themselves as analyzing the behaviors of private individuals and then advising "the" government as to what should be done:

> Most modern economic theory describes a world presided over by a *government* (not, significantly, by governments), and sees this world through the government's eyes. The government is supposed to have the responsibility, the will and the power to restructure society in whatever way maximizes social welfare; like the US Cavalry in a good Western, the government stands ready to rush to the rescue whenever the market "fails", and the economist's job is to advise it on when and how to do so. Private individuals, in contrast, are credited with little or no ability to solve collective problems among themselves. This makes for a distorted view of some important economic and political issues.  (Sugden 1986, p. 3)

Illustrative of this distorted view, and of direct relevance to the analysis of institutional change in CPR settings, is a study by Rolph (1982, 1983) concerning efforts to regulate CPRs, including the set of southern California groundwater basins examined in Chapter 4. Having described the general problem of overuse in relation to such resources, Rolph indicates that "the government (any of the three branches) is called upon to allocate user rights as a means of limiting a production or a consumption activity" (Rolph 1983, p. 51). In regard to the groundwater users, she writes that "they turned to the government for a program that would limit use equitably among the existing users" (Rolph 1983, p. 51). She was puzzled by what appeared to her to be a contradiction in that users were allowed to acquire private property rights to what was a public or a communal resource. She argues that "if the government had foreseen a future shortage of the resource, it might have laid claim to it in 'the beginning,' before any users had made investments" (Rolph 1983, p. 51). As she puzzles about options, she asks this:

As the government steps in to limit use, should it simply allocate complete property rights to a small sub-group of the users while stripping the rest of their limited communal rights? Alternatively, should it take the resource from its present users and redistribute it? Or should it first take away and then sell back the resource to its present users? (Rolph 1983, pp. 51–2)

What I find remarkable about Rolph's observations in regard to the groundwater cases is that the only policy actor she sees as being relevant is the amorphous, fictitious, and omnicompetent entity called "the government." The users are viewed as turning to "the government for a program," rather than themselves struggling to find workable and equitable solutions to difficult problems within arenas provided by courts, by legislative bodies, and by local authorities.

The models that social scientists tend to use for analyzing CPR problems have the perverse effect of supporting increased centralization of political authority. First, the individuals using CPRs are viewed as if they are capable of short-term maximization, but not of long-term reflection about joint strategies to improve joint outcomes. Second, these individuals are viewed as if they are in a trap and cannot get out without some external authority imposing a solution. Third, the institutions that individuals may have established are ignored or rejected as inefficient, without examining how these institutions may help them acquire information, reduce monitoring and enforcement costs, and equitably allocate appropriation rights and provision duties. Fourth, the solutions presented for "the" government to impose are themselves based on models of idealized markets or idealized states.

We in the social sciences face as great a challenge in how to address the analysis of CPR problems as do the communities of people who struggle with ways to avoid CPR problems in their day-to-day lives. The theoretical enterprise requires social scientists to engage in model-building,[20] but not limit theoretical inquiry to that specific level of discourse. We need to appreciate the analytical power that can be derived from the prior intellectual efforts of important contributors such as Hobbes, Montesquieu, Hume, Smith, Madison, Hamilton, Tocqueville, and many others.[21] Contemporary studies in the theory of public and social choice, the economics of transactions costs, the new institutional economics, law and economics, game theory, and many related fields[22] are making important contributions that need to be carried forward in theoretically informed empirical inquiries in both laboratory and field settings.

216

# Notes

## 1. REFLECTIONS ON THE COMMONS

1  Attributed to Merrill M. Flood and Melvin Dresher and formalized by Albert W. Tucker (R. Campbell 1985, p. 3), the game is described (Luce and Raiffa 1957, p. 95) as follows: "Two suspects are taken into custody and separated. The district attorney is certain that they are guilty of a specific crime, but he does not have adequate evidence to convict them at a trial. He points out to each prisoner that each has two alternatives: to confess to the crime the police are sure they have done, or not to confess. If they both do not confess, then the district attorney states he will book them on some very minor trumped-up charge such as petty larceny and illegal possession of a weapon, and they will both receive minor punishment; if they both confess they will be prosecuted, but he will recommend less than the most severe sentence; but if one confesses and the other does not, then the confessor will receive lenient treatment for turning state's evidence whereas the latter will get 'the book' slapped at him. In terms of years in a penitentiary, the strategic problem might be reduced" to the following:

|  | Prisoner 2 | |
| --- | --- | --- |
| *Prisoner 1* | Not confess | Confess |
| Not confess | 1 year each | 10 years for prisoner 1<br>3 months for prisoner 2 |
| Confess | 3 months for prisoner 1<br>10 years for prisoner 2 | 8 years each |

R. Kenneth Godwin and W. Bruce Shepard (1979), Richard Kimber (1981), Michael Taylor (1987), and others have shown that commons dilemmas are not always prisoner's dilemma (PD) games. Dawes (1973, 1975) was one of the first scholars to show the similarity of structure.

2  Hardin's model easily translates into the prisoner's dilemma structure. Many problems related to the use of common-pool resources (CPRs) do *not* easily

217

translate. Simple games such as "chicken" and "assurance" games are better representations of some situations (M. Taylor 1987). More complex games involving several moves and lacking dominant strategies for the players are better able to capture many of the problems involved in managing CPRs.

3 Hardin recommends "mutual coercion, mutually agreed upon" as a solution to the problem, but what "mutual agreement" means is ambiguous given his emphasis on the role of central regulators; see Orr and Hill (1979) for a critique.

4 A howling debate raged for some time, for example, regarding whether the number of participants involved was positively, negatively, or not at all related to the quantity of the good provided (Buchanan 1968; Chamberlin 1974; Frohlich and Oppenheimer 1970; McGuire 1974). Russell Hardin (1982) resolved the controversy to a large extent by pointing out that the effect of the number of contributors was largely dependent on the type of collective benefits being provided – whether or not each unit of the good was subtractable. Thus, the initial debate did not lead to clarification until implicit assumptions about the type of good involved had been made explicit.

5 J. A. Moore (1985, p. 483), reporting on the education project for the American Society of Zoologists.

6 See, for example, Berkes (1987), Berkes and Kislalioglu (1989), Berkes and Pocock (1981), A. Davis (1984), K. Martin (1979), Matthews and Phyne (1988). For strong critiques of Canadian policy, see Pinkerton (1989a,b) and Matthews (1988).

7 Michael Taylor (1987) analyzes the structure of Hobbes's theory to show that Hobbes proposed the creation of a Leviathan in order to avoid the equilibrium of situations structured like prisoner's dilemmas. See also Sugden (1986).

8 Stillman (1975, p. 13) points out that those who see "a strong central government or a strong ruler" as a solution implicitly assume that "the ruler will be a wise and ecologically aware altruist," even though these same theorists presume that the users of CPRs will be myopic, self-interested, and ecologically unaware hedonists.

9 The form of regulation used in Game 2 would be referred to in the resource economics literature as a "pure quota scheme." Alternative regulatory instruments that are frequently proposed are a "pure licensing scheme" and a "pure tax scheme." As Dasgupta and Heal (1979) point out, however, it is "the" government in each of these schemes that takes control of the resource and sets up the regulatory scheme. "The idea, in each case, is for the government to take charge of the common property resource and to introduce regulations aimed at the attainment of allocative efficiency" (Dasgupta and Heal 1979, p. 66). All of the models of these various schemes assume that the costs of sustaining these systems are nil (as in Game 2). Dasgupta and Heal repeatedly stress that these costs are *not* nil in field settings and may affect whether or not any of them actually will solve a commons problem or the relative efficiency of one scheme versus another. But Dasgupta and Heal's careful warnings about the importance of the relative costs of various constitutional arrangements are rarely heeded in the policy literature.

10 More accurately, the sum of the two types of errors must be less than 0.50, given the fixed parameters of this game, for the restructured game to have a (C, C) equilibrium. I am grateful to Franz Weissing, who suggested this par-

ticular analysis for illustrating the problem of incomplete information on the part of a central agency.

The last two decades of work in social-choice theory also have revealed other problems that may be involved in any system where a collective choice about policy must be reached through mechanisms of collective choice. Even if complete information is available about the resources, problems associated with cycling and/or agenda control can also occur (McKelvey 1976, 1979; Riker 1980; Shepsle 1979a).

11 This overlooks the fact that in a dynamic setting the decision whether to manage the meadow at a sustainable level or to "mine" it rapidly will depend delicately on the discount rate used by the private owner. If the discount rate is high, the private owner will "overuse" a commons just as much as will a series of unorganized co-owners. See Clark (1977) for a clear statement of how overexploitation can occur under private property.

12 And it should be pointed out that the private-rights system is itself a *public* institution and is dependent on public instrumentalities for its very existence (Binger and Hoffman 1989).

13 My thanks again to Franz Weissing, who suggested this symmetric version of the contract-enforcement game. I had originally modeled Game 5 giving one herder the right to offer a contract, and the second herder only the right to agree or not agree to it.

14 See the interesting paper by Okada and Kleimt (1990), in which they model a three-player contract-enforcement game using the rule that any two (or three) persons who agree can set up their own contract to be enforced by an external agent. They conclude that three persons will not make use of a costless enforcement process, whereas two may. The article helps to illustrate how very subtle changes in conditions make important differences in results.

15 Williamson (1983) argues, however, that the numbers of actual unresolved PD situations in long-term business relationships have been exaggerated because economists have overlooked the contracts that businesses negotiate to change the structure of incentives related to long-term contracts.

16 Much of the literature in the new institutional economics tradition has stressed the importance of private orderings in the governance of long-term private contracts (Galanter 1981; Williamson 1979, 1985).

17 When considerable competition exists among arbitrators for the job of monitoring and enforcing, one can assume that arbiters are strongly motivated to make fair decisions. If there is no competition, then one faces the same problem in presuming fair decisions as one does in relation to a public bureau with monopoly status.

18 Simply iterating the PD game is not a guaranteed way out of the dilemma. The famous "folk theorem" that cooperation is a possible perfect equilibrium outcome is sometimes misrepresented as asserting that cooperation is the only equilibrium in repeated games. In addition to the "all cooperate at every iteration" equilibrium, many other equilibria are also possible. Simple repetition without enforceable agreements does not produce a clear result (Güth, Leininger, and Stephan 1990).

19 Private orderings frequently are mistaken for *no* order, given the absence of an official formal legislative or court decision. See Galanter (1981) for a review of the extensive literature on private orderings.

20 The formal game-theoretical structures and outcomes of this and three other sets of rules for allocating fishing sites are analyzed by Gardner and E. Ostrom (1990).

21 See, for example, the cases contained in National Research Council (1986), McCay and Acheson (1987), Fortmann and Bruce (1988), Berkes (1989), Pinkerton (1989a), Ruddle and Akimichi (1984), Coward (1980), and Uphoff (1986c). In addition to these collections, see citations in F. Martin (1989) for the extensive literature contained in books, monographs, articles, and research reports. There are also common-property institutions that break down when challenged by very rapid population growth or changes in the market value of the products harvested from the CPR. As discussed in Chapter 5, however, fragility of common-property systems is much more likely when these systems are not recognized by the formal political regimes of which they are a part.

22 That the "remorseless logic" was built into Hardin's assumptions, rather than being an empirical result, was pointed out by Stillman (1975, p. 14): "But the search for a solution cannot be found within the parameters of the problem. Rather, the resolution can only be found by changing one or more of the parameters of the problem, by cutting the Gordian knot rather than untying it."

23 See Shepsle (1979a, 1989a), Shepsle and Weingast (1987), Williamson (1979, 1985), North and Weingast (1989), and North (1981).

24 One can search the development literature long and hard, for example, without finding much discussion of the importance of court systems in helping individuals to organize themselves for development. The first time that I mentioned to a group of AID officials the importance of having an effective court system as an intervention strategy to achieve development, there was stunned silence in the room. One official noted that in two decades of development work she had never heard of such a recommendation being made.

2. AN INSTITUTIONAL APPROACH TO THE STUDY OF
SELF-ORGANIZATION AND SELF-GOVERNANCE IN CPR
SITUATIONS

1 For physical resources, this translates into the relation between usage and natural deterioration, on the one hand, and investments made in maintenance and repair, on the other hand (E. Ostrom, Schroeder, and Wynne 1990).

2 Let me state at this point that the term "appropriator" is used in some legal systems to denote a person who has a particular legal *claim* to withdraw resource units. In Chapter 4, for example, certain groundwater pumpers are referred to as "appropriators" in a legal sense as those whose claim to water is not based on their using water on their own land; it is based on a "first-in-time, first-in-right" basis. Other than in Chapter 4, I always use the term "appropriator" to refer to all individuals who actually withdraw or somehow utilize the resource units of a CPR, regardless of the source of their legal claim to do so. Some actual appropriators may have no legal claim (e.g., squatters). In Chapter 4, I try to indicate carefully when the term is being used as a legal term for right-holders and when it is being used in the more general sense that I have just defined.

3  See, for example, the debate about the effect of group size on the provision of a good, as summarized by Hardin (1982, ch. 3).
4  The early work on public goods was written by Bowen (1943) and P. Samuelson (1954, 1955). See the distinction between public goods and CPRs in V. Ostrom and E. Ostrom (1977a). For recent reviews of the literature on collective goods, see Cornes and Sandler (1986).
5  Thus, this distinction between a public good and a CPR is nontrivial. A person who contributes to the provision of a pure public good does not really care who else uses it, or when and where, so long as enough other individuals share the cost of provision. A person who contributes to the provisions of a CPR cares a great deal about how many others use it, and when and where, even if the others all contribute to its provision.
6  See Radnitzky (1987) and Stroebe and Frey (1980) for a similar approach.
7  The concept of average yield may not be meaningful in regard to all biological resources (Schlager 1989).
8  See Berkes (1989) for a description of the strategies temporarily adopted by the Cree Indians near Hudson's Bay when an influx of nonnative trappers threatened the beaver stock. Legislation passed in 1930 legally recognized American-Indian communal and family territories, allowing the Cree to anticipate long-term survival for a key CPR. Since 1930, the Cree have successfully managed the beaver stock using the rules that had been tested by centuries of trial and error prior to the arrival of Europeans on the North American continent.
9  See Coleman (1987c, 1990) and Opp (1979, 1982, 1986) for extended analyses of the relationship between norms and rational-choice theory.
10  Sequential, contingent, and frequency-dependent behaviors may, of course, occur in unorganized settings. Some very interesting game-theoretical results have relied on the potentialities of individuals to rely on such forms of coordinated activities alone, without changing the underlying structures (Kreps et al. 1982; Levhari and Mirman 1980; Schelling 1978).
11  An important aspect of organizing a legislative process, for example, is the set of rules that specify the steps through which a bill must be processed before it becomes a law.
12  Changing the positive and negative inducements is the type of intervention that has received the most attention in the social sciences.
13  Alchian and Demsetz (1972) overtly posit that the key problem underlying reliance on a firm to organize behavior, rather than reliance on the independent actions of buyers and sellers in a market institution, is that of an interdependent production function. When the production function is interdependent, the marginal contribution of any one owner of an input factor will depend on the level of other inputs. One cannot tell from an examination of outputs alone how much any individual contributed. Rewarding inputs requires high levels of monitoring that are not needed when factors are combined additively. Williamson (1975), drawing inspiration from Coase (1937), argues that this is only one source of the need for organized firms. Williamson relies more on the costs of transacting in a market in which all act independently, as contrasted with a firm in which individuals agree ex ante to coordinate their activities ex post.
14  This stylized version does not do full justice to the extensive work on the theory of the firm, and I certainly do not recommend any policy prescriptions

221

on the basis of this sketch. Because my purpose is only to show how the theory solves the collective-action problem, I am presenting only this barebones outline. Readers are advised to see the work of Coase (1937), Alchian and Demsetz (1972), and Williamson (1975, 1985).

15 This discussion of the theory of the state draws most heavily on the work of scholars who base their theory of the state on Hobbes; it does not reflect the full range of debate about the theory of the state (Breton 1974; Levi 1988a; Niskanen 1971; M. Taylor 1987). My purpose in discussing the theory of the firm and the theory of the state is not to explore those theories but to point up the absence of an accepted theory for how individuals self-organize without an "external" leader who obtains most of the benefits. As Vincent Ostrom has so well demonstrated (1986a, 1987, 1989), when the "theory of the state" is used as the theory underlying a concept of democratic self-governance, basic contradictions exist. As long as a single center has a monopoly on the use of coercion, one has a state rather than a self-governed society.

16 Both are also subject to limits imposed by span-of-control problems: The cost of monitoring increases with the size and diversity of a firm or a state.

17 See Feeny (1988b) for an insightful discussion of the supply of institutions.

18 See, for example, the studies by Schelling (1960), Elster (1979), Brennan and Buchanan (1985), Levi (1988a,b), Shepsle (1989a), North and Weingast (1989), and Williamson (1985).

19 Reading a working paper by Shepsle (1989a) made me recognize how important this problem is to understanding CPR problems, as well as many other problems of interest to an institutional analyst.

20 This is how the literature on the "economics of crime" models the decision to comply or not (Becker 1968; Ehrlich 1973; Ehrlich and Brower 1987); for an insightful critique, see Tsebelis (1989).

21 Elster is not completely sure that the dilemma of mutual monitoring is always "decisive." He points to the possibility that tasks may be organized so that monitoring can be done without additional effort.

22 Assuming, of course, that the empirical observations are valid and the differences between predictions and observations are substantial.

23 Ciriacy-Wantrup and Bishop (1975) carefully distinguished between an open-access CPR, in which no one has any property rights, and a closed-access CPR, in which a well-defined group owns property in common. "Common-property resources" is a term that is still used inappropriately in many instances to refer to both open-access and closed-access CPRs.

24 Exactly how one models this depends on many underlying parameters. One that is essential to the prediction of full rent dissipation is that the underlying appropriation function (usually called a production function in this literature) is characterized by diminishing returns (Dasgupta and Heal 1979, p. 56). Although this is a reasonable assumption to make in many environments, the dependence of the incentive structure on underlying parameters, such as the shape of the appropriation function, is a key point I am trying to make. CPRs vary substantially in regard to their values on these underlying parameters. Two CPRs identical in almost all respects, except the range of variation found in regard to a important underlying parameter, may need quite different representations in terms of their strategic structures.

25 A third appropriation problem has to do with technological externalities.

Because none of the cases in this volume clearly illustrates this problem, I do not discuss it here; see Gardner, E. Ostrom, and Walker (1990).

26 This intimate relationship between solving appropriation problems and solving provision problems has frequently been ignored by contemporary designers of large-scale irrigation systems. It has almost uniformly been assumed that because farmers' interests are so clearly affected by the construction of field canals and the maintenance of distribution works, they will simply organize themselves to take care of providing and maintaining these small-scale works once the large-scale public works have been provided by a national government. But that assumption is based on two fallacies. The first is that the simple presence of a collective benefit is sufficient to assure that individuals will organize to obtain it. The second is that farmers who are not assured a reliable supply of water will make significant investment in provision (R. Chambers 1981).

27 See Frey (1988), Brennan and Buchanan (1985), Buchanan (1977), and Buchanan and Tullock (1962).

28 "Common knowledge" is an important assumption frequently used in game theory and essential for most analyses of equilibrium. It implies that all participants know $x$, that the participants know that each of the others knows $x$, and that the participants know that each of the others know that each of the others knows $x$ (Aumann 1976).

29 Heckathorn (1984) models this as a series of nested games.

30 These levels exist whether the organized human activity is public or private. See Boudreaux and Holcombe (1989) for a discussion of the constitutional rules of homeowner associations, condominiums, and some types of housing developments.

31 See, for example, Alexander Field's critiques of the work of institutional theorists who have attempted to develop rational-choice theories of institutional choice (Field 1979, 1984).

32 In designing the constitution of an irrigation community, for example, setting up a legislative body requires determining how many representatives there should be. Determining the number of representatives will be affected by the physical layout. If there are 5 canals, having one representative from each canal may work well. If there are 50 canals, the participants may want to cluster canals into branches in order to select representatives. Whatever constitutional choice is made about how many (and how to select) representatives, the effects on appropriation practices will come about as a result of decisions made at both a collective-choice level and an operational level. It is extremely difficult to predict these with any exactitude prior to experience in a particular setting.

### 3. ANALYZING LONG-ENDURING, SELF-ORGANIZED, AND SELF-GOVERNED CPRs

1 A substantial debate has been engendered among institutional economists and economic historians over the issue of whether or not long-enduring institutions are optimally efficient. The way the question is addressed in many instances leads to an automatic yes or no answer, depending on what variables are considered as constraints on the problem. If information and transactions

costs are not considered, no real-world institution can ever be optimally efficient. If all information and transactions costs are included as fixed constraints, all long-enduring institutions are automatically optimally efficient. Neither position is very useful in evaluating institutions. I prefer to argue that optimality is not well defined in a changing environment, including the capacity to change the institutional rules themselves. One must use criteria other than optimal efficiency to evaluate long-enduring institutions (Binger and Hoffman 1989; Furubotn and Richter 1989; Harris 1989; North 1989).

2 As Demsetz (1967, p. 354) stated his concerns about negotiation costs, "it is conceivable that those who own these rights, i.e., every member of the community, can agree to curtail the rate at which they work the lands if negotiating and policing costs are zero. Each can agree to abridge his rights. It is obvious that the costs of reaching such an agreement will not be zero. What is not obvious is just how large these costs may be. Negotiating costs will be large because it is difficult for many persons to reach a mutually satisfactory agreement, especially when each hold-out has the right to work the land as fast as he pleases. But, even if an agreement among all can be reached, we must yet take account of the costs of policing the agreement, and these may be large also."

3 I had hoped to include an analysis of the persistence of "common lands" in feudal and medieval England. The famous "enclosure acts" of British history have been presented in many history books as the rational elimination of an obviously inefficient institution that had been retained because of an unthinking attachment to the past for an overly long time. Recent economic historians, however, have provided an entirely different picture of English land-tenure systems before the enclosure acts and even of the process of gaining enclosure itself (Dahlman 1980; Fanoaltea 1988; McCloskey 1976; Thirsk 1959, 1967). Many of the manorial institutions share broad similarity with the long-enduring institutions described in this chapter: a clear-cut definition of who is authorized to use common resources; definite limits (stinting) on the uses that can be made; low-cost enforcement mechanisms; local rule-making arenas to change institutions over time in response to environment and economic changes. Common-field property institutions were transported to New England, where they flourished for close to 100 years, until exclusion costs became low enough and/or transactions costs rose to produce a slow evolution from larger to smaller commons, eventuating in private tenure (B. Field 1985a,b). Even the presumed increased efficiency of enclosure has come into question. R. C. Allen (1982) concludes, for example, that the eighteenth-century enclosures of open fields *redistributed* the existing agricultural income, rather than expanding total income through enhanced efficiency (Yelling 1977).

4 In personal correspondence, Netting clarifies that citizens in Törbel were "rigidly restricted to descendants in the male line, and the children of women who married outside men were excluded, even though these women and their offspring could inherit private property." Netting reflects that Törbel is a case of a "closed corporate community" in the sense developed by Wolf (1986), because "citizenship closes access to communal resources both to members of neighboring communities who might be direct competitors and to national or colonial states attempting to wrest control from local inhabitants."

5 Restrictions on the use of common grazing lands based on the "home feed

base" of the user were common throughout most of feudal Europe. The Forest Service and Bureau of Land Management in the United States currently allocate grazing permits based on the home feed base of the applicant and the carrying capacity of the grazing area (Ciriacy-Wantrup and Bishop 1975).

6 Stevenson (1990) examines milk yields for 245 grazing areas in Switzerland and finds that milk yields from common property fall below the yields for private-property alps, but he does not include production or transactions costs in his analyses, and thus no conclusions can be reached concerning efficiency. He finds that grazing pressure on the Swiss commons is *lower* than on private land.

7 The communally organized forests in Törbel appear to have been well managed through the years, as were the meadows, but some Swiss villages were not able to manage their forests as well as they managed their meadows. Some of the commonly owned forests were divided among villagers to become individually owned woodlots. The lots generally were too small for effective management, and they degenerated until intervention occurred in the nineteenth century (Ciriacy-Wantrup and Bishop 1975). Price (1987) provides an overview of the development of legislation in Valais, Graubünden, and Bern.

8 Villages that are no longer dependent on their commons for essential forest products complementary to agricultural productions frequently have leased the land and used that income to finance other village projects. See Sharma (1984), as well as McKean's work, for a discussion of the uses of leases.

9 Hayami (1975) comments on the substantial asset that village organization in Japan has been for modern development, in contrast to many Asian countries. The same point is stressed by Sharma (1984), who describes the extensive participation of villagers from all walks of life in village governance and the consequent organizational skills that exist at the village level.

10 Many Muslims remained for a long time in the territories recaptured by the Spanish crown. As individual Muslim families departed, their land and homesteads were granted to Spanish families. Considerable effort was expended to determine how the irrigation systems worked and to maintain the water-distribution procedures as they had operated prior to the reconquest. In 1244, for example, Don Peregrin, one of the knights of James I, ordered several Muslims who had been irrigation officials before the reconquest to appear and "take an oath on pain of their persons and goods" to "tell the truth about the waters, in what way they used to apportion them in the time of the Moors" (Glick 1970, p. 233).

11 Limited parcels of land in the eastern part of Spain have acquired irrigation rights since the reconquest as new irrigation projects have expanded the supply of water.

12 The medieval term for this same position was *cequier*.

13 See Glick (1970, pp. 64–8) and the references he cites for a discussion of the history of the tribunal and the dispute over its origins.

14 The syndic is the agent of the *hereters* and is removable by them. In medieval times, the syndics of Valencia were selected for a limited and nonrenewable term by election, lottery, or competitive bidding. The Tormos Canal, for example, used a competitive bidding system. At a public meeting of the *hereters*, the person who submitted the lowest price to administer the canal was assigned responsiblity to administer the canal for three years at the price set in

his bid. Each bidder had to estimate how large a staff he would need to employ in order to monitor the use of the canals by the irrigators and allocate water in times of drought without conflict erupting. He also needed to estimate the cost of cleaning the central canals once a year and monitoring the work of the *hereters* in cleaning the canal frontage that bordered their lands. The total bid of the lowest bidder was divided into pro rata sums assigned to the *hereters* according to the amounts of *regadiu* land owned, and thus proportional to the amounts of water obtained (Glick 1970, p. 38). Where a syndic was elected, he also had to determine an annual budget and submit it to the *hereters* for approval prior to their obligation to pay a pro rata assignment of the costs of managing the canal. In modern times, the syndics are elected for a two-year term and can succeed themselves. The assessment rate is now determined annually by an executive committee chaired by the syndic.

15 These rules are both complex and very specific. Maass and Anderson (1986, p. 27) provide a summary of the procedures used on the Bennager Canal. "The first laterals that draw from this canal are two small ones, with rights to continuous water, serving approximately 13 ha each. Shortly thereafter the water encounters its first lengua by which it is divided into two continuous streams in two laterals. The right lateral receives one-third of the water and is called *Terç*, meaning one-third in Valencian. With the aid of a gated control structure, Terç then supplies two regions. Water is run in a lateral to Alacuás on Wednesdays and Thursdays and in one to Picaña on the remaining days of the week."

"The two-thirds of the water that flows into the left lateral of the first divisor is separated subsequently into two equal streams by a lengua called the White Cross. Immediately the left one of these streams is further divided into two equal parts, and each of these then supplies smaller laterals and farms by turn, one after the other. The right lateral at the White Cross supplies four channels that run water in succession, one day each."

"This system is interrupted every Thursday for sixteen hours when all the water available at the White Cross is diverted to a single lateral called Thursday (*Dijous* in Valencian) that serves 12 ha and irrigates at these hours only. For two weeks in a row the sixteen hours are those after sunrise on Thursday; for the third week they are the hours before sunrise on Friday, an arrangement designed to distribute the burden of irrigating at night. For the remaining eight hours on Thursdays the water is divided normally at the White Cross, but that flowing into the right lateral is given each week in succession to one of the four channels served by that lateral in order to preserve the proportions and the timing used normally in that service area."

16 Glick indicates that the "picture of daily irrigation problems and the methods used to deal with them" represented by the fine books of Castellón "should be applicable to the Valencian huerta as well" (1970, p. 54).

17 For a researcher who has ridden with police officers in high-crime districts of metropolitan areas, this is an amazing level of activity.

18 The somewhat higher percentage (58 as contrasted to 42) of infractions due to error or negligence, instead of overt illegal attempts to obtain water, represented a slightly higher recorded infraction rate.

19 Glick's reflection on this infraction rate is as follows: "Again, this is indicative of the way in which the fine structure fine-tunes the system. In Castellón the

ditch rider imposed the fines summarily. The more formal, weekly court in Valencia no doubt reflects greater demand for water, hence stiffer penalties, including the humiliation of being called before the Tribunal" (T. F. Glick, personal communication).

20 In personal correspondence to me, Glick indicates the following: "The role of fines in Castellón appears to have been designed, first, to make the system more flexible. The fines for cheating are set low enough so that if you really need some more water it's worth the fine. In this sense it's another kind of internal switch. The system countenances low-level cheating. High-level cheating (or challenging the ditch rider) lands you in the king's court, so it was pretty clear where the limit of personal risk lay. Second, it helps maximize the efficiency of the distribution arrangements, inasmuch as careless waste of water is fined. Third, low-level damage to a neighbor's field or to public property is included in the fine structure; this acts to head off conflict between individuals which, if allowed to fester, could be detrimental to the entire community."

21 When the irrigators in Alicante decided to construct Tibi Dam, they appealed to the crown for assistance: "Philip the Second responded with protection and limited aid. He gave license to the city of Alicante to build the dam and to borrow money for this purpose. Although he refused to provide capital because the work would in good part benefit existing landowners, he agreed, after obtaining approval from the church, to assign the proceeds of tithes and first fruits from the lands to be benefited (that is, 10 percent of their crops) to the city to amortize the costs of building the dam. . . . Finally, he agreed that authority and responsibility for distributing water from the dam would remain with the city so that the farmers did not lose control over their destinies to any significant degree" (Maass and Anderson 1986, pp. 119–20).

22 When landholding new-water rights are converted to nonagricultural purposes, the water rights associated with this land revert to the irrigation community, because these rights cannot be sold. Thus, the permanent holdings of the irrigation community increase slowly over time.

23 Maass also reports that the market appears to be very efficient: "To a foreigner who has had an opportunity to study the detailed reports of individual rotations, the close agreement among the hypothetical length of a rotation (determined by the number of rights), the hours and minutes of water actually released from the regulating basins, and the hours and minutes of albalaes collected from farmers is uncanny. Thus shareholders who claim their scrip either use it or sell it – the market is efficient, and the scrip that are not claimed are sold at auction by the syndicate. The surprisingly short periods of running water not covered by scrip are almost always accounted for by minor breaks and disruptions in the distribution network and ordinary canal losses" (Maass and Anderson 1986, p. 116).

24 A private firm pumps groundwater from deep wells near Villena, located about 70 km from Alicante. Farmers can purchase Villena water by the hour, which is then delivered in the community's canals on those days when Tibi water is not being delivered. Another alternative is water brought by a private firm from the lower reaches of the Segura River delta. That firm had already invested in massive pumps to lift the water out of the delta and transport it to several nearby communities, and in 1924 the Alicante irrigation syndicate

funded the extension of a canal by 25 km so that this water could be delivered to Alicante. This water is sold in a daily auction, but the minimum and maximum prices are predetermined under a provision of the initial concession by the national government allowing the firm to export Segura River water. Relationships between Alicante irrigators and both of these private firms have been conflict-ridden and tense at many junctures in their history.

25 Wittfogel (1957), in his brief discussion of Spanish irrigation institutions after the reconquest, does not distinguish between the "Spanish absolution" of Castile and the more democratic institutions of eastern Spain. For some time it has been the accepted wisdom that the well-organized sheepherders guild (the Mesta) was responsible both for increasing the power of the Castilian monarch and for retarding development in Castile by delaying the development of well-specified property rights in land (Klein 1920). However, recent work by Nugent and Sanchez (1980), using an approach that is quite consistent with the one adopted herein, raises some substantial questions about that conventional view.

26 For an interesting account of the path of evolutionary change in North America, as contrasted with South America, see North (1986a).

27 Until 1923, when the first government-financed irrigation project was constructed, the communal irrigation society was the only form of irrigation management in the Philippines. In 1982 there were approximately 5,700 community irrigation systems in the Philippines, serving approximately 45% of the irrigated area (World Bank 1982, p. 8). For an interesting account of the early efforts to stimulate irrigation-service associations in the Philippines, see Bromley, Taylor, and Parker (1980).

28 Additional *atars* may be issued if a new irrigation canal is added to an old system by new members, who can acquire shares by constructing the new works and then bearing their share of maintenance for the entire system.

29 The position of a cook seems strange, but at each of the major work seasons of the *zanjera*, all those working are fed by the cooperative, which is one of the positive inducements used to encourage participation in the extremely difficult labor required by these systems. The cook is very important in this system!

30 I seriously doubt that the farmers would be willing to contribute this high a tax rate in monetized form, even if they were operating in a fully monetized economy. When a farmer contributes labor, he knows how the tax is being allocated, whether or not it is being used for the purpose for which it was levied. When a farmer contributes money, he may fear that it will be diverted to the pockets of bureaucrats or put to other uses beyond the purpose for which it was contributed.

31 Siy points out that this figure underestimates the actual amount of labor supplied to construction and maintenance, because the families of *zanjera* members and members of neighboring *zanjeras*, who receive the drainage waters of this sytem, also contribute labor for major projects. Siy estimates that at least 1,000 additional person-days are contributed by those who do not have direct obligations (Siy 1982, p. 95).

32 Siy refers to the labor contributed to the maintenance of the system as a "voluntary" contribution. Given that there is a high probability that non-participation will be sanctioned by members of the *zanjera* and/or the federation, calling this a voluntary contribution is misleading. What *is* voluntary is

joining or not joining the *zanjera*. Those who do not want to abide by the rules can obtain a good price for their land and thus exit. The price of this voluntary decision to join or remain a member, however, is to forgo discretion whether or not to contribute a certain amount of labor each year.

33 Although the level of participation described by Siy is very high, it is not unique in Third World settings. Pradhan (1984) describes an equally sophisticated irrigation system – the Chattis Mauja system – constructed 150 years ago in Nepal, covering 7,500 acres of land irrigated by farmers living in 54 different villages. Also a federal structure, it is organized at village, district, and central levels, in addition to working informally with three other farmer-managed systems. The Chattis Mauja system has a strong record for mobilizing labor input – over 60,520 man-days during 1981 – from at least 3,000 farmers working to desilt the main canal and other arduous tasks.

34 It appears, however, that those who own less than a full *atar* share have a somewhat higher absentee rate, particularly those who own less than a fourth of a share, but this is not true in regard to the contributions of materials by members owning less than a full share (Siy 1982, p. 99)

35 Computed from Siy (1982, p. 144, Table 38).

36 I do not think it is possible to elucidate necessary *and* sufficient principles for enduring institutions, as it takes a fundamental willingness of the individuals involved to make any institution work. No set of logical conditions is sufficient to ensure that all sets of individuals will be willing and able to make an institution characterized by such conditions work.

37 It is sometimes argued that the rules defining common property need not be as completely specified and detailed as those defining private property. Runge (1986, pp. 33–4) argues, for example, that "if common property – the individual right to joint use – is the norm, comparatively fewer claims must be assigned and defined. Less clarity in the assignment of rights (at least by Western standards) may also result. However, this is balanced against reduced social costs of assignment and definition." This is true if one means that the physical boundaries for individual use do not have to be mapped, but only the boundaries of the resource. It is certainly not true in regard to the detailed rules that are necessary for governing how the common owners are to appropriate from and provide for the resource.

38 On the other hand, that external authorities did not meddle (with the exception of Alicante) was very important. An appropriator who was unhappy about the way rules were enforced in one of these systems was not able to go to a politician at a higher level and get a reversal in return for political support. Thus, external authorities did not *unglue* the structure that local appropriators had put together. This stands in contrast to several of the cases discussed in Chapter 5.

39 A high level of quasi-voluntary compliance is present in other long-serving CPR institutional arrangements. The Chisasibi Cree, for example, have devised a complex set of entry and authority rules related to the fish stocks of James Bay, as well as the beaver stock located in their defined hunting territory. Fikret Berkes (1987, p. 87) describes why these resource systems and the rules used to regulate them have survived and prospered for so long: "effective social mechanisms ensure adherence to rules which exist by virtue of mutual consent within the community. People who violate these rules suffer not only

a loss of favour from the animals (important in the Cree ideology of hunting) but also social disgrace. This is no light matter, as seen in the case of the beaver boss who was forced to abandon his position because he neglected to remove his traps at the end of the trapping season."

40 In some systems not described in this chapter, guards are paid a proportion of the crop at the end of the year. With this type of payment, the guard's income is dependent on keeping the reliability of the system as high as possible so that the farmers being served can produce as much on their fields as possible.

41 See the discussion in Harsanyi and Selten (1988, pp. 19–20) about self-commitment moves in noncooperative games. The particular self-commitment move that I suggest here is less extreme that a commitment to follow the rules in every instance as long as everyone else also follows the rules in every instance. Given that modest levels of rule-breaking continue to occur in all long-enduring CPR institutions, while the overall level of rule conformance is very high, I think that my statement of the self-commitment move captures the commitment of appropriators in field settings.

## 4. ANALYZING INSTITUTIONAL CHANGE

1 See William Blomquist's reports (1987a,b, 1988a–e, 1989, 1990) for more detailed analyses of the origins of the institutions for governance and management of the three basins described here, plus analyses of several other basins that have devised different institutional arrangements to achieve self-governing systems.

2 The actual costs of imported water far exceed the wholesale price charged by the Metropolitan Water District of Southern California (MWD) for imported water, because considerable portions of the capital costs of constructing the aqueducts bringing water from the Colorado River and from northern California have been paid from property taxes and are not reflected in the wholesale prices charged by MWD.

3 The stock of water in a groundwater basin also is of value – independent of its future use as a subtractable quantity of water. The stock of water held in a basin holds "the water being pumped closer to the land surface, which reduces pumping costs" (Nunn 1985, p. 872). These cost savings are collective benefits available to all pumpers.

4 See Louis Weschler (1968) and William Blomquist (1988d) for discussions of the settlement in Orange County, where producers overtly rejected the idea of a legal settlement of rights and established the Orange County Water District in the early 1930s to administer a pump tax and replenish the basin by a variety of means. Blomquist (1988e) discusses a still different set of water rights that developed in the San Fernando Valley because of the strong "pueblo rights" of the city of Los Angeles.

5 The information presented in this section is based on the work of Blomquist (1988a).

6 The city of Pasadena was the logical initiator of litigation. The city owned overlying land and used water on that land, in addition to being a senior appropriator from the basin.

7 A proportionate cutback is an example of a solution that conforms to Reinhard Selten's general equity principle (Selten 1978b), whereby some individuals ($n$)

are allocated some acre-feet of water ($s$) according to a standard of distribution that defines how much water ($s_i$) will be allocated to each group member ($i$). The weight ($w_i$) assigned to each group member is a historical-use rate. An equitable distribution is one that satisfies the following condition:

$$\frac{s_1}{w_1} = \frac{s_2}{w_2} = \ldots = \frac{s_n}{w_n}$$

8  It is interesting to note that the procedure used in the Raymond Basin case, and subsequently in West Basin, Central Basin, and San Gabriel Basin, leads to a "solution" to this problem that is close to but not the same as that recommended by Nash (1950): point C. Mutual prescription has not been uniformly adopted as "the" solution concept used in all southern California groundwater litigations. In the San Fernando Valley, for example, the city of Los Angeles had been granted and has tenaciously defended a preeminent right to water. The California Supreme Court overturned an initial effort by the trial court to impose a mutual-prescription solution on all parties. The California Supreme Court found, in essence, that the mutual-prescription solution was an equitable solution, but it was not the only equitable solution that could be used in these types of situations (*City of Los Angeles v. City of San Fernando*, Superior Court Case No. 650073, 1968) (Blomquist 1988e). Water producers in Chino Basin also negotiated a settlement that allocated water rights that was broadly similar to the mutual-prescriptioin solution, but took into account a variety of specific problems that would have arisen if that formula had been applied in a mechanical fashion (Lipson 1978). I appreciate the opportunity to have discussed the logic of this outcome with Roy Gardner.

9  The judge in such a case is in a delicate position. The proposed solution was truly radical and was not based on any of the existing water-rights doctrines. If he accepted a negotiated settlement that he could not justify in his finding, he would be overruled by a higher court. On the other hand, there was no clear-cut alternative on which to base his decision. He was in as uncertain a situation as were the litigants.

10  *City of Pasadena v. City of Alhambra et al.*, Superior Court Case C-1323.

11  Cal. 2d 908, 207 P.2d 17 (1949).

12  The case was appealed, and a costly and time-consuming appeal procedure could not be avoided.

13  Thus, an N of 19 producers could function as an effective coalition to control most of the production from the basin; see Schelling (1978) on the concept of a minimal effective group.

14  One-half of the $25,000 allocated for that purpose came from federal funds, one-fourth was paid for by the county, and the remaining one-fourth was allocated on a pro rata basis to the nine signatory communities.

15  Although there is insufficient space in this chapter to discuss the structure and operational characteristics of the West Basin Water Association, the importance of its activities can hardly be overemphasized. The formal voting rules of the association prevented any potential subgroup from dominating the decisions made within the association. Given the voluntary status of the association, no actions were taken by the association until a consensus was reached. Because actions were being pursued in many different arenas at the same time, major water producers could coordinate activities and monitor the perfor-

mances of public officials (and their fellow water producers) in the context of the regular quarterly meetings, the Executive Committee meetings, and the meetings of the working committees of the association. See E. Ostrom (1965) for a detailed discussion of the operational characteristics of the association.

16 The policy of open files was also of immense value to my research; as a young graduate student, I was shown the filing cabinets and invited to read and make copies of any or all correspondence, minutes, reports, etc., contained therein.

17 In 1945 the Dominguez Water Corporation withdrew over 10,000 acre-feet from the basin, or about 15% of the total withdrawals.

18 The reason for the change in position was well documented, because once city officials recognized how exposed they were, they also had to recommend to the citizens of Inglewood that the city join the West Basin Water District to obtain MWD imported water. The mayor had vigorously opposed such a move only three years before. The mayor was repeatedly asked for a clarification for his change of heart. The following statement was printed in the September 26, 1950, *Inglewood Daily News*: "I have been asked many times the reason why I now support Metropolitan Water District, in view of my opposition to it in 1947. This is a very reasonable question and I feel that it is my obligation to answer this question. . . .

"On October 24, 1945, a case was filed in the Superior Court [that] asked that the Superior Court determine the rights of all water producers in the West Coast Basin and to allocate the available water therein equitably among all of the water producers.

"When this case was filed, your City Council employed the legal firm of Stewart, Shaw, and Murphy to defend the City of Inglewood on this action. . . . I quote from a letter received by the City Council from Arvin B. Shaw, Jr., 'I believe that there is a reasonable ground to hope to establish for the City of Inglewood, a preferred position, based on priority of water rights as an appropriator of water for many years.' . . .

"Some time prior to the filing of a California Water Service Company suit, there had been pending in another section of Los Angeles County a case known as the 'Raymond Basin Case.' This case was in many points substantially similar to the one in which we were being sued. . . . The substantial and pertinent portion of the Supreme Court decision was to the effect that all water users from a common basin must be treated exactly alike.

"On May 10, a conference participated in by William Renshaw, water engineer, F. R. Coop, administrative officer, and myself, was held with Arvin B. Shaw. . . . While much of the information given us by Shaw was in confidence, I have received his permission to quote from a confidential letter as follows: 'The decision of the Supreme Court in the Pasadena case, however, is to my mind, clear to the effect that you would not be given priority and that all overlying users in the West Basin, as well as appropriators, would be treated on an equal basis of right; in substance, would be required to prorate water production downward to a point which is within the safe yield of the Basin.'"

19 A major factor in the success of the committee was that T. B. Cosgrove was appointed to it; he was the attorney for the Dominguez Corporation and other related firms. Prior to his appointment to the Settlement Committee, he had vigorously fought against the litigation and strongly articulated a position that the Dominguez rights were superior to those of the others using the basin. No

one was likely to agree to curtail production without Dominguez participating. Cosgrove came to play an active role on the committee. By the time an agreement had been drafted, he had changed his strategy to one of cooperation with other water producers. In fact, one member of the committee gave him credit for drafting the form of the interim agreement, and he was commended for his outstanding contribution to the committee (West Basin Water Association, minutes, August 26, 1954). Cosgrove did not, as a result, obtain as many water rights for his firm as he might have if he had continued his opposition (see note 22).

20 They later defined "Prescriptive Rights, 1949" as "the highest continuous production of water by each user for beneficial use in any five-year period prior to October 1, 1949, as to which there was no cessation of use by it during any subsequent continuous five-year period prior to October 1, 1949" (interim agreement, p. 2). The 1944 water year was selected for comparison because many producers thought that initiating litigation in 1945 would lead to a determination of rights based on the water year that had just been completed.

21 See Mnookin and Kornhauser (1979) for a discussion of bargaining procedures related to private matters, such as divorce settlements, that also occur in the shadow of the law.

22 Because an authoritative list of rights as of 1944 was never compiled, it is difficult to determine exactly who won and who lost in this fight over the proportionate sharing of the basin. The shift was not very large, in any case. In digging back through the referee's report and the final stipulated agreement, my best estimate of the relative positions of the 35 largest producers from the basin is the following:

| | Estimated water rights, 1944 | % | "Prescriptive Rights, 1949" | % |
|---|---|---|---|---|
| *Overlying landowners* | | | | |
| 12 industrial firms | 16,135 | 36 | 25,876 | 41 |
| 8 large agricultural users | 2,061 | 5 | 1,628 | 3 |
| | 18,196 | 41 | 27,504 | 44 |
| *Appropriators* | | | | |
| 9 public districts or municipalities | 9,764 | 22 | 14,375 | 23 |
| 6 private utilities | 16,179 | 37 | 20,889 | 33 |
| | 25,943 | 59 | 35,264 | 56 |
| Total | 44,139 | 100 | 62,768 | 100 |

The California Water Service slipped from estimated rights of just over 5% to prescriptive rights of just under 5%. The Dominguez Water Corporation, which had opposed a settlement until T. B. Cosgrove was asked to head the committee of attorneys, slipped from estimated rights of 18% to prescriptive rights of 15%.

23 The city of El Segundo and Standard Oil withdrew water from wells located to the west of Hawthorne and near to the coast. Their fields consequently lay

233

in the path of the saltwater wedge moving at an accelerated rate toward the pumping trough beneath Hawthorne. Standard Oil had already reduced its own water withdrawals severely in 1952, because it feared that salt water would soon engulf its well lying between Hawthorne and the sea. Under the interim agreement, Standard Oil pumped about two-thirds of its "rights." El Segundo also was not pumping its full rights during that time period, for the same reason. The city of Inglewood, lying to the north of Hawthorne and inland, was not threatened by immediate saltwater intrusion, but Inglewood's pumping costs were considerably increased as a result of the lowered water table.

24 In September of 1957, for example, officials from Torrance, Inglewood, and El Segundo met with representatives of the city of Hawthorne "in an effort to persuade the City of Hawthorne to become a part of the Interim Agreement and petition to curtail pumping." The Inglewood official reporting on the meeting stated that "Hawthorne City officials had indicated that they would take the matter under consideration but that press releases implied that there was small likelihood that the City would become a party to the Agreement" (WBWA, Executive Committee, minutes, July 12, 1957, p. 4).

25 Many of the small producers had abandoned their rights as imported water became generally available to the basin. Others had sold their rights to the larger producers once the interim agreement had been signed and an active market for water rights had developed.

26 The total expenditure for the watermaster service for 1985 in Raymond Basin was $112,471, and in West Basin $151,800 (Watermaster reports for 1985).

27 See Blomquist (1990) for a description of the process in the San Gabriel Basin. Participants in that basin adopted several of the cost-saving strategies developed in the Central Basin case. Blomquist is just now completing studies in three additional basins – San Fernando, Chino, and Mojave – in which legal and environmental conditions are quite different. No settlement has yet been reached in Mojave, where the asymmetries of the interests of various parties are far greater than in any of the other cases involved. See the discussion of the Mojave case in Chapter 5. The city of Los Angeles holds a preeminent water right in the San Fernando Valley, and the final court decision adjudicating rights in that basin is quite different from those in the basins that relied on mutual prescription. The settlement in Chino Basin was reached by producers drawing on the experiences of all of these other basins.

28 Carl Fossette, the executive director of both associations, as well as the director of the Upper San Gabriel Water Association, played a remarkable role in helping the water producers in all of these interlinked basins to change the structures of institutions affecting their behaviors. His importance derived from several factors: (1) The number of overlapping positions he finally held. In addition to his role as executive director of three private water associations, he eventually became the general manager of the West Basin Municipal Water District, the Central Basin Municipal Water District, the Upper San Gabriel Municipal Water District, and the Central and West Basin Water Replenishment District. (2) The duration of his activities. He was appointed to his first position in 1946 and continued an active role in all three of the basins until he retired in 1974. Even after retirement at age 67, he continued an active role as a director representing Central Basin on the board of directors of the

Metropolitan Water District of Southern California, where he was vice-chairman during 1980–2 (Fossette and Fossette 1986, p. iv). (3) His tolerance for conflict and his commitment to conflict resolution. Fossette was able to sit through tough bargaining situations without losing his temper. The association minutes document his repeated efforts to bring contesting parties together in informal working settings to try to work out mutually agreeable relationships. (4) His ability to represent the interests of West, Central, and San Gabriel water producers to external agencies, including California state legislators. Fossette became the chief advocate for proposals developed within these basins that needed support from countywide, regionwide, or statewide public agencies.

29  Markets for water rights have emerged in all of the southern California basins that used litigation to assign defined water shares to parties. In all of these cases, agricultural users have slowly sold their rights to water companies or utilities, who can utilize the rights to avoid building expensive surface storage facilities. See R. Smith (1988) for a discussion of the advantage of tradable water rights.

30  Interview by Elinor Ostrom with John Johams of the watermaster service, November 17, 1960.

31  *Dominguez Water Corporation v. American Plant Growers, Inc.* Case 668,965, Superior Court, State of California, County of Los Angeles.

32  The parties in Raymond Basin changed their watermaster in recent years; so the threat of a change is credible.

33  For a surface storage facility, one can empty and fill the reservoir frequently without harming the structure itself. The degrees of freedom in raising and lowering the water levels in a groundwater basin are considerably less than those involved in the use of a surface reservoir.

34  The possibilities included the Los Angeles County Flood Control District and the Metropolitan Water District of Southern California, both of which had decided interests in seeing that the water basins in the area were regulated. Water producers in West Basin and Central Basin wanted to cooperate with these larger agencies, but not be completely dependent on them.

35  The wide representation involved in this group led one observer of the process to comment that "the Committee of Twelve was made up of engineers, attorneys and representatives of irrigation districts, water districts, farm bureaus, cities, private utilities and the State of California itself. Into that group came a variety of viewpoints and a diversity of problems which was most beneficial. Instead of recommending solutions for particular areas or groups, the ideas of this committee were bound to be cross-sectional in their scope" (James K. Krieger, "Progress in Ground Water Replenishment," mimeograph April 15, 1955, p. 2).

36  In a report to the West Basin Water Association, Louis Alexander, a member of the "Committee of Twelve" active in both West Basin and Central Basin, stated that "the original concept for the bill was that an assessment on pumping only would be provided and . . . no ad valorem tax would be permitted. . . . [T]he farm element in the State had insisted upon an ad valorem tax rate provision and . . . the present bill represents a compromise between the two points of view" (West Basin Water Association, minutes, April 12, 1955, p. 8). The president of the association had called a special meeting of the full associa-

tion to consider a draft of both pieces of legislation before he acted to approve the final draft within the Committee of Twelve. At that meeting, he and other members of the Committee of Twelve were asked many questions and subjected to some criticism for not having accomplished all that the members of the association had wanted, but the members finally voted unanimously to support the drafts.

37 James Krieger explained that provision in the following way: "Certain existing public agencies believed that they had the facilities to accomplish replenishment. Some of these agencies had the facilities to replenish groundwater basins, but no means of raising funds to purchase the water to do the replenishment. They felt that they should be permitted to do the job, and that no new public corporation should usurp their functions" (Progress in Ground Water Replenishment," mimeograph, April 15, 1955, p. 6).

38 In other words, if the district comprised only West Basin, then the West Basin producers could sue the Central Basin producers to pressure them into curtailing their production. If the Central Basin producers controlled the district, they might not let the district initiate legal proceedings against them.

39 Each of those agencies had substantial threat power over the proponents of the new district, because the boundaries of the proposed district had to be approved by the Department of Natural Resources, and the district itself had to be approved by the voters. Significant opposition at either stage would substantially raise the costs of gaining approval and threaten the likelihood of approval. Among the issues that had to be resolved at that stage of the negotiations was the formula for distributing the costs of replenishment. The city of Los Angeles, for example, strongly opposed any imposition of a property tax on its residents to pay for the construction of the barrier, because its taxpayers had borne a higher burden through the years to pay for imported water, while the taxpayers in the other cities had received the benefit of much lower water costs. By using "zones-of-benefit districts" within the Los Angeles County Flood Control District, which did not include portions of the city of Los Angeles, to pay for barrier construction, a cost-distribution formula was developed that was agreeable to all parties.

40 The costs are also less than the total operating costs in neighboring Orange County, where producers did not litigate their water rights, but instead developed only a replenishment program without any control over withdrawal rates. The focus of their management program, therefore, has been entirely on the "supply side" of the equation (Blomquist 1987a).

41 The story of this negotiation is extremely interesting, and it illustrates the vitality and creativity of a polycentric public-enterprise system. See E. Ostrom (1965) for a detailed discussion of the early process, and see more recent reports of the Central and West Basin Water Replenishment District for later developments.

42 A reader might wonder why a flood-control district would be in the business of supplying replenishment services in the first place. When the Los Angeles Flood Control District was first established in 1915, it was given strong powers over both flood control and water conservation. Once it had lined most of the rivers in the county, the district emphasized water conservation in an effort to maintain its survival as a large-scale engineering firm in the public arena.

43 Several private firms in the area serve as the watermasters for other basins; so

the Department of Water Resources does not have monopoly authority to perform this service.

44 Those who have rights to the largest proportions of water to be withdrawn also pay the largest proportions of the pump tax, which is then used to replenish the basin and pay for the monitoring arrangements that exist. Property owners who have benefited from the provision of an effective water system in an arid region pay low property taxes to support the modest administrative structure involved. Because the rules were devised basin by basin, they are tailored quite specifically to the unique aspects of each groundwater basin.

45 The process described here is somewhat similar to the "learning by doing" that occurs in the development of complex technologies; see Rosenberg (1982) and Nelson and Winter (1982). Because this is a dynamic process of selecting among various rules, it is likely to have aspects of path dependence similar to those of technological change (Arthur 1989; David 1985).

46 This is another application of Selten's equity principle; see note 7.

47 All rules share a common syntax: Defined persons with particular attributes filling specific positions are (required, forbidden, or permitted) to take named actions under specified conditions.

48 See von Wright (1951, 1963) for an introduction to the foundations of deontic logic. The modal form of the three deontic operators is as follows: must not (forbid), must (require), and may (permit). John R. Commons continually used these modal operators to characterize the basic structure of working rules (Commons 1957).

49 See, for example, the discussion by Shimanoff (1980, pp. 43–6) regarding why permission should not be included as a deontic operator to define rules.

50 This distinction characterizes my previous work (E. Ostrom 1985b).

51 See Buchanan (1975, p. 59), who characterizes the origin of a constitution as a "leap out of the anarchistic jungle."

52 Any change in the parts of the syntax of a rule, identified in note 47, would constitute a change in a rule. Rules can change without producing changes in the outcomes likely to be produced in the resulting situation. Following Gardner and E. Ostrom (1990), I reserve the term "reform" for a change in a rule that produces a new outcome preferred to the outcome produced prior to the change in the rule.

## 5. ANALYZING INSTITUTIONAL FAILURES AND FRAGILITIES

1 Rent dissipation is defined in Chapter 2 in the section "Appropriation Problems."

2 Central-government encouragement and even financing of "modern" fishing vessels have caused similar conflicts between inshore and offshore fishers in many other locations. See McGoodwin (1980) for a description of this problem in Mexico. Dasgupta (1982, p. 17) describes how modern fishing vessels in India have been able to ignore historical rights of traditional inshore fishers.

3 William Blomquist (1989) describes this case in considerable detail, and I am much indebted to him for his insights and analysis based on his fieldwork.

4 The Karave caste is known for being entrepreneurial and oriented toward trading and other forms of acquiring wealth: "Nor was caste a significant barrier against the conversion of economic gains into social mobility. . . . The

[Karave] lack the ranked subsections which are found among" other castes (Alexander 1982, p. 233).

5 A description of the way these nets are used is provided later.

6 One way to think of what happened is illustrated in Figure 5.2. Prior to the increase in the price of fish, the marginal and average returns to be derived from the use of each additional net can be represented by $MR_1$ and $AR_1$. With a uniform marginal cost of constructing a net, fishers would have maximized their economic return by constructing $X_1$ nets, where the marginal return would equal marginal cost. Because they were already dissipating rent before the price increase, the fishers probably were close to the point where average return would intersect the marginal-cost curve, say $X_2$. When a substantial increase in the price occurred, both the marginal-return and average-return curves would be shifted dramatically upward. The optimal economic return would then be at $X_3$. It would appear that the fishers were constructing new nets beyond that point, say at $X_4$. They may not have suffered full rent dissipation, because shares in the nets were still actively sought. Full rent dissipation would occur at $X_5$. So the lure of continuing profits (even with negative marginal returns) would always tempt more fishers to enter. This analysis was developed in a very useful discussion with Jimmy Walker.

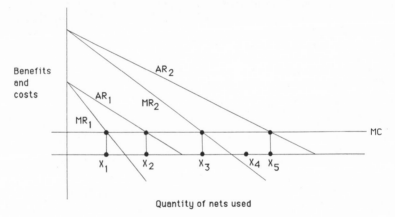

Figure 5.2. Rent dissipation in a fishery.

Paul Alexander's comment on reading this interpretation in an early draft of this manuscript was that he "would put more weight on political motives and the marked disparities in the returns to individual nets, in explaining why entry increased when marginal returns were negative, and probably recognized as such by the fishermen" (personal communication, August 2, 1988).

7 No matter how well a set of rules operates under one set of environmental and economic conditions, major changes – such as the price for a resource unit quadrupling – represent a substantial challenge to the capacity of an old set of rules to continue to produce outcomes that are efficient and fair.

8 Up to 1972, only Taiwan, Japan, and Korea experienced more rapid growth in the yield of paddy rice (N. T. Uphoff, personal communication).

9 The introduction of high-yield varieties has, in some villages, been associated with lower, rather than higher, yields (Byrne 1986).

10 This is not to imply that the participants are permanently trapped in this set of incentives, even though the social and political structures generating these incentives are difficult to change. It is particularly poignant that such vicious circles have been created in a country with a rich and very long history of successful irrigation using a diversity of indigenous institutions (Gunasekera 1981; Leach 1961, 1980).

11 Leach describes the system in effect during the 1950s in a single village that depended on a much smaller restored bund: "Whenever the Old Field is to be cultivated it is essential for the whole village to adhere closely to a predetermined program of work, for when the tank sluices are open the whole field can take water and when the sluices are shut the whole field must run dry. No plowing can be done on a dry field, but once the water has been let in to soften the earth, work must proceed everywhere simultaneously. Thereafter, to avoid loss by evaporation, the plowed fields must be sown and the crops carried through to harvest with the least possible delay.

"There must, therefore, be agreement about the dates on which the sluice will be opened, the date at which sowing will be completed, the varieties of rice that will be sown, and the dates at which it is planned to have harvest ready and the field drained. Under rules in force in 1954 the Village Cultivation Officer held a village meeting at the beginning of each cultivation season and formally agreed on these various dates with the assembled villagers" (Leach 1980, p. 108). Leach reports that this strict regimen was actually followed while he was there.

12 The British authorities were quite uncertain about what type of administrative and judicial arrangements they should establish, and they organized and reorganized both the administrative and conflict-resolution mechanisms related to irrigation several times during British rule. At each change, a key debate focused on how much authority could be entrusted to "native" tribunals or administrative officials. See Roberts (1980) for an excellent review of the 1856–71 period of British rule in Ceylon.

13 The recurring necessity for the exertion of considerable effort by British AGAs is revealed in a report by Edward Elliott, an AGA from 1863 to 1896, supervising a number of smaller irrigation systems (among other tasks). His report for 1871, as quoted by Roberts (1980, p. 200), contained the following: "Each year shows that incessant personal attention on the part of the Assistant Agent is necessary to carry out irrigation works by villages; to simply order the . . . Headmen to carry out any work may sound very fine, but, practically, the results are small, unless the Headmen be encouraged and supported by the Assistant Agent taking an active interest in their efforts; if the villagers see this and know that once they agree to any undertaking, everyone must contribute and that no shirking is allowed, all will combine cheerfully to carry out the work. But endless watching and numerous inspections are necessary."

14 Water meetings of this type have occurred in Sri Lanka for centuries (Gunasekera 1981). See the discussion of these institutions by Uphoff (1983).

15 The earlier land-tenure system in some parts of Sri Lanka had greatly reduced the level of conflict between head-enders and tail-enders, on the smaller tanks at least. The fields to be irrigated from a tank were laid out and assigned in

such a way that each farmer was assigned one block of land to farm in the top third of the area to be irrigated, another block in the middle section, and one block in the lower section. Thus, all farmers had a motivation to try to find ways of getting water to the tail end of the system. Further, when water shortages required a cutback, it was relatively easy to decide not to water the bottom third of the fields. Everyone participated in the sharing of this risk, and the mechanism for determining which fields would be watered was built into the design of the fields themselves (Leach 1961, 1980).

16  Fladby describes the patterns of interaction on a tract in Kirindi Oya during the early 1980s in the following manner: "The directing of water in [the minor agricultural season, when water is the scarcest] is similar to an early 19th century diplomatic Major Power game: No rules are sacred, alliances are formed, every move is answered with a counter-move and in the long run the only guiding line is self-interest. The role of the authorities is like that of an ineffectual trans-national organization . . . with some formal power, but without means to enforce it" (Fladby 1983, p. 191).

17  The increasingly partisan nature of the relationship between MPs and district administrative systems is described by Craig (1981).

18  A report by A. T. Corey (1986) lays out some of the severe problems faced on the huge Mahaweli set of projects planned to develop or improve water supply for 900,000 acres of land for over 200,000 new settlers (Jayawardene 1986). Among the problems Corey notes related to "Turnout Area H" are these: (1) Of the 119 allotments in the area, only 83 had received water during the year of his investigation. (2) Of those 83, only 49 received water through authorized project outlets; the rest obtained water through unauthorized cuts. (3) Rotation of water, where practiced at all, was haphazard. (4) An unauthorized breach was taking all of the water from one ditch, even though the downstream farmer had notified authorities and was afraid to take further action for fear of being "hammered" by the offending farmer (Corey 1986, pp. 158–9; Lundqvist 1986).

19  The deputy director for water management in the Irrigation Department told one member of the Gal Oya project team that if they could make progress in Gal Oya, they "could make progress anywhere else in the country" (Uphoff 1985c, p. 44).

20  In a personal communication, Norman Uphoff stresses that the decision to hire college graduates was initially taken to avoid hiring individuals with political connections, and the enhanced capacity of the IOs to communicate with the ID staff was an unforeseen but very positive consequence.

21  Exigencies in the field reduced the time available for data collection and pushed IOs into action earlier than planned.

22  Membership in FCOs and DCOs was at times a delicate issue, because many actual irrigators did not have legal claims to the water they used. A frequent accommodation to this problem was to involve all actual irrigators in the FCOs, and only legal irrigators in the DCOs. Some rotations had to be abandoned because farmers who "were using drainage water from the system for unauthorized cultivation broke open the closed gates" (Uphoff 1986a, p. 218, note 18).

23  Actually, farmer-representatives took the initiative to set up such area councils shortly after FCOs were formed and before many DCOs were in place. This

was possible because the program was not implementing a preconceived "blueprint," but wanted farmers to regard those organizations as their own and take responsibility for them.

24 Uphoff (1985c, note 32) discusses the change in official orientation: "One surprising but dramatic evidence of current ID responsiveness seen on the visit last January was the ID breaking down a freshly-built measuring weir off the Uhana branch canal to reduce its impediment to flow into a particular distributory. In the redesign meetings, farmers had insisted the size of the offtake for this D-channel was too small, but the ID insisted its calculations supported no change. When it became clear to the ID's Deputy Director himself that not enough water was reaching the tail-end of that distributory command area, he agreed to enlarge the offtake as soon as flow in the branch canal ceased and in the meantime to increase flow into the D-channel as much as possible, even if it cost the ID some funds and embarrassment. Actually, the respect it would gain from such an act of good faith should well outweigh those costs. We were pleased and surprised to find the Chief Irrigation Engineer for the district himself out checking the flow to the tail of the channel at 9:30 on a Sunday morning when we were making our own inspections (which he did not know about)."

25 Uphoff reports in a personal communication that one of the field-workers in Gal Oya, Nancy St. Julien, argued that free-riding has two faces: one that shows itself at the time of trying to establish a form of organization, and another that shows itself when their work has to be done to keep organized cooperation continuing. In this case, the first type of free-riding was harder to overcome, evidently, than the second type. The external IO was important in attempting to overcome the inertia of years of mistrust and unwillingness to work together. Sustaining the benefits of cooperation, once they became evident, was not as difficult.

26 Types of successful intervention strategies similar to those employed in Gal Oya have been used in the Philippines (D. Korten 1980; F. Korten 1982), in Nepal (Rahman 1981), in Bangladesh (D. Korten 1980), and in Thailand (Rabibhadena 1980).

27 Grate's Cove, Fermuse, and Twillingate in Newfoundland all use an annual lottery. A limited set of boats is eligible to participate in the lottery, which then is used to assign those vessels to particular locations. As described by one fisher, "we have a cod trap draw. There are only ten berths available and there are only ten crews fishing 'em. If a fellah has a berth one year he can enter the draw the next" (Matthews and Phyne 1988, p. 17). See also K. Martin (1979) and McCay (1978, 1979).

28 Similar findings concerning the development of property rights to fishing zones are described by Acheson (1975), Andersen (1979), and Faris (1972).

29 Subsidizing the purchase of new technologies has been a frequent strategy of national governments in relationship to fisheries, with results that have at times been disastrous. The effort to finance the acquisition of a new technology presumes that local fishers will not adopt efficient new technologies without external aid. The conservatism of fishers in regard to the use of new technologies may reflect an awareness that the management of complex resource systems depends on a delicate balance between the technologies in use and the entry and authority rules used to control access and use. If the adapta-

tion of new technologies is accelerated, the relationship between the rules and technologies in use may become seriously unbalanced. This is particularly the case when the rules have come about through long processes of trial and error and fishers do not possess legal powers to devise new rules and get them enforced. A focus on "production costs" alone, rather than on the total of production costs, transaction costs, and enforcement costs, leads to a narrow interpretation of efficiency (North 1986a,b). The rapid introduction of a "more efficient" technology by an outside authority can trigger the very "tragedy of the commons" that the same public officials presume will occur if they do not regulate the use of these fisheries. See Cordell and McKean (1986) for a discussion of the effects of the subsidization of a new technology on the Bahian coast of Brazil by national authorities.

30 A clear policy statement was contained in a federal policy guide issued in 1976: "In an open-access, free-for-all fishery, competing fishermen try to catch all the fish available to them, regardless of the consequences. Unless they are checked, the usual consequence is a collapse of the fishery: that is, resource extinction in the commercial sense, repeating in the fishery context 'the tragedy of the commons'" (Government of Canada 1976).

31 Such a vested system would need to be relatively complex and involve autonomy *and* exposure to scrutiny by external authorities regarding the legitimacy of the local rules.

## 6. A FRAMEWORK FOR ANALYSIS OF SELF-ORGANIZING AND SELF-GOVERNING CPRs

1 If the only anomalies were the cases described in this book, one could overlook a few cases that could not be explained. But these cases were selected to be illustrative of many others that are similarly difficult to explain using current theories.

2 The importance of information and transaction costs is stressed in the work of North (1978, 1981, 1989) and Williamson (1979, 1985).

3 For an insightful discussion of situational analysis, see Farr (1985).

4 Heckathorn and Maser (1987) stress that in many institutional-choice situations the decision is not between one alternative and the status quo rules, but rather among a series of proposed alternatives. They recommend that one view the process of narrowing the alternatives as a bargaining process. This is a useful way of understanding the elimination of various alternative sets of rules, but the final decision is between the best alternative set that individuals identify and the set of status quo rules in use.

5 That there is always a set of status quo rules (see discussion in Chapter 4) and that they remain in effect until changed helps to clarify the final choice made in these situations at any particular time. That a set of status quo rules will stay in effect until changed also stabilizes the structure of operational situations. A new set of rules must be perceived as generating more benefits than costs to at least a minimum winning coalition (whatever that may be) in an institutional-choice situation.

6 This list is the result of my effort to understand what I have read in many case studies at a more general level. I presume that this list will be refined over time

as propositions are more rigorously developed and tested. In other words, these are my informed conjectures subject to refutation.

7 If that were the case, the group would be a privileged group in Olson's terminology (1965).

8 Because the process of governing affects the future costs of governing, these processes are recursive. Decisions made within a structure will affect that structure in the future.

9 Tocqueville, in *The Old Regime and the French Revolution* (1955), deals with the general case in which there are uniform rules, but many seek exceptions for their situations. This generates a strict-rule/law-enforcement regime in which everyone comes to view the law as an obstacle to a reasonable course of action. The potentials for corruption are obviously great.

10 See Wade (1988) for an intriguing analysis of a CPR system in India that was managed entirely outside the formal governance system of India and was sustained by paying regular bribes to regional and national officials.

11 Institutional-choice processes are thus path-dependent (David 1988).

12 The relationships of the community to shared norms and internal norms and discount rates obviously could be developed much further than I have done in this sketch. Given the limitations of what can be covered in any one work, I have focused much more on factors directly affecting benefits and costs, as well as the role of designed rules as compared with evolved norms. The extensive work of James Coleman (1990) on norms is directly relevant to the argument that I am making here.

13 The empirical fact of massive numbers of failures is consistent with modern economic theory, but not the focus of its attention. If one attempted to explain why some firms fail, but others do not fail, one would need a theoretical apparatus different from that used for predicting characteristics of survivors at equilibria. The question being pursued in this study is why some CPR appropriators succeed and others fail to change the structures of incentives they face, and simple benefit maximiation is not a useful theoretical assumption for this purpose.

14 The difficulty and typical biases involved in estimating benefits and costs of future capital structures – whether physical irrigation works or the rules to be used to allocate irrigation water – are well documented in Chapter 5 of Ascher and Healy (1990). Ascher and Healy carefully document an almost universal bias toward overestimating benefits and underestimating costs of large-scale irrigation projects in Third World settings.

15 For good summaries of this extensive literature, see Dawes (1988) and Hogarth and Reder (1987).

16 The first attempt to create a special district in West Basin failed, at least in part because of a massive rainstorm that occurred on election day. The quantity of water in the gutters was substantially augmented by the efforts of one city administration that opposed the creation of a new district: They opened all of the fire hydrants for a "routine" flushing (Fossette and Fossette 1986, pp. 28–9).

17 Because many models *assume* the first two characteristics, they are not even considered. Recently, however, several scholars have explored the results produced by rules that have strong distributional effects and the importance of "grandfathering" current appropriations in order to gain agreement to rule

changes (Johnson and Libecap 1982; Karpoff 1989; Welch 1983).

18  Where local institutions already exist and appropriators find them to work well, given the problems they face, considerable resistance may be expected if other rules are imposed. Local appropriators may attempt to continue an "illegal" rule system for as long as they can make it viable, either because of lack of enforcement by central officials or because of the capacity to bribe central officials to ignore what is happening at the local level.

19  It is not just when external officials make rules that local appropriators try to present the facts of local situations in their favor. One can expect that tendency in all cases. But it will be difficult for a set of appropriators to convince others who are familiar with the local circumstances of "facts" that are at variance with the experience and advantage of those others, whereas it will be easier to sell such "facts" to individuals who are not familiar with the local situation.

20  See, for example, Gardner and E. Ostrom (1990), where we model the effects of four different rule configurations used to organize appropriations activities in inshore fisheries. There we compare equilibrium outcomes that are achieved when fishers follow specific rules in different physical environments. We do not claim to have developed a universal model of inshore fishery environments, nor do we claim to have explored all relevant rule configurations. Because we are developing models guided by a general framework, we recognize the part of the general terrain to which our models are relevant. Within that terrain, we are able to make precise predictions about equilibria and the logical relationships among the variables overtly included in the model.

21  See the recent publications by V. Ostrom (1987, 1989, 1990) for examples in which the work of these scholars provides the foundation for modern political theory.

22  Readers are referred to the list of references for the many important recent works by Buchanan, Coase, North, Shepsle, and Williamson that are substantially adding to our understanding of how institutions work.

# References

Acheson, J. M. 1975. The Lobster Fiefs: Economic and Ecological Effects of Territoriality in the Maine Lobster Industry. *Human Ecology* 3:183–207.

Acheson, J. M. 1988. *The Lobster Gangs of Maine.* Hanover, N.H.: University Press of New England.

Advisory Commission on Intergovernmental Relations. 1987. *The Organization of Local Public Economies.* Washington, D.C.: Advisory Commission on Intergovernmental Relations.

Agnello, R. J., and L. Donnelly. 1950. Property Rights and Efficiency in the Oyster Industry. *Journal of Law and Economics* 18:521–33.

Ahmed, M. 1980. BRAC: Building Human Infrastructure to Serve the Rural Poor. In *Meeting the Basic Needs of the Rural Poor*, ed. P. Coombs, pp. 362–468. London: Pergamon Press.

Alchian, A. 1950. Uncertainty, Evolution, and Economic Theory. *Journal of Political Economy* 58:211–21.

Alchian, A., and H. Demsetz. 1972. Production, Information Costs, and Economic Organization. *American Economic Review* 62:777–95.

Alchian, A., and H. Demsetz. 1973. The Property Rights Paradigm. *Journal of Economic History* 33:16–27.

Alexander, P. 1977. South Sri Lanka Sea Tenure. *Ethnology* 16:231–55.

Alexander, P. 1979. Evolution and Culture. In *Evolutionary Biology and Human Social Behavior. An Anthropological Perspective*, eds. N. A. Chagnon and W. Irons, pp. 59–78. North Scituate, Mass.: Duxbury Press.

Alexander, P. 1982. *Sri Lankan Fishermen: Rural Capitalism and Peasant Society.* Australian National University Monographs on South Asia, No. 7. Canberra: Australian National University.

Allen, P. M., and J. M. McGlade. 1987. Modelling Complex Human Systems: A Fisheries Example. *European Journal of Operational Research* 30:147–67.

Allen, R. C. 1982. The Efficiency and Distributional Implications of 18th Century Enclosures. *Economic Journal* 92:937–53.

Alt, J. E., and A. Crystal. 1983. *Political Economics.* Berkeley: University of California Press.

Andersen, R. 1979. Public and Private Access Management in Newfoundland

# References

Fishing. In *North Atlantic Maritime Cultures: Anthropological Essays on Changing Adaptations*, ed. R. Andersen, pp. 299–336. The Hague: Mouton.

Arnold, J. E. M., and J. G. Campbell. 1986. Collective Management of Hill Forests in Nepal: The Community Forestry Development Project. In *Proceedings of the Conference on Common Property Resource Management*, National Research Council, pp. 425–54. Washington, D.C.: National Academy Press.

Arthur, W. B. 1989. Competing Technologies, Increasing Returns and Lock-in by Historical Events. *Economic Journal* 99:116–31.

Ashby, W. R. 1956. *An Introduction to Cybernetics*. New York: Wiley.

Ashby, W. R. 1960. *Design for a Brain. The Origin of Adaptive Behavior*, 2nd ed. New York: Wiley.

Ascher, W., and R. Healy. 1990. *Natural Resource Policymaking: A Framework for Developing Countries*. Durham, N.C.: Duke University Press.

Attwood, D. M., and B. S. Baviskar. 1987. Why Do Some Cooperatives Work But Not Others? A Comparative Analysis of Sugar Cooperatives in India. *Economic and Political Weekly* 22:A38–56.

Aumann, R. J. 1973. Subjectivity and Correlation in Randomized Strategies. *Journal of Mathematical Economics* 1:67–96.

Aumann, R. J. 1976. Agreeing to Disagree. *Annals of Statistics* 4:1236–9.

Aumann, R. J. 1987. Correlated Equilibrium as an Expression of Bayesian Rationality. *Econometrica* 55:1–18.

Axelrod, R. 1981. The Emergence of Cooperation Among Egoists. *American Political Science Review* 75:306–18.

Axelrod, R. 1984. *The Evolution of Cooperation*. New York: Basic Books.

Axelrod, R. 1986. Modeling the Evolution of Norms. *American Political Science Review* 80:1095–111.

Axelrod, R., and D. Dion. 1988. The Further Evolution of Cooperation. *Science* 242:1385–90.

Baack, B. 1982. Testing the Impact of Exclusive Property Rights: The Case of Enclosing Common Fields. In *Explorations in the New Economic History*, eds. R. L. Ransom, R. Sutch, and G. M. Walton, pp. 257–72. New York: Academic Press.

Bacdayan, A. S. 1980. Mountain Irrigators in the Philippines. In *Irrigation and Agricultural Development in Asia*, ed. E. W. Coward, Jr., pp. 172–85. Ithaca, N.Y.: Cornell University Press.

Bagnoli, M., and B. L. Lipman. 1986. Can Private Provision of Public Goods be Efficient? Working paper, University of Michigan at Ann Arbor.

Barry, B., and R. Hardin. 1982. *Rational Man and Irrational Society? An Introduction and Source Book*. Beverly Hills: Sage.

Barry, N. 1982. The Tradition of Spontaneous Order. *Literature of Liberty* 5:7–58.

Bates, R. H. 1985. The Analysis of Institutions. Paper presented at a seminar on institutions, sponsored by USAID/ST, Washington, D.C.

Bates, R. H. 1988. Contra Contractarianism: Some Reflections on the New Institutionalism. *Politics and Society* 16:387–401.

Beardsley, R. K., J. Hall, and R. E. Ward. 1959. *Village Japan*. University of Chicago Press.

Becker, G. S. 1968. Crime and Punishment: An Economic Approach. *Journal of Political Economy* 76:169–217.

246

# References

Bell, F. W. 1972. Technological Externalities and Common Property Resources: An Empirical Study of the U.S. Lobster Industry. *Journal of Political Economy* 80:148–58.

Bendor, J., and D. Mookherjee. 1985. Institutional Structure and the Logic of Ongoing Collective Action. Working paper, Stanford University.

Bentley, A. 1949. *The Process of Government.* Evanston, Ill.: Principia Press.

Berkes, F. 1984. Ecology and Resource Management Terminology. Paper presented to the Panel on Common Property Resource Management of the National Academy of Sciences, Washington, D.C.

Berkes, F. 1985a. The Common Property Resource Problem and the Creation of Limited Property Rights. *Human Ecology* 13:187–208.

Berkes, F. 1985b. Fishermen and "The Tragedy of the Commons." *Environmental Conservation* 12:199–206.

Berkes, F. 1986a. Local-Level Management and the Commons Problem: A Comparative Study of Turkish Coastal Fisheries. *Marine Policy* 10:215–29.

Berkes, F. 1986b. Marine Inshore Fishery Management in Turkey. In *Proceedings of the Conference on Common Property Resource Management*, National Research Council, pp. 63–83. Washington, D.C.: National Academy Press.

Berkes, F. 1987. Common Property Resource Management and Cree Indian Fisheries in Subarctic Canada. In *The Question of the Commons*, eds. B. McCay and J. Acheson, pp. 66–91. Tucson: University of Arizona Press.

Berkes, F., ed. 1989. *Common Property Resources. Ecology and Community-Based Sustainable Development.* London: Belhaven Press.

Berkes, F., D. Feeny, B. J. McCay, and J. M. Acheson. 1989. The Benefits of the Commons. *Nature* 340:91–3.

Berkes, F., and M. Kislalioglu. 1989. A Comparative Study of Yield, Investment and Energy Use in Small-Scale Fisheries: Some Considerations for Resource Planning. *Fisheries Research* 7:207–24.

Berkes, F., and D. Pocock. 1981. Self-Regulation of Commercial Fisheries of the Outer Long Point Bay, Lake Erie. *Journal of Great Lakes Research* 7:111–16.

Binger, B. R., and E. Hoffman. 1989. Institutional Persistence and Change: The Question of Efficiency. *Journal of Institutional and Theoretical Economics* 145:67–84.

Binswanger, H. P., and V. W. Ruttan. 1978. *Induced Innovations: Technology, Institutions, and Development.* Baltimore: Johns Hopkins University Press.

Blaikie, P., and H. Brookfield. 1987. *Land Degradation and Society.* London: Methuen.

Blomquist, W. 1987a. Getting Out of the Commons Trap: Variables, Process, and Results in Four Groundwater Basins. Paper prepared for the Common Property Resource Management Conference, Workshop in Political Theory and Policy Analysis, December 4–5, Indiana University, Bloomington.

Blomquist, W. 1987b. Getting Out of the Trap: Changing an Endangered Commons to a Managed Commons. Ph.D. dissertation, Indiana University.

Blomquist, W. 1988a. *The Performance of Groundwater Management: Volume 1, Raymond Basin.* Workshop in Political Theory and Policy Analysis. Bloomington: Indiana University.

Blomquist, W. 1988b. *The Performance of Groundwater Management: Volume 2, West Basin.* Workshop in Political Theory and Policy Analysis. Bloomington: Indiana University.

# References

Blomquist, W. 1988c. *The Performance of Groundwater Management: Volume 3, Central Basin.* Workshop in Political Theory and Policy Analysis. Bloomington: Indiana University.

Blomquist, W. 1988d. *The Performance of Groundwater Management: Volume 5, Orange County.* Workshop in Political Theory and Policy Analysis. Bloomington: Indiana University.

Blomquist, W. 1988e. *The Performance of Groundwater Management: Volume 6, The San Fernando Valley.* Workshop in Political Theory and Policy Analysis. Bloomington: Indiana University.

Blomquist, W. 1989. *The Performance of Groundwater Management: Volume 8, The Mojave River Basin.* Workshop in Political Theory and Policy Analysis. Bloomington: Indiana University.

Blomquist, W. 1990. *The Performance of Groundwater Management: Volume 4, San Gabriel Basin.* Workshop in Political Theory and Policy Analysis. Bloomington: Indiana University.

Blomquist, W., and E. Ostrom. 1985. Institutional Capacity and the Resolution of a Commons Dilemma. *Policy Studies Review* 5:383–93.

Blumel, W., R. Pethig, and O. van den Hagen. 1986. The Theory of Public Goods: A Survey of Recent Issues. *Journal of Institutional and Theoretical Economics* 142:241–309.

Boudreaux, D. J., and R. G. Holcombe. 1989. Government by Contract. *Public Finance Quarterly* 17:264–80.

Bowen, H. R. 1943. The Interpretation of Voting in the Allocation of Economic Resources. *Quarterly Journal of Economics* 58:27–48.

Braybrooke, D. 1985. The Insoluble Problem of the Social Contract. In *Paradoxes of Rationality and Cooperation,* eds. R. Campbell and L. Sowden, pp. 277–305. Vancouver: University of British Columbia Press.

Brennan, G., and J. Buchanan. 1985. *The Reason of Rules.* Cambridge University Press.

Breton, A. 1974. *The Economic Theory of Representative Government.* Chicago: Aldine.

Breton, A., and R. Wintrobe. 1982. *The Logic of Bureaucratic Conduct.* Cambridge University Press.

Bromley, D. W. 1984. Property Rights and Economic Incentives in Resource and Environmental Systems. Agricultural economics staff paper series, No. 231, University of Wisconsin.

Bromley, D. W. 1986. Opening Comments. In *Proceedings of the Conference on Common Property Resource Management,* National Research Council, pp. 1–5. Washington, D.C.: National Academy Press.

Bromley, D. W. 1989. *Economic Interests and Institutions: The Conceptual Foundations of Public Policy.* Oxford: Blackwell.

Bromley, D. W., ed. 1990. *Essays on the Commons.* Madison: University of Wisconsin Press.

Bromley, D. W., and D. P. Chapagain. 1984. The Village Against the Center: Resource Depletion in South Asia. *American Journal of Agricultural Economics* 66:868–73.

Bromley, D. W., D. C. Taylor, and D. E. Parker. 1980. Water Reform and Economic Development: Institutional Aspects of Water Management in Developing Countries. *Economic Development and Cultural Change* 28:365–87.

# References

Buchanan, J. M. 1968. *The Demand and Supply of Public Goods*. Chicago: Rand McNally.

Buchanan, J. M. 1975. *The Limits of Liberty*. University of Chicago Press.

Buchanan, J. M. 1977. *Freedom in Constitutional Contract. Perspectives of a Political Economist*. College Station: Texas A&M University Press.

Buchanan, J. M. 1987. The Constitution of Economic Policy. *American Economic Review* 77:243–51.

Buchanan, J. M., and G. Tullock. 1962. *The Calculus of Consent: Logical Foundations of Constitutional Democracy*. Ann Arbor: University of Michigan Press.

Bullock, K., and J. Baden. 1977. Communes and the Logic of the Commons. In *Managing the Commons*, eds. G. Hardin and J. Baden, pp. 182–99. San Francisco: Freeman.

Byrne, J. A. 1986. The Decline in Paddy Cultivation in a Dry Zone Village of Sri Lanka. In *Rice Societies: Asian Problems and Prospects*, eds. I. Norlund, S. Cederroth, and I. Gerdin, pp. 81–116. London: Curzon Press.

California, State of, Department of Water Resources, *Report on Watermaster Service in West Coast Basin Watermaster Service Area*, annual reports for water years 1944–5 through 1984–5.

Campbell, D. T. 1982. Legal and Primary-Group Social Controls. *Journal of Social and Biological Structures* 5:431–8.

Campbell, R. 1985. Background for the Uninitiated. In *Paradoxes of Rationality and Cooperation*, eds. R. Campbell and L. Sowden, pp. 3–41. Vancouver: University of British Columbia Press.

Carruthers, I., and R. Stoner. 1981. Economic Aspects and Policy Issues in Groundwater Development. World Bank staff working paper No. 496, Washington, D.C.

Cave, J. A. K. 1984. *The Cold Fish War: Long-Term Competition in a Dynamic Game*. Santa Monica, Calif.: Rand Corporation.

Central and West Basin Water Replenishment District. 1987. *Annual Survey Report on Ground Water Replenishment*. Glendale, Calif.: Bookman, Edmmonston Engineering.

Chamberlin, J. 1974. Provision of Collective Goods as a Function of Group Size. *American Political Science Review* 68:707–16.

Chambers, J. D., and G. E. Mingay. 1966. *The Agricultural Revolution, 1750–1880*. New York: Schocken Books.

Chambers, R. 1981. In Search of a Water Revolution: Questions for Canal Management in the 1980s. *Water Supply and Management* 5:5–18.

Chapagain, D. P. 1984. Managing Public Lands as a Common Property Resource: A Village Case Study in Nepal. Ph.D. dissertation, University of Wisconsin.

Cheung, S. 1970. The Structure of a Contract and the Theory of a Non-Exclusive Resource. *Journal of Law and Economics* 13:45–70.

Chomsky, N. 1965. *Aspects of the Theory of Syntax*. Cambridge, Mass.: MIT Press.

Chomsky, N. 1975. *Reflections on Language*. New York: Random House.

Chomsky, N. 1978. *Rules and Representation*. New York: Columbia University Press.

Christy, F. T., Jr. 1982. Territorial Use Rights in Marine Fisheries: Definitions and Conditions. FAO technical paper No. 227, Food and Agricultural Organization of the United Nations, Rome.

Ciriacy-Wantrup, S. V., and R. C. Bishop. 1975. "Common Property" as a Con-

249

# References

cept in Natural Resource Policy. *Natural Resources Journal* 15:713–27.

Clark, C. W. 1976. *Mathematical Bioeconomics.* New York: Wiley.

Clark, C. W. 1977. The Economics of Over-exploitation. In *Managing the Commons,* eds. G. Hardin and J. Baden, pp. 82–95. San Francisco: Freeman.

Clark, C. W. 1980. Restricted Access to Common-Property Fishery Resources: A Game-Theoretic Analysis. In *Dynamic Optimization and Mathematical Economics,* ed. P. T. Liu, pp. 117–32. New York: Plenum Press.

Clark, C. W., G. Munro, and A. Charles. 1985. *Fisheries: Dynamics, and Uncertainty, in Progress in Natural Resource Economics,* ed. A. Scott, pp. 99–119. Oxford University Press (Clarendon Press).

Coase, R. H. 1937. The Nature of the Firm. *Economica* 4:386–405.

Coase, R. H. 1960. The Problem of Social Cost. *Journal of Law Economics* 3:1–44.

Cole, J. W., and E. R. Wolf. 1974. *The Hidden Frontier: Ecology and Ethnicity in an Alpine Valley.* New York: Academic Press.

Coleman, J. S. 1987a. Externalities and Norms in a Linear System of Action. Working paper, Department of Sociology, University of Chicago.

Coleman, J. S. 1987b. Free Riders and Zealots: The Role of Social Networks. Working Paper, Department of Sociology, University Chicago.

Coleman, J. S. 1987c. Norms as Social Capital. In *Economic Imperialism. The Economic Approach Applied Outside the Field of Economics,* eds. G. Radnitzky and P. Bernholz, pp. 133–55. New York: Paragon House.

Coleman, J. S. 1990. *Foundations of Social Theory.* Cambridge, Mass.: Harvard University Press.

Commons, J. R. 1957. *Legal Foundations of Capitalism.* Madison: University of Wisconsin Press.

Copes, P. 1983. Fisheries Management on Canada's Atlantic Coast: Economic Factors and Socio-Political Constraints. *Canadian Journal of Regional Science* 6:1–32.

Cordell, J. C., and M. A. McKean. 1986. Sea Tenure in Bahia, Brazil. In *Proceedings of the Conference on Common Property Resource Management,* National Research Council, pp. 85–113. Washington, D.C.: National Academy Press.

Corey, A. T. 1986. Control of Water within Farm Turnouts in Sri Lanka. Proceedings of a Workshop on Water Management in Sri Lanka, Documentation Series No. 10. Agrarian Research and Training Institute, Colombo, Sri Lanka.

Cornes, R., and T. Sandler. 1986. *The Theory of Externalities, Public Goods, and Club Goods.* Cambridge University Press.

Courtois, P. J. 1985. On Time and Space Decomposition of Complex Structures. *Communications of the ACM* 28:590–603.

Coward, E. W., Jr. 1979. Principles of Social Organization in an Indigenous Irrigation System. *Human Organization* 38:28–36.

Coward, E. W., Jr. 1980. *Irrigation and Agricultural Development in Asia: Perspectives from Social Sciences.* Ithaca, N.Y.: Cornell University Press.

Coward, E. W., Jr. 1985. Technical and Social Change in Currently Irrigated Regions: Rules, Roles and Rehabilitation. In *Putting People First,* ed. M. M. Cernea, pp. 27–51. Oxford University Press.

Craig, J. 1981. Continuity and Change in Sri Lanka's District Administration: A Political Perspective. In *Studies in Decentralization* (issue No. 3 of *Manchester Papers on Development*). Department of Administrative Studies, University of Manchester.

# References

Cruz, M. C., L. B. Cornista, and D. C. Dayan. 1987. *Legal and Institutional Issues of Irrigation Water Rights in the Philippines.* Laguna: University of the Philippines at Los Baños, Agrarian Reform Institute.

Cruz, W. 1986. Overfishing and Conflict in a Traditional Fishery: San Miguel Bay, Philippines. In *Proceedings of the Conference on Common Property Resource Management,* National Research Council, pp. 115–35. Washington, D.C.: National Academy Press.

Dahlman, C. 1980. *The Open Field System and Beyond: A Property Rights Analysis of an Economic Institution.* Cambridge University Press.

Dales, J. H. 1968. *Pollution, Property, and Prices: An Essay in Policy-making and Economics.* University of Toronto Press.

Dani, A. A., C. J. N. Gibbs, and D. W. Bromley. 1987. *Institutional Development for Local Management of Rural Resources.* Honolulu: East-West Center.

Dasgupta, P. S. 1982. *The Control of Resources.* Oxford: Blackwell.

Dasgupta, P. S., and G. M. Heal. 1979. *Economic Theory and Exhaustible Resources.* Cambridge University Press.

David, P. A. 1985. Clio and the Economics of QWERTY. *American Economic Review* 75:332–7.

David, P. A. 1988. Path-Dependence: Putting the Past into the Future of Economics. Working paper, Department of Economics, Stanford University.

Davis, A. 1984. Property Rights and Access Management in the Small-Boat Fishery: A Case Study from Southwest Nova Scotia. In *Atlantic Fisheries and Coastal Communities: Fisheries Decision-Making Case Studies,* eds. C. Lamson and A. J. Hanson, pp. 133–64. Halifax: Dalhousie Ocean Studies Programme.

Davis, L. E., and D. C. North. 1971. *Institutional Change and American Economic Growth.* Cambridge University Press.

Dawes, R. M. 1973. The Commons Dilemma Game: An N-Person Mixed-Motive Game with a Dominating Strategy for Defection. *ORI Research Bulletin* 13:1–12.

Dawes, R. M. 1975. Formal Models of Dilemmas in Social Decision Making. In *Human Judgment and Decision Processes: Formal and Mathematical Approaches,* eds. M. F. Kaplan and S. Schwartz, pp. 87–108. New York: Academic Press.

Dawes, R. M. 1988. *Rational Choice in an Uncertain World.* New York: Harcourt Brace Jovanovich.

Dawes, R. M., J. McTavish, and H. Shaklee. 1977. Behavior, Communication, and Assumptions About Other People's Behavior in a Commons Dilemma Situation. *Journal of Personality and Social Psychology* 35:1–11.

Dawkins, R. 1976. *The Selfish Gene.* Oxford University Press.

De Alessi, L. 1980. The Economics of Property Rights: A Review of the Evidence. *Research in Law and Economics* 2:1–47.

De Alessi, L. 1987. Nature and Methodological Foundations of Some Recent Extensions of Economic Theory. In *Economic Imperialism. The Economic Approach Applied Outside the Field of Economics,* eds. G. Radnitzky and P. Bernholz, pp. 51–76. New York: Paragon House.

de los Reyes, R. P. 1980. *47 Communal Gravity Systems: Organizational Profiles.* Quezon City: Institute of Philippine Culture.

de Saussure, F. 1960. *Course in General Linguistics.* London: Peter Owen.

de Silva, N. G. R. 1981. Farmer Participation in Water Management: The Minipe

251

# References

Project in Sri Lanka. *Rural Development Participation Review* 3:16–19.
Demsetz, H. 1967. Toward a Theory of Property Rights. *American Economic Review* 62:347–59.
Dosi, G. 1988. Technical Change, Institutional Processes and Economic Dynamics: Some Tentative Propositions and a Research Agenda. Working paper, Department of Economics, University of Rome.
Dove, M. R. 1986. Peasant versus Government Perception and Use of the Environment: A Case-Study of Banjarese Ecology and River Basin Development in South Kalimantan. *Journal of Southeast Asian Studies* 17:113–36.
Downs, A. 1967. *Inside Bureaucracy.* Boston: Little, Brown.
Durham, W. H. 1979. Toward a Coevolutionary Theory of Human Biology and Culture. In *Evolutionary Biology and Human Social Behavior. An Anthropological Perspective*, eds. N. A. Chagnon and W. Irons, pp. 39–58. North Scituate, Mass.: Duxbury Press.
Ehrenfield, D. W. 1972. *Conserving Life on Earth.* Oxford University Press.
Ehrlich, I. 1973. Participation in Illegitimate Activities: A Theoretical and Empirical Investigation. *Journal of Political Economy* 81:521–64.
Ehrlich, I., and G. D. Brower. 1987. On the Issue of Causality in the Economic Model of Crime and Law Enforcement: Some Theoretical Considerations and Experimental Evidence. *American Economic Review* 77:99–106.
Elkin, S. L. 1985. Economic and Political Rationality. *Polity* 18:253–71.
Elster, J. 1979. *Ulysses and the Sirens: Studies in Rationality and Irrationality.* Cambridge University Press.
Elster, J. 1989. *The Cement of Society. A Study of Social Order.* Cambridge University Press.
Esman, M. 1986. The Maturing of Development Administration. Paper presented to the American Society for Public Administration, Anaheim, California.
Fanoaltea, S. 1988. Transaction Costs, Whig History, and the Common Fields. *Politics and Society* 16:171–240.
Faris, J. C. 1972. *Cat Harbour: A Newfoundland Fishing Settlement.* University of Toronto Press.
Farr, J. 1985. Situational Analysis: Explanation in Political Science. *Journal of Politics* 47:1085–107.
Feeny, D. H. 1982. *The Political Economy of Productivity: Thai Agricultural Development, 1880–1975.* Vancouver: University of British Columbia Press.
Feeny, D. H. 1986. Conference on Common Property Resource Management: An Introduction. In *Proceedings of the Conference on Common Property Resource Management*, National Research Council, pp. 7–11. Washington, D.C.: National Academy Press.
Feeny, D. H. 1988a. Agricultural Expansion and Forest Depletion in Thailand, 1900–1975. In *World Deforestation in the Twentieth Century*, eds. J. F. Richards and R. P. Tucker, pp. 112–43. Durham, N.C.: Duke University Press.
Feeny, D. H. 1988b. The Demand for and Supply of Institutional Arrangements. In *Rethinking Institutional Analysis and Development: Issues, Alternatives, and Choices*, eds. V. Ostrom, D. Feeney, and H. Picht, pp. 159–209. San Francisco: Institute for Contemporary Studies Press.
Field, A. J. 1979. On the Explanation of Rules Using Rational Choice Models. *Journal of Economic Issues* 13:49–72.
Field, A. J. 1984. Microeconomics, Norms, and Rationality. *Economic Develop-*

# References

*ment and Cultural Change* 32:683–711.

Field, B. C. 1984. The Evolution of Individual Property Rights in Massachusetts Agriculture, 17th–19th Centuries. *Northeastern Journal of Agricultural and Resource Economics* 14:97–109.

Field, B. C. 1985a. The Evolution of Property-Rights Institutions: Common Lands in Early Massachusetts Agriculture. Paper presented at the annual meeting of the Economic History Association, September, New York.

Field, B. C. 1985b. The Optimal Commons. *American Journal of Agricultural Economics* 67:364–7.

Field, B. C. 1986. Induced Changes in Property-Rights Institutions. Research paper series 86–1, Department of Agricultural and Resource Economics, University of Massachusetts, Amherst.

Fladby, B. 1983. Household Viability and Economic Differentiation in Gama, Sri Lanka. Occasional paper 28, Department of Social Anthropology, University of Bergen.

Forman, S. O. 1967. Cognition and the Catch: The Location of Fishing Spots in a Brazilian Coastal Village. *Ethnology* 6:405–26.

Fortmann, L., and J. W. Bruce, eds. 1988. *Whose Trees? Proprietary Dimensions of Forestry*. Boulder: Westview Press.

Fossette, C., and R. Fossette. 1986. *The Story of Water Development in Los Angeles County*. Downey, Calif.: Central and West Basin Water Replenishment District.

Freeman, M. M. R. 1989. Graphs and Gaffs: A Cautionary Tale in the Common-Property Resources Debate. In *Common Property Resources*, ed. F. Berkes, pp. 92–109. London: Belhaven Press.

Frey, B. S. 1988. Political Economy and Institutional Choice. *European Journal of Political Economy* 4:349–66.

Frohlich, N., and J. A. Oppenheimer. 1970. I Get By with a Little Help from My Friends. *World Politics* 23:104–20.

Fudenberg, D., and E. Maskin. 1986. The Folk Theorem in Repeated Games with Discounting or with Incomplete Information. *Economica* 54:533–54.

Furubotn, E. G., and R. Richter. 1989. Editorial Preface. *Journal of Institutional and Theoretical Economics* 145:1–5.

Gadgil, M., and P. Iyer. 1989. On the Diversification of Common-Property Resource Use by Indian Society. In *Common Property Resources*, ed. F. Berkes, pp. 240–72. London: Belhaven Press.

Galanter, M. 1981. Justice in Many Rooms: Courts, Private Ordering, and Indigenous Law. *Journal of Legal Pluralism* 19:1–47.

Gardner, R. 1987. A Theory of Spoils System. *Public Choice* 54:171–85.

Gardner, R., and E. Ostrom. 1990. Rules and Games. *Public Choice*.

Gardner, R., E. Ostrom, and J. M. Walker. 1990. The Nature of Common-Pool Resource Problems. *Rationality and Society* 2:335–58.

Ghai, D., and A. Rahman. 1981. The Small Farmers' Groups in Nepal. *Development* 1:23–8.

Giddens, A. 1979. *Central Problems in Social Theory: Action, Structure and Contradiction in Social Analysis*. Berkeley: University of California Press.

Gilles, J. L., and K. Jamtgaard. 1981. Overgrazing in Pastoral Areas: The Commons Reconsidered. *Sociologia Ruralos* 21:129–41.

Glick, T. F. 1970. *Irrigation and Society in Medieval Valencia*. Cambridge, Mass.: Harvard University Press.

253

# References

Godwin, R. K., and W. B. Shepard. 1977. Population Issues and Commons Dilemmas. *Policy Studies Journal* 6:231–8.

Godwin, R. K., and W. B. Shepard. 1979. Forcing Squares, Triangles and Ellipses into a Circular Paradigm: The Use of the Commons Dilemma in Examining the Allocation of Common Resources. *Western Political Quarterly* 32:265–77.

Gordon, H. S. 1954. The Economic Theory of a Common-Property Resource: The Fishery. *Journal of Political Economy* 62:124–42.

Government of Canada. 1976. *Policy for Canada's Commercial Fisheries.* Ottawa: Government of Canada.

Gray, R. F. 1963. *The Sonjo of Tanganyika. An Anthropological Study of an Irrigation-based Society.* Oxford University Press.

Grofman, B., and J. Pool. 1975. Bayesian Models for Iterated Prisoner's Dilemma Games. *General Systems* 20:185–94.

Grossinger, R. S. 1975. The Strategy and Ideology of Lobster Fishing on the Back Side of Mt. Desert Island, Hancock County, Maine. Ph.D. dissertation, University of Michigan.

Gulland, J. A. 1974. *The Management of Marine Fisheries.* Bristol: Scientechnica.

Gunasekera, W. 1981. *The Role of Traditional Water Management in Modern Paddy Cultivation in Sri Lanka.* Japan: United Nations University.

Gupta, A. K. 1985. Managing Common Properties: Some Issues in Institutional Design. Paper presented at the Common Property Resource Management Conference, sponsored by the Board on Science and Technology, National Research Council, April 21–6, Annapolis, Maryland.

Güth, W. 1985. An Extensive Game Approach to Modelling the Nuclear Deterrence Debate. *Zeitschrift für die gesamte Staatswissenschaft* 141:525–38.

Güth, W., W. Leininger, and G. Stephan. 1990. On Supergames and Folk Theorems: A Conceptual Discussion. In *Game Equilibrium Models, Vol. 2: Methods, Morals, and Markets,* ed. R. Selten. Berlin: Springer-Verlag.

Haefele, E. T., ed. 1974. *The Governance of Common Property Resources.* Baltimore: Johns Hopkins University Press.

Hamilton, A. 1981. The Unity of Hunting-Gathering Societies: Reflections on Economic Forms and Resource Management. In *Resource Managers: North American and Australian Hunter-Gatherers,* eds. N.M. Williams and E.S. Hunn, pp. 229–48. Boulder, Colo.: Westview Press.

Hardin, G. 1968. The Tragedy of the Commons. *Science* 162:1243–8.

Hardin, G. 1978. Political Requirements for Preserving our Common Heritage. In *Wildlife and America,* ed. H. P. Bokaw, pp. 310–17. Washington, D.C.: Council on Environmental Quality.

Hardin, R. 1971. Collective Action as an Agreeable N-Prisoner's Dilemma. *Behavioral Science* 16:472–81.

Hardin, R. 1982. *Collective Action.* Baltimore: Johns Hopkins University Press.

Harris, F. H. deB. 1989. Comment. *Journal of Institutional and Theoretical Economics* 145:85–94.

Harriss, J. C. 1977. Problems of Water Management in Hambantota District. In *Green Revolution,* ed. B. H. Farmer, pp. 364–76. Boulder, Colo.: Westview Press.

Harriss, J. C. 1984. Social Organisation and Irrigation: Ideology, Planning and Practice in Sri Lanka's Settlement Schemes. In *Understanding Green Revolutions,* eds. T. P. Bayliss-Smith and S. Wanmali, pp. 315–38. Cambridge University Press.

# References

Harsanyi, J., and R. Selten. 1988. *A General Theory of Equilibrium Selection in Games*. Cambridge, Mass.: MIT Press.

Hayami, Y. 1975. *A Century of Agricultural Growth in Japan*. Minneapolis: University of Minnesota Press.

Hayami, Y., and M. Kikuchi. 1982. *Asian Village Economy at the Crossroads: An Economic Approach to Institutional Change*. Baltimore: Johns Hopkins University Press.

Hayami, Y., and V. W. Ruttan. 1985. *Agricultural Development: A Global Perspective*, rev. ed. Baltimore: Johns Hopkins University Press.

Hayek, F. A. 1973. *Law, Legislation and Liberty*, 3 vols. University of Chicago Press.

Head, J. G. 1962. Public Goods and Public Policy. *Public Finance* 17:197–219.

Hechter, M. 1984. When Actors Comply: Monitoring Costs and the Production of Social Order. *Acta Sociologica* 27:161–83.

Heckathorn, D. D. 1984. A Formal Theory of Social Exchange: Process and Outcome. *Current Perspectives in Social Theory* 5:145–80.

Heckathorn, D. D., and S. M. Maser. 1987. Bargaining and Constitutional Contracts. *American Journal of Political Science* 31:142–68.

Heilbroner, R. L. 1974. *An Inquiry Into the Human Prospect*. New York: Norton.

Hesselberg, J. 1986. Lack of Maintenance of Irrigation Facilities: Experiences from Southern Sri Lanka. In *Rice Societies: Asian Problems and Prospects*, eds. I. Norlund, S. Cederroth, and I. Gerdin, pp. 72–80. London: Curzon Press.

Hofstadter, D. R. 1979. *Godel, Escher, Bach: An Eternal Golden Braid*. New York: Basic Books.

Hogarth, R. M., and M. W. Reder, eds. 1987. *Rational Choice: The Contrast between Economics and Psychology*. University of Chicago Press.

Holt, S. J., and L. M. Talbot. 1978. *New Principles for the Conservation of Wild Living Resources*. Wildlife monographs, No. 59, Washington, D.C.: Wildlife Society.

Humboldt, W. von. 1836. *Ueber die Verschiedenheit des menschlichen Sprachbaues*. Berlin: Druckerei der Koniglichen Akademie der Wissenschaften.

Hwang, S. 1985. Constitutional Choice and the Individual Calculus of Voting. Ph.D. dissertation, Indiana University.

International Irrigation Management Institute. 1986. *Participatory Management in Sri Lanka's Irrigation Schemes*. Digana Village via Kandy, Sri Lanka: IIMI.

Irons, W. 1979. Natural Selection, Adaptation, and Human Social Behavior. In *Evolutionary Biology and Human Social Behavior. An Anthropological Perspective*, eds. N. A. Chagnon and W. Irons, pp. 4–39. North Scituate, Mass.: Duxbury Press.

Isaac, R. M., and J. M. Walker. 1986. Group Size Effects in Public Goods Provision: The Voluntary Contribution Mechanism. Working paper, Department of Economics, University of Arizona.

Isaac, R. M., and J. M. Walker. 1988. Communication and Free-Riding Behavior: The Voluntary Contribution Mechanism. *Economic Inquiry* 26:585–608.

Isaac, R. M., J. M. Walker, and S. H. Thomas. 1984. Divergent Evidence on Free Riding: An Experimental Encameration of Possible Explanations. *Public Choice* 43:113–49.

Jacobs, J. 1961. *The Death and Life of Great American Cities*. New York: Random House.

# References

Jayawardene, J. 1986. The Training of Mahaweli Turnout Group Leaders. In *Participatory Management in Sri Lanka's Irrigation Schemes*, International Irrigation Management Institute. Digana Village via Kandy, Sri Lanka: IIMI.

Jenson, M. C., and W. H. Meckling. 1976. Theory of the Firm: Managerial Behavior, Agency Costs and Ownership Structure. *Journal of Financial Economics* 3:305–60.

Jodha, N. S. 1986. Common Property Resources and Rural Poor in Dry Regions of India. *Economic and Political Weekly* 21:1169–81.

Johnson, D., and D. Anderson, eds. 1988. *The Ecology of Survival: Case Studies from Northeast African History*. London: Crook.

Johnson, O. E. G. 1972. Economic Analysis, the Legal Framework and Land Tenure Systems. *Journal of Law and Economics* 15:259–76.

Johnson, R. N., and G. D. Libecap. 1982. Contracting Problems and Regulation: The Case of the Fishery. *American Economic Review* 72:1005–22.

Kahneman, D., and A. Tversky. 1979. Prospect Theory: An Analysis of Decision Under Risk. *Econometrica* 47:263–91.

Kaitala, V. 1986. Game Theory Models of Fisheries Management–A Survey. In *Dynamic Games and Applications in Economics*, ed. T. Basar, pp. 252–66. Berlin: Springer-Verlag.

Kaminski, A. in press. *The Withering Away of the Communist State: The Design, Institutional Structure, and Change of the Soviet System*. San Francisco: Institute for Contemporary Studies Press.

Karpoff, J. M. 1989. Limited Entry Fisheries. *Land Economics* 4:386–93.

Karunatilleke, T. H. 1986. Farmer Participation in Water Management in the Mahaweli Projects. In *Participatory Management in Sri Lanka's Irrigation Schemes*, International Irrigation Management Institute. Digana Village via Kandy, Sri Lanka: IIMI.

Kasyanathan, N. 1986. The Farmer Organization Component in Final Impact Assessment Study of the Gal Oya Water Management Project. Manuscript, ARTI Research Study Series, Colombo, Sri Lanka.

Kaufman, H. 1960. *The Forest Rangers. A Study in Administrative Behavior*. Baltimore: Johns Hopkins University Press.

Kaufmann, F. X., G. Majone, and V. Ostrom. 1986. *Guidance, Control, and Evaluation in the Public Sector*. New York: Walter de Gruyter.

Keesing, F. M. 1962. *The Ethnohistory of Northern Luzon*. Stanford University Press.

Kimber, R. 1981. Collective Action and the Fallacy of the Liberal Fallacy. *World Politics* 33:178–96.

Kisangani, E. 1986. A Social Dilemma in a Less Developed Country: The Massacre of the African Elephant in Zaire. In *Proceedings of the Conference on Common Property Resource Management*, National Research Council, pp. 137–60. Washington, D.C.: National Academy Press.

Kiser, L. L., and E. Ostrom. 1982. The Three Worlds of Action. A Metatheoretical Synthesis of Institutional Approaches. In *Strategies of Political Inquiry*, ed. E. Ostrom, pp. 179–222. Beverly Hills: Sage.

Klein, J. 1920. *The Mesta. A Study in Spanish Economic History, 1273–1836*. Cambridge, Mass.: Harvard University Press.

Knapp, K., and H. J. Vaux. 1982. Barriers to Effective Ground-Water Management: The California Case. *Groundwater* 20:61–6.

# References

Koestler, A. R. 1959. *The Sleepwalkers*. New York: Macmillan.

Korten, D. C. 1980. Community Organization and Rural Development: A Learning Process Approach. *Public Administration on Review* 40:480–511.

Korten, F. F. 1982. *Building National Capacity to Develop Water Users' Associations: Experience from the Philippines*. World Bank staff working paper No. 528, Washington, D.C.

Kreps, D. M., P. Milgrom, J. Roberts, and R. Wilson. 1982. Rational Cooperation in the Finitely Repeated Prisoner's Dilemma. *Journal of Economic Theory* 27: 245–52.

Kreps, D. M., and R. Wilson. 1982. Reputation and Imperfect Information. *Journal of Economic Theory* 27:253–79.

Krieger, J. H. 1955. Progress in Ground Water Replenishment in Southern California. *Journal of the American Water Works Association* 47:909–13.

Leach, E. R. 1961. *Pul Eliya, a Village in Ceylon: A Study of Land Tenure and Kinship*. Cambridge University Press.

Leach, E. R. 1980. Village Irrigation in the Dry Zone of Sri Lanka. In *Irrigation and Agricultural Development in Asia: Perspectives from the Social Sciences*, ed. E. W. Coward, Jr., pp. 91–126. Ithaca, N.Y.: Cornell University Press.

Leonard, D. E., and D. R. Marshall. 1982. *Institutions of Rural Development for the Poor: Decentralization and Organizational Linkages*. Berkeley: University of California, Institute of International Studies.

Levhari, D., and L. H. Mirman. 1980. The Great Fish War: An Example Using a Dynamic Cournot-Nash Solution. *Bell Journal of Economics* 11:322–34.

Levi, M. 1988a. *Of Rule and Revenue*. Berkeley: University of California Press.

Levi, M. 1988b. The Transformation of Agrarian Institutions: An Introduction and Perspective. *Politics and Society* 18:159–70.

Levine, G. 1980. The Relationship of Design, Operation, and Management. In *Irrigation and Agricultural Development in Asia: Perspectives from the Social Sciences*, ed. E. W. Coward, Jr., pp. 51–62. Ithaca, N.Y.: Cornell University Press.

Lewis, D. K. 1969. *Convention: A Philosophical Study*. Cambridge, Mass.: Harvard University Press.

Lewis, H. T. 1980. Irrigation Societies in the Northern Philippines. In *Irrigation and Agricultural Development in Asia: Perspectives from the Social Sciences*, ed. E. W. Coward, Jr., pp. 153–71. Ithaca, N.Y.: Cornell University Press.

Lewis, T. R., and J. Cowens. 1983. Cooperation in the Commons: An Application of Repetitious Rivalry. Vancouver: University of British Columbia, Department of Economics.

Libecap, G. D. 1989. Distributional Issues in Contracting for Property Rights. *Journal of Institutional and Theoretical Economics* 145:6–24.

Libecap, G. D., and S. N. Wiggins. 1985. The Influence of Private Contractual Failure on Regulation: The Case of Oil Field Unitization. *Journal of Political Economy* 93:690–714.

Liebenow, J. G. 1981. Malawi: Clean Water for the Rural Poor. American University Field Staff Reports, Africa, No. 40.

Lipson, A. J. 1978. *Efficient Water Use in California: The Evolution of Groundwater Management in Southern California*. Santa Monica, Calif.: Rand Corporation.

Lloyd, W. F. 1977. On the Checks to Population. In *Managing the Commons*, eds.

257

# References

G. Hardin and J. Baden, pp. 8–15. San Francisco: Freeman.

Luce, D. R., and H. Raiffa. 1957. *Games and Decisions: Introduction and Critical Survey.* New York: Wiley.

Lumsden, M. 1973. The Cyprus Conflict as a Prisoner's Dilemma. *Journal of Conflict Resolution* 17:7–32.

Lundqvist, J. 1986. Irrigation Development and Central Control: Some Features of Sri Lankan Development. In *Rice Societies: Asian Problems and Prospects*, eds. I. Norlund, S. Cederroth, and I. Gerdin, pp. 52–71. London: Curzon Press.

Maass, A., and R. L. Anderson. 1986. *. . . and the Desert Shall Rejoice: Conflict, Growth and Justice in Arid Environments.* Malabar, Fla.: R. E. Krieger.

McCay, B. J. 1978. Systems Ecology, People Ecology, and the Anthropology of Fishing Communities. *Human Ecology* 6:397–422.

McCay, B. J. 1979. "Fish Is Scarce": Fisheries Modernization on Fogo Island, Newfoundland. In *North Atlantic Maritime Cultures: Anthropological Essays on Changing Adaptations*, ed. R. Andersen, pp. 155–88. The Hague: Mouton.

McCay, B. J. 1980. A Fishermen's Cooperative, Limited: Indigenous Resource Management in a Complex Society. *Anthropological Quarterly* 53:29–38.

McCay, B. J., and J. M. Acheson. 1987. *The Question of the Commons: The Culture and Ecology of Communal Resources.* Tucson: University of Arizona Press.

McCloskey, D. N. 1976. English Open Fields as Behavior Toward Risk. In *Research in Economic History: An Annual Compilation, Vol. 1*, ed. P. Uselding, pp. 124–70. Greenwich, Conn.: JAI Press.

McGoodwin, J. R. 1980. The Human Costs of Development. *Environment* 22:25–31.

McGuire, M. 1974. Group Segregation and Optimal Jurisdictions. *Journal of Political Economy* 82:112–32.

McGuire, R., and R. McC. Netting. 1982. Leveling Peasants? The Maintenance of Equality in a Swiss Alpine Community. *American Ethnologist* 9:269–90.

McHugh, J. L. 1972. Jeffersonian Democracy and the Fisheries. In *World Fisheries Policy: Multidisciplinary Views*, ed. B. J. Rothschild, pp. 134–55. Seattle: University of Washington Press.

McKean, M. A. 1982. The Japanese Experience with Scarcity: Management of Traditional Common Lands. *Environmental Review* 6:63–88.

McKean, M. A. 1986. Management of Traditional Common Lands (*Iriaichi*) in Japan. In *Proceedings of the Conference on Common Property Resource Management*, National Research Council, pp. 533–89. Washington, D.C.: National Academy Press.

McKean, R. 1975. Economics of Trust, Altruism, and Corporate Responsibility. In *Altruism, Morality and Economic Theory*, ed. E. S. Phelps, pp. 29–44. New York: Russell Sage.

McKelvey, R. D. 1976. Intransitivities in Multidimensional Voting Models and Some Implications for Agenda Control. *Journal of Economic Theory* 2:472–82.

McKelvey, R. D. 1979. General Conditions for Global Intransitivities in Formal Voting Models. *Econometrica* 47:1085–111.

MacKenzie, W. C. 1979. Rational Fishery Management in a Depressed Region: The Atlantic Groundfishery. *Journal of the Fisheries Research Board of Canada* 36:811–26.

Madduma Bandara, C. M. 1984. Green Revolution and Water Department: Irriga-

# References

tion and Ground Water in Sri Lanka and Tamil Nadu. In *Understanding Green Revolutions. Agrarian Change and Development Planning in South Asia*, eds. T. P. Bayliss-Smith and S. Wanmali, pp. 296–314. Cambridge University Press.

Magnusson, D., ed. 1981. *Toward a Psychology of Situations: An Interactional Perspective*. Hillsdale, N.J.: Erlbaum.

Majone, G. 1986. Policy Science. In *Guidance, Control, and Evaluation in the Public Sector*, eds. F. X. Kaufmann, G. Majone, and V. Ostrom, pp. 61–70. New York: Walter de Gruyter.

Margolis, J. 1955. A Comment on the Pure Theory of Public Expenditures. *Review of Economics and Statistics* 37:347–9.

Marshak, P. 1987. Uncommon History. In *Uncommon Property: The Fishing and Fish Processing Industries in British Columbia*, eds. P. Marshak, N. Guppy, and J. McMullan, pp. 353–9. Toronto: Methuen.

Martin, F. 1989. *Common Pool Resources and Collective Action: A Bibliography*. Bloomington: Indiana University, Workshop in Political Theory and Policy Analysis.

Martin, K. O. 1979. Play by the Rules or Don't Play at All: Space Division and Resource Allocation in a Rural Newfoundland Fishing Community. In *North Atlantic Maritime Cultures: Anthropological Essays on Changing Adaptations*, eds. R. Andersen and C. Wadel, pp. 277–98. The Hague: Mouton.

Marwell, G., and R. E. Ames. 1979. Experiments on the Provision of Public Goods. I: Resources, Interests, Group Size, and the Free-Rider Problem. *American Journal of Sociology* 84:1335–60.

Marwell, G., and R. E. Ames. 1980. Experiments on the Provision of Public Goods. II: Provision Points, Stakes, Experience and the Free-Rider Problem. *American Journal of Sociology* 85:926–37.

Maser, S. M. 1985. Demographic Factors Affecting Constitutional Decisions. *Public Choice* 47:121–62.

Matthews, R. 1988. Federal Licensing Policies for the Atlantic Inshore Fishery and Their Implementation in Newfoundland, 1973–1981. *Acadiensis: Journal of the History of the Atlantic Region* 17:83–108.

Matthews, R., and J. Phyne. 1988. Regulating the Newfoundland Inshore Fishery: Traditional Values versus State Control in the Regulation of a Common Property Resource. *Journal of Canadian Studies* 23:158–76.

Matthews, R. C. O. 1986. The Economics of Institutions and the Sources of Growth. *Economic Journal* 96:903–18.

Menger, K. 1963. *Problems in Economics and Sociology* (translated from the 1883 German edition). Urbana: University of Illinois Press.

Messerschmidt, D. A. 1986. Collective Management of Hill Forests in Nepal: The Community Forestry Development Project. In *Proceedings of the Conference on Common Property Resource Management*, National Research Council, pp. 455–80. Washington, D.C.: National Academy Press.

Mnookin, R. H., and L. Kornhauser. 1979. Bargaining in the Shadow of the Law: The Case of Divorce. *Yale Law Journal* 88:950–97.

Moore, J. A. 1985. Science as a Way of Knowing–Human Ecology. *American Zoologist* 25:483–637.

Moore, M. P. 1979. The Management of Irrigation Systems in Sri Lanka: A Study in Practical Sociology. *Sri Lanka Journal of Social Sciences* 2:89–112.

Moore, M. P. 1980. *Approaches to Improving Water Management on Large-Scale*

# References

*Irrigation Schemes in Sri Lanka.* Occasional Publication Series, No. 20, Agrarian Research and Training Institute, Colombo, Sri Lanka.

Musgrave, R. A. 1959. *The Theory of Public Finance: A Study in Public Economy.* New York: McGraw-Hill.

Myhrmann, J. 1989. The New Institutional Economics and the Process of Economic Development. *Journal of Institutional and Theoretical Economics* 145:38–58.

Nash, J. F. 1950. The Bargaining Problem. *Econometrica* 18:155–62.

National Research Council. 1986. *Proceedings of the Conference on Common Property Resource Management.* Washington, D.C.: National Academy Press.

Nebel, B. J. 1987. *Environmental Science,* 2nd ed. Englewood Cliffs, N.J.: Prentice-Hall.

Needler, W. H. 1979. Evolution to Canadian Fisheries Management: Towards Economic Rationalization. *Journal of the Fisheries Research Board of Canada* 36:716–24.

Negri, D. H. 1989. The Common Property Aquifer as a Differential Game. *Water Resources Research* 25:9–15.

Neher, P. A. 1978. The Pure Theory of the Muggery. *American Economic Review* 68:437–45.

Nelson, R., and S. Winter. 1982. *An Evolutionary Theory of Economic Change.* Cambridge, Mass.: Harvard University Press.

Netting, R. McC. 1972. Of Men and Meadows: Strategies of Alpine Land Use. *Anthropological Quarterly* 45:132–44.

Netting, R. McC. 1976. What Alpine Peasants Have in Common: Observations on Communal Tenure in a Swiss Village. *Human Ecology* 4:135–46.

Netting, R. McC. 1981. *Balancing on an Alp.* Cambridge University Press.

Netting, R. McC. 1982. Territory, Property, and Tenure. In *Behavioral and Social Science Research: A National Resource,* eds. R. McC. Adams, N. J. Smelser, and D. J. Treiman, pp. 446–501. Washington, D.C.: National Academy Press.

Niederer, A. 1956. *Gemeinwerk im Walis: Bruerliche Geminschaftsarbeit in Vergangenheit and Gegenwart.* Basel: G. Krebs.

Niskanen, W. 1971. *Bureaucracy and Representative Government.* Chicago: Aldine-Atherton.

Nitzan, S., and E. Ostrom. 1989. *The Nature and Severity of Inefficiency in Voluntary Provision of Mixed Public Goods.* Bloomington: Indiana University, Workshop in Political Theory and Policy Analysis.

Norgaard, R. B. 1981. Sociosystem and Ecosystem Coevolution in the Amazon. *Journal of Environmental Economics and Management* 8:238–54.

Norman, C. 1984. No Panacea for the Firewood Crisis. *Science* 226:676.

North, D. C. 1978. Structure and Performance: The Task of Economic History. *Journal of Economic Literature* 16:963–78.

North, D. C. 1981. *Structure and Change in Economic History.* New York: Norton.

North, D. C. 1986a. Institutions, Economic Growth and Freedom: An Historical Introduction. Paper presented at a symposium on economic, political, and civil freedom sponsored by the Liberty Fund and managed by The Fraser Institute, October 5–8, Napa Valley, California.

North, D. C. 1986b. The New Institutional Economics. *Journal of Institutional and Theoretical Economics* 142:230–7.

260

# References

North, D. C. 1989. Final Remarks–Institutional Change and Economic History. *Journal of Institutional and Theoretical Economics* 145:238–45.

North, D. C., and B. R. Weingast. 1989. Constitutions and Commitment: The Evolution of Institutions Governing Public Choice in 17th Century England. St. Louis: Washington University, Center in Political Economy.

Nugent, J. B., and N. Sanchez. 1989. The Efficiency of the Mesta: A Parable. *Explorations in Economic History* 26:261–84.

Nunn, S. C. 1985. The political Economy of Institutional Change: A Distributional Criterion for Acceptance of Groundwater Rules. *Natural Resources Journal* 25: 867–92.

Oakerson, R. J. 1978. The Erosion of Public Highways: A Policy Analysis of the Eastern Kentucky Coal-Haul Road Problem. Ph.D. dissertation, Indiana University.

Oakerson, R. J. 1985. The Meaning and Purpose of Local Government: A Tocqueville Perspective. Working paper, Advisory Commission on Intergovernmental Relations. Washington, D.C.

Oakerson, R. J. 1986. A Model for the Analysis of Common Property Problems. In *Proceedings of the Conference on Common Property Resource Management*, National Research Council, pp. 13–30. Washington, D.C.: National Academy Press.

Oakerson, R. J. 1988. Reciprocity: A Bottom-Up View of Political Development. In *Rethinking Institutional Analysis and Development: Issues, Alternatives, and Choices*, eds. V. Ostrom, D. Feeny, and H. Picht, pp. 141–58. San Francisco: Institute for Contemporary Studies Press.

Okada, A., and H. Kleimt. 1990. Anarchy and Agreement – A Game Theoretical Analysis of Some Aspects of Contractarianism. In *Game Equilibrium Models. Vol. II: Methods, Morals, and Markets*, ed. R. Selten. Berlin: Springer-Verlag.

Oliver, P. 1980. Rewards and Punishments as Selective Incentives for Collective Action: Theoretical Investigations. *American Journal of Sociology* 85:356–75.

Oliver, P., and G. Marwell. 1985. A Theory of the Critical Mass. I. Interdependence, Group Heterogeniety, and the Production of Collective Action. *American Journal of Sociology* 91:522–56.

Olson, M. 1965. *The Logic of Collective Action. Public Goods and the Theory of Groups*. Cambridge, Mass.: Harvard University Press.

Ophuls, W. 1973. Leviathan or Oblivion. In *Toward a Steady State Economy*, ed. H. E. Daly, pp. 215–30. San Francisco: Freeman.

Ophuls, W. 1977. *Ecology and the Politics of Scarcity*. San Francisco: Freeman.

Opp, K. D. 1979. The Emergence and Effects of Social Norms. *Kyklos* 32:775–801.

Opp, K. D. 1982. The Evolutionary Emergence of Norms. *British Journal of Social Psychology* 21:139–49.

Opp, K. D. 1986. The Evolution of a Prisoner's Dilemma in the Market. In *Paradoxical Effects of Social Behavior*, eds. A. Diekmann and P. Mitter, pp. 149–68. Vienna: Physica-Verlag.

Orbell, J. M., and L. A. Wilson. 1978. Institutional Solutions to the N-Prisoners' Dilemma. *American Political Science Review* 72:411–21.

Orr, D. S., and S. Hill. 1979. Leviathan, the Open Society, and the Crisis of Ecology. In *The Global Predicament. Ecological Perspectives on World Order*, eds. D. W. Orr and M. S. Soros, pp. 457–69. Chapel Hill: University of North

# References

Carolina Press.

Ostrom, E. 1965. Public Enterpreneurship: A Case Study in Ground Water Management. Ph.D. dissertation, University of California at Los Angeles.

Ostrom, E. 1985a. Are Successful Efforts to Manage Common-Pool Problems a Challenge to the Theories of Garrett Hardin and Mancur Olson? Working paper, Workshop in Political Theory and Policy Analysis, Indiana University.

Ostrom, E. 1985b. The Rudiments of a Revised Theory of the Origins, Survival, and Performance of Institutions for Collective Action. Working paper, Workshop in Political Theory and Policy Analysis, Indiana University.

Ostrom, E. 1986a. An Agenda for the Study of Institutions. *Public Choice* 48:3–25.

Ostrom, E. 1986b. A Method of Institutional Analysis. In *Guidance, Control, and Evaluation in the Public Sector*, eds. F. X. Kaufmann, G. Majone, and V. Ostrom, pp. 459–75. New York: Walter de Gruyter.

Ostrom, E. 1986c. Multiorganizational Arrangements and Coordination: An Application of Institutional Analysis. In *Guidance, Control, and Evaluation in the Public Sector*, eds. F. X. Kaufmann, G. Majone, and V. Ostrom, pp. 495–510. New York: Walter de Gruyter.

Ostrom, E. 1987. Institutional Arrangements for Resolving the Commons Dilemma: Some Contending Approaches. In *The Question of the Commons: The Culture and Ecology of Communal Resources*, eds. B. J. McCay and J. M. Acheson, pp. 250–65. Tucson: University of Arizona Press.

Ostrom, E. 1989. Microconstitutional Change in Multiconstitutional Political Systems. *Rationality & Society* 1:11–50.

Ostrom, E., L. Schroeder, and S. Wynne. 1990. *Institutional Incentives and Rural Infrastructure Sustainability*. Washington, D.C.: U.S. Agency for International Development.

Ostrom, E., and J. Walker. 1990. Communication in a Commons: Cooperation without External Enforcement. In *Contemporary Laboratory Research in Political Economy*, ed. T. R. Palfrey. Ann Arbor: University of Michigan Press.

Ostrom, V. 1980. Artisanship and Artifact. *Public Administration Review* 40:309–17.

Ostrom, V. 1982. A Forgotten Tradition: The Constitutional Level of Analysis. In *Missing Elements in Political Inquiry: Logic and Levels of Analysis*, eds. J. A. Gillespie and D. A. Zinnes, pp. 237–52. Beverly Hills: Sage.

Ostrom, V. 1985a. The Constitution of Order in Human Societies: Conceptualizing the Nature and Magnitude of the Task in Institutional Analysis and Development. Paper presented at International Political Science Association meetings, July 15–20, Paris.

Ostrom, V. 1985b. Opportunity, Diversity, and Complexity. Paper presented at the conference Multi-Actor Policy Analysis: The Scope and Direction of Policy Recommendations, July 23–5, University of Umea, Sweden.

Ostrom, V. 1986a. Constitutional Considerations with Particular Reference to Federal Systems. In *Guidance, Control, and Evaluation in the Public Sector*, eds. F. X. Kaufmann, G. Majone, and V. Ostrom, pp. 111–25. New York: Walter de Gruyter.

Ostrom, V. 1986b. A Fallabilist's Approach to Norms and Criteria of Choice. In *Guidance, Control, and Evaluation in the Public Sector*, eds. F. X. Kaufmann, G. Majone, and V. Ostrom, pp. 229–49. New York: Walter de Gruyter.

Ostrom, V. 1987. *The Political Theory of a Compound Republic: Designing the*

## References

*American Experiment*, rev. ed. Lincoln: University of Nebraska Press.

Ostrom, V. 1989. *The Intellectual Crisis in American Public Administration*, 2nd rev. ed. University of Alabama Press.

Ostrom, V. 1990. *American Federalism: A Great Experiment*. San Francisco: Institute for Contemporary Studies Press.

Ostrom, V., R. Bish, and E. Ostrom, 1988. *Local Government in the United States*. San Francisco: Institute for Contemporary Studies Press.

Ostrom, V., D. Feeny, and H. Picht. 1988. *Rethinking Institutional Analysis and Development: Issues, Alternatives, and Choices*. San Francisco: Institute for Contemporary Studies Press.

Ostrom, V., and E. Ostrom. 1977a. Public Goods and Public Choices. In *Alternatives for Delivering Public Services. Toward Improved Performance*, ed. E. S. Savas, pp. 7–49. Boulder: Westview Press.

Ostrom, V., and E. Ostrom. 1977b. A Theory for Institutional Analysis of Common Pool Problems. In *Managing the Commons*, eds. G. Hardin and J. Baden, pp. 157–72. San Francisco: Freeman.

Ostrom, V., C. M. Tiebout, and R. Warren. 1961. The Organization of Government in Metropolitan Areas: A Theoretical Inquiry. *American Political Science Review* 55:831–42.

Panayoutou, T. 1982. Management Concepts for Small-Scale Fisheries: Economic and Social Aspects. FAO Fisheries Technical Paper No. 228, Rome.

Perera, J. 1986. The Gal Oya Farmer Organization Programme: A Learning Process? In *Participatory Management in Sri Lanka's Irrigation Schemes*, International Irrigation Management Institute, Digana Village via Kandy, Sri Lanka: IIMI.

Picardi, A. C., and W. W. Seifert. 1977. A Tragedy of the Commons in the Sahel. *Ekistics* 43:297–304.

Picht, C. 1987. Common Property Regimes in Swiss Alpine Meadows. Paper presented at a conference on advances in comparative institutional analysis at the Inter-University Center of Postgraduate Studies, October 19–23, Dubrovnik, Yugoslavia.

Pinkerton, E., ed. 1989a. *Co-operative Management of Local Fisheries. New Directions for Improved Management and Community Development*. Vancouver: University of British Columbia Press.

Pinkerton, E. 1989b. Competition Among B.C. Fish Processing Firms. In *Uncommon Property: The Fishing and Fish Processing Industries in British Columbia*, eds. P. Marshak, N. Guppy, and J. McMullan, pp. 66–91. Toronto: Methuen.

Plott, C. R. 1979. The Application of Laboratory Experimental Methods to Public Choice. In *Collective Decision Making: Applications from Public Choice Theory*, ed. C. S. Russell, pp. 137–60. Baltimore: Johns Hopkins University Press.

Plott, C. R., and R. A. Meyer. 1975. The Technology of Public Goods, Externalities, and the Exclusion Principle. In *Economic Analysis of Environmental Problems*, ed. E. S. Mills, pp. 65–94. New York: Columbia University Press.

Popper, K. R. 1967. Rationality and the Status of the Rationality Principle. In *Le Fondements Philosophiques des Systems Economiques Textes de Jacques Rueff et Essais Rediges en son Honneur*, ed. E. M. Classen, pp. 145–50. Paris: Payot.

Posner, R. A. 1980. A Theory of Primitive Society, with Special Reference to Law. *Journal of Law and Economics* 23:1–53.

Powers, R. B. 1987. Bringing the Commons into a Large University Classroom.

# References

*Simulation and Games* 18:443–57.

Pradhan, P.P. 1980. *Local Institutions and People's Participation in Rural Public Works in Nepal.* Ithaca, N.Y.: Cornell University, Rural Development Committee.

Pradhan, P. P. 1984. Chattis Mauja Irrigation System: Community Response in Resource Management. Paper for Social Science Research Council–Indian Institute of Management, Bangalore Seminar, January 4–7.

Price, M. 1987. The Development of Legislation and Policy for the Forests of the Swiss Alps. Working paper, Research Program on Environment and Behavior, University of Colorado.

Prigogine, I. 1978. Time, Structure, and Fluctuations. *Science* 201:777–85.

Raadschelders, J. 1988. Dutch Water Control Systems, 900–1990. Colloquium presentation at the Workshop in Political Theory and Policy Analysis, October 24, Indiana University.

Rabibhadena, A. 1980. *The Transformation of Tambon Yokkrabat, Changwat Samut Sakorn.* Bangkok: Thammasat University.

Radnitzky, G. 1987. Cost–Benefit Thinking in the Methodology of Research: The "Economic Approach" Applied to Key Problems of the Philosophy of Science. In *Economic Imperialism. The Economic Approach Applied Outside the Field of Economics*, eds. G. Radnitzky and P. Bernholz, pp. 283–331. New York: Paragon House.

Rahman, A. 1981. *Some Dimensions of People's Participation in the Bloomni Sena Movement.* Geneva: United Nations Research Institute for Social Development.

Rapoport, A. 1966. *Two-Person Game Theory. The Essential Ideas.* Ann Arbor: University of Michigan Press.

Rapoport, A. 1985. Provision of Public Goods and the MCS Experimental Paradigm. *American Political Science Review* 79:148–55.

Rapoport, A., and A. M. Chammah. 1965. *Prisoner's Dilemma: A Study in Conflict and Cooperation.* Ann Arbor: University of Michigan Press.

Raub, W., and T. Voss. 1986. Conditions for Cooperation in Problematic Social Situations. In *Paradoxical Effects of Social Behavior: Essays in Honor of Anatol Rapoport*, eds. A. Diekmann and P. Mitter, pp. 85–103. Vienna: Physica-Verlag Heidelberg.

Rhodes, R. E., and S. J. Thompson. 1975. Adaptive Strategies in Alpine Environments: Beyond Ecological Particularism. *American Ethnologist* 2:535–51.

Riker, W. H. 1980. Implications for the Disequilibrium of Majority Rule for the Study of Institutions. *American Political Science Review* 74:432–47.

Riker, W. H., and P. C. Ordeshook. 1973. *An Introduction to Positive Political Theory.* New York: Prentice-Hall.

Roberts, M. 1980. Traditional Customs and Irrigation Development in Sri Lanka. In *Irrigation and Agricultural Development in Asia*, ed. E. W. Coward, Jr., pp. 186–202. Ithaca, N.Y.: Cornell University Press.

Rolph, E. S. 1982. Government Allocation of Property Rights: Why and How. Technical report, Rand Corporation, Santa Monica, California.

Rolph, E. S. 1983. Government Allocation of Property Rights: Who Gets What? *Journal of Policy Analysis and Management* 3:45–61.

Rose-Ackerman , S. 1977. Market Models for Water Pollution Control: Their Strengths and Weaknesses. *Public Policy* 25:383–406.

Rosenberg, N. 1982. *Inside the Black Box: Technology and Economics.* Cambridge

# References

University Press.

Roumasset, J. A. 1985. Constitutional Choice for Common Property Management: The Case of Irrigation Associations. Paper presented at the National Academy of Sciences Workshop on Common Property Resource Management in Developing Countries.

Ruddle, K., and T. Akimichi, eds. 1984. *Maritime Institutions in the Western Pacific*. Osaka: National Museum of Ethnology.

Runge, C. F. 1981. Common Property Externalities: Isolation, Assurance and Resource Depletion in a Traditional Grazing Context. *American Journal of Agricultural Economics* 63:595–606.

Runge, C. F. 1984a. Institutions and the Free Rider: The Assurance Problem in Collective Action. *Journal of Politics* 46:154–81.

Runge, C. F. 1984b. Strategic Interdependence in Models of Property Rights. *American Journal of Agricultural Economics* 66:807–13.

Runge, C. F. 1986. Common Property and Collective Action in Economic Development. In *Proceedings of the Conference on Common Property Resource Management*, National Research Council, pp. 31–60. Washington, D.C.: National Academy Press.

Samuelson, L. 1987. A Note on Uncertainty and Cooperation in an Infinitely Repeated Prisoner's Dilemma. *International Journal of Game Theory* 16:187–95.

Samuelson, P. A. 1954. The Pure Theory of Public Expenditure. *Review of Economics and Statistics* 36:387–9.

Samuelson, P. A. 1955. A Diagrammatic Exposition of a Theory of Public Expenditure. *Review of Economics and Statistics* 37:350–6.

Sandford, S. 1983. *Management of Pastoral Development in the Third World*. New York: Wiley.

Sawyer, A. 1989. The Evolution of Autocracy in Liberia. Unpublished manuscript, Workshop in Political Theory and Policy Analysis, Indiana University.

Schaaf, J. 1989. Governing a Monopoly Market Under Siege: Using Institutional Analysis to Understand Competitive Entry into Telecommunications Markets, 1944–1982. Ph.D. dissertation, Indiana University.

Scharpf, F. W. 1985. Ideological Conflict on the Public–Private Frontier: Some Exploratory Notes. Working paper, Wissenschftszentrum, Berlin.

Scharpf, F. W. 1987. A Game-Theoretical Explanation of Inflation and Unemployment in Western Europe. *Journal of Public Policy* 7:227–58.

Scharpf, F. W. 1988. The Joint Decision Trap: Lessons from German Federalism and European Integration. *Public Administration* 66:239–78.

Scharpf, F. W. 1989. Decision Rules, Decision Styles, and Policy Choices. *Journal of Theoretical Politics* 1:151–78.

Schelling, T. C. 1960. *The Strategy of Conflict*. Oxford University Press.

Schelling, T. C. 1978. *Micromotives and Macrobehavior*. New York: Norton.

Schelling, T. C. 1984. *Choice and Consequence: Perspectives of an Errant Economist*. Cambridge, Mass.: Harvard University Press.

Schlager, E. 1989. Bounding Unboundable Resources: An Empirical Analysis of Property Rights and Rules in Coastal Fisheries. Working paper, Workshop in Political Theory and Policy Analysis, Indiana University.

Schlager, E., and E. Ostrom. 1987. Common Property, Communal Property, and Natural Resources: A Conceptual Analysis. Working paper, Workshop in Poli-

# References

tical Theory and Policy Analysis, Indiana University.

Schmid, A. A. 1986. Neo-Institutional Economic Theory: Issues of Landlord and Tenant Law. In *Contract and Organization: Legal Analysis in the Light of Economic and Social Theory*, eds. T. Daintith and G. Teubner, pp. 132–41. New York: Walter de Gruyter.

Schotter, A. 1981. *The Economic Theory of Social Institutions*. Cambridge University Press.

Scott, A. D. 1955. The Fishery: The Objectives of Sole Ownership. *Journal of Political Economy* 63:116–24.

Scott, A. D. 1979. Development of an Economic Theory on Fisheries Regulation. *Journal of the Fisheries Research Board of Canada* 36:725–41.

Scott, A. D. 1982. Regulation and the Location of Jurisdictional Powers: The Fishery. *Osgoode Hall Law Journal* 20:780–805.

Searle, J. 1969. *Speech Acts: An Essay in the Philosophy of Language*. Cambridge University Press.

Selten, R. 1975. Reexamination of the Perfectness Concept for Equilibrium Points in Extensive Games. *International Journal of Game Theory* 4:25–55.

Selten, R. 1978a. The Chain Store Paradox. *Theory and Decision* 9:127–59.

Selten, R. 1978b. The Equity Principle in Economic Behavior. In *Decision Theory and Social Ethics*, eds. H. W. Gottinger and W. Leinfellner, pp. 289–301. Dordrecht: D. Reidel.

Sen, A. K. 1967. Isolation, Assurance, and the Social Rate of Discount. *Quarterly Journal of Economics* 81:172–224.

Sen, A. K. 1986. Prediction and Economic Theory. *Proceedings of the Royal Society of London* 407:3–23.

Sharma, P. N. 1984. Social Capability for Development: Learning from the Japanese Experience. *Regional Development Dialogue* (special issue), pp. 41–86.

Shepsle, K. A. 1979a. Institutional Arrangements and Equilibrium in Multidimensional Voting Models. *American Journal of Political Science* 23:27–60.

Shepsle, K. A. 1979b. The Role of Institutional Structure in the Creation of Policy Equilibrium. In *Public Policy and Public Choice*, eds. D. W. Rae and T. J. Eismeier, pp. 249–81. Beverly Hills: Sage.

Shepsle, K. A. 1989a. Discretion, Institutions, and the Problem of Government Commitment. Working paper, Cambridge, Mass.: Harvard University, Department of Government.

Shepsle, K. A. 1989b. Studying Institutions. Some Lessons from the Rational Choice Approach. *Journal of Theoretical Politics* 1:131–49.

Shepsle, K. A., and B. R. Weingast. 1984. Legislative Politics and Budget Outcomes. In *Federal Budget Policy in the 1980's*, eds. G. Mills and J. Palmer, pp. 343–67. Washington, D.C.: Urban Institute Press.

Shepsle, K. A., and B. R. Weingast. 1987. The Institutional Foundations of Committee Power. *American Political Science Review* 81:85–104.

Shimanoff, S. B. 1980. *Communication Rules. Theory and Research*. Beverly Hills: Sage.

Shubik, M. 1982. *Game Theory in the Social Sciences. Concepts and Solutions*, 2 vols. Cambridge, Mass.: MIT Press.

Sinn, H. W. 1984. Common Property Resources, Storage Facilities and Ownership Structures: A Cournot Model of the Oil Market. *Economica* 51:235–52.

Siy, R. Y., Jr. 1982. *Community Resource Management: Lessons from the Zanjera*.

# References

Quezon City: University of the Philippines Press.

Smith, R. J. 1981. Resolving the Tragedy of the Commons by Creating Private Property Rights in Wildlife. *CATO Journal* 1:439–68.

Smith, R. T. 1988. *Trading Water: An Economic and Legal Framework for Water Marketing*. Washington, D.C.: Council of State Policy and Planning Agencies.

Smith, V. L. 1969. On Models of Commercial Fishing. *Journal of Political Economy* 77:181–98.

Snidal, D. 1979. Public Goods, Property Rights, and Political Organizations. *International Studies Quarterly* 23:532–66.

Snidal, D. 1985. Coordination Versus Prisoner's Dilemma: Implications for International Cooperation and Regimes. *American Political Science Review* 79:923–47.

Sobel, J. H. 1985. Utility Maximizers in Iterated Prisoner's Dilemmas. In *Paradoxes of Rationality and Cooperation*, eds. R. Campbell and L. Sowden, pp. 306–19. Vancouver: University of British Columbia Press.

Speck, F. G., and W. S. Hadlock. 1946. A Report on Tribunal Boundaries and Hunting Areas of the Malecite Indians of New Brunswick. *American Anthropologist* 48:355–74.

Stevenson, G. G. 1990. *The Swiss Grazing Commons: The Economics of Open Access, Private, and Common Property*. Cambridge University Press.

Stillman, P. G. 1975. The Tragedy of the Commons: A Re-Analysis. *Alternatives* 4:12–15.

Stroebe, W., and B. S. Frey. 1980. In Defense of Economic Man: Towards an Integration of Economics and Psychology. *Zeitschrift für Volkswirtschaft und Statistik* 2:119–48.

Sugden, R. 1986. *The Economics of Rights, Co-operation, and Welfare*. Oxford: Blackwell.

Tang, S. Y. 1989. Institutions and Collective Action in Irrigation Systems. Ph.D. dissertation, Indiana University.

Taylor, J. 1988. The Ethical Foundations of the Market. In *Rethinking Institutional Analysis and Development: Issues, Alternatives, and Choices*, eds. V. Ostrom, D. Feeny, and H. Picht, pp. 377–88. San Francisco: Institute for Contemporary Studies Press.

Taylor, M. 1987. *The Possibility of Cooperation*. Cambridge University Press.

Taylor, M., and H. Ward. 1982. Chickens, Whales and Lumpy Goods: Alternative Models of Public Goods Provision. *Policy Studies* 30:350–70.

Telser, L. G. 1980. A Theory of Self-enforcing Agreements. *Journal of Business* 53:27–44.

Thirsk, J. 1959. *Tudor Enclosures*. Pamphlet No. 41. London: Historical Associations.

Thirsk, J. 1964. The Common Fields. *Past and Present* 29:3–25.

Thirsk, J. 1967. *The Agrarian History of England and Wales*. Cambridge University Press.

Thomson, J. T. 1977. Ecological Deterioration: Local-Level Rule Making and Enforcement Problems in Niger. In *Desertification: Environmental Degradation in and around Arid Lands*, ed. M. H. Glantz, pp. 57–79. Boulder: Westview Press.

Thomson, J. T., D. Feeny, and R. J. Oakerson. 1986. Institutional Dynamics: The Evolution and Dissolution of Common Property Resource Management. In

267

# References

*Proceedings of the Conference on Common Property Resource Management,* National Research Council, pp. 391–424. Washington, D.C.: National Academy Press.

Tocqueville, A. de. 1955. *The Old Regime and the French Revolution.* Garden City, N.Y.: Meridian Books.

Townsend, R., and J. A. Wilson. 1987. An Economic View of the Commons. In *The Question of the Commons,* eds. B. J. McCay and J. M. Acheson, pp. 311–26. Tucson: University of Arizona Press.

Troost, K. K. 1985. The Medieval Origins of Common Land in Japan. Paper presented at the American Historical Association meetings, December.

Truman, D. B. 1958. *The Governmental Process.* New York: Knopf.

Tsebelis, G. 1989. The Abuse of Probability in Political Analysis: The Robinson Crusoe Fallacy. *American Political Science Review* 83:77–91.

Tsebelis, G. 1990. *Nested Games: Political Context, Political Institutions and Rationality.* Berkeley: University of California Press.

Tullock, Gordon, 1965. *The Politics of Bureaucracy.* Washington, D.C.: Public Affairs Press.

Ullmann-Margalit, E. 1978. *The Emergence of Norms.* Oxford University Press.

Uphoff, N. T. 1983. *Rural Development and Local Organization in Asia. Vol. 2. East Asia.* New Delhi: Macmillan.

Uphoff, N. T. 1985a. Fitting Projects to People. In *Putting People First,* ed. M. M. Cernea, pp. 359–95. Oxford University Press.

Uphoff, N. T. 1985b. Summary of January 1985 Trip Report on Farmer Organization Program in Gal Oya, Sri Lanka. Manuscript, Cornell University.

Uphoff, N. T. 1985c. People's Participation in Water Management: Gal Oya, Sri Lanka. In *Public Participation in Development Planning and Management: Cases from Africa and Asia,* ed. J. C. Garcia-Zamor, pp. 131–78. Boulder: Westview Press.

Uphoff, N. T. 1986a. Activating Community Capacity for Water Management in Sri Lanka. In *Community Management: Asian Experience and Perspectives,* ed. D. C. Korten, pp. 201–19. West Hartford, Conn.: Kumarian Press.

Uphoff, N. T. 1986b. *Local Institutional Development: An Analytical Sourcebook with Cases.* West Hartford, Conn.: Kumarian Press.

Uphoff, N. T. 1986c. *Getting the Process Right: Improving Irrigation Water Management with Farmer Participation.* Boulder: Westview Press.

Vanberg, V., and J. Buchanan. 1989. Interests and Theories in Constitutional Choice. *Journal of Theoretical Politics* 1:49–62.

van de Kragt, A. J. C., J. M. Orbell, and R. M. Dawes. 1983. The Minimal Contributing Set as a Solution to Public Goods Problems. *American Political Science Review* 77:112–22.

Veliz, C. 1980. *The Centralist Tradition of Latin America.* Princeton University Press.

von Wright, G. H. 1951. Deontic Logic. *Mind* 60:48–74.

von Wright, G. H. 1963. *Norms and Action. A Logical Enquiry.* London: Routledge & Kegan Paul.

Wade, R. 1986. Common Property Resource Management in South Indian Villages. In *Proceedings of the Conference on Common Property Resource Management,* National Research Council, pp. 231–57. Washington, D.C.: National Academy Press.

# References

Wade, R. 1988. *Village Republics: Economic Conditions for Collective Action in South India.* Cambridge University Press.

Walker, J., R. Gardner, and E. Ostrom. 1990. Rent Dissipation and Balanced Deviation Disequilibrium in Common Pool Resources: Experimental Evidence. In *Game Equilibrium Models. Vol. II: Methods, Morals, and Markets,* ed. R. Selten. Berlin: Springer-Verlag.

Wallis, J. J. 1989. Towards a Positive Economic Theory of Institutional Change. *Journal of Institutional and Theoretical Economics* 145:98–112.

Ward, H. 1989. Testing the Waters: Taking Risks to Gain Reassurance in Public Goods Games. *Journal of Conflict Resolution* 33:274–308.

Ways and Means Committee. 1945. *Report.* Downey, Calif.: West Basin Water Association.

Weissing, F., and E. Ostrom. 1990. Irrigation Institutions and the Games Irrigators Play. In *Game Equilbrium Models. Vol. II: Methods, Morals, and Markets,* ed. R. Selten. Berlin: Springer-Verlag.

Welch, W. P. 1983. The Political Feasibility of Full Ownership Property Rights: The Cases of Pollution and Fisheries. *Policy Sciences* 16:165–80.

Weschler, L. F. 1968. *Water Resources Management: The Orange County Experience.* California Government Series No. 14. Davis: University of California, Institute of Governmental Affairs.

Wiegandt, E. B. 1977. Communalism and Conflict in the Swiss Alps. Ph.D. dissertation, University of Michigan at Ann Arbor.

Wiggins, S. N., and G. D. Libecap. 1985. Oil Field Unitization: Contractual Failure in the Presence of Imperfect Information. *American Economic Review* 75:368–85.

Williamson, O. E. 1975. *Markets and Hierarchies: Analysis and Antitrust Implications.* New York: Free Press.

Williamson, O. E. 1979. Transaction Cost Economics: The Governance of Contractual Relations. *Journal of Law and Economics* 22:233–61.

Williamson, O. E. 1983. Credible Commitments: Using Hostages to Support Exchange. *American Economic Review* 83:519–40.

Williamson, O. E. 1985. *The Economic Institutions of Capitalism: Firms, Markets, Relational Contracting.* New York: Free Press.

Wilson, J. A. 1977. A Test of the Tragedy of the Commons. In *Managing the Commons,* eds. G. Hardin and J. Baden, pp. 96–111. San Francisco: Freeman.

Wilson, J. A. 1986. Subjective Probability and the Prisoner's Dilemma. *Management Sciences* 32:45–55.

Wilson, R. K. 1985. Constraints on Social Dilemmas: An Institutional Approach. *Annals of Operations Research* 2:183–200.

Witt, U. 1986. Evolution and Stability of Cooperation Without Enforceable Contracts. *Kyklos* 39:245–66.

Witt, U. 1987. How Transaction Rights Are Shaped to Channel Innovativeness. *Journal of Institutional and Theoretical Economics* 143:180–95.

Wittfogel, K. A. 1957. *Oriental Despotism. A Comparative Study of Total Power.* New Haven, Conn.: Yale University Press.

Wittgenstein, L. 1953. *Philosophical Investigations.* Oxford: Basil Blackwell & Mott.

Wolf, E. R. 1986. The Vicissitudes of the Closed Corporate Peasant Community. *American Ethnologist* 13:325–9.

269

## References

World Bank. 1982. *Philippines Communal Irrigation Development Project.* Washington, D.C.: World Bank.

Wynne, S. 1986. Information Problems Involved in Partitioning the Commons for Cultivation in Botswana. In *Proceedings of the Conference on Common Property Resource Management*, National Research Council, pp. 359–89. Washington, D.C.: National Academy Press.

Wynne, S. 1988. The Land Boards of Botswana: A Problem in Institutional Design. Ph.D. dissertation, Indiana University.

Yang, T. S. 1987. Property Rights and Constitutional Order in Imperial China. Ph.D. dissertation, Indiana University.

Yelling, J. A. 1977. *Common Field and Enclosure in England, 1450–1850.* Hamden, Conn.: Archon.

Young, O. R. 1982. *Resource Regimes. Natural Resources and Social Institutions.* Berkeley: University of California Press.

# Index

Acheson, J. M., 220n21, 241n28
action
  arena, 54
  collective, *see* collective action
  independent, 38–40
  interdependent, *see* interdependent
    situations
  world of, 45–6
Aegean Sea, 144–6
Agency for International Development
  (AID), 220n24
Agrarian Research and Training Institute
  (ARTI), 168–9, 171–2, 189
Akimichi, T., 220n21
Alanya, Turkey, 18–21, 47–8, 95–6, 143,
  179–80, 185, 188
  *see also* Turkish inshore fisheries
Alchian, A., 207, 221n13, 221–2n14
Alexander, L., 235–6n36
Alexander, P., 149–56, 237–8n4, 238n6
Alhambra, California, 111, 231
Alicante, Spain
  *Huerta* of, 78–81, 92, 180, 182, 227n21,
    227–8n24, 229n38
  *see also* Spanish *huertas*
Allen, R. C., 224n3
American Plant Growers, Inc., 235
Andersen, R., 241n28
Anderson, R. L., 70, 71, 73, 77–82,
  226n15, 227n21n23
appropriation, 30–3, 47–50, 55–6,
  222–3n25, 223n26
  *see also* design principles, congruent
    rules
appropriative rights, 107–8

appropriators, 30–1, 33–8, 220n2, 244n18
  *see also* appropriation
Aragon, kingdom of, 81
arbitrator, 17
Aristotle, 2
Arnold, J. E. M., 23, 178
Arthur, W. B., 237n45
Ascher, W., 159, 243n14
Asia, 144, 165, 225n9
*atar*, 82, 85–6, 228n28, 229n34
Aumann, R. J., 125, 223n28
authority
  central, 10–11, 13–14, 17–18, 20, 22,
    143–4, 156–7, 159–60,
    166, 175–8, 181, 205, 213–16,
    218n8n9, 237n2; *see*
    *also* centralization
  external, 17, 93, 110, 172–3, 190,
    201–2, 211–13, 229n38
    241n26
  local, 155, 200–2
  *see also* design principles, nested
    enterprises
authority rules, *see* rules, authority
Axelrod, R., 7, 36, 93, 95

Bacarra-Vintar federation of *zanjeras*,
  Philippines, 83–8, 180, 189
  Nibinib, 86
  Sto. Rosario, 85–6
  Surgui, 85
Bacarra-Vintar River, 83–4
Baden, J., 3
Bahia, Brazil, 177, 241–2n29
Bandara, M., 158

271

# Index

# Index